D1616199

SHAKE
HEAVEN
& EARTH

Peter Bergson and the Struggle
to Rescue the Jews of Europe

LOUIS RAPOPORT

gefen גפן
publishing house בית הוצאה לאור

JERUSALEM ◆ NEW YORK

Typesetting: Marzel A.S. – Jerusalem

Cover Design: David Grossman

Reproduction of photos: Procolor

**Publication of this book was made possible by a grant from
the Institute for Mediterranean Affairs**

Edition 9 8 7 6 5 4 3 2

Gefen Publishing House	Gefen Books
POB 36004	12 New Street
Jerusalem 91360, Israel	Hewlett, NY 11557, USA
972-2-538-0247	516-295-2805
isragefen@netmedia.net.il	gefenbooks@compuserve.com

Printed in Israel   *Send for our free catalogue*

Library of Congress Cataloging-in-Publication Data
Rapoport, Louis.
Shake heaven and earth: Peter Bergson and the struggle
to rescue the Jews of Europe / Louis Rapoport
Includes bibliographical references (p. 264) and index.

ISBN: 965 229 182 X

1. Kook, Hillel, 1915- . 2. Revisionist Zionists—Biography. 3. Holocaust, Jewish (1939-1945).
4. Jews— United States—Politics and government. 5. Zionism—United States. 6. World War, 1939-1945—
Jews—Rescue. 7. United States. War Refugee Board. 8. United States—Ethnic relations. I. Title.
DS151.K59R37 1999
956.94'001'0924
[B]—DC19

88-6694
CIP

Contents

In loving memory of Louis Rapoport
my husband, our father

Sylvia, Ehud, Adi, Avigal, Michal

My gratitude to an extraordinary woman, Nili Kook, for all she has done to make the publication of this book possible. Also my heartfelt appreciation to Nili Kook and Dr. Becky Kook-Doron for their knowledge of the subject and their valuable comments on the text.

Sylvia Rapoport
June 1998

ACKNOWLEDGMENTS

This book starts and ends with Hillel Kook, alias Peter Bergson. Contact with him over the past three years has been an enlightening experience. My interest in the Bergson group was first sparked by my friend Sol Stern. In the course of my research, I have been helped by friends and colleagues, and by former members of the Bergson group as well as their foes. Special thanks to Samuel Merlin, Sir Isaiah Berlin, Harry Louis Selden, Max Lerner, Prof. Michael J. Cohen, Prof. Martin Gilbert, Prof. Monty Penkower, Nahum Kook, Batya Kook, Nili Kook, Helen Brown Sherman, Shoshana Raziel, Dr. Alexander Rafaeli, Dr. Carl Hermann Voss, and Paul O'Dwyer. The late Yitshaq Ben-Ami, the late Rabbi Morton Berman and the late Dr. Israel Goldstein were most helpful.

Documents on the Bergson group are available at several archives in the United States, Israel and Britain, the main ones being the Sterling Library at Yale University, the Jabotinsky archives in Tel Aviv, the Institute for Mediterranean Affairs in New York, the Public Record Office in London, the FDR Library at Hyde Park, the National Archives in Washington, and the Zionist Archives in Jerusalem. Many other documents are available from the U.S. Government under the Freedom of Information Act. Thanks to Raymond Teichman at the FDR Library, Abraham J. Peck of the American Jewish Archives, Nathan M. Kaganoff of the American Jewish Historical Society, Dr. Michael Heymann of the Zionist Archives, and J.M. Armstrong of the Institute of Historical Research at the University of London.

Most of all, my appreciation is to my wife, Sylvia, who gave me the time to write while she managed our four small children amid the complications of daily life in Israel.

Louis Rapoport
Jerusalem, September 21, 1986

FOREWORD

The explosiveness of the issue cannot be underestimated. Enemies of the Jewish people lap up any evidence that some Jews, however inadvertently, may have prevented other Jews from being saved from the Nazi exterminators. The Germans killed five or six million Jews, but, they say ingenuously, there were accomplices to the deed, by acts of omission or commission: not only State Department and British Foreign Office and Catholic church officials, but even Zionist and Jewish leaders outside occupied Europe.

Unfortunately, there is more than a kernel of truth to the allegation that Jewish leaders in the Free World – fearful of anti-Semitism or blinded by ideology, or victims of narcissism and overweaning pride – caused inestimable damage to the people they claimed to represent. But it is a complex question that simply cannot be portrayed in black-and-white terms, and the measure of responsibility is yet to be determined. In order to assess the question of what American Jews and Zionists did or did not do during the Holocaust, an increasing number of scholars and journalists is focusing on the role of one non-establishment Jewish activist, a Palestinian nationalist revolutionary who led an unorthodox, highly visible campaign to save lives.

Hillel Kook used the alias Peter Bergson when he struggled to rally Americans to rescue Jews condemned by Hitler's Germany. He assumed the alias to protect the family name, including that of his uncle, then chief rabbi of Palestine and the foremost figure in modern Judaism. Kook/Bergson is still haunted by his belief that as many as one million Jews could have been saved from Nazi satellite states –

principally Hungary and Rumania – if the Zionist and Jewish establishment had devoted its energies to pressure the U.S. Government to undertake political action to save European Jews. What these leaders did instead was to promote their vision of Zionism, or promote themselves, giving vent to the selfish ambition and self-righteousness so common to organization and religious professionals, doing everything they could to stop the young activists who they thought were challenging their authority.

Bergson was, to some minds, a Runyonesque, Hollywood-like creature, a "nuisance diplomat," while others saw him as a courageous "new Jew," a man with a prophetic mission. What he and his colleagues managed to do was to wiggle out of the straitjacket of Zionist politics, in order to break the silence surrounding the "Final Solution." The record of their achievements refutes those who still claim that "nothing could be done." Something *was* done, and a great deal more could have been achieved had the establishment Zionist and Jewish organizations not concentrated so much of their efforts on destroying the "Bergson group," instead of on prodding the Roosevelt administration to undertake a program of rescue for the condemned Jews of Europe.

It was not an easy task. The fact of the extermination, even after the genocide was officially verified, simply did not penetrate into people's consciousness. This lack of reaction was widespread, and not confined to Jewish and Zionist leaders. It may be true that people simply do not have the capacity or the courage to face such unimaginable horrors. During the course of the war, they lived in a kind of penumbra where the truth did not disturb their ordinary routines. Historian-philosopher Sir Isaiah Berlin, for example, a Russian-born Jew and a Zionist who was also chief information officer at the British embassy in Washington during the war, says today that he was not aware of the extermination until 1944 or 1945. Berlin was as brilliant and as perceptive as they come. But in a November 2, 1983, letter to the author, the Oxford dean said that "no Zionist leader told me about systematic extermination until 1945." What then could be expected of the "head" of American Jewry Stephen Wise, a theatrical rabbi and a much dimmer light by comparison?

To the Bergsonites, the first and most natural reaction to the news of systematic extermination that emerged in 1942 was to scream, and then to organize. Bergson's youth was no doubt one factor in overcoming the constraints binding the Jewish leadership. In Palestine, Bergson had falsified his age to become a member of the Haganah defense at sixteen, and after a few years, he became a leader in the Irgun underground. Later, as the Irgun's chief emissary in Europe on the eve of the war, his dedication broadened as he became aware of the situation facing Poland's Jews, who were living on a tinder box.

The Palestinian core group and its American supporters which Bergson led in the United States was militant and audacious in a way that was foreign, and ultimately threatening, to American Zionists. And the broader Jewish leadership in America was frozen by the fear of increasing anti-Semitism in their own backyard. Instead of mounting a political campaign to press the reluctant Allies to undertake action on behalf of European Jews, the main issue became how to "liquidate" – in Jewish Agency leader Nahum Goldmann's term – Peter Bergson and his colleagues.

Today, when he recalls those agonizing years, Hillel Kook/Peter Bergson never uses the term Holocaust. The word, he notes, is of Greek origin, and means a burnt sacrifice, a sin offering. The Jews did not die on an altar. They were not sacrificed by the Nazis; they were murdered. If history construes that any sacrifice was offered, it was surely by the Free World: the State Department and the British Foreign Office, and, to a lesser yet significant extent, the Zionist and Jewish establishment.

A growing number of younger writers and historians is now beginning to accept that view, criticizing the "utter passivity," as some put it, of the Jewish leadership outside Nazi Europe. In response, another group of historians, reflecting the view of past and present leaders of the Jewish establishment, have renewed the bitter attacks on the Bergson group of forty years ago, accusing them of being charlatans who never saved any Jews, or upstarts who tilted at windmills. In contrast, these historians portray the wartime Jewish leadership as having done everything possible in a historical context in which the Jewish establishment was "powerless."

In the United States, the issue of the response of the Zionist and Jewish establishment to the extermination has become a stormy issue within the Jewish community. A private commission, headed by former Supreme Court Justice Arthur Goldberg, was set up in 1981 to study these questions. Its work was interrupted for some months after it broke up in dissension over the charges that it was an attempt to "rewrite history," and counter-charges that establishment American Jewry was once again acting to suppress the true story. But on March 21, 1984, *The New York Times* reported that the study had been completed and that it concluded that America's major Jewish organizations showed laxity, and failed to act forcefully on behalf of the doomed Jews of Europe. The subject of the Bergson group was all but ignored (I believe, simply because it was too hot to handle), but commission members Justice Goldberg and Rabbi Arthur Hertzberg wrote an article in the *Los Angeles Times* in which Bergson/Kook's outstanding activist role was noted and praised. The commission's report, though critical of the establishment, tried to please everyone, and therefore pleased no one. By hedging on "the Bergson question," it missed the heart of the story.

History is usually written by the "winners." This book is an attempt to recover a figure from the past relegated by some to the "losers." He was a man of courage and vision who stood against the tide of passivity at the most desperate moment in Jewish history in two thousand years. Kook and his colleagues have not yet received adequate recognition for their achievements in mobilizing public opinion and pressuring President Roosevelt to create the War Refugee Board in 1944, the one concrete step taken by the U.S. Government that resulted in the saving of thousands of Jewish lives in Hitler's Europe.

Part of the reason the story of the Bergson group has never really been told is Kook himself, who wants to put the past to rest. His concerns are with the problems of today's Jews in Israel and elsewhere. Although he grants interviews and his story pops up from time to time (as in the 1983 BBC documentary *Auschwitz and the Allies*, or as the pivotal figure in Laurence Jarvik's documentary *Who Shall Live and Who Shall Die*, shown on PBS in 1983), he has remained as elusive as mercury since his friend and co-activist Ben Hecht profiled him in 1954 in *A Child of the Century*, in which Kook was characterized as "a man of history."

It is my purpose to finally tell this long-suppressed story, and to show why questions that arose during the extermination are relevant today. The story would be worth telling merely for the fact that the Bergsonites broke the circle of silence around the Holocaust and helped achieve the creation of a rescue agency, albeit too little too late. Equally important, however, is that out of their struggle with the problems confronting world Jewry during the war years, they developed a challenging approach to "the Jewish question" and how it should be resolved in the post-war period, an approach that still remains vital.

This maverick group also played a crucial, little-known role towards speeding the timetable for Israeli independence, and came to grips with what independence would mean. Bergson and some of his colleagues grappled with the problem of Jewish identity. What does it mean to create a "Jewish" state, as Bergson asked in his confrontation with Chaim Weizmann, what is an Israeli, and what does Israeli citizenship mean in terms of the Jewish People? Bergson raised searching intellectual questions that still have not been resolved and which present Israel with terrible dilemmas on the basic issues of nationality and religion, the Palestinians, war and peace. Kook, the secular son of Judaism's leading rabbinical family, confronted the problem of the mixture of Jewish nationality and Jewish religion in ways that were disturbing to those who believe that separation of Israeli nationality from Judaism would only compromise the uniqueness of the Jews, and solve nothing. Although his ideas are discussed by leading Israeli intellectuals, the debate is far removed from the average Israeli, whose concerns are with security and economic survival.

This book is not a standard biography, but rather the story of a unique and crucial chapter of Jewish history that has been kept in the closet. Uncovering this buried history, and tracing the development of Hillel Kook's ideas, has been an eye-opening experience for me, an American-born journalist who emigrated to Israel in 1973. Despite an ingrained skepticism, I have come to believe that Kook's history and his message are vital to Israel and to the Jews.

During the era, Zionist leaders like Rabbi Wise and Nahum Goldmann told the State Department that Kook/Bergson was as big a threat as Hitler to the well-being of American Jewry. While Jews 3,000 miles away were being gassed, these leaders feared that Bergson would bring pogroms to America. Instead, he was instrumental in bringing about the creation of the War Refugee Board, which, with its emissaries like Raoul Wallenberg of Sweden, saved as many as 200,000 Jews from liquidation. Ideological blinders and the chronic hunger for staying in power prevented the establishment Jewish and Zionist leaders from doing what Bergson did, dropping everything but the issue of rescue.

Professor David Wyman's *The Abandonment of the Jews*, the award-winning 1985 book on American policy during the Holocaust, went beyond Arthur Morse's groundbreaking 1965 best-seller *While Six Million Died*, which chronicled the ignominious role of the State Department and President Roosevelt concerning rescue policy. Wyman included American church groups and – finally – the American Jewish and Zionist establishment among those who impeded rescue.

His book was extremely cautious; it had to be, as this is one of the most sensitive issues of our time. But he did not hold back in his praise of the young maverick who called himself Peter Bergson.

This book focuses on Bergson/Kook and explores the theme of what is to be learned from this historical period in relation to the present problems facing Israel and the Jews of the world. The Holocaust years prove how fragile and problematic is the much vaunted unity of the Jewish People – something that often exists only in the world of speeches and testimonials. The established Jewish leadership during World War II refused to change the agenda of their lives, while the Bergson group employed groundbreaking tactics to get their message across. In this case, the "war between the Jews" was unilateral, a tragic and destructive campaign led by Rabbi Wise, Nahum Goldmann, Congressman Sol Bloom, and others, many of whom have since been ensconced in the Zionist pantheon.

During the war years, the Zionists said openly and continually that the future of Palestine deserved top priority over the rescue issue. Only in recent years have survivors of that era, such as former Zionist leader Rabbi Israel Goldstein, admitted that they may have been wrong. Their war on the Bergsonites, their blind devotion to ideology, and their petty internecine fighting were tragically negligent at a time when they should have dropped all else in pursuit of Judaism's holiest imperative: the saving of life.

INTRODUCTION

It gives me great pleasure, tinged with personal sadness, to write this introduction. Louis Rapoport was a friend with whom I, like so many others, had long hours of animated conversation. He was also an author from whose books – which he sometimes showed me in typescript or in proof – I derived enormous satisfaction, gaining knowledge and insight. His interests ranged widely but had a central focus. He sought to uncover the reality, however uncomfortable, in historical inquiry that is an essential, but all-too-rare, quality.

Peter Bergson and his small but determined group always fascinated Louis. It is, therefore, very good indeed that the fruits of his dedicated work are now to be published and, most importantly, to be read by a wide circle. This circle will include not only those who knew Louis and his earlier books, but those for whom, alas he will only be known posthumously. *Shake Heaven and Earth* carries with it the torch that Louis always carried with him – the torch of persistent research, bold discovery, and passion for truth.

Sir Martin Gilbert
Merton College, Oxford
March 1998

CHAPTER ONE

THE MAKING OF A HEBREW
REVOLUTIONARY

For the Jewish People of the modern era, Eastern Europe was a house of bondage and torment, akin to the Egypt of the Pharaohs. Though Eastern Europe was the crucible of Zionism, it was also the slaughterhouse of a great Jewish culture. In the era of World War I, the "Jewish problem" was so graphic that great numbers of Jews became either Zionists or socialists – or both. It was a violent, tempestuous part of the world, for the Jews most of all. Jewish people had no rights and were the main objects of persecution. They faced the reality that they had no future – national, personal, or religious – among the Russians, Poles, or other Slavic peoples.

The East European volcano was the cradle for many of the leaders who helped bring about the dream of Israel: Eliezer Ben-Yehuda, Ahad Ha'am, A.D. Gordon, David Ben-Gurion, Ze'ev Jabotinsky, Chaim Weizmann, Golda Meir, Menachem Begin, and scores of others, including many whose names have been virtually forgotten today. The cruel realities of Russia, Poland, and their satellites shaped their lives as well as their thoughts.

Hillel Kook, the man who one day would lead a crusade to save European Jews fleeing before Hitler's consuming fire, was born in July 1915 in the town of Kruk, Lithuania, near the Latvian border, while the Great War was raging. If there had been a royal family among pious Jews, it would have been the Kooks, a famed rabbinical clan which had helped keep the flame of Judaism alive through centuries in Exile.[1] Hillel's father, Dov Kook, a large man with a full black beard, was a renowned scholar and a regional chief rabbi. Many of Hillel's uncles, cousins and one of his brothers were prominent rabbis. Dov's brother, Avraham Yitzhak Hacohen Kook, Hillel's uncle, would become the first chief rabbi of Palestine and was already considered, at age fifty, to be Judaism's leading spiritual figure of the modern era, a genius who towered above those around him.[2]

Hillel's mother, Rebecca, came from another respected family, the Schockens, well-to-do merchants and members of the hassidic Lubavitch sect. She taught each of her children to read Hebrew before they went to *heder*, Talmud-Torah schools. The Jews lived separately from the Lithuanian and Russian peasants. They spoke a special dialect of Yiddish and saw no reason to speak the local language or adopt the customs of their neighbors. Their religion ruled their outlook on life. Everything was related to the Torah, the Talmud, and the rabbinic tradition.

In the spring of 1915, when Rebecca was pregnant with Hillel, the last of her eight children, the Russians ordered the expulsion of all Jews from Lithuania, on the pretense of their having been "pro-German" in the war. Russian military authorities unleashed squads of pogromists who attacked the Jews. The czar's regime, as it had been for decades, was the greatest tormentor and enemy of the Jews, who were without legal protection in Eastern Europe until after the war's end. When the expulsion order came, Rabbi Dov Kook and his large family were among the hundreds of thousands of Jewish refugees desperately scrambling for shelter – it was not the first time that Jewry exemplified the human condition carried to its extreme.

The Kooks were far more fortunate than most other Jews, because they had money from Rebecca's family. This enabled them to buy horses and carriages for the journey, first to the town of Birz, where they were put up by members of the Schocken family, and then to the Ukraine, where fugitives of every kind had fled for centuries.[3] The Kooks settled in Yelizavetgrad (called Kirovgrad today) in the south-east Ukraine, where there was a large and vital Jewish population.

Dov and Rebecca Kook and their brood lived with other relatives in a compound of buildings that were banded together by a wooden stockade – a kind of fort in the midst of the political, economic, and social upheavals that convulsed the vast Russian empire. Chaos reigned in the Ukraine from 1917, the year of the revolution, until 1921. As Russia was torn by civil war, four rival armies crisscrossed the ravaged Ukraine, each army's favorite target being the Jews. Thousands of Jews escaping from the battlefront areas poured into Yelizavetgrad, where Jews dominated much of the town's economy, controlling flour mills, liquor and tobacco factories. But the town was not much of a refuge. In 1919, "partisans" belonging to the anti-Bolshevik force of the czarist ex-officer, Commander Grigoriev, massacred some three thousand Jews in Yelizavetgrad, where Dov Kook was chief rabbi, and went on to kill thousands more in the region. (Grigoriev was caught and executed by the anarchist army commander Nestor Makhno, the only army commander who attempted to restrain his men from killing too many Jews.)[4]

The Ukrainian nationalists led by Simon Petlura carried out pogroms on an even wider scale, as did the troops of Deniken's reactionary White Army, whose Don Cossack cavalry pillaged, raped, and murdered with the cry, "Strike at the Jews and Save Russia!" The Polish army also entered the Ukraine and joined the bloodletting against the Jews, who had been restricted to the Pale of Settlement by the czars. When the Bolsheviks entered Yelizavetgrad, they closed down Jewish institutions and suppressed Jewish communal life.

The Jews were being slaughtered because they were a pariah people who had no nation of their own, no army to defend them or to carry out retribution. Lenin, the new embattled czar of Russia, reaffirmed the belief that there was no basis for a separate Jewish nation.

Two of Hillel's brothers were injured in different pogroms. In the worst pogrom, when Rabbi Dov Kook and his sons, Rafael and Herzl, were out of town, Grigoriev's men invaded and ransacked the Kook's home. Rebecca fled with her youngest, four-year-old Hillel (the family called him "Hilka"), and her four girls: Batya, Sonia, Tzila, and Nehama. Fifteen-year-old Nahum, who stayed behind, was shot in the chest, the bullets penetrating his lungs. The pogromchiks left him for dead. Rebecca and her children hid in the cellar in the courtyard, where other Jewish mothers were sheltering their children, trembling in fear. Hillel's mother warned her little boy not to cry out, or she would have to clasp her hand over his mouth, as another young mother was doing to her child. They stayed in the cellar for hours. When they emerged, they found Nahum at death's door and the streets of the town literally flowing with blood. The experience was indelibly branded into Hillel Kook's soul: His earliest memories were of Jews being shot, or cut down with swords or axes.[5] Nahum was brought by cart to the hospital, where the doctors said there was no hope for him. But somehow, he survived. In offering thanks to God for what was considered a miraculous recovery, he took a vow to become a doctor. This was pleasing to Rebecca, who wanted two of her sons to become rabbis, and the other two to become physicians.[6]

Scrawny little "Hilka," the runt of her litter, was her favorite. She wanted him to become a rabbi, like his father and his eldest brother, Rafael. He was a precocious boy who preferred to play with older children, and Hillel always pretended that he was older than his true age. Once, in a game with bigger boys, he fell and severely cut his lower lip. When the wound healed, it left his mouth slightly crooked. Rebecca felt he was more vulnerable than ever. She and Dov continued to tutor him at home.

In a second pogrom, the Kook family also escaped death, although they were thoroughly terrorized. Two drunk partisans entered their home and said they were going to cut off Rafael's hand. The young rabbi (one day, he would become chief rabbi of Tiberias, one of the four Jewish holy cities) was forced to place his hand on the table. One of the peasants lifted his sword, clasped like an executioner's axe, and came down hard on Rafael's hand – only he used the flat side of the sword. It was just a joke. The two men left laughing, their arms full of loot.

Between the pogroms (during these repeated attacks on over 500 communities, some 60,000 Jews were killed), there was hunger. On the rare occasions when Hillel was allowed to venture into the streets with one of his brothers or sisters, he saw other children who were victims of the great famine, their bellies swollen from malnutrition. Jews in East Europe learned early on that they could lose their lives at the whim of their gentile neighbors, that an ordinarily warm and friendly peasant could suddenly become red-eyed drunk, rave about the Christ-killers and their gold, and carve up a Jewish mother, father, or child without the slightest remorse. An idyllic day could suddenly turn into pure horror, as in the Isaac Babel story, "My Dovecote."

Rabbi Dov Kook and the rest of his family were different from the great majority of their fellow Orthodox Jews in that they were Zionists. His older brother, the Talmudic genius Rabbi Avraham Kook (known as Rav Kook), had gone to Palestine in 1904, the year that Theodor Herzl, the secular founder of the Zionist political movement, had died. Rav Kook was a pioneer, intent on synthesizing the secular Zionism of Herzl with the spiritual awakening that he deemed crucial for national revival. The mystical Rav Kook was unique in the religious-Zionist camp in that he was open to socialist Zionists, for he believed that the return to Zion – by atheist farmers or Talmudic scholars or by any other Jews – meant that the Redemption was at hand.[7] He believed that the Jews were marked by God to carry out the Divine plan, and that Jewish nationalism was a stage in that development.

In 1921, Rav Kook became the Ashkenazi chief rabbi of Palestine. He kept in close touch with his large family in the Ukraine, urging them to join him in the Holy Land. But Dov Kook felt he couldn't leave yet; besides being the chief spiritual leader of the area, he was also in charge of distributing relief packages sent to the Jews by the American Relief Association. The Kook family's *aliyah*, or "ascension" (emigration) to the Holy Land was also delayed when the Bolsheviks arrested Dov for his Zionist activities. His release was brought about only with the help of prominent Jews in the West.

Rabbi Rafael Kook, Hillel's eldest brother, was the first to go to Palestine. Soon afterwards, he arranged visas and housing for the rest of the family, who finally left Russia in 1925, traveling steerage class from Odessa on a ship named after Lenin, who had recently died. They felt they were on their way to freedom, which meant "to be at home."[8] After the week-long journey to Jaffa, the Kooks disembarked into waiting dinghies, and were rowed to the shore of the Promised Land by Arab laborers. The house that awaited them, not far from Rav Kook's house and his yeshiva, was on Eben Yeshua Street near new Jerusalem's main thoroughfare, Jaffa Road. There were no comforts – no electricity or water – and malaria and typhus were rampant in the small, dusty town that Jerusalem then was. But Dov Kook and his family felt that they were "home" at last.

Ten-tear-old Hillel was enrolled in a Talmud-Torah school, and later in the yeshiva established by his uncle. The yeshiva was immediately different from most of the other Orthodox institutions, in that the language of instruction was Hebrew, not Yiddish. (Most Orthodox Jews felt it was blasphemy to use the tongue of Scripture for daily discourse.) The spirit was different, too, as Rav Kook continued to build bridges between the religious and the non-observant.

Hillel Kook's first friend in the yeshiva was an intense youth four years his senior, David Raziel, also the scion of a dynasty of rabbis. Raziel immediately took Hillel under his wing. Hillel was a frail, spindly boy, with cold, clear, light-blue eyes. He was handsome, despite the scar that made his mouth appear to be slightly twisted on the right side. During the course of the next few years, Raziel, a driven nationalist and future commander of the Irgun underground, tutored Hillel in everything from boxing to philosophy. He gave his small friend *The Grey Wolf*, a book about Turkey's Kemal Ataturk, an inspirational figure to young Zionists because he dramatically changed the course of his country.

Both Raziel and Kook would eventually leave Rav Kook's yeshiva for a secular education. They felt that studying the Talmud was not enough. Raziel, however, remained observant, while Hillel drifted away. By his fifteenth birthday, he felt that belief had to come from within, and that ritual was an imposition. Although he still believed in God, he could no longer believe in the *mitzvot*, the 613 commandments that are at the heart of Orthodox Judaism. It seemed absurd to him that God was concerned about preserving the ancient dietary laws, or that it mattered whether or not he ate meat off a dish that once held cheese. There may have been other reasons as well. After six formative years in Palestine, Hillel had acquired a strong new identity – a Hebrew, living in the land where his ancestors had lived. For centuries in exile, the Torah and the Talmud had been a "portable fatherland," in Heine's phrase. But for Hillel Kook and many other members of his generation in Palestine, the Exile ended, and the struggle for independence began.

The residence of the Chief Rabbi was a focal point and communications center for Palestinian Jewry – religious and secular – and Rav Kook's lean young nephew spent much of his time there. He had grown bored with yeshiva study, and much more exciting things were happening at his uncle's house. Rav Kook was intimately involved in political as well as religious affairs – he was sometimes called "High Priest of the Rebirth" – and when Jews were killed by Arabs, it was reported immediately to the Chief Rabbi. When the Mufti, Haj Amin al-Husseini, the political and religious leader of the Palestinian Arabs, ordered attacks on Jews praying at the Western Wall – the last vestige of the Temple – Rav Kook called on the Jews to defend their holiest shrine.

The 1929 Arab riots in Palestine, in which over 500 Jews were slain in the streets, brought back Hillel's memories of the pogroms he had witnessed as a young boy. All around Jerusalem, in the Musrara quarter and the Old City, Jews were being cut down. In Hebron, scores of yeshiva students Hillel's age were massacred, and the town became *judenrein*.[9] He was very much under the influence of Raziel, who remained his closest friend and, like him, he vowed to take part in the nascent Haganah, the defense movement of the *yishuv* (the Jewish community in Palestine). The British Mandate authorities, who had ruled Palestine since capturing it from the Turks in 1917, were doing little to protect the Jews from the marauders. In the ensuing years, their attitude would harden further. Lord Josiah Wedgwood,[10] a fiercely pro-Zionist Member of Parliament, would call British-ruled Palestine "the land of anti-Semitism *par excellence*." The British, who blamed Arab unrest on the growing Jewish immigration, would not allow Jews to possess arms, leaving them at the mercy of the Arabs. But after the traumatic events of 1929, many Jews ignored the British laws; it was a turning point in the history of the Yishuv. At Hillel's yeshiva, as at many other religious and secular Jewish schools following the Hebron massacre, military training was introduced clandestinely.

At nineteen, Raziel joined the Haganah defense force, with his young protege soon following. For the riots[11] of 1929 taught the youths a basic lesson: Where the Jews had illegal arms, they successfully resisted attack; where they had none, they were slaughtered.

In 1930, David Raziel entered the recently founded Hebrew University of Jerusalem[12] to study philosophy. He joined the El-Al fraternity,[13] founded by historian Joseph Klausner, a nationalist maverick on the mainly socialist faculty, which included Martin Buber and Judah Magnes. A good deal of antagonism was engendered between the predominantly dovish faculty and the many nationalistic students.

Students like Raziel and his Polish-born classmate Avraham Stern – a fervent poet and member of the Hulda group, to the right of El-Al – rejected the notion espoused on campus that the Jews were a spiritually and ethically superior people who should not resort to violence in a struggle for independence. They were already involved in revolutionary activities against the British rulers.

Hillel Kook took part in El-Al activities as Raziel's "little brother" but did not attend classes at the university until the fall of 1932, when he registered as a non-matriculated student. He felt himself psychologically handicapped because he was much younger than the others, and because he had not ventured far from his religious education, which he felt was limiting. Later, in his underground life, he would become used to working with people who were five, ten or thirty or more years older, and what had been a handicap would become one of his strengths. Meanwhile, he went where Raziel went. "Raziel was his rebbe," Hillel's sister Batya would recall.[14]

In April 1931 Raziel, Stern, Kook and other young nationalists followed the Haganah's Jerusalem commander, Avraham Tehomi, when he split from the defense force dominated by the labor-Zionists to form a more "nationally representative" group of fighters. It was called "Haganah Bet" (Haganah 'B'),[15] and would soon evolve into the *Irgun Zvai Leumi* (the National Military Organization). Tehomi felt that the Haganah had been too socialist-party oriented, and he sought the support of religious and middle-class groups. Some saw the Irgun as the emerging army of the bourgeoisie. Others felt it was a natural outgrowth of the Jabotinsky youth movement, Betar.[16]

The youthful Hillel could not help but be impressed by Tehomi, a military figure with piercing eyes and a withered right hand. Tehomi coined the phrase "Hebrew Army," using the word Hebrew to underline the national aspect of the Jewish People.

Kook was not as favorably impressed by Stern, who was an intellectual leader among the nationalist students at the small university.[17] As yet, Stern showed little trace of the fanaticism that would mark his future career, when he would break bitterly with Raziel and the Irgun to form the Fighters for the Freedom of Israel, or *Lehi* – what the British, and the labor-socialists, called "the Stern Gang." Hillel was disturbed by the vain and aloof Stern, who combed his black hair constantly and who wrote poetry that Kook thought revealed a strong death wish. In the spring of 1932, Stern wrote the lyrics for a song that was to be performed at the graduation of the first Irgun cadet class, which included Raziel, Stern, and Kook, who had learned the use of arms and explosives under Tehomi's tutelage. Stern's song, "Unknown Soldiers,"[18] combined poetry and mythic history as integral ingredients of national revolution. It became the anthem of the Irgun, and later of the Sternists, and eventually an early Israeli folksong. Hillel was disturbed by the words, especially the line, "our dream is to die for our nation," and he told Stern that they had just finished a course on how to protect themselves in combat, that they should not be dreaming of dying but of living. Stern's reply was that Kook obviously didn't understand poetry.

Stern was regarded as a loner, and he especially exasperated Raziel, who thought him a snob and a pedant. Even the way Stern opened an ink bottle and slowly dipped his pen irked Raziel. The two young men, and their respective girl friends, hated each other. Soon after the cadet course, Stern went to Italy to continue his studies. He did not tell his colleagues that he was also smuggling arms for Tehomi.

Kook at that time never thought of himself or his friends as revolutionaries – he believed that the term was the province of the far left. His view was that social issues had to be subordinated to the struggle for national liberation. He thought of the Communists as enemies of the Jews, a belief stemming from his religious upbringing and his childhood experience in Russia, where the Bolsheviks had imprisoned his father for being a Zionist. On campus, he engaged in heated debate with Communists and fellow-travelers who criticized those who focused on one people – the Jews – when only "world revolution" could bring "liberation." Kook, greatly influenced by the writings of Vladimir Ze'ev Jabotinsky, founder of revisionist Zionism, argued that Jewish national goals had to be their main concern, and that the main task was to make the Jews "normal," like any other people, with the eventual aim of national independence. When Norman Bentwich, a prominent "dovish" British labor-Zionist, spoke at the university on February 10, 1932, stink bombs were thrown by nationalist students, who shouted "Go talk with the Mufti."[19] Police were called in to restore order. Kook was standing on a chair shouting that the police were arresting people, at which point *he* was arrested. When he was released the next day, Raziel reprimanded him: His arrest could have endangered underground activities.

By the time he was eighteen, Kook was cutting most of his classes, devoting himself almost entirely to Irgun activities in the belief that the underground would one day become the "liberation army of the Hebrew nation." Despite his age – four years younger than most of his comrades – he rose quickly, taking a leading role in the Irgun's propaganda and fund-raising activities, and in the campaign to boycott Germany.[20] In 1935 he became an Irgun liaison between the organization's military wing and its civilian supporters and persuaded Chief Rabbi Kook to write a letter to help raise money for the Irgun – the appeal urged people to support this "holy work of saving Jews."[21]

Around the same time, Hillel arranged for the clandestine printing of the first arms manual in Hebrew, *The Pistol*, written by Raziel and Stern. In order to throw off the British, the front piece of the book said it was published by the "Union of Jewish Veterans in Danzig." Hillel also stored illegal arms in the Talmud research center run by his father, Dov, and Ya'acov Herzog, member of another famed rabbinical clan. Dov, now a distinguished-looking man whose full beard was turning gray, knew and approved of Hillel's activities, although they never talked about it.[22] The Irgun was growing up, its membership increasing from about 300 in 1933 to 2000 in 1936.

Hillel was no longer living at home. He held a part-time job at Hadassah hospital in the center of town, where his brother Nahum practiced medicine. For three months, he "house sat" for Prof. Klausner and his wife, while they were abroad. Just before they left, Mrs. Klausner had told Hillel that "knowing how young people are these days" he might be tempted to have parties or bring girls to the house. She made him promise he would not. But soon after they left, Kook broke his promise.

The inner circle of Irgun officers, which was still more of a social group than a central command, continued to hold long discussions in a house in the Bukharian quarter in Jerusalem. They often went with their girl friends to the Vienna Cafe in Zion Square. None of the Irgun leaders could afford to go to the terrace of the King David Hotel. Quiet, parochial Jerusalem had no night life to speak of; socializing was done in private homes.

The youths kept in good physical shape. The husky Raziel continued to box with scrawny Hillel, on one occasion breaking one of the latter's front teeth. They were inseparable, trekking into the Judean hills to practice shooting, taking apart and assembling arms, discussing the basic issues of how to deal with Arab attacks and the eventual need for unity with the mainstream Haganah.

The military training the Irgun leaders underwent was put to use during the 1936 Arab disturbances. Kook commanded a group of Irgunists stationed in the settlement of Motza, just outside Jerusalem, when it came under fire from the Arab village of Kolondia. Their transport from Jerusalem was provided by Yitshaq Ben-Ami, one of the only Irgun members to possess a car, a rare luxury. One of the young Irgunists who served under Kook, Eliahu Amikam, greatly admired Hillel's style, describing him years later as "a golden youth" and "a kind of prince, both in the fraternity and in the Irgun... He was a ladies' man, a *bon vivant*, and a Raziel protege. He was very bright and ambitious, with British manners and a great name – Kook. It meant a lot."[23]

Behind the Arab uprising that began in April 1936 and lasted for three years was a decade of rising Arab national fervor in Syria, Egypt, and Palestine. In the Thirties, with the great influx of Jews into Palestine after the advent of Hitler, the Yishuv's population nearly doubled, fueling Arab fears. Palestinian Arabs believed that the British were intent on pursuing the Zionist aims set out in the 1917 Balfour Declaration, with its promise of a "national home" in Palestine for the Jewish People. The end of an economic boom in 1935, coupled with rising Arab unemployment, exacerbated the situation and provided fertile ground for incitement by the Mufti, who had provoked the 1929 uprising as well.

In 1937, Tehomi, who had created the Irgun when he left the Haganah in 1931, now left the Irgun and returned to the Haganah, taking much of the top command with him. The decimated Irgun struggled for existence. In the vacuum, the new Irgun command was taken over by the young guard, which included Raziel, Stern and Kook. The three men and their closest comrades were "like monks giving up their private lives for the nation," according to one early member of the Irgun.[24]

But if they were monks, they were of the variety that went to parties, drank wine, and made love to young women. Yet, in spite of this, there was near total devotion to the cause. It was like an army company underground. The experience of working in a tight-knit, disciplined military organization would one day be a major factor in the success of the Bergson group in America.

Kook, like other Irgun leaders, assumed an underground name – his first alias was "Eitan." He was the youngest member of the inner circle, called the *Suhba* (Arabic for fellowship). The young men constantly engaged in political arguments that lasted deep into the night, discussing for the most part the controversial ideas of Ze'ev Jabotinsky. The militant nationalist Zionists felt that it was Jabotinsky who had assumed Herzl's mantle, and that he alone would bring about the Jewish state through a bold political struggle. His foes, mainly socialist Zionists, considered him a militarist, a proto-fascist. In truth, Jabotinsky (not unlike Herzl) was a complex man, a nineteenth-century liberal humanist, with a romantic streak and a radical vision of what the Jews had to do to achieve self-determination.

Jabotinsky, who was born in 1880, was the man who, early in the Zionist movement, planted the seeds for a Jewish army. As a young journalist, he had organized a Jewish self-defense corps in Odessa in 1903 when pogroms were threatening. In the ensuing years, he gained a wide following through his writings and speeches. He was an Anglophile, like Chaim Weizmann, head of the rival stream of Zionism, which emphasized colonization rather than political action. Jabotinsky did not think that the Turkish rulers of Palestine or the Arabs would ever accept a Jewish state in Palestine. When World War I broke out, he tried to persuade the British to establish a Jewish Legion that would fight alongside the Allies.[25] He was opposed by the War Office, assimilated British Jews and most Zionists – except Weizmann. David Ben-Gurion, who would eventually become Israel's first prime minister, and Yitzhak Ben-Zvi, who would become its second president, wanted to fight alongside the Turks, against the Allies.

Jabotinsky's friend Joseph Trumpeldor, a one-armed hero of the Russo-Japanese war and already a legendary figure among the early Zionist settlers in Palestine,[26] teamed up with a colorful British colonel, John Henry Patterson, to form the Zion Mule Corps. The story of the corps is a little-known chapter of Zionist history – most American Jews of the era never heard of it. The 650-man unit served heroically in the Gallipoli campaign and was disbanded in 1916. Jabotinsky, who helped to form the corps, kept pushing for his far more ambitious goal of a Jewish Legion to fight on the Palestine front, for he felt that a Jewish army was an historical necessity. His wish came true in 1917, the year of the Balfour Declaration, which called for a Jewish national home in Palestine. It was then that Jabotinsky, who served as a lieutenant, and Lt. Col. Patterson, put the legion together. It included many British and Russian Jews, as well as Palestinian Jews. The legion fought under General Allenby and took part in the great British victory at Damascus. In 1918, most of the Jewish young men in Palestine volunteered for the legion, but it was demobilized at the end of the war.

In 1920, when anti-Jewish riots broke out in Jerusalem, the British confined Jewish troops to their barracks. In reaction, Jabotinsky formed two companies of self-defense units: the Jerusalem Haganah. British Mandate authorities arrested Jabotinsky and nineteen others for illegal possession of arms. They were soon pardoned, but Jabotinsky was barred from Palestine, and he was never to return.

Jabotinsky differed sharply with the Zionists led by Weizmann in many ways. He pressed for mass immigration of Jews to Palestine, while the mainstream Zionists pursued a policy of selective immigration, preferring young people ideologically committed to building up the land. Jabotinsky had a mass following among Jews in many countries, especially in eastern Europe and Palestine. In the mid-Twenties, he had split with the majority of Zionists, setting up the Revisionist Party. Throughout the 1930s, Jabotinsky, though physically removed from Palestine, remained the mentor and nominal leader of the young Irgunists of the Yishuv. For Hillel Kook and his friends, the short, homely Jabotinsky was a larger-than-life figure, "the greatest Jew since Moses," the man who would lead the Jews to independence in the Promised Land.[27] Jabotinsky wrote a song that expressed Jewish yearnings for *both* banks of the Jordan, "the one which is ours, and the other one which is ours too." Alongside this sacred stream, Jabotinsky dreamed, his son would dwell in happiness and plenty with Moslems and Christians alike.[28]

In 1935, Jabotinsky pulled out of the umbrella Zionist Congress and founded the New Zionist Organization, an attempt to counter the minimalist policies favored by the "practical Zionists," who governed the Yishuv under the British.

During the Arab uprising of 1936-1939, the basic issue dividing the military arms of the two Zionist camps, the Haganah and the much smaller Irgun, was over how to react to indiscriminate Arab attacks. The practical Zionists under Ben-Gurion advocated a policy of "self-restraint." The Haganah of 1936 instructed its members not to let the smell of blood go to their heads, and declared that the proper response to Arab outrages was to build a new settlement. At Hadassah hospital in central Jerusalem, Dr. Nahum Kook treated a steady flow of Jews wounded in the Arab riots. Hillel was still working there, too. It was hard to avoid the smell of blood.

The young Irgun leaders marched to a different drummer than the members of the Haganah, more in tune with a patriotic, Polish-Russian nationalist trend than the Marxist-Tolstoyan tradition of the labor-socialist leaders of the Yishuv. The Irgunists believed in a policy of "response" – taking the lives of innocent Arabs in reprisal for the murder of innocent Jews. The issue of retaliation was reduced to a basic question of morality: Does one punish any Arab when one can't find the actual killers? This was the issue that split the Irgun in 1937, with Tehomi going back to the Haganah. Raziel and others – Kook, too, was involved – set up a retaliation unit. If Arabs continued to shoot indiscriminately at buses carrying Jews, the Irgun would react in kind. Tehomi said that he could understand their motivation, but he could not condone their activities. Jabotinsky in Europe, whom Tehomi recognized as the honorary head of the Irgun in 1935, was also opposed to retaliation at first. But in any case, he was too far removed from the events in Palestine to affect policy.

Raziel had become an inspirational figure to many of the Irgunists and their sympathizers. The former yeshiva student had become the complete soldier, obsessed with military matters – intensive training, obtaining weapons and ammunition. "We are not building just another Haganah," he told Irgun member Yitshaq Ben-Ami, "we are laying the foundation of our national army."[29] Raziel would become the mythic Hebrew Soldier, "the first soldier of rebellious Judea," as the Herut party newspaper would call him years after his death.

Raziel detested the intrigues and complications of politics and thought of himself as a pure military man, while Kook, his protege, already at age twenty-two was beginning to show that he was purely a political animal, a propagandist and a diplomat. He shied away from the activities of some of the more radical rank-and-file Irgun members and sympathizers.

Raziel's girl friend and future wife, Shoshana, was involved with the *Brit Habiryonim* group (roughly, "the tough guys' league"), an extremist sect led by Abba Achimeir, an admirer of Mussolini's who systematically attacked "the Marxists," and who, like Stern, constantly preached the virtues of death and sacrifice. Shoshana thought Kook was too much of a gentleman, a "dandy" in the underground, and she could not understand why David was so attached to and interested in him.[30]

There were continuing splits among the young nationalists, but they were mostly over personality and power conflicts, rather than over issues such as the holding up of banks to finance revolutionary activities. All of the Irgunist leaders were greatly influenced by a series of articles in 1937 by nationalistic, romantic poet Yonatan Ratosh (the future leader of the "Canaanite" movement).[31] The articles, entitled "Our Eyes Are Raised Towards Sovereignty," called for a rebellion against the British to achieve independence. Ratosh expressed in that one basic goal the spirit of many members of his generation throughout the Zionist spectrum.

In the years prior to World War II, the confrontation between the political Zionists and practical Zionists grew sharper and more pronounced. To the political Zionists it seemed the practical Zionists wished to build the Jewish state farm by farm, cow by cow. Jabotinsky insisted that the program of the political Zionists was also very practical, just not as romantically "photogenic" as a cow or a kibbutz. He believed in dramatic diplomatic methods, and this is what Kook found so appealing. Jabotinsky dealt exclusively with political issues, pressing the British to live up to the Mandate and the Balfour Declaration, to give Jews a national home. The practical Zionists thought his timetable was unrealistic. They kept their focus on pragmatic goals, creating "facts on the ground."

The name-calling between the two camps (Jabotinsky's people were called "fascists," while the practical Zionists were labeled "Bolsheviks") was symptomatic of most revolutionary movements, and of the general animosity between socialists and nationalists, even though the lines between them were often blurred. The two main streams of Zionism, blinded by the flames of conflicting ideology, were each unable to see any good on the other side.

In spite of popular conceptions (then and now), Jabotinsky was *not* a militarist. He was an intellectual, a diplomat and a fighter, a kind of composite of Mazzini, Garibaldi and Cavour, who had brought about the Italian national revolution. He emphasized military preparedness, because he advocated an independent Jewish country which, he believed, could not come into being without a Jewish army.

Hillel Kook first met Jabotinsky when the Irgun command sent him on a mission to Warsaw in September 1937 to consult with the political leader of the movement. The refined, intellectual Jabotinsky had an immediate impact on the brash twenty-two-year-old Irgun emissary, who was greatly impressed by Jabotinsky's cultured personality. Those who came into close contact with the writer-linguist-soldier often could not help emulating him, even in the choice of attire. He was always immaculately dressed, as had been Herzl, but that was already Kook's style.

In the ensuing three years, the boyish Irgun representative developed a close working relationship with the much older Jabotinsky. Nonetheless, everything about Jabotinsky was highly formal, and the two men never called each other anything but "Sir."

Jabotinsky had tens of thousands of followers in Poland, where he had one main goal: a ten-year plan to evacuate 1.5 million East European Jews to Palestine.

Under the system of treaties formulated at the 1919 Versailles Peace Conference, the Jews of eastern Europe, unlike their assimilated brethren living in the freedom of western Europe, were granted social and cultural autonomy. Their legal status, after centuries of persecution, was now that of any other national minority. But there was one major difference between them and their neighbors, a distinction that would facilitate their extermination: the Jews were an ethnic minority with no homeland, no territory where they could constitute a local majority of the population. These Jews were recognized as a distinctive national group by friends and foes alike, but politically, there was no recognition of their national rights.

Jabotinsky, pro-British, believed that that great democracy could eventually be moved to bring about the promised Jewish state in Palestine. In a dramatic appearance before the Royal Commission on Palestine – the Peel Commission – in London in early 1937, Jabotinsky described the position of Jews in eastern Europe as a potential disaster of historic magnitude, a "calamity," an "earthquake."[32] Without direct reference to the Hitler menace, he said that the "frozen stampede" – meaning the Jewish masses – was living on a volcano. "We have got to save millions, many *millions*," he emphasized passionately. Jabotinsky argued that although there were "two rights" in Palestine, the Jews had a greater need than did the Arabs and, therefore, the greater right. Chaim Weizmann, who also appeared before the commission, reiterated the longstanding majority Zionist policy on immigration, the antithesis of Jabotinsky's position: Palestine's shaky economy could only absorb a fraction of the Jews of Europe, Weizmann said, echoing the position of the British Colonial Office. Only a few, selected Jews could find a haven in the promised homeland. Millions of others would have to be left to their fate. In a report on the Peel Commission to the Twentieth Zionist Congress meeting in Zurich, he said: "The old ones will pass, they will bear their fate or they will not. They are dust, economic and moral dust in the cruel world."[33]

In Poland, Hillel Kook's immediate task was to raise funds for the Irgun underground in Palestine, to work not only with the Jewish masses, the "frozen herd," but also with the cosmopolitan upper classes in Warsaw, the capital whose population was one third Jewish. Jabotinsky ordered the Revisionist party to help Kook, to hear his case at a meeting of party leaders. It would prove an eye-opening lesson for Kook, as he dealt for the first time with organization Jews in the Diaspora.

The agenda of the Revisionists' central committee conference, which was held in a private Warsaw house, was in Yiddish; Kook was listed on the agenda as the second speaker. But they never got past the first item – the election of officers. It seemed to him that bureaucratic matters took precedence over hearing about the Irgun or the realities of Palestine, where the Arab uprising was continuing. Organization Jews seemed to him a world apart, and he never attended another such meeting.

It is a widespread historical misconception that the Irgun was an arm of the Revisionists. The Irgun was always totally separate from the party founded by Jabotinsky. It was a homegrown Palestinian liberation movement. As an individual, Jabotinsky in his twilight years considered himself an Irgunist, and he was often at odds with his own Revisionist party, which sought to control the Irgun. The young Irgunists regarded the Revisionists almost as adversaries, constantly trying to pressure "Jabo" to force the Irgun into the party structure. When the Revisionists' "foreign minister" (and future Jabotinsky biographer) Joseph Schechtman insisted on accompanying Kook, the Irgun's emissary, to a meeting at the Polish Foreign Ministry, Kook balked and Jabotinsky backed him up. The Irgun and the Revisionists would always remain separate entities.[34]

One of the men who had taken part in the Revisionist central committee meeting in the Warsaw house was Samuel Merlin, a young journalist who, though secretary-general of the Revisionist party in Poland, had become fed up with the petty concerns of party politics. The brooding, soft-spoken Merlin, born in Kishinev, Moldavia, in 1910, was soon swayed to the Irgun by Kook (who assumed the alias "Peter Swartzman" during his stay in Poland) and by Avraham Stern, who visited Poland periodically from 1938 to 1939. The young Turks of the Irgun maintained that their only recourse was violence against the British administration in Palestine, that the fuse had been lit by the forces of history. The Irgunists still thought of the diminutive Jabotinsky as a giant, but the Irgun felt it was essential to search for a way around the revered leader, who continued to favor political solutions over the use of force. "In the beginning, God created politics," Jabotinsky told Merlin, his one-time secretary.[35] The task of maintaining clear-cut separation and independence from the Revisionist movement fell to Kook, who began to engage in intricate political stratagems in order to circumvent Revisionist attempts to speak for the Irgun.

Kook's experiences in Poland were an awakening. The dapper, handsome and self-confident young man was brought closer to his childhood experience in pogrom-haunted eastern Europe, which contrasted sharply with the relatively hopeful atmosphere of Palestine where he had grown up. He had read and heard that the Jews of Poland were living on the brink, but the day-to-day reality of ghetto life and the rueful poverty of the Jewish masses stunned him. He lived in a boarding house in the Jewish quarter, where the Betar office was located. He took his meals with Merlin and Nathan Yellin-Friedman (a future left-wing leader of the Stern group) at a kosher *pension*. The well-dressed young nationalist revolutionary had come a long way from the *shtetl*, but as he walked among his brethren, his heart went out to them, and he rededicated himself to bringing as many Jews as possible to Palestine. He saw for himself that Jabotinsky was not exaggerating when he said that there were three or four million Jews in the East who were begging for salvation.

Poland wanted to get rid of the Jews – ten percent of the country's population and over a quarter of the urban population – and the Polish government helped finance Jewish immigration activities.[36] Thus, paradoxically, a community of interest was shared by the Zionists and anti-Semitic Polish students chanting "Jews to Palestine."

Kook did some organizing work among poor Jews, but he devoted most of his time to Jews of a different class: the intellectual, bohemian and political circles that revolved around a wealthy and well-connected young couple: university professor Henryk Strassman, a Jabotinsky supporter and Polish army reserve officer, and his wife Lilliane, a former leftist intellectual who had been hostile to the ideas of Jewish nationalism. Kook moved easily in the Strassmans' *salon*. His social success helped his political activities, a foreshadowing of his later work in America.

Pogroms had swept across Poland a few weeks after Kook's arrival, and his immediate task was to help organize the first Irgun military units in the country. Meanwhile, the main support group, the Strassman's broad circle of friends, formed an organization called the Jordan Club, and put out a highly professional Polish-language newspaper called *Jerozolima Wyzwolona*, or "Liberated Jerusalem."

The Irgun in Warsaw later put out another newspaper, *Die Tat* (The Deed), in Yiddish, edited by Merlin and Yellin-Friedman. The symbol of *Jerozolima Wyzwolona* was later adopted by the Irgun in Palestine: a hand holding a rifle over a map of the whole of Palestine – both banks of the Jordan – with the Hebrew words *rak kach*, "only thus."[37]

Kook, while organizing the Irgun cells in Poland, also continued to raise funds, and became a key figure in the Irgun's most vital project – "illegal" immigration to Palestine. Among those with whom he worked were Mordechai Strelitz, Chaim Lubinsky, Yosef Katznelson, Jabotinsky's son Eri, Yitshaq Ben-Ami, Aryeh Ben-Eliezer, Merlin, and the "notorious" Avraham Stavsky.[38] In the ensuing years, several of these men would work under Kook's direction in the United States, trying to save European Jews through different means.

The British, according to the terms of the League of Nations Mandate, were supposed to foster immigration of Jews to Palestine, but since they were now in fact acting to curb Jewish immigration, the Zionists believed it was their right and responsibility to smuggle Jews into the territory. In the 1920s, when there had been virtually no restrictions on immigration, few Jews wanted to go to Palestine. But with the Nazi takeover of Germany in 1933, great numbers of Jews clamored for the limited number of British immigration certificates available.

In the summer of 1937, Moshe Galili, a young Palestinian studying in Italy, devised plans for exploiting Palestine's long coastline to smuggle in large numbers of Jews. On his own, he organized a pilot run, bringing seventeen immigrants on a motorized sailboat from Greece to Palestine. Upon his arrival, he immediately contacted Raziel and sold him on the idea of transporting Jews to Palestine on a large scale.[39] It would not require great expenditures because the immigrants would pay their own way.

It was a particularly appealing idea because the mainstream Zionists' Jewish Agency, which administered the relatively small number of available British certificates for Palestine, excluded ideological opponents. When Jabotinsky broke away from the World Zionist Organization in 1935 and set up the New Zionist Organization, the Agency cut off his followers' share of the quota. In the years before Galili's operation, some labor-Zionists had engaged in similar activities, but the Jewish Agency was opposed on the grounds that it might hamper legal entry of labor-Zionists.

Within months, the innovative Irgun operation grew substantially. Kook was still in Poland in the summer of 1938.[40] But as the immigration project developed,

Raziel decided that Hillel should be stationed in London, Jabotinsky's main headquarters, in order to be closer to the leader of the movement, to become the liaison between Jabotinsky and the Irgun, and to further the immigration work, which had become a joint enterprise of the Revisionists, the Irgun, the New Zionist Organization (NZO) and the Betar youth organization. He was also to travel to the various European cities where the immigration movement was concentrated, and to keep in close touch with the Irgunists in Poland. In the capital of the British empire, Kook learned more lessons in basic politics, fending off continuing Revisionist attempts to infringe on the Irgun's independence. On one occasion Revisionist functionaries stole an Irgun communication from Kook's overcoat and brought it to Jabotinsky. The letter revealed how the Irgun found it necessary to work around "Jabo" (a nickname no one would dare use to his face), in order to avert control by the Revisionists. Jabotinsky was greatly upset at the realization of how great a gulf separated his followers.

In the period from 1937 to 1940, the Irgun's "illegal" immigration operation saved anywhere from nine thousand to twenty-five thousand European Jews.[41] The Nazis were not opposed to the exodus – in fact SS officials, including Adolf Eichmann, encouraged the Irgun's immigration efforts.[42] Germany was still years away from the "Final Solution," though Hitler vowed in many of his speeches that if war came, the Jews of Europe would be annihilated.

After Hitler's annexation of Austria and Czechoslovakia in 1938, the Irgunists no longer restricted selection of immigrants to supporters of their Zionist camp. This contrasted sharply with the policy of the Jewish Agency, which barred anyone but their own from entering Palestine. The Zionist organizations in Palestine, the United States and England attacked the Irgunists for using "floating coffins" – an apt enough description for most of the vessels that Kook and his comrades could hire – to bring to Palestine "undesirable elements" from among the Jews of Europe.[43]

The foremost concern of the Irgun groups, located in several European capitals, was to get Jews to Palestine, no matter how. But the immigration operation also provided fringe financial benefits for the different – often competing – organizations involved, and this, inevitably, exacerbated the rivalry among them. There was continuing cooperation in the field between the Irgun and Betar, the latter headed by Jabotinsky's son, Eri. Most of the immigrants were, in fact, drawn from the youth movement. Nevertheless, conflicts persisted, especially between the Irgunists and the functionaries of the NZO. This led Jabotinsky to call a meeting in Paris, in order to resolve the conflict.

Kook, who was on a trip to Poland when Jabotinsky summoned him for the meeting, was joined by Raziel, who had just arrived in Poland from Palestine. It had been eighteen months since they had seen each other, and there was much to talk about on the train from Warsaw to Paris. Although the dispute over immigration was important, they talked for hours about a potentially far more damaging conflict – the personality clash between Raziel and Stern. It was apparent, long before the sharp ideological differences between the two charismatic men emerged, that a schism was coming, and that the movement itself was threatened internally.

At the conference in Paris, held in a house on Victor Emmanuel III Boulevard, there was a heated debate, with Kook insisting that the Irgun refused to be subordinate to the NZO. It was decided that an overall command for the immigration work be appointed: Eri Jabotinsky for Betar; Kook for the Irgun; and one so-called neutral, Joseph Katznelson, as chairman.[44]

Mainstream Zionists all over the world condemned the Irgun's immigration efforts, and Reform Rabbi Stephen Wise, the undisputed leader of organized American Jewry, called Jabotinsky a "traitor" for preaching evacuation of over a million eastern European Jews. Many liberal Jews like Dr. Wise condemned the idea of mass emigration because they felt it would constitute acquiescence in the expulsion of the Jews. Furthermore, Wise claimed, the Jabotinsky movement was guilty of bringing unselected, "unsuitable" Jews to Palestine. As the United Palestine Appeal's director Henry Montor wrote, "No responsible person has ever said that Palestine could hold all the millions of Jews who need shelter." Montor condemned those who ignored the "need" for selecting Jews "worthy" of settling in Palestine: "I think it is fair to point out that many who have been brought into Palestine by the Revisionists [sic] have been prostitutes and criminals."[45]

Between American Zionists like Montor and a Palestinian Zionist like Kook, or his colleagues, there was a huge gap in understanding the facts in the field. The Irgunists felt that they were saving the Jewish family, and it did not matter at that point in history if an uncle was never going to milk a cow on the kibbutz, or that he was lazy or drank too much. He had every right to get out of the cauldron of Europe and to be brought to Palestine. They could not tell him that "your credentials aren't good enough to be a New Jew; go back to Poland." Yet that was the openly stated position of many mainstream Zionists – even after the war had begun, as Montor's letter shows.

The British government led the chorus of condemnation against the immigration effort that Kook helped coordinate throughout eastern and central Europe. In a House of Commons debate on April 26, 1939, Colonial Secretary Malcolm MacDonald was queried about the policy of turning back shiploads of Jews fleeing the Nazis. When asked if they were being sent back to concentration camps, he replied: "The responsibility rests on those responsible for organizing illegal immigration."[46] A few weeks later, the British government put the official seal of doom on European Jewry when it issued the White Paper, virtually closing the gates of Palestine to the millions who were about to die.

Kook was shocked to find that, although the Zionists led by Weizmann and Ben-Gurion strongly condemned the infamous White Paper, they continued to obstruct efforts by the Irgunists to circumvent it. (The extent of the betrayal would not be known for years, with the release of previously secret documents.) An indication of how far the Zionist leadership would go is given by the fact that Ben-Gurion's close aide, Arthur Lourie, political secretary of the Jewish Agency, gave British authorities the names and countries of origin of ships chartered by the Irgunists.[47]

The White Paper, issued on May 17, 1939, restricted Jewish immigration to Palestine to 75,000 over a five-year period, and also stipulated that there would be no immigration whatsoever after 1944 without Arab approval. It also severely limited Jewish land purchases. The White Paper may have pacified rebellious Palestinian Arabs and the Arab and Moslem world, but it also set off the Jewish revolt against the British in Palestine. On the day it was issued, David Raziel and the rest of the Irgun High Command in Jerusalem decided for the first time to attack British targets.

Everywhere in the world, doors were shutting on the Jews; the month of May 1939 also witnessed the tragic affair of the *S.S. St. Louis* and the defeat in Congress of the Wagner refugee bill. The *St. Louis*, a Hamburg-American Line ship, sailed from Germany on May 13 and headed for Cuba. Over 700 of the 900 passengers thought they were bound for the United States, having gone through a preliminary, labyrinthine immigration process. To the horror of all the passengers, the ship was turned away, first by the Cubans and then by the Americans. A few American journalists and clergymen called it one of the most shameful episodes in the history of the so-called "haven for the oppressed," the United States. American Jewish organizations, worried about the strong anti-Semitism enveloping America, refused to press the government for visas or to criticize the Roosevelt administration.[48]

It appears in retrospect that the *St. Louis* was a test case for the Nazis. It confirmed their theory that the democracies were unconcerned about the fate of the Jews, and it therefore advanced the prospects for a "Final Solution" to the "Jewish problem." The American Joint Distribution Committee, the aid arm of the American Jewish Committee, did finally succeed in finding refuge in various European countries for the passengers of that ship, but most of them would eventually perish in Hitler's death camps.

Organized American Jews, led by Rabbi Wise, had not only let down the *St. Louis* passengers, but they also failed to press for passage of the Wagner bill, which had called for the admission of 20,000 "German" refugee children. The term "German" was used instead of "Jewish" in the draft of the bill because of the prevailing aversion to bringing Jews to America, led, among others, by the anti-Semitic "tobacco senator" Robert Reynolds of North Carolina. The bill was enthusiastically supported by such prominent Americans as Eleanor Roosevelt, Herbert Hoover, and entertainer Eddie Cantor. But the cautious attitude of American Jewish leaders guaranteed that the bill would be defeated when it came before Congress that fateful May. The Jewish leaders feared that they would be suspected of "double loyalty." Wise, faced by the fierce opposition of the Jew-hating American right, was determined to keep a low profile, and he urged other Jewish leaders to do the same.[49] Wise insisted that the Jewish community – five million strong at that time – refrain from publicity while the bill was under consideration. The "timidity" of Rabbi Wise[50] was construed by American anti-Semitic groups, such as the Silver Shirts, the Ku Klux Klan, the American Legion, and the Daughters of the American Revolution, as a symbol of indifference. The exclusionary racist philosophy of Father Coughlin, Henry Ford, Joseph Kennedy, Charles Lindbergh and other American Firsters and their fellow travelers, prevailed.

Through the first six months of 1939, Hillel Kook, using Jabotinsky's London headquarters as his home base, continued to work on immigration efforts in Europe, traveling frequently to Poland, the center of Jewish life in Europe.

In mid-August, Jabotinsky cabled Kook and asked him to go to the Twenty-First Zionist Congress meeting in Geneva, and to use the occasion to propagandize for Irgun policy. Kook organized a group including Chaim Lubinsky, Alexander Rafaeli and Lilliane Strassman from Warsaw to attend the congress, which was convening in the shadow of Hitler's war. Jabotinsky, after meeting with Kook's group in southern France, told his Revisionist "foreign minister" and biographer, Schechtman, that he saw in the youthful Irgunists a "real quest for some policy more adequate to the (present) period."[51]

In the drive down from Paris on the way to Switzerland, Kook, who had used the alias "Eitan" in Palestine and "Peter Swartzman" in Europe, chose a new name – Peter Bergson. There was a certain compulsion in the underground to use aliases, but there were also sound reasons. As a member of the Irgun leadership, Kook now had a price on his head. He also wanted to protect the family name, the most revered in Orthodox Judaism. He chose the name Bergson from his father's name, Dov (Hebrew for "bear"). "Son of Bear" became Bergson; he was also a staunch admirer of the Polish-born Jewish philosopher Henri Bergson.

In Palestine, the Kook family knew that Hillel was on a mission on behalf of the nascent Hebrew nation, and in the years to come, they would follow with pride reports of "Peter H. Bergson's" progress, though news of him came only through word of mouth or clippings sent through the mail. Under the British rulers of Palestine, the very mention of the name Peter Bergson in the press or on the radio would be subject to censorship.

CHAPTER TWO

THE RIGHT TO FIGHT: THE IDEA OF A JEWISH ARMY

During the morning hours of September 1, 1939, Germany's Blitzkrieg invasion of Poland began, setting off World War II. At that moment all hope was shattered for millions of Jews.

Ze'ev Jabotinsky, as well as most Jewish leaders, was caught by surprise; he had told Merlin, Kook, and others that war was not in the cards because the loss of human life would be too staggering to contemplate.[1] A day after the outbreak of war, Jabotinsky proposed formation of a Jewish army to fight alongside the Allies, a force formed on the lines of the World War I Jewish Legion, which he had created and which had helped Britain to wrest Palestine from the Turks. But this time, the British, mindful of the need to maintain good relations with the Arabs, would reject the idea out of hand. In his proposal – made during talks with the French cabinet minister Anatole de Monzie – Jabotinsky described a force that would be the nucleus of a true national army, comprised of Palestinian Jews and volunteers from Jewish communities around the world.[2] Jabotinsky issued an appeal to Jews worldwide to fight alongside the French and British. "The Jewish nation's place is... on all the fronts where these countries fight."[3]

Jabotinsky's legendary activities during World War I made it all too easy to misinterpret him as saying that Jews should be separated into a Jewish army. Even the most fervent Zionist recognized that the overwhelming majority of American Jews felt they were Americans first, and that the primary allegiance of most French

Jews was to the French – not to the Jewish nation. Jabotinsky and some of his followers recognized the problems of Jewish identity that were made manifest by the Zionist movement. In World War I, few thought there was a conflict of identity when French Jews fought German Jews (in the manner in which, say, a number of socialists and anarchists refused to fight like-minded people who happened to be of different nationalities). But now there emerged a fundamental conflict between the Jewish claim for total equality as members of other nations and the struggle for total equality for the emerging Jewish nation in Palestine.

Jabotinsky declared that the Jewish people saw themselves as an ally in the war against their primary enemy, the Nazis; and he would continue for the remaining ten months of his life to seek recognition of the Jews as a co-belligerent. In December, Chaim Weizmann submitted a proposal of his own for the formation of a Jewish force, a single division to be included in the British army. But neither of the two Jewish leaders' plans was acceptable to the British, for it was obvious to them, and to the Arab nations, that a well-equipped Jewish army, comprised mainly of Palestinian Jews, would work toward the Zionist goal once the war was over. Jabotinsky also declared that the differences between the British and the Jewish people over Palestine should be suspended because of the war. Never, he said, through the long centuries of persecution, was there a greater need for the Jews to be armed for self-defense.

When the war broke out, tens of thousands of Palestinian Jews voluntarily registered for military service with the British, including large numbers of underground fighters who grudgingly accepted Jabotinsky's call to fight with England, which "until recently... was our partner in Zion."[4] The Palestinian Jews were not subject to conscription because Palestine was a League of Nations mandate territory, but 130,000 (out of a population of about 550,000 – or nearly 25%) registered for service through the Jewish Agency, six times the percentage of the Palestinian Arab population that volunteered. But the Jews were officially discouraged by the British. In Palestine, all news items relating Jews with the war effort were censored, as was the very word "Zionism."[5] The British were right to fear that a Jewish army could potentially be a force that would fight British colonialism. Jabotinsky urged, however, that everything be subordinated to the struggle against Hitler, and it was clear that a Jewish army would be a formidable force.

Jabotinsky's appeal to the underground to cooperate with Britain caused a rift in the Irgun, which had been attacking British targets since the issuance of the

White Paper four months before the war broke out. But that was not the only issue involved. The personality conflict and rivalry between Raziel and Stern were coming to a head. Both Raziel and Stern were regarded by most of their followers as almost Messianic figures. Stern was perceived as "the prophet speaking truth, but unable to effect it," while Raziel was "the Biblical king, able to rule, but making mistake after mistake, apparently due to a lack of political insight."[6] Raziel, who had been caught and imprisoned in Palestine on the eve of the war, approved Jabotinsky's decision. But Stern, also in prison, disagreed vehemently, preaching that the British were the occupiers of Palestine, and therefore the number-one enemies of the Jews. Stern and his supporters referred to Jabotinsky as an "ex-activist leader," a lackey of the British. Needless to say, Jabotinsky, who regarded Stern's position as suicidal, was greatly disturbed by these developments.[7] But the split between Stern and Raziel, and Raziel's mentor Jabotinsky, was to grow wider.

In February 1940, Jabotinsky, rebuffed by the British, left Europe for the United States, in order to launch a public campaign for the idea of a Jewish army in Palestine, an army that would be a concrete step towards creation of the Jewish nation. He was fully aware of the controversial nature of such a step in still-neutral America. Jabotinsky sent an appeal to David Ben-Gurion, the head of the Jewish community in Palestine, to Weizmann, and to leaders of the United States Jewish community to establish a central focal point, in order to evaluate information and to plan action. The campaign for a Jewish army would focus, at certain moments during the war, on the safety of the Jewish community in Palestine and the steps that should be taken to stop the advance of the Germans in the Near East and North Africa. But all along, it was based on the concept that there was only one answer to the physical threat against the Jewish People – a physical answer, a Jewish army.[8]

Hillel Kook, a.k.a. Peter Bergson, was eager to go back to Palestine from England, but at Jabotinsky's urging, he prepared to go to America to join him. Already in the spring of 1939, a Jabotinsky delegation had gone to the United States, consisting of Lt. Col. John Henry Patterson, the maverick British officer who had commanded the Jewish Legion in World War I; Robert Briscoe, a Jewish member of the Irish parliament; and Palestinian Irgunists Chaim Lubinsky and Yitshaq Ben-Ami. Ben-Ami had established a small office in New York, organizing and directing a non-sectarian group called the American Friends of a Jewish Palestine, the first pro-Irgun organization in America.[9]

In the months before Bergson's departure for America in June 1940 to take part in Jabotinsky's campaign, he engaged in a frantic attempt to raise funds in England for the *Sakarya*, an Irgun ship guided by Jabotinsky's son, Eri, brought over 2,000 refugees down the Danube route to Palestine, underscoring the fact that even with war raging, it was still possible to get Jews out, even from territories under Nazi control. Eri Jabotinsky, in a dispatch from Rumania, informed his colleagues that "as long as this is happening, we will continue our work."[10] He called for intensive fund raising.

Since the day after the war broke out six months earlier, the Irgun had sent fourteen barely seaworthy ships out of Europe; but the mainstream Zionist movement continued to attack their efforts. In the United States, Rabbi Stephen Wise issued a statement to the press in November 1939, condemning "the activities of independent organizations seeking to duplicate or parallel the work of the Jewish Agency." Wise ignored the fact that at that time the Jewish Agency's own activities were extremely limited. The *South African Zionist Review* also deprecated the Irgun's efforts. "These people are dumped into Palestine without regard for their usefulness to the country. No screening or selection is attempted."[11] This attitude was spelled out in detail by Henry Montor, head of the United Palestine Appeal,[12] in a letter to a Maryland rabbi on February 1, 1940.[13] "Selectivity" was an absolute necessity in immigration to Palestine, he said, and that meant labor Zionists, not Revisionists or other "radical" Zionists. Like Wise, he condemned "irresponsible parties" for the way they were transporting Jews down the Danube – they were turning the plight of these Jews into a public issue, while the Jewish Agency was working discreetly. He charged that most of the "Revisionists" responsible for organizing the exodus of the so-called illegals were only in it for the money. Since they were solely "concerned with the profit motive," they were more than willing to take the "unsuitable" – old people, even "prostitutes and criminals – certainly an element which cannot contribute to the upbuilding of a Jewish national home." He reiterated the position of Weizmann that Palestine could not absorb great numbers of European Jews. Montor was simply being frank, and the present plight of the Jews seemed to concern him less than the post-war plans for a state. But this was still over two years before the first news of the systematic extermination of Europe's Jews was revealed, and his words, in retrospect, seem callous when considered out of their historical context.

The *Sakarya* was intercepted by the British on February 13, 1940, and the passengers, many of them Jews from Germany, were interned, and later released and allowed to stay, except for six Hungarian Jews who were sent back to war-torn Europe. British High Commissioner Harold MacMichael's decision was not based on humanitarian considerations, but on the need to avoid "any measures which, by inflaming Jewish opinion," might immobilize some British forces. In any case, the British had decided, in July 1939, that the number of interned "illegals" would henceforth be deducted from the quota set by the White Paper.[14] Eri Jabotinsky, who was responsible for saving 2,200 lives, was arrested and imprisoned for bringing "illegals" to Palestine.

The ship that brought Peter Bergson to America traveled in a convoy, and the passenger vessel that proceeded his was torpedoed by the Germans. On board the *Scythia*, a British vessel that he had boarded in Southampton, Bergson reflected on the darkness descending on Europe, the volcano that had finally erupted. The Europe he left in June was shattered by the fall of France and with fears that the Nazis were about to invade England. The Jewish struggle was part of the greatest battle ever against a consummate evil. America was clearly the world's only hope for salvation, but President Roosevelt was struggling against the majority sentiment to stay out of the war.

Ze'ev Jabotinsky was naturally in a grim mood when he met Bergson upon the young Irgunist's arrival in New York. For the leader who had not believed the war would come, the news of the Jewish suffering in Poland was crushing. Jabotinsky was working on a book, *The War and the Jew*, which included a call for the establishment of a Jewish army to help fight the Nazis, and the creation of a Jewish state in Palestine.[15] Jabotinsky had drawn a crowd of over 5,000 in an address at the Manhattan Center on March 19, 1940, in which he promoted his ideas for the Jewish force. This aroused the ire of Rabbi Wise, especially since the British ambassador, Lord Lothian, had lent his name as a sponsor of the rally. The rabbi led a delegation of important American Jewish leaders to the British envoy to protest Lothian's action and to attack Jabotinsky's "adventurous scheme." Lord Lothian withdrew his support from a second rally, scheduled for June 25.[16]

Soon after Bergson disembarked in New York, Jabotinsky told him that the split between Stern and Raziel was now final, and that each had taken a small group of Irgunists with him. In fact, what had happened was that the majority had dropped out altogether, leaving the Irgun in disarray. Jabotinsky described the small group of Irgunists now in America, including the recently arrived Samuel Merlin, as a "cut-off battalion." Jabotinsky was deeply disturbed by Stern, who believed in indiscriminate terror, including the shooting of British police and soldiers on sight. Stern derided the Irgun's code of honor in choosing its targets, and its decision to cooperate with the British in the war effort.[17]

In the first weeks after Bergson's arrival, the twenty-five-year-old (his mustache made him look just a bit older) felt confused and bewildered by the war situation, by the distance from Palestine where his two friends Raziel and Eri Jabotinsky were imprisoned, and by the startling uniqueness of the America he was confronting. In his mind, he had always equated the Jews of America with the Jews of Europe, and it took him some time to realize that the Jews he met were *part* of America, in a way that was fundamentally different from the relationship of most European Jews to their countries. In Poland, Bergson and the others had found that even assimilated Jews like the Strassmans were vitally involved with Palestine. But in the city of New York, with its two million Jews, Bergson and his colleagues were confronted with general indifference about Palestine, and little grass-roots Zionist activity.

Palestinians Ben-Ami, Lubinsky, Alexander Rafaeli, and the others who had tried to raise money for the Irgun's illegal immigration effort in 1939 and for the post-White Paper campaign against the British, had worked on a very small scale.[18] None of them could be described as particularly dynamic personalities who could mobilize a large number of important supporters. Moreover, they were working under a stigma – they represented a small minority of the Jews in Palestine, and their movement was associated with terrorism by the mainstream Zionists. Jabotinsky was reviled as a "neo-fascist," and his followers were blamed, probably unjustly, for the 1933 killing of labor Zionist leader Arlosoroff. They were, in short, outsiders in every way. In any case, their fund-raising efforts before Bergson came were a failure, and Ben-Ami did not succeed in conveying the sense of urgency to the people the group was trying to reach.[19] In April 1940, Merlin, at the behest of Bergson in London, left Europe to join the small group in New York. They bided their time until Bergson could join them.

When Bergson took over in mid-1940, he soon learned the lesson that the others knew all too well: that the established Jewish organizations were fossilized and often led by self-righteous, unenlightened men concerned mainly with the prestige of office. But there was something *positive* about being unacceptable to them, about being forced to work outside the establishment in order to advance the Jewish cause. That cause was now no longer illegal immigration – which had become much more difficult after the fall of France – but promoting the idea of a Jewish army.

The group realized early on that they had to avoid the pitfall of confining their activities to Jews, and pursued a non-sectarian approach. Opposition to their efforts came not only from mainstream Zionists, but from the Revisionist party in the United States as well – just as in Poland and elsewhere in Europe. Soon after Bergson took over, the Revisionists tried to pressure Jabotinsky to disband the group. The Revisionists contended that the Irgun was an underground organization, and that they therefore "shouldn't have letterhead" as did the party.[20] But the Palestinians claimed that their "American Friends" organization was a non-sectarian United States group which was independent and free to support the general cause of a free Palestine.[21]

Under Bergson's authority (he was regarded by the others as their military commander in a civilian situation), the Ben-Ami group functioned much more effectively, in spite of frequent disagreements and bruised egos.[22] Bergson had "very definite ideas, dislikes and loves," and a dominating personality, especially to those, like Alex Rafaeli, who regarded themselves as soldiers under his command.[23] Merlin, too, thought of the Irgun as a pyramid, with the soldiers on the bottom, their individualistic tendencies of necessity suppressed. By contrast, those in the top rank could give vent to their individualism. In general, they could not stand one another. Bergson, Raziel's protege, felt very close to his friend and mentor, who was rotting in a Palestine jail; even Jabotinsky did not mean as much to him. Merlin, who had been very close to Stern, had mixed feelings about Bergson – he admired him greatly, but resented his youthful arrogance and steely-eyed contemptuousness for the opinions of lower-ranking Irgunists. But Merlin took Jabotinsky at his word when he said that the "cut-off battalion" was the only surviving cohesive Irgun group engaged in political and propaganda activities.

A few weeks after Bergson's arrival, he and Merlin took an apartment together at 3 East 63rd Street, paying $60 a month rent. It took a few days to get the phone connected and, in the interim, Bergson imposed on a neighbor down the hall. She was an attractive twenty-year-old woman from Kansas City, Betty Keane Caplan. She would eventually be recruited into Bergson's committee – and a few years later, her relationship with Bergson would become much more. But for now, the relationship between the dark-haired young woman with almond-shaped eyes and Bergson, five years her senior, was one of friendship only. She learned that the young Palestinian Jew was using an alias, and she told her sister Rose, a Broadway actress, that he was an extremely articulate and intriguing man.

Soon after moving in, Bergson and Merlin threw a party for Jabotinsky, during which an attempt was made to make peace between the Irgun group and the American Revisionists. But few Revisionists came – they were barely on speaking terms with the young Irgunists. Jabotinsky himself was becoming increasingly vocal about where his sympathies lay: with the Raziel-Bergson camp of the Irgun.[24]

It took several months for Bergson to organize a broader-based group than the original American Friends of a Jewish Palestine, one that had the potential to mobilize public opinion on the issue of a Jewish army, which was still strenuously opposed by the British. In June 1940, a few weeks after Dunkirk, Lord Lothian, the British envoy to the United States, who had previously expressed support for Jabotinsky because of his pro-British position, contemptuously dismissed calls for a Jewish army. The ambassador associated the call with the Irgun, which was "an illegal organization concerned with political terrorism."[25] Jabotinsky, bitterly disappointed, lashed out at the British for refusing to treat the Jewish People as an allied nation. But the British would never change their view, and the Irgun would always be regarded as an enemy organization – even when the British secretly sent Irgun leader David Raziel and some of his men on a fatal commando mission against the Nazis.

In the late 1930s and early forties, American Jewish organizations were paralyzed by fear of a growing and virulent anti-Semitism in the United States. Hatred of the Jews was rife. The magazine *Fortune*, in its April 1939 issue, commented on the opposition of most Americans to admitting Jewish refugees into the country, and said that Hitler and his German-American Bund could safely conclude that "Americans don't like Jews much better than do the Nazis."

A few months earlier, on November 13, 1938, four days after the *Kristallnacht* pogrom in Germany, American Jewish organizations exhibited their anxieties about home-grown anti-Semitism by adopting a resolution against holding any public demonstrations or mass meetings. The umbrella American General Jewish Council's resolution said that there should not be large Jewish meetings "in any place other than in a place of worship."[26]

The leaders' fears were far from being groundless. Anti-Semitism was well-organized by American fascist movements, like the Silver Shirts and the Ku Klux Klan, boasting membership in the millions. In 1942, at the time the news of the

Holocaust was first documented, the Silver Shirts advocated an "alien registration day" for persons of "Hebrew blood"; ghettoization of all Hebrews; and removal of their civil rights. Such sentiments were strong not only among the masses. Some of the most prominent men in the country, such as American Firsters Charles Lindbergh, Henry Ford and Joseph Kennedy, were openly anti-Jewish in preaching isolationism. In July 1942, a Gallup poll showed that one American in six believed that their enemy, Hitler, was "doing the right thing" to the Jews. There was widespread fear of aliens, and Jews were often falsely accused of being "draft dodgers."[27]

In this general atmosphere, the young Palestinians in their newly-organized committee recognized that the Zionist and Jewish establishment had to contend with the accusations of the anti-Semitic American right that fighting Hitler was really a war to save Jews. But they could not understand why the leadership was so immobilized, why there was so little imagination or daring.

The major Jewish organizations in America were in continual competition for funds and for getting credit for such projects as the boycott of German goods. Because their concentration was often focused on internal power struggles, the organizations frequently failed to cooperate on major issues – or they displayed a minimalist posture. By April 1941, the leaders of Dr. Wise's American Jewish Congress were "paranoid about every action taken by their groups."[28] Disorder and disagreement permeated every aspect of the American Jewish community's plans to help Hitler's victims.

For years, Rabbi Wise was engaged in a bitter struggle for power with the more activist Zionists led by Rabbi Abba Hillel Silver and Emanuel Neumann, whose militancy would be constantly spurred by the growing appeal of the Bergson group. "Every one of those factions thought that they were following the right path," one of the establishment leaders would say forty years later.[29]

In August 1940, American Orthodox rabbis were pressing the big Jewish organizations to save 2,800 rabbis and yeshiva students in Lithuania by demanding that the State Department grant non-quota visas for them. But at a major conference of the Joint Distribution Committee, the American Jewish Congress, B'nai B'rith, HIAS (Hebrew Immigrant Aid Society), the Zionist Organization of America, and other groups, Stephen Wise, the keynote speaker, expressed the cautious belief that it was important to absorb 300-500 of the Lithuanian religious figures – and only for reasons of "Jewish culture." He did not feel it was feasible to resettle large numbers of Jews in the United States, and he disavowed the use of pressure on the government to issue visas.[30] In truth, organized American Jewry had never really been involved in political work, only in fund-raising. David Ben-Gurion was contemptuous of United States Jews and felt American Zionists would have to change radically, in order to fulfill a vital role in bringing about the creation of a Jewish state.[31] The failure of the organizations to act – at the August 1940 conference and on many other occasions – was symptomatic of the malaise of inactivity into which American Jewish organizations had fallen prior to World War II.

The "Bergsonites," as they would soon become known, were not bound by the usual constraints of the establishment organizations. They thought of themselves as political creatures, and an *ad hoc* group working in an emergency situation. It was soon to become evident that there was a greater need for fresh initiative, a new outlook. Their first goal was to engage in political work for creation of a Jewish army, which, for the Jews, was not some quixotic goal, but *the* issue – as some prominent intellectuals on both the right and left understood.[32]

But the group suffered a major blow two months after Bergson's arrival. Ze'ev Jabotinsky died suddenly at age sixty while on a visit to a Betar camp in upstate New York in August 1940. His death had a profound effect on the "cut-off battalion," which nevertheless was determined to carry on his work. Bergson believed the only way to achieve Jabotinsky's dream of a Jewish army was to launch a massive propaganda campaign to create the appropriate public climate. It was an ambitious goal, and in order to attain it, the group felt it would be necessary to mobilize a wide body of support among Americans, both Jewish and non-Jewish, and of all political persuasions.

Peter Bergson – whom his colleagues described as "handsome," "arrogant," "brilliant" – envisioned it on a grand scale, and he had the complex of personal attributes to pull it off. His experience in Palestine, Poland and England gave him a certain polish, so that by the time Bergson started work in the United States, he had shed any provincial traits he may have had.[33] Within a year, the group, under Bergson's direction, began to show impressive successes in its political and propaganda activities. Bergson was not shy, and he had a certain charisma that drew important people to him. He had no difficulty in recruiting many prominent Jews and non-Jews to fight for Jewish national rights: Among those who would support the Jewish army campaign were almost one-third of the Senate; a hundred congressmen; the top echelon of the War Department; cabinet members; even leftist intellectuals like Hannah Arendt, a refugee from Germany who thought that a Jewish army would bring pride to her beleaguered people and create a new image, "a new sense of Jewish identity."[34]

In late May 1941, Bergson was devastated by the news of his best friend's death. The British mandate authorities had freed David Raziel soon after the war broke out. Some eighteen months later, British intelligence in Cairo sent him and some of his men on a sabotage mission to Habaniya, Iraq. The target was oil depots which served the *Luftwaffe*. Part of the arrangement with the British was an unspoken agreement that the Irgunists would try to capture the pro-Nazi Mufti of Jerusalem, Haj Amin al-Husseini, who had taken refuge in Baghdad with the German-aligned government of Rashid Ali. But Raziel was killed on May 20 in a German bombing attack near the oil fields. The British never acknowledged during the war that they had pardoned some members of the Irgun and the Haganah and had sent them on suicide missions to Iraq and Vichy-held Syria. Bergson received the news in a telegram from Palestine and was in a state of shock for days.[35] It was a much greater blow personally than was Jabotinsky's death, for Raziel and Bergson had been like brothers. It took some time for Bergson to regain the momentum he had built up, but he was soon inspiring politicians and well-known personalities to urge the allies to allow the organization of all-Jewish military units in Palestine.

The Jewish army idea was vital. Since Germany was the mortal enemy of the Jewish People, it was only natural that Palestinian Jews and Jews who became stateless because of Hitler should combine into a distinct military force to fight with the Allies as a co-belligerent. It would have been important to the general war effort, as well as helping the imperiled Jews of Europe. In the eyes of the occupied nations, such an army would have enhanced the position of the Jews, who were thought of only as victims. The army idea stemmed from the conviction that there was a need to stress the national identity of those Jews who, in the Europe of Hitler, belonged to no other nation but the Jewish one. American Jews, British Jews, would not join such an army – they were part of their native countries. The army would be composed of stateless European Jews and the Jews of Palestine. But there was a certain confusion about what a Jewish army meant. The Bergsonites would later use the term "Hebrew" – a precursor of "Israeli" – to define the Jewish nationality, as distinct from the Jewish religion of nationals of other states.

A few intellectuals recognized the differences between the position of the mainstream Zionists, who spoke of a Jewish armed force recruited in Palestine to serve under British command, and the Bergson committee's call for an army of Palestinian *and* stateless European Jews that would serve under a general Allied command. The difference was a question of national identity.[36] In essence, the Zionist establishment agreed with the injurious allied perception of the stateless Jews as being "Germans" or "Poles." They were interested in nothing more than a Jewish brigade. But in September 1941, the Zionist Organization of America adopted a resolution that closely paralleled the position of the Bergson group. However, when Peter Bergson approached the ZOA and offered to cooperate, and to subordinate his own group's activities in the name of Zionist unity, he was rebuffed.[37]

The Bergsonites viewed the need for a Jewish army as self-evident. The group's old name was shed, and the Committee for a Jewish Army formally launched its campaign on December 4, 1941, three days before Pearl Harbor and America's entry into the war. (Once America was no longer neutral, it became necessary to make it even clearer that the Jewish army was not meant for American Jews; the Organization's name was lengthened to Committee for a Jewish Army of Stateless and Palestinian Jews.)

The convention launching the committee was held in Washington, D.C., chaired by Dr. Samuel Hardin Church, head of the Carnegie Institute, and journalist Pierre van Paassen. Bergson was named as National Director of the Jewish army group, and the national committee included thirteen senators (Harry Truman among them), retired generals and admirals, leading clergymen and labor leaders (William Green of the AFL and Philip Murray of the CIO), writers and entertainers, such as Rex Stout, Louis Bromfield, Max Lerner, Lowell Thomas, Eddie Cantor, and Ben Hecht. Secretary of War Henry Stimson sent a telegram of support to the newly-formed committee, saying that, "Free men everywhere are arming for the defense of democracy." Rear Admiral E.E. Yarnell, in joining the committee, emphasized the need for a Jewish army based in Palestine and predicted that the near East would become the main theater of operations during the coming year. Dr. Church in his opening address did not hide the fact that the proposed army of 200,000 Jews in Palestine would have another task after helping to defeat Hitler. The army would then be "in Jerusalem, under the aegis of England and America... we want a Jewish government to be established there...."[38]

Bergson, in subsequent meetings with Stimson and other defense officials, suggested that the proposed army be formed under American command and be based in North Africa. Stimson established a committee headed by an anti-Zionist Jew, a Colonel Greenbaum, to investigate the logistics of such an army. The panel's report was entirely negative, but Stimson himself remained interested.[39] And

Secretary of the Navy Frank Knox advocated the creation of a Jewish army to stop the German thrust towards the Mosul oil fields of Iran.[40]

Within weeks of the committee's formal launching, the first of several major congressional resolutions sponsored by the Bergson group was introduced in the House of Representatives by New York Congressman Andrew L. Somers, an Irish-American who would become one of the most active supporters of the committee through the coming years. The resolution urged the President to press Britain to permit the organizing of Jewish military units in Palestine. In April 1942, Senator Edwin Johnson of Colorado urged the Senate to help implement the Bergson group's proposals. The prominent Democratic senator, who became national chairman of the Jewish army committee and who later chaired the Senate Armed Forces Committee, emphasized that the Bergson organization was non-partisan and non-sectarian, and that the force it was fighting to create would be similar to the Free French or Free Serbs or other armies of the oppressed peoples. It was made abundantly clear that American Jews naturally would continue to serve in the United States armed forces.

Over a period of about six months, Bergson and his colleagues managed to raise enough money among a circle of about two hundred supporters to pay for the first of scores of full-page newspaper and magazine advertisements promoting a Jewish army. The advertisement in *The New York Times* in January 1942, entitled "Jews Fight for the Right to Fight," drew a tremendous public response.[43] Such large ads with political messages were a fairly recent phenomenon, and the Bergsonites would master this innovative form for getting across a political message. The text of the ad said that 200,000 Palestinian and stateless Jews were "eager to fight back and avenge." Over 135,000 Palestinians had volunteered for service as soon as war broke out more than two years earlier. "They are still waiting to be called to the colors." Formation of such a force in Palestine was a vital Allied interest, the message said, for it would protect the Suez Canal, free Anzac (Australian and New Zealand) forces from the Middle East for combat elsewhere, and be of great strategic importance to the Allied cause, while giving the Jewish People an opportunity to strike back at its tormentors.

The Jewish army advertisement was praised by some newspaper columnists, but it was a different story at *The New York Times* itself, for publisher Arthur Sulzberger opposed the entire Zionist idea. The very word "Jew" appearing in bold type was reportedly upsetting to Sulzberger, as it was to other assimilationists, for it was an opprobrious word, and "news about Jews" was usually buried on the newspaper's obit page.[44] The official Zionists also continued to press for President Roosevelt to urge the British to allow a Jewish force to serve in Palestine. But they differed with the Bergsonites in seeking exclusively British instead of Allied command, and excluding stateless European Jews. Though there was much common ground in the two positions and a desperate need for unity, such was not forthcoming.[45]

In the United States of the war years, many Americans were bewildered about the status of the Jews in the world – most could not understand the need for the Zionist movement at all. Peter Bergson, according to friends and foes alike, had a knack for breaking through the ring of confusion, for reaching gentile political leaders and turning them into ardent supporters of "Hebrew liberation." Senator Johnson, like several of his colleagues – former isolationst Guy Gillette of Iowa and Elbert Thomas of Utah, for example – was one of those who met frequently with the young Palestinian and remained a Bergson group activist for years to come. Under Bergson's tutelage, he came to understand what may have seemed obvious: the basic difference between American Jews, who were an integral part of the American nation, and Palestinian and stateless Jews, who clamored for sovereignty in their own country.

Johnson's activities on behalf of the Bergson group soon brought him under attack from both the Zionist establishment, which opposed the "upstarts" from the very beginning, and the Jewish assimilationists, whose greatest fear was that they would face charges of dual loyalty. At a Washington rally held by the Bergson committee in September 1942 at the Mayflower Hotel, Johnson said that "the most embarrassing objection to the organization of a Jewish army which I have encountered is that advanced by certain Jewish circles in America. They seem to fear that the creation of a Jewish army somewhere on this earth will raise the issue of Jewish separation within the United States."[46]

The Bergson group was adamant that the committee should embrace both Jews and non-Jews, in contrast to the mainstream Zionists, whose own organizations were exclusively Jewish. The make-up of the committee leadership and its advertisements reflected this non-sectarian approach. The full-page appeal in the *Washington Post* of May 25, 1942, was signed by, among others, Reinhold Niebuhr, Paul Tillich, A. Philip Randolph, Sir Cedric Hardwick, Lowell Thomas, as well as by prominent Jews, such as composer Arnold Schoenberg and actor Melvyn Douglas, whose wife, Congresswoman Helen Gahagan Douglas, a California liberal, also became active in the committee. Helen Douglas arranged the first of several meetings between Bergson and Eleanor Roosevelt at the White House. But Mrs. Roosevelt would show only sporadic and reserved support for the Bergson group's later campaign for a government agency to rescue European Jews.

None other than Lord Halifax, the new British ambassador in Washington, viewed the Bergson group's army campaign as extremely effective and with considerable apprehension. In a June 17, 1942, message to the Foreign Office, he said that the Bergsonites had caused the Zionist camp to split into "extremists" and "moderates."[47] The moderates were identified as Chaim Weizmann and his followers, such as Wise and Nahum Goldmann, while Ben-Gurion and Rabbi Abba Hillel Silver – the Republican firebrand from Cleveland – were among the "extremists."

Halifax reported that the Bergson group had "set up a great agitation directed at the Prime Minister... and Weizmann no doubt felt that he must weigh in with an appeal of his own, if he was not to appear too moderate altogether. Weizmann's moderation is of great value to us here, and it is our impression that he is fighting a difficult battle." Halifax urged that if any concession toward setting up a Jewish force were contemplated, it was in Britain's interest to ignore the Bergson group and give full credit to Weizmann, in order to "show that moderation pays." The British regarded Bergson as a radical more extreme even than Ben-Gurion. Only Weizmann, in their view, could be "reached." Halifax on another occasion urged Weizmann to "do something" about the Bergsonites, because he felt their call for a Jewish army was harming U.S.-British relations.[48]

Weizmann's failure to make the Jewish army a major issue was a calamity for the Jewish People. He "spoke deprecatingly of a 'so-called Jewish Army,' and, after five years of war, accepted the 'Jewish Brigade,' which another spokesman of the Jewish Agency (the quasi-governmental body in pre-state Palestine) hastened to diminish in importance."[49] Weizmann and his followers were blind to the import of Jabotinsky's idea, which would have meant, at the very least, implicit recognition of Jewish national rights. The British felt that this would only arouse the Arab and Moslem world, and in the midst of the Nazi onslaught, this was something they could not allow. It seemed to be a legitimate concern, but it also most assuredly meant that an "Israeli army" of 200,000 would never be allowed to fight the Nazis – the Jews' worst enemy in history. Only in the last months of the war did the British finally make a token gesture in response to widespread demands for a Jewish army, setting up the Jewish Brigade, which was far too little and much too late.

The British, like the Americans, Russians and others, including assimilationist Jews, stubbornly refused to recognize national rights for the stateless Jews and the Jews of Palestine. Thus, the Jews were condemned early on by the Allies, who failed to recognize the Jewish nation and its rights as a co-belligerent. The very word "Jew" was avoided constantly in major Allied conferences and declarations – they were "Poles" or "refugees." The refusal to recognize the Jews as a nation made it possible to abandon them during the Holocaust. The "Final Solution" – the systematic genocide of European Jews – began in January 1942, but the climate and mental set which would countenance the Nazis' worst crimes were created earlier.

Just before his death in 1940, Jabotinsky had realized the perfidiousness of British policy and finally lashed out at that country, despite its heroism in facing Hitler, for it had refused to treat the threatened Jews as an Allied people. He had campaigned for a Jewish army not only to defend the Jews of Palestine, but as an instrument to speed the redemption of the Land of Israel in what seemed to him to be the opening of the Messianic era. His legacy was left to the "cut-off battalion." The Bergson group, which included his only son, Eri, would now carry his idea to a wider audience than Jabotinsky had ever been able to reach.

CHAPTER THREE

THE FRONT PAGE

Ben Hecht, the towering and dynamic "reporter's reporter" of the post-World War I era who also became America's leading screenwriter in the 1930s, "bumped into history" one day in April 1941 when he met an intense young man called Peter Bergson at the 21 Club in Manhattan.[1] Bergson had first contacted Hecht by letter after reading a lashing column by him in the liberal newspaper, *PM*, in which he assailed American Jewish personalities who were reluctant to speak out as Jews against Hitler's onslaught. As Hecht would recall in his autobiography, *A Child of the Century*, "the letter contained a mysterious ferment that led me to invite for a drink, unknowingly, the political head of the not yet notorious Palestinian underground called the Irgun Zvai Leumi."[2]

Bergson liked the older man immediately – he was earthy, smart, and sophisticated. He told Hecht about Jabotinsky, of whom Hecht had never heard, and the struggle for Palestine. Nor had Hecht ever heard of Weizmann, the man who had obtained the Balfour Declaration from the British. Bergson was struck that Hecht was both a thoroughly integrated American and a proud Jew. He ran counter to Bergson's conceptions about American Jews.

In turn, the twenty-six-year-old Bergson was perceived by Hecht as a proud and mysterious "Hebrew hero." Bergson converted the much older man almost immediately, becoming "another Sinbad" in Hecht's adventure-filled life – "a Sinbad bringing greater risks than any of the diamond-shine peddlers who had preceded him."[3]

Hecht regarded Bergson and the other Palestinians he met as "perfect Jews" and "Jewish knights," subscribing to the general Zionist myth that would become much more prevalent later, namely, that Jews born or raised in the Promised Land are in all ways superior to other Jews. In the last twenty years of his life (he died in 1964), Hecht's often blustery prose expressed a Jewish macho that was narrow and unattractive. But the author of thirty-five books, a thousand articles, and seventy classic screenplays (including *The Front Page, Scarface, Gunga Din, Wuthering Heights* and *Spellbound*), though seen by some critics as a "self-hating Jew" suddenly reborn, was a vibrant, remarkably talented man who possessed a visionary's sense, foreseeing that the Jews of Europe "would die like a single child on a bayonet."[4]

Ben Hecht was Bergson's most important recruit because he was a believer, and one of the most talented people anywhere, a man who could achieve great results from his assiduous endeavors in promoting the Bergsonite cause. He was a formidable playwright and a honky-tonk showman, eager to turn the spotlight on issues of which most Americans were ignorant, or which they wished to ignore. Bergson, Merlin, Ben-Ami and other "knights" convinced him that a Jewish army would join General Wavell's African campaign, and tip the balance in favor of the free world. "Imagine the kind of soldiers these Jews will make against the Germans," Bergson told him. "Do you realize that an army with such a spirit can actually change the course of the war in Africa?"[5]

Bergson's argument had tremendous appeal for Hecht, who had visions of Jewish boxer Maxie Baer splattering Germany's Max Schmeling in the ring. Although Hecht may have had some doubts about the Bergson group, he dismissed them early on. "The fact that they were possibly Mad Hatters was less important to me than that they were Jews of gallantry and good health."

Hecht was an angry man who felt that powerful American Jews were shamelessly silent. He recalled how Hollywood's fifty leading movie moguls had been cowed by the anti-Semitic former film tycoon, Ambassador to Britain Joseph Kennedy, who virtually ordered them not to protest as Jews against the Nazis, or the world would feel that this was a "Jewish War."

Early in 1942, Hecht, feeling out of character as a man with a cause, brought the Jewish army campaign to Hollywood. His wife, Rose, and Miriam Heyman, a Palestinian and one of Bergson's aides, helped organize a meeting at the Twentieth Century Fox commissary. Hecht got David O. Selznick to co-sign a telegram that was sent to a thousand Hollywood personalities. Most of the movieland bigwigs

were appalled by the idea, but Hecht picked up additional support from director
Ernst Lubitsch, and even some of those who had balked at Hecht's invitation, like
Harry Warner, showed up. So did Charlie Chaplin, who had never before attended
any "Jewish affair," lest he give credence to the persistent rumor that he was a Jew.[6]
Chaplin joined Hecht and Bergson for dinner after the rally to discuss the Jewish
army idea, but though he expressed keen interest, he would not commit himself,
then or later.

At the rally itself, the first speaker was Senator Claude Pepper of Florida. Hecht
and Bergson had brought him to the rally from outside the Lakeview Country Club
– Jews were not permitted inside the dining room.

Bergson, Heyman and actor Burgess Meredith spoke for the cause to general
applause. The speech by Colonel John H. Patterson, however, was embarrassingly
strident. When the former lion hunter,[7] founder of Nairobi, and commander of the
World War I Jewish Legion, attacked Britain's policy on Palestine as anti-Semitic,
he drew cat calls. Several members of the audience stalked out, including, in
Hecht's words, a "London Jew" who had become a Hollywood director (and who
told the FBI the next day that Colonel Patterson was a Nazi agent).[8] The
uncomfortable silence that followed the walk-out was broken by gossip columnist
Hedda Hopper, who made the first pledge. A total of $130,000 was promised, but
only $9,000 was raised. Although it was a disappointing haul, it was enough to
expand the committee's office operation in New York.

Hecht, who had reluctantly agreed to become a co-chairman of the army
committee, soon turned into an indefatigable fund-raiser. Years later, his life-long
friend and sometime collaborator (*The Front Page*), Charles MacArthur, would ask
Bergson what he had done to Hecht to keep him involved so long and so
passionately, for he had never known Ben to be interested in anything for more than
a month.[9] MacArthur thought that it had to do with Bergson's personality. Bergson
responded that Hecht's involvement stemmed from the fact that the committee's
goals struck deep chords in his soul, giving expression to his Jewish identity. Hecht
did not relate to the Jewish religion, but through Bergson, he discovered the Jews
as a nationality.[10]

Shortly after the Hollywood rally, Hecht called a meeting in New York of thirty
prominent writers, musicians and artists, and made a plea for the Jewish army
cause. But of those assembled in the elegant home of playwright George S.
Kaufman, only Moss Hart and Kurt Weill came forward. Novelist Edna Ferber
accused Hecht of libeling the British and thereby helping Hitler and Goebbels.

Ferber would remain bitterly opposed to the committee, and she tried to persuade her close friend, novelist Louis Bromfield, to sever his ties to the movement. Bromfield told her that he did not agree, and that he would continue to give speeches and write regularly for the Bergsonites' publications.[11]

Hecht's participation in the campaign for a Jewish army drew fire from many Reform rabbis and from Stephen Wise's American Jewish Congress. Like Ferber, they called him a propagandist for Hitler and Goebbels, because he was so sharply critical of Britain's Palestine policy.[12] Hecht had met Wise before the advent of the Bergson group and had taken an instant, strong dislike to him. Anyone who possessed such a sonorous and impressive voice as Wise, Hecht would say, was "either a con man or a bad actor."[13]

Hecht poured his great energies into the publicity campaign, never taking seriously the charges by organizations such as B'nai Brith that the Bergsonites' newspaper ads, some of which attacked State Department policy, would fan the fires of United States anti-Semitism. On many projects Hecht teamed up with Arthur Szyk, the Polish-born artist whose drawings illustrated the committee's ads and publications over the years. Szyk became a one-man art department for the Bergsonites, who he felt were the true disciples of Jabotinsky. "They follow in his footsteps – they don't stand in them," he wrote in *The Answer*, a monthly publication edited by Merlin and issued by the Bergson group after 1943.[14] Szyk, illustrator of Flaubert, the *Haggadah*, and later, of Israel's Declaration of Independence, was appalled by the attitude of the establishment: "The old leaders have changed from lovers of Zion into chasers after prestige, and are ready to stake all, the 'all' of others, provided they remain unchallenged in their position of dubious eminence... One of the mandarins once asked me what he should do with 'those young men.' My reply was, 'Condemn them if you must, but pray to the Almighty for their success.'"[15]

Prominent people from all walks of life worked as hard for the army committee and its successors. Attorney Louis Nizer, who emceed many Bergson group events, was one of those who refused to quit, despite intense pressure on him from the Jewish establishment.

Composer Kurt Weill, who had become world famous after his collaboration with Berthold Brecht on *The Threepenny Opera*, was a product of the Bohemian world of post-World War I Berlin. He, too, would become committed to the Jewish cause. He wrote most of the music for the Bergson group's propaganda pageants,

including the 1943 spectacle *We Will Never Die*, and later *A Flag Is Born*, both of
which were written by Hecht.

Perhaps the group's most effective friend in Washington was Oscar Chapman,
a southerner who was Assistant Secretary of the Interior and later Interior
Secretary. Chapman was one of the many devoted Christians who helped the
movement, because he believed in its basic humanitarian goals. Chapman
eventually persuaded Interior Secretary Harold Ickes to become honorary chairman
of the Washington branch of the army committee's successor, the Emergency
Committee to Save the Jewish People of Europe.[16] Chapman's friend, Fowler
Harper, U.S. Solicitor General, became one of the group's leading activists and
eventually a full-time consultant. The non-sectarian committee gave gentiles the
means to show their feelings on "Jewish matters."

Missouri's Senator Harry Truman at first refused to lend support to the army
committee because he was confused about the Jews' national status – *which* Jews
was the committee talking about? In a letter to Congressman Somers in January
1942, Truman wrote: "...I think the best thing for the Jews to do is to go right into
our army as they did in the first war and make the same sort of good soldiers as
they did before. It is an honorable undertaking to organize an Army for Palestine
but I think American citizens ought to serve in the American Army."[17] But after
meeting with Bergson, Truman changed his mind about lending his name to the
committee and offered his support. It was after Truman's association with the
committee that its ads and statements made clear that the army it advocated
forming would not include U.S. or British Jews.[18]

Father Flanagan of Boys Town accepted membership on the committee, saying
that he thought the movement would have considerable influence "and create
sympathy on the part of the whole world to try to right the wrongs that have been
committed against the Jewish People."[19] But Harvard Professor J. Anton de Haas,
one of those who declined to join, wrote that he was "not certain that the cause of
Judaism itself will be well served by such an undertaking." He feared that the
reaction to such an army would frighten the Moslem world. Indeed, Princeton Prof.
Philip Hitte, the Arab-American historian of the Arab world, declined membership
because "it appears from a careful reading of your literature that you have another
objective in mind," namely using such an army to carry out the Zionist program in
Palestine.[20] The majority of those invited to join did so, including labor leader
William Green, Clare Booth Luce, Dorothy Parker, Herbert Hoover, Jimmy Durante,
Billy Rose, and sister and brother Stella and Luther Adler.

Stella Adler, the statuesque actress who brought the Stanislavsky "method" to America, was one of the committee's most fervent activists from 1942 onwards. She held dozens of parlor meetings in her West Side Manhattan apartment and brought many prominent people to the movement from the entertainment and business worlds. She later recruited one of her students, Marlon Brando, to take a leading role in the Bergson committee's *A Flag Is Born*. "It was one of the most important experiences of my life," Adler would recall forty years after the events. "The people were men of value, aristocrats of the mind, with social responsibility and the force to do something about it."[21]

For personalities like composer/showman Billy Rose, the committee was not a passing fancy but a cause to which he devoted himself. When he died in 1966, his work with the Bergson group was commended by a former foe of the committee, Jerusalem Mayor Teddy Kollek.[22]

Scholars of various political persuasions worked with the committee, issuing policy papers and articles. They included Isaac Zar, a Zionist journalist who came out of the Ben-Gurion/Poalei Zion (workers of Zion) tradition; Prof. Johan Smertenko of Barnard College, one of the few Revisionists to support the group; and Prof. A.S. Yahuda, an Arabist. Journalists who took part in many Bergson group activities included Pierre van Paassen, Quentin Reynolds, Lowell Thomas, Max Lerner, Frances Gunther, Curt Riess and Herbert Moore.

On Capitol Hill, the two key supporters were Senator Guy Gillette, who would later become full-time head of one Bergson group committee, and Congressman Will Rogers, Jr. At war's end, the sixty-six-year old Gillette, a former isolationist, gave a speech in Washington saying that he had been among those who were skeptical at first about the persecution and extermination of European Jews. But through his contact with the young Palestinians, he learned the truth about the Holocaust and believed it was not "just a Jewish or Hebrew problem, but an urgent question for all humanity."[23]

Will Rogers, Jr., who was part-Indian and had long been involved in human rights struggles, was deeply influenced by Bergson. After the group shifted its emphasis to the rescue issues, he devoted himself to the campaign to get President Roosevelt to set up a special agency to save Jews. Bergson and Hecht "slowly began to convince me," said Rogers, "that a mass murder was going on over there... and in what I like to think is the good old American tradition, I thought that every activity and every action and every wheel should be turned to try to get these people out." Like Adler, Max Lerner and many others, in retrospect he considered his association with the Bergson group one of the highlights of his life. "They were an alert, wonderful group, with a great moral fervor."[24]

In addition to the well-known personalities attracted to the Jewish Army Committee in 1942 and to its later incarnations (the group in 1943 was transformed into the Emergency Committee to Save the Jewish People of Europe, which was succeeded by the Hebrew Committee for National Liberation in 1944), there were hundreds of volunteers and paid workers involved in the Bergson group, which eventually had offices in half a dozen major cities. As with many grass-roots organizations, much energy and enthusiasm was generated by the sense workers had that they were working for a great cause: recognition of the Jewish nation and its right to fight the oppressor.

Peter Bergson always emphasized that the committee was a group effort, and the Palestinians under his direction felt that without the group, Bergson could not have achieved anything. "With his brilliance and talent of persuasion," he was able to win over important people, Merlin would recall. Without the group, "little could have been realized," while the group without Bergson "would not have prevailed." But working together, the group with Bergson as "the commander and the star" proved to be a formidable combination.[25]

Details of office work were not Bergson's strong points, according to Merlin. He had other functions. "He worked very fast, attracting people and keeping them. They had all been told that we were no-good terrorists, or shady characters. Peter managed to overcome this resistance. The work the committee undertook required a superhuman effort, a lot of organizing and routine office work. Peter didn't do much of that – he had other tasks. He had the power of knowing what he wanted. He thought big. Secondly, he had ideas about how to affect public opinion and the government. He couldn't sit at his desk for long. He'd get an idea, and then go out and throw himself into developing his inspiration. He'd champion an idea; and he never took no for an answer."[26]

In Merlin's estimation, Peter Bergson's magnetic personality was "one of the main causes of our success. He had a natural genius for winning over prominent people to the cause and becoming close friends with people like Will Rogers and Senator Thomas, for example, and they're the ones who pushed the Rescue Resolution," which led to the creation of a U.S. rescue agency.

Bergson's exposure to the American experience helped him to transcend the limitations and parochialism of the nationalistic comrades he left behind in

Palestine. People like Ben Hecht and Will Rogers, Jr., awakened him to the uniqueness of America and of the Jewish experience there. Bergson was primarily a "doer," but the important ideas that he developed about Jewish identity were the result of his exposure to life in the "home of the free." There was no tradition of freedom, no Tom Paines or Thomas Jeffersons in the eastern European countries where most of the world's Jews lived. Despite the very real anti-Semitism in America, it was for the most part a freedom-loving country, and Bergson had great hopes that the American people, Jewish and gentile, would help in the struggles of European and Palestinian Jews.

In the estimation of virtually everyone who came in contact with him, Peter Bergson in his mid-twenties was attractive, persistent, sophisticated, abrasive, argumentative, aggressive – very smart. He has been variously described as "lean, handsome and brilliant," "provocative and arrogant," and "a dapper young man and a smooth talker."[27] Hecht thought him overly argumentative, and characterized some of the group meetings as "lame affairs." But he loved the man.

Older men like Hecht and Senator Thomas were attracted by Bergson's energy and devotion to his cause. He seemed at times not to have any private life at all, to be a "Hebrew monk" as he had been in Irgun as a youth. Of course, he did not devote every moment to the movement. Women were drawn to him and he to them. He felt comfortable in the salons of the sophisticated and wealthy, and he enjoyed the milieu of successful artists, journalists and politicians. He looked good, and he spoke well; his single-mindedness and passion only added to his allure.

The foes of the Jewish Army Committee and its successor organizations used the term "Bergson group" or "Bergsonites" because it is often easier to focus on an individual, to seek personification of an organization or a movement. In turn, leaders and members of the committee itself came to accept the characterization. In due course, the Palestinians accepted Bergson as their senior officer, as if they were still functioning as a military unit of Irgun in Palestine. It was natural, then, that the American volunteers who worked for the committee would also come to think of Bergson as their leader. Thus, when the group became the central object of attack by both the Zionist and anti-Zionist Jewish establishment, the spotlight fell on Peter Bergson.

But the anti-Zionists – the American Jewish Committee headed by Judge Joseph Proskauer, and the smaller American Council for Judaism headed by Lessing Rosenwald – were not *obsessed* by the Bergsonites, as was the American Zionist establishment headed by Rabbi Wise, who had been the dominant figure in

American Jewry for thirty years by the time the young Palestinians appeared on the scene.

At one time or another, and often simultaneously, Stephen Wise was president or chairman of a bewildering number of organizations, among them: the American Jewish Congress, which he founded; the Zionist Organization of America; the United Palestine Appeal; the World Jewish Congress, which he co-founded with Nahum Goldmann; and the American Jewish Conference, an umbrella group of dozens of U.S. Jewish and Zionist organizations. In addition, he presided over a Reform synagogue and seminary, edited one of his organization's magazines, and lectured frequently. Wise, born in 1874, had established his reputation before World War I as a fighting liberal, an advocate of pacifism and a showman of the synagogue, where his mellifluous, "Shakespearean" voice enthralled his congregants. He was not considered exceptionally bright, and questions had been raised about the authorship of his doctoral thesis. The rabbi, according to a generally admiring biographer, craved recognition and "mass adulation" throughout his life. "Many of his critics, and not a few of his friends, considered Stephen Wise so egocentric a personality that he never could play the role of supporting actor to another star; he had to occupy center stage."[28] There could be no tolerance for a rival Zionist personality like the firebrand Rabbi Abba Hillel Silver of Cleveland, or for a rising star such as young Bergson. Wise once had been considered a great progressive and champion of the underdog, but these accomplishments were all in the past. In 1942, he was a doddering old man who clung to his many high offices and continued to assume the posture of a great Jewish statesman. "The harder the post, the higher the duty of sticking to it, of holding out to the grim end," he once wrote to his wife, who was loyal to him in spite of doubts raised by rumors of her husband's philandering. The man who tenaciously held the reins of a dozen organizations throughout the Holocaust years saw no contradiction when he told his American Jewish Congress as early as May 1929 that, "One of the most serious evils in Jewish life grows out of the all but perpetual tenure of Jewish office."[29] Fear, egotism, and vanity ruled his judgment. His health was poor, yet he insisted on maintaining a staggering, impossible work schedule.

Although Wise was regarded as a demi-god by the organization Jews around him, a "prophet in the wilderness" to his admirers, he was mostly bluster, a speechifier with arcane, ordinary ideas about "honor" and "duty." As prophet, he will be best remembered for his scornful rejoinder just before the war, when British

Prime Minister Chamberlain suggested that Jewish refugees from Hitler go to the former German colony of Tanganyika. "I would rather have my fellow Jews die in Germany than live in lands which bear the imprint of yesterday's occupation by Germany," Wise said.[30]

President Franklin Delano Roosevelt, whom Wise called "Boss" or "Chief," regarded the rabbi as pompous and a pest, and once wrote to him, "...you care more for personal publicity than for good government." FDR delighted in teasing "Stevey," who acted like an awed courtier whenever he visited the White House. But the results of this absurd relationship would help compound the tragedy of the Jews of Europe. Even his admirers concede that Wise's loyalty to Roosevelt "blinded his judgment," and his reliance on FDR would have "terrible results."[31] But in the Reform synagogue, where Judaism took on trappings of the Protestant churches, the people loved Dr. Wise's dramatic, showy sermons accompanied by solemn music. The house-lights would dim and go out except for a single spotlight on his leonine head, and "the long-maned Wise spread his arms wide, held out his open-palmed hands in supplication, and with measured beat poured forth his peroration, 'Give us mercy – Rahem...'."[32]

Although it is inconceivable and clearly slanderous to say that American Jewish and Zionist leaders were opposed to saving European Jews, when evaluating the wartime activities of such leaders as Rabbi Wise, one can conclude that they may as well have been. Wise would soon inspire and help orchestrate a "dirty tricks" and informing campaign against Bergson and the other young "upstarts," who he believed were challenging his power and who he said would increase anti-Semitism in America. Within the Zionist Organization of America (ZOA), where he wielded great influence, a special department was set up whose sole objective was to deal with "the Bergson problem." Wise apparently also set up a similar task for Nahum Goldmann, the Jewish Agency of Palestine's representative in America and leader, with Wise, of the World Jewish Congress.[33]

In September 1941, when the ZOA did an about-face on the Jewish army idea and passed a resolution along the lines of the Bergsonites' stated goals, yet continued its campaign against the Bergsonites (to the point of rejecting Bergson's direct conciliatory proposals), it became clear that the mainstream Zionists recognized no one but themselves as the organization charged with the welfare of the Jewish People. There could only be "a single address," according to Goldmann, who saw himself as "a president of presidents." In the world of organized Jewry, Goldmann's ego was as inflated as Wise's, but he was in a different league altogether. Goldmann was both brilliant and highly educated. The Lithuanian-born man of many nationalities (he eventually had seven passports) admitted to having authoritarian traits: "It was even said that I was the dictator of American Jewry," he would boast in a memoir.[34] But the real "king" of American Jewry, however impotent, was Dr. Wise, a far less sophisticated man. Nahum Goldmann might be more aptly described as his Richelieu.

Goldmann, a sworn enemy of Jabotinsky and the nationalistic Jewish movement, wanted total control of world Jewry concentrated in his hands, and said so unabashedly. The World Jewish Congress, which he had set up with Wise, was "the single address" in his mind. Goldmann thought Wise "was very naive politically, and used to confess that he always needed an oracle... me." And Wise "only acted out of love. I have never met a man with such love for others."[35]

But the great humanitarian rabbi was on the verge of senility; rather than loving his fellow man, he became paranoid at the most critical moment in Jewish history, allowing himself to become obsessed with the Bergson group until, towards the war's end, he would tell people that Peter Bergson was planning to murder him in the street.

Wise was in close touch with his friend, Edgar Hoover from April 25, 1941, on, asking to be interviewed by FBI agents.[36] The subject of the information he relayed to the FBI over the next two years remains classified to this day, as it would, according to the Department of Justice, "constitute an unwarranted invasion of the personal privacy of another person or reveal the identity of a confidential source." Did Stephen Wise provide the FBI with information on Peter Bergson and his group's activities? This is a serious question, but the answer remains hidden in the Bureau's secret files. In any case, when Wise complained to Hoover that the FBI's New York office did not respond speedily enough to his requests, Hoover immediately chastised the head of the New York office for "delinquency."[37] The agents interviewed Wise at the Jewish Institute of Religion, site of the Free Synagogue, on West 68th Street.

The efforts of Wise and other Jewish leaders against the Bergsonites were often alluded to but rarely spelled out. For example, in March 1942, the American Emergency Committee for Zionist Affairs issued a manifesto, warning its members to avoid individuals or groups "who are not prepared to accept the authority or the policies of the Zionist movement."[38] Wise, in his hatred for Jabotinsky, could not countenance an "offshoot" group from the stream of Zionism that included the Revisionists and the Irgun. He believed Bergson was "dangerous" because of his obvious appeal, and "opposed the Bergson committee for the same reason he detested the parent body, for its irresponsibility."[39]

The mainstream Zionist leaders were also involved in a bitter struggle among themselves, mainly between Democrat Wise and Republican Silver, who attacked Wise for not being militant enough in pursuit of the Zionist goal of a Jewish state. Silver also characterized Wise as senile, prompting Wise to write: "If I am [senile], I don't feel it… Working for a great people is to work by the side of the littlest men. I suppose I must test my soul by enduring it a little longer."[40] Meyer Weisgal, Chaim Weizmann's factotum in America and an old friend of Wise's, left the rabbi's umbrella Zionist Emergency Committee in March 1942, along with other prominent leaders such as Emanuel Neumann and Wise's friend David Petegorsky, because of the energy-consuming internal dissension, what he called (in a letter to Wise) "the poison of years of hate and prejudice and distrust for one another" that typified Jewish politics.[41] Neumann said he resigned because of the Zionist establishment's "inadequacy" and inaction."[42] The poison Weisgal referred to would prove fatal for European Jews who prayed that their American brethren would act on their behalf.

On January 20, 1942, in the wooded Berlin suburb of Wannsee, Reinhard "Hangman" Heydrich of the SS presided over a meeting of fourteen other heads of Nazi agencies and laid out plans for the "Final Solution," the code-word for the extermination of the Jews. Hundreds of thousands of Jews had been shot by the mobile *Einsatzgruppen* SS units, but now the slaughter was to be systematic and total.

In the free world, the mass atrocities by the death's head units were known, but they were regarded as occasional massacres rather than genocide. The Rumanians, Nazi allies, were also murdering tens of thousands of Jews, and the Nazi crimes were thought of in the same way – blood pogroms, not genocide.

As the Nazi functionaries planned the extermination of the Jewish People, 769 Jewish refugees who had fled the bloodbath in Rumania were taken out of Europe on a riverboat. The ship, the *Struma*, broke down and drifted in the Black Sea until it reached Istanbul, where it was quarantined for five weeks while Jewish organizations around the world appealed to the British to give Palestine immigration certificates to these "illegals." Stephen Wise cabled the passengers and said that the certificates would be forthcoming. But Britain's Colonial Secretary, Lord Moyne, said that if the *Struma* passengers were allowed to land in

Palestine, it would have "a deplorable effect throughout the Balkans in encouraging further Jews" to follow the same escape route.[43] Moyne, who was close to Churchill, said that the Turks should be urged to send the boat back. British officials maintained that Nazi agents might be among the Jews, the same argument used by State Department officials to block the entry of Jewish refugees to the United States.

The Turks towed the *Struma* out to the Black Sea, and on February 24, 1942, the ship exploded and sank, with only one survivor. The incident would hasten the Palestinian Jewish revolt against the British. It showed just how helpless the Jews were, just how little their lives were regarded even by the great upholders of democracy and freedom, and just how impotent Jewish leaders like Wise were. Albert Einstein saw the *Struma* affair as a curtain-raiser for the coming Apocalypse, but he was a definite minority.

As the last hopes for refuge faded, the pace of extermination quickened. In June 1942, the underground Jewish Bund in Poland drew up an exhaustive report on the murder of 700,000 East European Jews and smuggled it out to the Polish government-in-exile in London. But even though the Bund report was broadcast on the BBC and confirmed by independent sources, it got relatively little play in the world press. The American Jewish Congress, B'nai Brith and the Jewish Labor Committee sponsored a protest rally at Madison Square Garden on July 21, and Churchill and Roosevelt sent messages of support, but it was a low-keyed affair that somehow failed to focus on the issues. The point was still not understood – that the Nazis had undertaken to exterminate an entire people. The enormity of the crime was outside the range of normal human comprehension. There was still no "hard" proof that a program of genocide was under way.

In August 1942, the World Jewish Congress representative in Geneva, Gerhart Riegner, received information "from a leading German industrialist – who had always proved to be a reliable source" that Hitler had ordered the extermination by gassing of all European Jews. Riegner claimed that he received the information directly, and for forty years since the event, he refused to divulge the name of the source. There have been questions about whether Riegner ever met the source, and speculation that the "mysterious messenger" was either Eduard Reinhold Schulte or Dr. Arthur Sommer. In any case, Riegner attempted to cable the information to his superior, Stephen Wise, through the American consulate. Both Riegner and Chaim Pozner, a Jewish Agency official in Geneva who had also received the report, relayed the information to the British as well.[44] In Britain, the "Riegner cable" was received by the Foreign Office and Member of Parliament Sidney Silverman, head of the British section of the World Jewish Congress. The State Department, in contrast to the British, refused to pass the cable on to Wise. He finally got the information on August 28 from Silverman in England.

The State Department suppressed news of the Nazi extermination plan on the grounds that it was "unsubstantiated," and Wise agreed to a request by Undersecretary of State Sumner Welles to sit on the news until the U.S. government could confirm it.[45] Although Wise was aware of the department's general hostility to the Jews, he apparently did not appreciate just how deep ran its opposition to helping the Jews of Europe. During the period when the State Department was concealing the Riegner cable from Wise, Paul Culbertson, of the Division of European Affairs, wrote a memo about the cable in which he said: "I don't like the idea of sending this on to Wise, but if the rabbi hears later that we had the message and didn't let him in on it he might put up a kick."[46]

Wise was not entirely passive in the months that followed: He did send a copy of the Riegner cable to Justice Felix Frankfurter, and he asked Treasury Secretary Henry Morgenthau to tell the "boss" about it.[47]

But the Jews trapped in Hitler's inferno knew very well that their American brethren were not doing enough. Two months before the Riegner telegram, Chaim A. Kaplan, a keen observer of the creation and destruction of the Warsaw Ghetto, recorded in his secret diary: "A joke is making the rounds: Rabbi Stephen S. Wise is helping. He has ordered the American Jews to say the memorial prayer for the departed souls of the Polish Jewry. His foresight is accurate."[48]

In the years since these events, many have asked why Wise consented to suppress the terrible news for so long. "How was he not driven mad by this secret?" wrote Auschwitz survivor Elie Wiesel. "How could other Jewish leaders pledge silence? How is it that they did not cry out in despair? More important, more disturbing is this question: What happened after Rabbi Wise was released from his pledge? Not much. Not much at all. Did he and the other Jewish leaders proclaim hunger strikes to the end? Did they organize daily marches to the White House? They should have shaken heaven and earth, echoing the agony of their doomed brethren; taken in by Roosevelt's personality, they in a way became accomplices to his inaction."[49]

At the end of November 1942, Sumner Welles told Wise that the reports of systematic extermination had been confirmed, and he finally authorized the rabbi to release the news. Wise chose to give out the news in the lowest of keys. He called a press conference in Washington, but apparently did not emphasize the importance of the event, or instruct his organizations to put the pressure on. The two most important American newspapers, the *New York Times* and the *Washington Post*, both owned by assimilated Jews, did not even bother to send their own reporters to the press conference, relying instead on the wire services. The influential rabbi could easily have telephoned his friend Arthur Krock, a Jew who headed the *Times* Washington bureau, or reporter James Reston, and asked one of them to attend. But apparently he did not do so. Therefore, the first officially confirmed news of the Holocaust, of the fact that two million Jews had already been exterminated, ended up as a tiny story on page 10 of the *Times*, tacked on to a longer report from the Polish government-in-exile in London, which said that a much smaller number – a total of 250,000 Polish Jews – had been killed by the Nazis since September 1939.[50] The story ran on Wednesday, November 25, on the day before Thanksgiving, dwarfed by an eye-catching House of Seagrams advertisement on the same page, which said: "We can be thankful that the Hudson, the Ohio and the Mississippi are not 'rivers of blood' – like the Volga and the Don." The Russian rivers were very much in the news that chilly day. On page one, the major war report was that the Nazi grip on Stalingrad had been broken. It was, in fact, the turning point of World War II. The 15,000 slain in the most recent fighting at Stalingrad was a terrible toll, but for the Jews, every day was a Stalingrad in terms of the number of deaths. Yet, the first confirmed news of this slaughter was buried in the back of the paper, among such stories as "Four Ways to Cut a Turkey," and way behind such featured page-one matter as a story about a shake-down attempt on a New York stirrup-pump distributor.

There was no follow-up to the Wise story, not even a mention in the *Times* Sunday "Week in Review" Section. The *Washington Post* also gave the story scant attention and buried it inside.

But it did not go entirely unnoticed. Peter Bergson read it at breakfast just before a scheduled meeting on Capitol Hill. The sudden revelation of horror left him trembling. During the course of his two years of endeavors to establish a Jewish army to fight Hitler, he had come to know of the great slaughter. But now he recognized that there was something radically different in the Wise statement from previous reports of atrocities against the Jews. It had never before been reported as a program of systematic extermination. Every time there was a news story that the Germans were incinerating Jewish bodies, disclaimers were made reminding readers of similar atrocity reports from World War I which had proved false.

Up to this moment, the brash and brilliant twenty-seven-year-old Bergson had been a conventional Zionist, albeit of the militant stripe. Wise's muted announcement struck him like a thunderbolt and changed the course of his life. He picked up the phone, called Assistant Secretary of State Adolph Berle and got an appointment to see him that morning. They had met on several occasions to discuss the Jewish army proposals, and despite attempts to discredit Bergson and his group, the doors in Washington were still open to him because, in Ben Hecht's words, Bergson "had a diplomatic bearing" and was "as persistent as a force of nature."[51]

Still, the State Department was none too friendly territory for Jews. The man who presided over the key Visa Division and "the Jewish problem," as well as forty-three other State Department fiefdoms, was the aristocratic Breckinridge Long, an FDR financial backer who had been ambassador to Italy and a great admirer of Mussolini's.

Long was far more interested in his thoroughbred horses, in Pimlico and the Kentucky Derby, than in the extermination of the Jews. In the detailed diary he kept throughout the war, he did not once refer to the genocide campaign, or to the death camps. Adolph Berle was a different sort and at least appeared to be attentive and concerned about the plight of the Jews. He made himself available to Bergson, who was unaware that Berle kept a complete dossier on him, which was passed on to other top officials.[52]

Bergson asked Berle if the news of the extermination and the United States confirmation were correct. Berle answered that there could be no doubts – two million Jews were already dead, and the Nazis planned to kill all of the remaining Jews of Europe. "What are you going to do about it?" Bergson asked.

"What can we do?" Berle replied, shrugging his shoulders. Later, he would be among the many who argued that Jews could not be saved till the war was won.[53] Bergson believed that if the murdered people had been Americans (or perhaps even Europe's gentiles), Berle would not have thrown up his hands so readily. It seemed to Bergson that since the Jews were not Berle's people, the official did not really regard it as his problem. Bergson thanked Berle for his time and said that he, at least, was certainly going to try to do something about it.

The news galvanized Bergson's small group into frenzied action. He went to New York that evening, and for the next few days, the Bergson group met continuously to map a campaign to stimulate the U.S. government to take specific actions to help save European Jews. They vowed to put the issue of the extermination on the front pages. Wise's announcement, they believed, should have been a bombshell, not a throwaway story on page ten. Slowly, the realization grew that they would have to depart completely from the pale of Zionist politics in order to break the silence surrounding the Final Solution. The Bergson group recognized immediately that all else – even the sacrosanct issue of a Jewish state in Palestine – had to be subordinated to the cause of rescue.

The reaction was essential – but the mainstream Zionists never made the transition, and it was clear from the outset that they would not do so. Four days after Wise's shocking announcement, 2,500 delegates, representing sixty-five Zionist organizations, convened at the Hotel Commodore in New York to discuss "the continued upbuilding of Palestine" and to map its post-war growth. Only as an afterthought did the delegates issue an incidental declaration calling for the United Nations to act immediately to stop "the reported program of Nazi Germany for the extermination of the Jews..."[54]

The Bergsonites, on the other hand, two months before Wise's announcement, were already looking beyond the goal of a Jewish army and were beginning to focus on the issues of the rescue. Since September 1942, committee activists had been gathering over 1,800 signatures of prominent figures for a Proclamation on the Moral Rights of the Stateless and Palestinian Jews. The proclamation, most of it composed by committee co-chairman Pierre van Paassen, said: "We shall no longer witness with pity alone, and with passive sympathy, the calculated extermination of the ancient Jewish People by the barbarous Nazis."

A news story about the group's arduous efforts to win support for the proclamation appeared towards the end of November; and on December 7, 1942, the proclamation and its huge list of sponsors appeared as a two-page spread in the New York Times. The ad assailed the Allied governments for not allowing 200,000 Jews to fight as a co-belligerent, pointing out that even tiny Luxembourg had the status of a full-fledged ally, but not the Jews, who had suffered "a hundred Rotterdams... a thousand Lidices."[55] The proclamation was signed by twenty-seven senators, twenty governors, and hundreds of other political leaders, top military men, writers, clergymen, labor leaders, industrialists, actors and artists, including Harry Truman, Herbert Hoover, Norman Chandler, Clare Booth Luce, Katherine Anne Porter, Harold Stassen, Humphrey Bogart, Eugene O'Neill, Bruno Walter, Sholem Asch, Mary Pickford, Langston Hughes, Cecil B. DeMille, Jimmy Durante, William Allen White, Paul Tillich and Aaron Copland. The proclamation featured an illustration by Arthur Szyk, showing a Jewish soldier with an upraised tommy gun, coming to the assistance of an old man, a woman and a child. The huge ad appeared in other newspapers across the country.

That same week, Wise wrote to FDR. "Dear Chief: I do not wish to add an atom to the awful burden which you are bearing... But do you know that the most overwhelming disaster of Jewish history has befallen Jews in the form of the Hitler mass massacres?" He then asked for a meeting, so that Roosevelt could "utter what I am sure will be your heartening reply."[56] To some historians, Wise's words appear "heartrending"; to others, they evoke an image of the pitiful *shtadlan*, the court Jew who puts his faith in princes.[57]

Wise's defenders say that the suppression of the news of the extermination for nearly three months "didn't really matter," since the Allies were still losing the war at that point and threats of retaliation "would have been hollow."[58] They deny categorically that demonstrations would have helped or that personal protest had any effect. On the dubious (or at least questionable) assumption that American Jews were "powerless," that there was nothing they could do, it is argued that it did not matter that they did not even try.[59]

In fact, the Jewish leadership did exercise power – to enforce silence, for example, when it was requested to do so by the government, or when it did so on its own initiative. On December 1, 1942, Wise boasted in a letter to FDR that "I succeeded together with the heads of other Jewish organizations in keeping [the Riegner report] out of the press."[60]

One factor which kept Wise from being "driven mad" by the terrible secret was the Zionist fixation on the main goal: Palestine. The Jews of Europe were never at the top of the agenda – not before and not after the Riegner cable; not at the Biltmore Conference in New York in May 1942, which was concerned with the post-war situation and the achievement of a Jewish commonwealth, nor at the American Jewish Conference in August 1943, when the extermination took a back seat to the question of Palestine. At the 1943 conference, Wise belatedly – and only temporarily – came to the realization that the rescue issue deserved top priority, but he was defeated by his rival, Rabbi Silver, and immediately reverted to the "Palestine first" formula.[61]

Wise's muted treatment of the news of the two million, however, after three months of keeping it out of the press entirely, may also indicate that he could not really bring himself to believe such a terrible truth. Two months before the Riegner cable, in June 1942, when the Allies received a remarkably detailed report on the systematic genocide from the Jewish Bund, Wise also held back from taking any forceful action, other than holding a single mass meeting at Manhattan's Madison Square Garden. There was no follow-up, no plan, no concerted campaign. In August, at a conference of Jewish publicists called by Wise's World Jewish Congress, WJC official Leon Kubowitski dismissed the Jewish Bund report on the Nazis' program to exterminate the Jewish population on Polish soil, saying, "Such things do not happen in the twentieth century."[62] Nor was the Riegner report Wise's first experience with State Department suppression of the news of the extermination. On July 17, 1942, when Rabbi Israel Goldstein, a Wise disciple and president of the Synagogue Council of America, submitted a report to Secretary of State Cordell Hull on the mobile gas chambers and mass shootings in Poland, the State Department suppressed the report.[63] As a result, the Jewish leaders did not – could not – protest publicly.

According to Yitshaq Ben-Ami, one of the core group of Palestinians, Bergson and Merlin, in the period after the Bund report and immediately before Wise's announcement, were as unbelieving of the systematic genocide as mainstream Zionists. "Peter did not believe the Germans would dare do what they were reported to be doing... Merlin argued that it was simply impossible to carry out physically the extermination on the scale which was being reported."[64] Ben-Ami was the only member of the group who had worked under the Nazis during the pre-war period, when the Irgun, with the assent of Gestapo men like Adolf Eichmann, was bringing thousands of European Jews to Palestine illegally. He felt he knew their organizational know-how and their techniques, and told the others that the Nazis were perfectly capable of carrying out the mass liquidation. But the difference between Bergson and Merlin on the one hand, and the establishment leaders on the other, was that once the facts *were* confirmed, the shock of the truth stayed with them, and all their other concerns were subordinated to the rescue issue.

On December 8, 1942, Wise led a group of Jewish leaders to meet with FDR at the White House and to present him with a detailed report on the known facts about the extermination. It was the only such meeting Roosevelt would hold with the leadership. Wise's inadequacy and unpreparedness were never more evident. The Jewish leaders had no concrete proposals to present, no ideas about what could be done – only a lament. FDR promised "to save those who may yet be saved." When the leaders asked Roosevelt to speak out about the extermination, the patrician president replied by quoting Longfellow, "the mills of God grind slowly, yet they grind exceedingly small."[65] Time was not on the side of the Jews. In the three months that Wise complied with the State Department's request for silence, hundreds of thousands were exterminated in Poland.

According to Wise's biographer, the rabbi was well aware that something could be done. For example, supply ships to England returned empty when they could have brought refugees – in 1943, 200,000 German and Italian POWs were brought by these ships to detention camps in America. Wise knew that the government could facilitate rescue efforts, but he "rarely pushed Roosevelt and this did give the administration the option to ignore Jewish pressure without fear of political retribution or public controversy."[66] The President had the "king of the Jews" in his pocket, and Wise was all too comfortable there.

Nor did Wise press the media. *Time, Life* and *Newsweek*, like the major dailies, ignored the extermination. The only voice outside the Jewish press to penetrate the silence was Ben Hecht's, who wrote a powerful article on the destruction of European Jews which appeared in the *American Mercury* and *The Reader's Digest* in February 1943.[67]

The Zionist and Jewish leaders did not press Roosevelt, and most Jewish historians writing on this period justify this by contending that "try as they might" the leaders "lacked the power" to force the U.S. government to act.[68] But to some observers it appears absurd to talk of the powerlessness of the establishment when the Bergson group of outsiders and the grass-roots movement they inspired were about to show great feats of "powerfulness" in the fourteen months following Wise's announcement – stepping up the public pressure until Roosevelt would be forced to set up an agency for the purpose of rescuing European Jews. The army committee's proclamation of Jewish rights, which appeared the day before Wise's meeting with FDR, had put it this way: "To commiserate is not enough. Our pity will not stay the doom of millions more... We will be judged guilty if we do not change our present remote attitude to a positive, bold course of moral action."[69] The signatories called on the U.S. government to recognize that the solution of the Jewish plight in Europe should be one of the paramount goals of democracy. Winning the war, of course, had to have top priority, but the war did not preclude rescue opportunities, particularly after November 1942, when the tide turned against the Nazis.

Not all of those approached by the committee agreed to sign the proclamation. Alf Landon, who had been the Republican candidate for president in 1936, wrote to van Paassen to express his opposition to the idea of a Jewish army (it would provoke the Arabs, he said) and to the committee's work in general. Referring to a recent Jewish Army Committee dinner addressed by Senator Pepper, Landon remarked: "I think such meetings... are doing the Jews and their friends a disservice in this country, as well as the cause of the United Nations. I said the same thing to Rabbi Stephen Wise a year or so ago..."[70]

But Landon's attitude was very much the exception. The proclamation and other committee ads elicited a tremendous response. Hecht's vigorous fund-raising and tens of thousands of small contributions made it possible for the Bergson group to expand its activities. The Palestinians no longer had to operate on a shoe-string. Bergson was now able to commute regularly between New York and Washington, where he met constantly with government officials, Supreme Court justices, congressmen and anyone who might be able to help the movement. "He had no respect for the great men whom he bagged with his persistence," Hecht wrote, "He respected only his cause."[71]

In mid-December 1942, the documented reports of the extermination resulted in the first Allied declaration directly condemning the Nazis' program of genocide againt the Jews. But this joint declaration came about largely because of British public opinion – there was no equivalent pressure coming from the American public, because the Jewish leadership had not initiated such a campaign. (The American Jewish Committee held its annual convention in January 1943, but none of its resolutions dealt with the extermination or rescue proposals. Wise's American Jewish Congress also virtually ignored the news. *The Jewish Exponent* of Philadelphia on February 19, 1943, condemned the Jewish and Zionist leadership for its part in the conspiracy of silence, for failing to arouse the rank and file. American Jews needed "flaming indictments" instead of "polite phrases," the newspaper said.)

But the Bergsonites were more determined than ever to fire American public opinion, and to publicize facts that others thought should be ignored or suppressed. Some of the language they used in their literature and ads had an undeniably shrill, off-putting tone, which was particularly offensive to the mandarins of the American-Jewish world.

The Bergson group's lobbying activities and propaganda campaign were augmented over the years by a series of rallies, pageants and benefit concerts. Zionist leaders, who often stylized the Bergsonites as "circus show people" (Hecht, in fact, had performed in the circus in his youth), were eventually spurred into undertaking similar activities, and even tried to steal the show. Indicative of this is a comment to be found in the minutes of a December 29, 1942, meeting of an American Jewish Congress planning committee: "...the matter of holding a Madison Square Garden meeting was revived, in view of the information that the Jewish Army Committee is planning a similar meeting."[72] Hecht, trying to achieve the unachievable – Jewish unity – called a meeting with Jewish leaders at the Algonquin Hotel in January 1943 and offered to merge the two rallies, but he was turned down.[73]

Wise simply "decided against it," according to his friend and first biographer, Dr. Carl Hermann Voss.[74] But in Hecht's version of the story, Wise called him and said, "I have read your pageant script, and I disapprove of it. I must ask you to cancel this pageant and discontinue all your further activities in behalf of the Jews. If you wish hereafter to work for the Jewish cause, you will please consuslt me and let me advise you," whereupon Hecht hung up on him.[75]

On March 1, 1943, the establishment organizations held their Manhattan rally a few days ahead of Hecht's pageant, *We Will Never Die* (typically, Hecht eschewed the more formally grammatical "We Shall Never Die"). A captive audience heard Chaim Weizmann assail the free world for not giving sanctuary to Hitler's victims. "Two million Jews have already been exterminated. The world can no longer plead that the ghastly facts are unknown or unconfirmed."[76] He called for negotiations with Germany through neutral countries for the release of the Jews. A resolution was adopted protesting the indifference of the United Nations to the fate of the Jews; and Rabbi Wise forwarded the resolution to Secretary of State Hull. The rally was packed, with a spillover of thousands. But in the months and years to come, there was no follow-up, and no other major event concerning the Holocaust was staged by the establishment organizations.

For Ben Hecht, speeches and prayers were not sufficient for getting the message across to the people. Hecht believed it was necessary to dramatize the extermination in order to reach the entire American public, most of whom either did not believe the reports, did not hear the news, or did not care about it. But the main target was those who did care, Jews and gentiles. America's top screenwriter knew the audience he was addressing when he conceived the memorial to the over two million who had been murdered so far. The pageant's rehearsal hall was jammed with thousands of applicants, eager to demonstrate solidarity with the Jews. On March 9, 40,000 people filled Madison Square Garden to watch the spectacle staged by Hecht and his friends Billy Rose, Moss Hart and Kurt Weill, with a cast that included some of the greatest Jewish actors of the time: Paul Muni,

Paul Henreid, Edward G. Robinson, Stella Adler and her brother Luther, and many other well-known artists.[77]

Hecht's script showed deep feeling, nobility, and a touch of *Kitsch*. A narrator, standing before two immense Tablets of the Law, read Hecht's words: "Before our eyes has appeared the strange and awesome picture of a folk being put to death, of a great and ancient people in whose veins have lingered for so long the earliest words and image of God...."

"They shall never die, though they were slaughtered with no weapon in their hands. Though they fill the dark land of Europe with the smoke of their massacre, they shall never die." They would be revenged against the German Goliath by a stronger land, America – "our David." Kurt Weill's score, which was based on *Kol Nidre* and other traditional Jewish religious melodies, added to the somberness of the memorial.

Billy Rose had persuaded Governor Thomas Dewey to proclaim the day of the pageant an official day of mourning in New York State. Upon hearing of this, Rabbi Wise led a delegation of twelve important Jews to Albany to try to change Dewey's mind. Wise warned the governor that he might lose most of New York City's Jewish vote if he "sided" with the Bergsonites, but Dewey refused to be dissuaded.[78]

The melodramatic pageant apparently struck the right chord, receiving nationwide press coverage and deemed an immediate success, a call to the conscience of the world. It went on tour to six major cities after its New York success, but Wise's American Jewish Congress succeeded in barring it from several other cities.[79] In Washington, Hecht's memorial pageant held at Constitution Hall was attended by Eleanor Roosevelt, diplomats from forty nations, hundreds of congressmen, and many other political figures and prominent personalities. The ambassadors sponsored the memorial, which was organized under the co-chairmanship of Senator Johnson and Bergson. In her nationally syndicated newspaper column, Mrs. Roosevelt wrote that "No one who heard each group come forward and give the story of what happened to it at the hands of a ruthless military will ever forget the haunting words, 'Remember us!'"[80]

In some ways, Eleanor Roosevelt was responsive to the work of the Bergson group and was able to overcome some of the patrician anti-Semitism that marked her younger years. The Bergsonites hoped to reach the President through her, as did many other groups advancing all manner of social issues. They could not know that FDR was contemptuous of his "soft-hearted" wife and her causes.

Speaking at the Washington pageant, Senator Johnson, the Bergson committee's national chairman, referring to an intensified Bergson advertising and lobbying campaign and the success of *We Will Never Die*, declared: "The conspiracy of silence which surrounded the Jewish disaster in Europe is definitely broken."[81] He said that the committee's campaign had awakened the conscience of America, "...therefore it will be sinful if we do not agree upon a policy of action to save the millions who survive."

As the pageant toured the country, the Bergson group, which now had bustling office operations in New York, Washington, Boston, Chicago, Philadelphia, Houston and Los Angeles, placed nationwide ads bannered, "Action – Not Pity, Can Save Millions Now!" A full page ad in the *Washington Post* of April 5, 1943, suggested several concrete steps for rescue, chief among which the transfer of Jews from Nazi satellite countries – such as Hungary and Rumania – to temporary havens in neutral countries. But the committee's credibility was under constant attack. On April 13, J. Edgar Hoover, citing "remarks by an Executive" of Wise's American Jewish Congress, submitted a report to the War Policies Unit of the Department of Justice, saying that the Bergson committee was led by "a group of thoroughly disreputable Communist Zionists."[82] Among the "Communists" and "dupes" he listed were Ben Hecht, composer Arnold Schoenberg, Max Lerner, and sculptor William Zorach. Previously, Justice Department memos based on establishment Zionist informants had described the committee as "fascist."

After the destruction of the Warsaw Ghetto in April-May 1943, the Jewish National Committee in underground Poland sent the following message to Jewish leaders in London: "The blood of three million Jews will cry out for revenge not only against the Hitlerite beasts, but against the indifferent groups that, worlds apart, did not do anything to rescue the nation that was sentenced to destruction." Earlier, the same group of fighters had condemned Jewish leaders in the free world for not doing more for their people in the most terrible days of Jewish history. During the previous year, after 1.8 million Polish Jews had been exterminated, the Jewish underground leaders told a Polish liaison officer, Jan Karski, who brought news of the Holocaust to London, what they thought the world Jewish leaders should do: "Let them accept no food or drink. Let them die a slow death while the world is looking on. Let them die. This may shake the conscience of the world."[83]

One man, Shmuel Zygelboym, a representatiave of Polish Jewry in Poland's government-in-exile in London, took the message to heart. He had lost his entire family, but the decision to commit suicide was not one of personal despair. His suicide, in May 1943, was a final protest against the passivity with which the world looked on and permitted the annihilation of the Jewish People. But Zygelboym's suicide would have no effect on Allied policy – he was not famous; he was not an American; he was not a Rabbi Wise.[84]

In April 1943, Britain and the United States called a conference ostensibly to discuss the "refugee" situation. In fact, it was an attempt to squelch the growing chorus of criticism of Allied policy towards the Jews. The meeting was set for remote Bermuda in order to head off attempts to "pressure" the conferees, whose deliberations were kept secret. The U.S. delegation included Robert B. Reams of the State Department, a former salesman whose anti-Semitism reportedly surpassed that of his superior, the aristocratic Breckinridge Long; Congressman Sol Bloom of New York, a man who "hung on the tails of the State Department," and Senator Scott Lucas of Illinois, floor leader of the Democrats and a man "eager to enhance his reputation for a possible vice-presidential bid in 1944.[85] Lucas, like Bloom and the other American delegates, knew nothing about the issue. He told the press, however, that he intended to study the refugee problem.[86]

The entire spectrum of Jewish and non-sectarian groups concerned with the fate of European Jews noted and condemned the dismal make-up of the American delegation. Rabbi Wise was among those who complained that Bloom was an inappropriate choice to represent Jewish interests at Bermuda, even though Bloom was a Zionist and a personal friend of Wise's. As one chronicler of these events put it, Bloom's "intellectual resources in general, and courage on the refugee issue in particular, were notably deficient."[87] Indeed, Bloom's intellect was an object of ridicule among bemused British diplomats.[88]

"Breck" Long, the immensely wealthy horse breeder, FDR financial backer, and one of four Assistant Secretaries of State, was the overseer of the American delegation, the man in charge of every facet of "the Jewish problem." There was no question about his attitude towards the Jews. Treasury Secretary Morgenthau, the only Jew in the Cabinet, but a careful and astute politician, had even told Long to his face that he was the biggest anti-Semite in the government.[89]

Long had met with Bergson several times, as well as with Wise. In his mind, he lumped all the Jews together, largely ignoring the obvious divisions among them. As the Bermuda Conference got under way, just as the Warsaw Ghetto uprising began, Long displayed this confusion, writing in his diary that the conference "...has taken a lot of nursing but is now in existence. One Jewish faction, under the leadership of Rabbi Stephen Wise, has been so assiduous in pushing their particular cause – in letters and telegrams to the President, the Secretary and Welles – in public meetings to arouse emotions – in full-page newspaper advertisements – in resolutions to be presented at the conference – that they are apt to produce a reaction against their interest. Many public men have signed their broadsides and Johnson of Colorado introduced their resolution into the Senate." He concluded with the trite argument resorted to over and over by closet anti-Semites: "One danger in it all is that their activities may lend color to the charges of Hitler that we are fighting this war on account of and at the instigation and direction of our Jewish citizens..."[90]

The American Jewish Congress program – a six-point rescue plan, and the activities of the Bergsonites, apparently were intertwined in Long's perception. He was also confused about the role of Senator Johnson: At this time he was National Chairman of the Bergson committee and not at all a member of "Wise's faction."

Wise wrote to Welles on behalf of the Joint Emergency Committee for European Jewish Affairs, the umbrella group of major Jewish organizations, appealing to him personally to turn Bermuda into an instrument for "rescuing a defenseless people who are otherwise doomed to complete annihilation."[91] But FDR was in complete agreement with Long that the conference should be low-key and held in a remote location like Bermuda. The President and Secretary Hull further ordered the U.S. delegates not to allow the subject of America's immigration laws to be brought up. In 1943, the immigration quota to the United States was set at 23,725, with the exception of the Depression year, 1933, the lowest in 110 years.[92]

At the conference, the Americans, especially Bloom, vigorously opposed a British proposal to establish a refugee camp for 3,000 in North Africa, saying that it might incur the hostility of the Arabs and could disrupt military operations. This was the President's view as well.[93]

The Bermuda Conference became little more than a sham, a meaningless gesture. The conference avoided any mention of rescue, and the delegates regarded it improper to even mention the word "Jew." The conferees, embarrassed by the poverty of their recommendations, decided to keep their report secret for "military" reasons.[94]

Bermuda was universally condemned as an utter failure. A "sad and sordid affair," Wise called it, while the New York Times termed Bermuda "pitifully inadequate."[95] The establishment Jewish leaders were upset by the indifference of U.S. officials, and at a meeting of the Joint Emergency Committee, Nahum

Goldmann "expressed the view that the time has come to change our policy. We have to oppose the American and British governments' attitude."[96] Although there was support for militant action, it was eventually rejected.

As soon as the conference ended, the Bergson group took out huge newspaper ads proclaiming that "To 5,000,000 Jews in the Nazi death trap, Bermuda was a 'Cruel Mockery'" – a phrase used by the London *Sunday Observer*.[97]

The Bergsonites' message charged that Bermuda was proof to Hitler that the Allies were not willing to act to save Jews, and thus gave him *carte blanche* to commit genocide: "Now we are witnessing a variety of attempts to justify the Bermuda failure, to wrap it in secret formulae, such as 'no dealing with Hitler,' or 'not to interfere with the prosecution of the war'... all this is just throwing sand into the eyes of public opinion."[98]

Senator Lucas was enraged by the general condemnation of the Bermuda Conference and by the Jewish Army Committee's ad in particular. At the height of the Holocaust, he delivered a classic speech on the Senate floor, prefacing his remarks by saying, "Some of my best friends I have in this country, Mr. President, are members of the Jewish faith."[99] Then Lucas lashed out at Bergson personally, playing on the general suspicion of foreigners – a bias used by the State Department to keep Jews out of America because "they might be Nazi spies."

"Mr. Bergson... is not even a citizen of this country," Lucas thundered. He said that the ad, which quoted a journalist as saying that the word "Jew" was all but omitted from the conference discussions, had fostered a "diabolical untruth."[100] Other senators rose to defend the beleaguered floor leader, and took up his line, saying that aliens have no rights to criticize senators, or congressmen like Bloom. Harry Truman, claiming that Lucas was his dear friend, asked that his name be removed as a supporter of the Jewish army group.[101]

At the height of the flap, Senator Johnson counselled Bergson to be on his guard and said that the FBI had probably tapped his phone.[102] Lucas seemed determined to have the young Palestinian deported, Johnson added. Tensions were soon relieved, however. Lucas was defeated for re-election in 1944. But Congressman Bloom, the powerful head of the House Foreign Relations Committee, never forgave the Bergsonites for their anti-Bermuda ads, and was intent on revenge.

Whenever Bergson met with government officials, he talked about rescue, not about the one-sided "War between the Jews" in which he was the main target. Wise and Goldmann, by contrast, rarely discussed rescue with legislators, but often complained about Bergson.

After one of these meetings, Interior Secretary Harold Ickes recorded in his diary that Bergson was "unhappy about the attitude of our State Department when it came to getting individual Jews out of danger. Apparently Breckinridge Long is still in charge of clearances for political refugees."[103] Ickes told Bergson and Congressman Will Rogers, Jr., that he was discouraged and had "practically given up" any thought of making pro-Jewish speeches "in view of the fact that they had to clear through the State Department, and the State Department objected if anyone proposed to do more than to merely utter words."[104]

Rogers had become extremely active by this time and accompanied Bergson to many meetings on Capitol Hill. It was a moral issue for him, "the Jews should be saved and never mind the rest of it."[105] He felt the only way to do something was to continue working with the Bergson group.

Shortly after Bermuda, when Bergson met with Breckinridge Long to talk about rescue proposals, the Assistant Secretary of State agreed to a long-standing army committee request to send a special Bergson group emissary to neutral Turkey, a key center for any rescue efforts; but Long sought a *quid pro quo*, asking whether the committee would now end its campaign. Bergson refused to give any such assurance. Clearly, the ads and the public attacks on the "conspiracy of silence" did affect Long, who felt that the Jews, including Wise, were out to get him.

The emissary the Bergson group wished to send to Turkey was Eri Jabotinsky. Bergson had exploited his contacts on the Hill to help free his friend from a British prison in Palestine. He had taken Ze'ev Jabotinsky's widow, Joanna, to see Republican Senator Robert A. Taft, whom she asked to help get her son out of detention in Palestine. The powerful Ohio senator interceded, and the British finally allowed Eri to join his comrades in the United States.[106]

The Bergson group's steady call for a Jewish army, which continued even after the committee switched its emphasis to the rescue issue, never ceased to upset both the British and the mainstream Zionists, who conferred on what to do about Bergson and his colleagues. In a discussion at the British embassy between Chaim Weizmann and the ambassador, Lord Halifax, on May 17, 1943, Halifax referred to a two-page advertisement in that day's *Washington Post* calling for the immediate mobilization of a Jewish army. Halifax said that the committee's activities were driving a wedge between the British and the Americans, and added that he knew Weizmann was trying to prevent this activity. "I can't prevent it, I simply can't,"

Weizmann replied.[107] But the British and the Zionists continued to exchange information on the Bergsonites, and to cooperate in attempts to stop the committee's activities.

The Bergsonites were as yet unaware of the extent of the machinations and conspiracies to quash them. They were preoccupied elsewhere, trying to put the issues that were buried at Bermuda and were reported in the back pages of newspapers into the spotlight. They felt that the plight of the European Jews and the possibility of saving at least some of them deserved better than page 10 treatment.

CHAPTER FOUR

THE EMERGENCY

In May 1943, the Bergson group drew up position papers for an Emergency Conference to Save the Jewish People of Europe, which was planned for late July. It was a direct reaction to the Bermuda fiasco – a public, grass-roots response to what was perceived by almost all U.S. Jewish leaders as an ignominy. Samuel Merlin was in charge of drawing up an agenda for the conference. In the discussions among the young Palestinians, Bergson came up with the idea that the main goal should be to press for the creation of a special U.S. governmental agency to save European Jews.[1]

Other people were thinking along the same lines at around the same time. Oscar Cox of the Lend Lease Administration talked to Treasury Secretary Morgenthau about a rescue agency in June 1943, and he would press for the idea again in December.[2] But the establishment leaders were still reluctant to focus on rescue for fear of weakening the campaign for a post-war commonwealth in Palestine. In May 1943, Nahum Goldmann told a meeting of the Zionist leadership that there was not enough manpower to campaign for rescue.[3]

Nor was the Congress acting effectively. In March, a resolution had been introduced in the Senate by Majority Leader Alben W. Barkley condemning Nazi atrocities "and especially the mass murder of Jewish men, women and children." But it said nothing at all about rescue, and went virtually unreported – the *New York Times* gave it three inches on page 12, omitting "Jews" from the headline.[4]

Meanwhile, the Bergson group promoted its forthcoming Emergency Conference, publicizing the big names who had agreed to take part. Predictably,

Rabbi Wise, from the moment he learned of it, tried to undermine the conference, letting the State Department know where he stood. Sumner Welles advised refugee expert Myron Taylor not to take part because the major Jewish organizations, and Wise in particular, "are strongly opposed to the holding of this conference [and] have done everything they could to prevent it." Wise also tried, unsuccessfully, to persuade his friend, Episcopal Bishop Henry St. George Tucker, to withdraw from the conference.[5]

Wise's efforts did not discourage the many important figures who became associated with the Emergency Conference and the Emergency Committee to Save the Jewish People of Europe, which emerged out of the six-day event. Herbert Hoover, Mayor LaGuardia, Senators Johnson, Gillette, Thomas and Langer, Dorothy Parker, and William Allan White were among the many prominent personalities who did not heed those who opposed the conference.[6] Bergson also got powerful support from William Randolph Hearst, who appeared genuinely concerned about the Jewish plight. His thirty-four newspapers gave full backing to the Emergency Conference and the subsequent activities of the Bergson group, consistently emphasizing one of Bergson's basic arguments: "Remember Americans, this is not a Jewish problem. It is a human problem."[7]

The conference convened in a hot and muggy New York on July 20, 1943. Senator Johnson and Max Lerner, one of FDR's favorite journalists, chaired the conference, which was held at the Hotel Commodore; and Roosevelt – for the first and only time – publicly acknowledged the existence of the Bergson group, cabling Lerner that the government had made "repeated endeavors to save those who could be saved," though to this day no evidence of any such effort has emerged.[8]

Secretary of State Hull also sent a cable, a bland message that an intergovernmental agency had been created to deal with "these problems."[9] Unbeknownst to the recipients, Hull's message was the final version of two previous drafts drawn up at the secretary's request by R.B. Reams, one of which showed how sensitive the State Department was becoming to the criticism leveled against it by the Bergson group: It denied that the Bermuda Conference was a farce or a cruel mockery, calling it "a sincere attempt on the part of the two governments concerned to rescue as many people as possible...." Hull vetoed the drafts and settled for the statement that rescue policy was under constant study, and that the "agency" would do something.[10]

In reading the messages to the conference, Lerner commented that Hull's agency was "catastrophically inadequate" and urged creation of a *special* agency (the

Bergson group's objective) capable of accomplishing something tangible.[11] Treasury Secretary Morgenthau, in another message to the conference, said that he felt certain they would come up with a plan of action. Although Cox had mentioned to him a month earlier that a special agency was needed, the idea apparently had not been worked out: "It is my earnest hope that out of your Emergency Conference will come a specific plan to relieve the criticial situation which exists among the Jewish people who are facing complete extinction in Nazi Europe... With so substantial a group of outstanding people backing your efforts, I feel confident that some plan, and some action, will certainly result."[12] The Bergsonites did, in fact, come up with a plan, and six months later, Morgenthau would use it.

The conference participants were not merely names adorning a letterhead. The panel on international relations included Lerner, Representatives Cellar, Dickstein, and Somers, and Count Carlo Sforza, leader of the Free Italian anti-fascist movement, and future foreign minister. Herbert Hoover chaired the Relief and Transportation Committee, which included representatives of Polish, French, Belgian and other relief organizations, as well as prominent business leaders such as Thomas Watson of IBM. The public opinion panel included Dorothy Parker, Nobel literature laureate Sigrid Undset (one of the Bergson group's most loyal and active supporters), labor leaders, college presidents and journalists. There were other committees on military affairs and on churches and synagogues. A total of 1,500 people took part in the conference.

In all, the conference's various subcommittees and groups, meeting over a six-day period, came up with nine major proposals for rescue, refuge and retribution, detailing such matters as how necessary transport could be worked out without hindering the war effort.

Two days after the conference got under way, Lerner published an article in the highly regarded newspaper *PM* entitled, "What about the Jews, FDR?"[13] In his appeal for action to save four million Jews facing death, Lerner condemned the British and American governments for their anti-Jewish policies. Relying heavily on Bergson's analysis of the situation, Lerner wrote: "Neither government recognizes that any Jewish problem exists. Both governments talk of the Jews as Polish nationals, or Czech nationals, or Hungarian nationals. Yet the fact remains that while Czechs are killed by the hundreds, Jews in Czechoslovakia are killed by the tens of thousands." And, he emphasized, what was more important, they were being killed as Jews. Lerner charged that "the State Department and Downing

Street avert their eyes from the slaughter" and called on FDR to take the lead and reverse the trend.[14]

Lerner was deeply impressed by the young Peter Bergson, whom he had first met a few months before the Emergency Conference. "He had one of the best natural public relations talents that I have ever seen... And he had much more as well – a stunningly clear vision of what was happening in the Holocaust and a hard determination to act on it."[15]

Lerner had wrestled with himself over whether he should get involved with the Bergsonites. Many of his journalist colleagues and left-wing friends regarded "the Jabotinsky group" as "fascist." It took guts to defy the establishment and work with Bergson, he felt, but he "had no choice but to swim against the stream at that point because so many Jewish lives were involved, and I am happy that I did."[16] But Lerner, soon after the conference, would succumb to pressure and quit as a Bergson group activist.

In the middle of the conference, Eleanor Roosevelt cabled Lerner that if the conferees could formulate a program of rescue action, she was certain the American people would do everything possible to resettle or evacuate European Jews. This was very much a reversal for her. In June, she had responded negatively to novelist Louis Bromfield's appeal to her to participate in the conference, replying that she could "not see what can be done until we win the war."[17] It showed that the holding of the Emergency Conference was vital in helping to disabuse important people out of the notion that nothing could be done until the war was over.

The general atmosphere at the conference was somber. Bergson took part in various panel discussions, and held late-night meetings with the subcommittee leaders to discuss the next day's events. He was consumed with work. His friend Ben Hecht did not take part in the conference; he was working "on deadline" on a script at his California home in Oceanside.

Bergson, since the day of Wise's announcement of two million dead, was a haunted man. He was one of the few outside the charnel house of Europe who was conscious of the horrible reality. He empathized completely and was able to devote his entire being to the cause of his tormented people. He was a man who did not display his emotions, except, perhaps, to the person closest to him. For over a year now, since the black days when it appeared that Rommel would reach Palestine, his relationship with Betty Caplan had intensified. But their romance was never public, and never got in the way of the cause to which they were both devoted.

At the closing session of the Emergency Conference (parts of which were broadcast to the nation over the Columbia radio network), Bergson, who was introduced as "the son of the new Palestinian nation," praised America and condemned it at the same time. He charged that the world's leading democracy was "not completely free of the onus and responsibility for what happened to two million Jews in Europe and for what may happen to four million more."[17] This was the message that got across, but elsewhere in the speech Bergson displayed something of the audacity – the chutzpah – that many found annoying about him. In all sincerity, he claimed that the Emergency Conference had begun "a movement to rehabilitate the fair name and the fine traditions of your great nation..."[18]

In another speech, his colleague, Alexander Rafaeli (Hadani), suggested that the special rescue agency, the focus of the conference, should be under the aegis of the United Nations.

Former President Hoover, in his closing address, reiterated the Bergson group's call for temporary measures as well as "long-term measures," including the establishment of temporary refugee stations in neutral countries, and food and relief, which had been refused by the Allies on the grounds that it would aid the Germans. (The establishment Jewish organizations would not offer a food and medical aid plan until September, when Nahum Goldmann presented a wide-ranging aid proposal – but one that contained no rescue measures, such as funds to bribe officials. Goldmann's plan got bottled up in the State Department and the Foreign Office, and nothing came of it, and the establishment made no protest in public about how even this strictly humanitarian plan was sabotaged.)[19]

The conferees concluded that the Jewish people of Europe constituted a specific problem that should not be dealt with as part of the general refugee issue. It passed a series of resolutions on military and political measures, transportation admission to Palestine, treatment of Jews in Axis satellites, and temporary asylum in neutral countries: Spain, Portugal, Ireland, Sweden, Switzerland and Turkey.[20]

The Emergency Conference resolved to transform itself into an ongoing operation, the Emergency Committee to Save the Jewish People of Europe, whose purpose would be to submit recommendations to congressmen, government officials including the President, and the public at large.

The Committee for a Jewish Army was no more. Events had changed, priorities had changed, and for the Bergsonites, the Emergency Committee was the natural outcome.

Among the Palestinians in the group, there was no dissension over policy or ultimate goals – all agreed that they must focus on mobilizing American public opinion to press for the establishment of the rescue agency. But personality clashes persisted, and there were disagreements on tactics and behavior. Ben-Ami, while conceding that Bergson was "a master public relations man" and an undaunted struggler ("he would retreat and lick his wounds, and the next day he would be ready for the next round"),[21] felt that he was "a catastrophe" in meetings with the organization's rank and file. The Bergson group at this point was comprised of a thirty-two member Executive Board, a paid staff of forty, and a steering committee of five co-chairmen. In addition, there were hundreds of volunteers who were active across the nation, local chairmen and vice-chairmen. Bergson, in Ben-Ami's eyes, "treated them awfully." Ben-Ami thought Bergson was "wrecking the work of people like Rafaeli, Ben-Eliezer and myself, which we were doing in the provinces and in the chapters and the branches."[22]

Two months after the Emergency Conference, Ben-Ami and Rafaeli went into the U.S. army (the U.S. government was frequently pressed by the British to induct the young group of Palestinians into the army), and the remaining group under Bergson decided to send Aryeh Ben-Eliezer back to Palestine to reorganize the Irgun. Rafaeli, who had been in charge of the committee's Chicago office, was replaced by an American supporter of the Irgun, Helen Brown Sherman, who, forty years later, recalls that "the men in this movement were all of the old-world European type... male chauvinists to the core. There were many women who did valuable work in public relations and allied fields who were never mentioned."[23]

Soon after the conference, on August 12, 1943, Bergson, co-chairman of the newly established Emergency Committee to Save the Jewish People of Europe, met with Secretary Hull and Breckinridge Long to discuss the key proposals of a rescue agency and the establishment of temporary shelters. Bergson was accompanied by committee co-chairman Dean Alfange, a prominent New York Liberal Party politician, and sculptor Jo Davidson. Hull would not commit himself to either proposal, but he said that he and Long would "consider" the committee's suggestions. Bergson also urged them to press the British to release the remaining 29,000 immigration certificates to Palestine under the White Paper, which had limited Jewish immigration to 75,000 over a five-year period beginning in 1939. Hull did say that he was in favor of the Emergency Committee's proposal to send commissions to Palestine, Spain and Turkey.[24] In the weeks after the Emergency Conference, the Bergson group also began to press for a congressional Rescue

Resolution, calling for the establishment of a special governmental agency to deal with the problem.

The Zionist establishment, meanwhile, continued to put the Palestine issue ahead of rescue. The umbrella organization of major Zionist and Jewish groups held a conference that contrasted sharply with the Bergsonites' Emergency Conference. At the American Jewish Conference, held from August 29 to September 2 at the Waldorf-Astoria, the delegates called for a Jewish commonwealth in Palestine, while rescue was not even on the agenda – the final resolution included rescue only as an afterthought.[25] It blasted the Bergson group's Rescue Resolution, charging that it was introduced "in complete disregard of the rescue program which is being actively pressed in Washington by representatives of Jewish agencies."[26] The main fault of the Rescue Resolution, according to the Conference, was that it "contains no reference to Palestine."[27]

The American Jewish Conference was a typical, rather stiff affair produced by the major organizations, opening with the singing of the verse from Psalms, *Hinei ma tov u'ma na'im, shevet achim gam yachad* – "How wonderful it is for brethren to be together in unity." But the facade of unity even within the establishment disintegrated in front of the delegates' eyes as the split between Rabbi Wise and Rabbi Silver became more apparent than ever. Silver, the fifty-year-old firebrand, could compete with Wise at his own game – the art of oration, a talent of immense importance to Jewish organization people, which often put form above content.

In setting up the conference, Wise had obtained the support of Judge Proskauer's non-Zionist American Jewish Committee by agreeing that the Zionists would not let the Palestine issue dominate this initial meeting of the new umbrella organization. It was a lapse that he would greatly regret, since it gave Silver a chance to go for his throat. In his opening speech to the distinguished assembly, Wise mentioned the ongoing extermination in passing but did not talk of pressing the U.S. government to take any special action. Monsky, too, had gone through the motions of urging rescue action, but most of his speech was about post-war reconstruction.[28]

Rabbi Silver, a Republican who disliked FDR, had little patience for the Democrat Wise, whom he thought "senile,"[29] or for Nahum Goldmann, whose imperious political style galled him. At the conference, Silver vilified Wise for giving in to the anti-Zionist Proskauer. "We finally have a slogan, a battlecry for a Jewish state," he said, "and you who claim to be a Zionist leader refuse to talk about it." Silver attacked Wise's *shtadlanut* role – the Jewish courtier in FDR's court – citing the psalmist's warning not to "put your trust in princes."[30]

Silver gave a rousing speech about the necessity for the commonwealth in Palestine, and showed clearly that he was about to supplant the revered, but less militant Wise. The Republican rabbi's only reference to rescue was an inadvertent but telling indictment of inflexible Zionism: "We cannot truly rescue the Jews of Europe unless we have free immigration to Palestine." It would be a sin "to ask merely for the right of asylum in our historic home."[31] Silver never explained why asylum – the whole rescue issue itself – was not worth fighting for.

Wise, upon being so severely humiliated by Silver, reverted to the Palestine-first position. His "lapse" had been only momentary – when Silver challenged him, Wise caved in, and rescue became a non-issue.

Only one delegate, Robert P. Goldman of Cincinnati, challenged Silver's approach.[32] The immediate problem was not Jewish homelessness and the Palestine issue, Goldman said, "the immediate problem, ladies and gentlemen, is rescue; and I don't care what else you say or how you characterize it, or what you say about me for saying it, that is the immediate problem and that is the problem we should be concerned with."[33] The push for Palestine would not help European Jews, he said. But the conference ignored him.

In the aftermath of the American Jewish Conference, a few isolated voices echoed Robert Goldman's sentiment. A mainstream Zionist journalist, David Eidelsberg, criticized the fact that the Palestine question had totally eclipsed the issue of rescue. "The first task should be to save the Jews for whom Palestine is needed," he wrote. "By waiting till the last moment to discuss this question and bypassing stereotyped resolutions, the leaders of the conference gave a signal to the powerful ministries that nothing can be done and that we have to wait till the war is over."[34]

With Silver and militant Zionism in the ascendancy, the American Jewish Committee pulled out of the umbrella organization; Wise's attempt at unity among the establishment Zionist and non-Zionist organizations was a failure.

The American Jewish Conference relegated the rescue issue to a subcommittee, an ineffectual unit called the Commission on Rescue headed by I.L. Kenan, the future head of the Zionist lobby in Washington. It did little more than conduct a campaign against the Bergson group's Rescue Resolution. The crucial fact is that, in the ensuing months, the American Jewish Conference never called a special assembly to deal exclusively with the extermination issue. In concentrating on the

"Bergson threat," the conference, in effect, helped to obstruct the rescue of thousands of Jews who could have been saved.

From the July 1943 Emergency Conference to Save the Jewish People of Europe to January 1944, when FDR finally set up the War Refugee Board, the Bergson committee's main focus was on getting Congress to pass a resolution urging the President to establish a special rescue agency. The Palestinian Jews, who had struggled since early youth for an independent Jewish homeland, were no less Zionistic than Rabbi Wise or Rabbi Silver, neither of whom had ever lived in Palestine (nor would they live in the future state of Israel). Bergson and his friends were militant Zionists, but from late 1942 until the end of the war it was clear to them that rescue came first. The committee's full-page ads, such as one which appeared in the *New York Times* in August 1943, said: "We all stand before the bar of humanity, history and God... We will all be judged if we do not create the machinery to save the Jewish people of Europe."[35] Nothing could be clearer. Yet organized American Jewry and the Zionist leadership never made a similar public declaration, nor did they subscribe to this belief.

Only a special agency, with no other duties, could perform the needed task, the Bergsonites believed. The agency would be independent of the State Department or the White House or any bureau of government, with no constraints. All of its activities would be related to the basic goals of rescue and relief, in one way or another. The agency would be able to implement a psychological warfare program, and to threaten retaliation unless the atrocities were stopped. That was the Bergsonites' vision. It appeared to be so straight-forward, practical and obvious, yet few others seemed to think that such an agency was necessary.

In September 1943, committee activist Rep. Will Rogers, Jr., wrote that "the big trouble – a fatal trouble – has been that there is no one agency, no single man... given the entire responsibility for this job of saving the Jews."[36] The aimlessness, he wrote, had resulted in "confusion and buckpassing, which spells utter inaction," which was why a special agency was essential, and why Rogers was the most active member of the House advocating the Rescue Resolution.[37]

Bergson brought up the Emergency Committee's proposals with Eleanor Roosevelt in August 1943. They met several times, the appointments being made by intermediaries like Max Lerner and Congresswoman Helen Gahagan Douglas, who, along with her Jewish husband, actor Melvyn Douglas, remained active in the Bergson group.[38]

Mrs. Roosevelt agreed to broadcast a shortwave radio message to the Jews of Europe on behalf of the Emergency Committee, and she passed on to FDR a copy of the recommendations of the Emergency Conference held in July, with special emphasis on the need for a rescue agency. The President sent a memorandum on August 16 to Miss Thompson, Eleanor's aide, saying, "I do not think this needs an answer at this time."[39] But the Bergson group would not relent on the proposal for a special rescue agency until Roosevelt did come up with "an answer" – the War Refugee Board – five months later. Bergson himself never let a meeting with a prominent official or personality go unrecorded – others had to be made aware that their colleagues were being briefed about the necessity for a concrete rescue program. On August 26, Morgenthau got a letter from Bergson concerning his recent discussions on rescue with Eleanor Roosevelt, Hull, Long and Attorney-General Biddle, and an ironic reminder that Jewish lives were not considered as valuable as *objets d'art*: "This week the State Department announced the formation of a special United States Commission to save European art and monuments. It is very laudable indeed, but at the same time there is no action on our repeated requests that a specific government agency be created to save 4,000,000 European Jews whom Hitler has sentenced to death."[40] He asked Morgenthau to urge creation of such an agency, and thanked the Treasury Secretary for a recent meeting with him.

In the death factories of Europe, hundreds of thousands of Jews filed quietly, or were being whipped and driven into gas chambers. They died painful, horrible deaths as the Zyklon B gas, manufactured by I.G. Farben, was discharged through the shower heads into the sealed chambers.

But even as late as July 1943, long after the systematic extermination had been confirmed, top British officials, among them V. Cavendish-Bentinck, chairman of the Joint Intelligence Committee, said that the Jews exaggerated atrocities "in order to stoke us up."[41] This attitude led to Britain's request that all references to the gas chambers be deleted from the Allies' Moscow Declaration of November 1, 1943, in which Nazi atrocities against everyone but Jews were mentioned. Nor was the State Department any less anti-Semitic than British officialdom. The list, topped by Long, included several high or middle-ranking officials, such as George Brandt, Wallace Murray, James Dunn, Ray Atherton, Howard Travers, R. Borden Reams and Paul Culbertson. The latter, chief of the Western European Division, was irked by Morgenthau's interest in the Jewish refugees, and denounced him in private as "that damned Jew in the Treasury."[42] Randolph Paul, one of the group of gentile Treasury officials who did everything possible to counteract the obstructionist deeds of the State Department, described Long and company as an American "underground movement... to let the Jews be killed."[43]

Since the fiasco in Bermuda in April 1943, the Bergson group had been demanding retaliation for crimes against the Jews. That month, the doomed Jews of the Warsaw Ghetto had smuggled out a desperate message to the free world via Jan Karski, the main Polish liaison officer with the underground. They pleaded with the Allies to threaten the German people with mass retaliation.

From the Emergency Conference in July 1943 until the end of the war, the Bergsonites continually submitted proposals for direct retribution, but the State Department's answers were negative. In rejecting one set of proposals, the department's Adolph Berle recommended at least a U.S. government denunciation of the systematic extermination. But Breckinridge Long opposed even this, saying that it would only further unify the Germans.[44]

The Bergson group, like the mainstream Zionists, had urged the bombing of the concentration camp incinerators and rail lines, to no avail. If the Allies had complied, many lives could have been saved. Bergson urged the U.S. to threaten to use gas against Germany if the Germans continued to use gas to exterminate Jews. He was greatly disappointed that the threat was never made,[45] in spite of the fact that early in the war, FDR threatened reprisals against Japan for using poison gas against China.[46] At the end of the war, the Americans would use weapons far more terrifying than poison gas on Japanese civilians in order to "save American lives," but in no case did the Jewish millions in Europe merit even consideration of protection through the threat of direct reprisals.

Bergson wired President Roosevelt suggesting that he retaliate against the Nazis as he would were French or English civilians being gassed. But the cable was sent on and soon lost in the bureaucratic thicket.[47] Bergson's position was summed up in a September 26, 1944, letter to the Joint Chiefs of Staff, in which he reiterated the point that the U.S. government had warned Germany it "would retaliate in kind" if the Germans used gas on any Allied population. If the Jewish people were included in the warning, "...it might induce Nazi Germany to stop the use of poison gas."[48] In any case, he said, such a warning was important in order to impress upon Germany the fact that, at the very least, the Allies were ready to include the Jews of Europe as human beings deserving the same consideration as other members of the United Nations.

A lengthy reply to Bergson's proposal was drafted by the Joint Strategic Survey Committee, after deliberation by Admiral William Leahy of the Navy, General H.H. Arnold of the Air Force, Commander-in-Chief George Marshall, and others. After the draft reply underwent several modifications, General Arnold recommended that no reply at all should be forthcoming. Finally, it was decided that a short letter from Admiral Leahy would do. Leahy wrote to the Bergson group that "from a military point of view, the proposal set forth in your letter does not come within their [the Joint Chiefs'] cognizance."[49]

The story behind that final answer to the eighteen-month effort by the Bergsonites to obtain a U.S. retaliatory pledge would remain buried in classified documents for a generation. One of the draft replies by the Joint Chiefs said that they "clearly recognize and are in sympathy with "the Bergson group's proposals "for drastic retaliatory action against Germany for use by that country of the lethal chamber as a means of executing non-combatants."[50] The use of poison gas in warfare had been a subject of continuing and careful study by the Joint Chiefs over a long period of time, and certain well-defined policies had been established. The Joint Chiefs of Staff re-examined these policies with the Bergson group's retaliation proposal in mind, but, in spite of its sympathies, decided that it was inadvisable for U.S. forces to use poison gas "at the present time."[51]

The Joint Chiefs, in a second of the series of draft replies, said that it was not logical or realistic to threaten gas warfare against Germany.[52] It gave several reasons: If the threat were made, the Joint Chiefs must be prepared to carry it out. The action would not stop the executions, since the Germans would then use other means, and this would unleash all restraint in the use of gas "and possible other inhuman methods of warfare" with a resulting great loss of life. Further, this retaliation would not fall on those primarily responsible for the atrocities.[53] This pronouncement was made while the Allies engaged in saturation bombings of cities, and while these same American military leaders were planning to drop "other inhuman methods of warfare" on Japanese civilians. The Jews of Europe were still not recognized as a nation, except by the Nazis, the other fascist movements, and the Zionists. As Bergson woud say, the core of the tragedy was the Allies' refusal to recognize Jewish nationhood. Roosevelt and the State Department would say that the Nazis were gassing "people"; it seemed they were physically incapable of acknowledging that the Germans were gassing the *Jewish* people. And the Zionist movement failed to drive this fundamental point home.[54]

Some of Bergson's more liberal friends cringed when he discussed the gas retaliation proposals. It was monstrous, they thought, and it was asking the United States to do too much. There was also internal debate among the Bergsonites over the issue. Newspapers did not choose to publish the proposals that appeared in committee press releases or in the text of speeches; clearly, for many the concept was simply too shocking.[55]

Bergson, however, continued to push the proposal. In a letter to Lord Halifax in 1944, he reminded the British ambassador of Churchill's vow to use poison gas against the Germans if it were used against any member of the United Nations.[56] The tragedy would continue, he warned, unless the British recognized what would soon become the Israeli nation, the Jews of Palestine, and the stateless Jews of Europe. Halifax never responded. Indeed, the British never replied to any of the hundreds of letters and telegrams they received from the Bergson group and its supporters.

It was not until mid-1944 that the Allies were willing to threaten Nazi satellite states with massive bombing if the deportations to the death camps continued. Roosevelt issued an ultimatum to Hungarian leaders, and Budapest was heavily bombed on July 2. Dictator von Horthy's reaction was to stop the deportations immediately.[57]

But would the threat to use poison gas in retaliation have influenced the Germans? Hitler himself had an obsession about gas (undoubtedly because he had been dosed with mustard gas in the last year of World War I). In 1924 he declared in *Mein Kampf* that it would have been good if thousands of Jews had been killed by poison gas at the outbreak of World War I.[58] From May 1943 onward, Hitler was being urged by Martin Bormann, Goebbels and Ley to use poison gas against enemy cities. The weapon these fanatic Nazis had in mind was Tabun, a nerve gas developed by I.G. Farben that was so lethal that a drop of it anywhere on the body killed a victim within minutes. But Hitler consistently refused to unleash poison gas on the Allies because of his great fear of retaliation – his experts believed, incorrectly, that the Allies had stockpiled great quantities of gases as lethal as Tabun.[59] For Hitler, gas was reserved for the Jews, and he knew there would be no threat of retaliation. The allies would not include the Jews in the blanket warning to the Nazis against using poison gas on any Allied military or civilian population, because the Jews were not regarded as a nation – a simple issue of national identity. Because the Jews lacked such recognition, the path was clear for the extermination of millions by gassing.

Bergson gradually came to understand why, when it came to the "Jewish question," the Allies never threatened to retaliate in kind against the Nazis. It was part of the general failure to pursue avenues of rescue, to ransom captive Israel. But even in the face of these failures and disappointments, he believed that it was still possible to save a million or two million lives, and that the American government could be moved to act.

Hillel Kook in his teens.

Hillel Kook's parents, Rabbi Dov HaCohen
and Rivka Kook.

Warsaw, October 1937. From right to left: Hillel
Kook, Shmuel Katz, Chaim Lubinsky.

Hillel Kook, center, in Washington in the 40s
with Menachem Begin and Etzel Representatives
from Israel.

From right to left: Hillel Kook, Senator Guy
M. Gillette, Menachem Begin, during the 40s.

Standing, far left: Hillel Kook, at right: Samuel
Weiser. In front of Hillel, sitting from left: Shmuel
Merlin, Alex Raphaeli (Hadani), Harry Selden and
Senator Guy M. Gillette.

Members of "The Hebrew Committee of National Liberation." From left to right: Theo Ben Nahum, Hillel Kook and Shmuel Merlin.

Hillel Kook in Paris in the 40s.

At a dinner organized in 1944 by "The Emergency Committee to Save the Jewish People of Europe" in honor of Dean Alfange. Hillel Kook, left, with Rep. Emanuel Celler.

A press conference of "The Hebrew Committee of National Liberation." Hillel Kook accompanied by Eri Jabotinsky, right, Congressman Will Rogers Jr., left, and Senator Guy M. Gillette, far left.

A speech given at a dinner by Ben Hecht, standing. To the right: Hillel Kook and
Rose Keane, at left Billy Rose.

2 CENTS in CITY (3 CENTS
LIMITS) Klsewhere
5½c a Month by Mail in U. S. A.
5½ Issues with Canada Editions &c.

23

Philadelphia, Thursday, April 22, 1943

RITTenhouse 5200—Bell
RACE 2445—Keystone

Entered as 2d-Class Matter Daily, Except Sunday, at the Postoffice at Phila.,
Pa., under the act of March 3, 1879.

"WE WILL NEVER DIE"

A memorial dedicated to the 2,000,000 Jewish dead of Europe

Written by .... BEN HECT	Musical Score by .... KURT WEIL
Produced by .... BILLY ROSE	Setting and Technical Direction by . S. SYRJALA
Directed by .... MOSS HART	Associate Designer : .... LEMUEL AYERS

PHILADELPHIA PRODUCTION

Supervised by .... S. SYRJALA	Orchestra—Conducted by ISAAC VAN GROVE
Staged by .... HERMAN ROTSTEN	Associate Conductor .... HENRI ELKAN
Lighting & Production Coordinator. YOLA MIL! ̂ ̂	

Hillel Kook, 1949, after release
from Israeli prison following the
"Altalena" incident.

Meeting with Andrei Gromiko, center. At
right, Hillel Kook, at left, Eri Jabotinsky.

"The Embassy" building, housing
the office of the "The Hebrew
Committee of National Liberation"
in May 1942, in Washington, DC.

1944. In front of "The Embassy" in
Washington, DC. From left to right:
Hillel Kook, Senator Guy M. Gillette,
Senator Andrew Somers.

Hillel Kook during the 1980s.

JEWS FIGHT FOR THE RIGHT TO FIGHT

"The vast majority of the members of the human race are on our side. Many of them are fighting with us, all of them are praying for us." —Franklin Delano Roosevelt.

The Jews of Palestine and the stateless Jews of the world do not only want to pray—THEY WANT TO FIGHT!!!!

"ANY NATION, ANY MAN WHO FIGHTS AGAINST NAZIDOM WILL HAVE OUR AID." — *Winston Churchill.*

200,000 JEWS OFFER THEIR SERVICES.

What are the Jews doing in this war?

In England, the United States and in Russia this question has an easy answer:

They are fighting.

But there are thousands upon thousands of Jews who are not fighting.

135,000 Fearless Palestinian Jews registered as volunteers for war service as soon as the war broke out. They want to defend their homeland and their very lives from attack by aggressors.

They are still waiting to be called to the colors.

Then there are the stateless Jews, the disinherited Jews, the ones driven from their homes by the great and evil violence of the Axis Powers.

They are scattered in every part of the world, young and courageous, who have only one dream—to fight under a flag that will carry them against the armies of Hitler.

They were the first victims of Hitler's hatred and aggression. Their relatives, their people are the most persecuted, the most starved, the most tortured under Hitler's yoke; they paid and are paying in actual human suffering infinitely more than any other people on earth.

They are eager to fight back and to avenge.

There is still another category of Jews—from countries not yet involved in the war—from South America and the Middle East. They feel that they, too, should have a part in the world struggle to defeat the enemies of civilization.

All of them are convinced that the Jewish people's place is on all the fronts where the democracies are fighting for those very foundations of society whose Magna Charta is the Bible.

They all want to unite in their own Freedom Army and to fight under their own Liberty Flag, under the supreme Allied Command.

There is nothing unprecedented in this demand: Jewish Legion fought in the last World War and participated in conquering Palestine.

To urge the materialization of this demand a Committee For a Jewish Army was organized and inaugurated on December 4, 1941, in Washington, D. C., a committee composed of men from all walks of American life who passionately believe in the victory of democracy and through that victory, in a better world for all, regardless of race or creed.

This Committee believes that with America's entrance into the war against the Axis, the question of a Jewish Army, based on Palestine, has become a direct and vital concern to the United States, since this army, 200,000 strong,

Will consolidate the Allied positions around the Suez Canal;

Will release a considerable part of the Anzac forces from the Middle East for combat in the Pacific, and thus

Will strengthen the defences of this hemisphere.

In these historic days when the greatest leaders and animators of world democracy, President Roosevelt and Prime Minister Churchill, are deliberating the vital problems of world strategy, this Committee wants to express its conviction that the organization of a Jewish Army will be of great strategic importance to the strength of the United Nations and an additional proof that this titanic struggle will be decided not solely by brute force, but by principles of justice and honor.

Churchill gave expression to this conviction in these immortal words:

"Without honor we could neither hope nor deserve to win this hard war."

Therefore, this committee feels that humanity, Christianity, the very ideals for which we are fighting this war, are embodied in the demand for a Jewish Army.

It is the conviction of this Committee that the Jewish flag must fly in this ultimate clash, that will probably be fought out in the Middle East, over the evangelic hills of Galilee.

This Committee demands the right for the Jews to go and fight for freedom under the walls of Jerusalem.

This Committee demands that the Jews be not slaughtered in Palestine as helpless children, but that they will be trained and will be given arms in their hands—arms, airplanes, tanks and guns.

This Committee demands that the Jewish People be heard, that the Jewish People takes its place in the ranks of free peoples of the earth.

This Committee demands that the Jews the world over should be given a chance to express and to demonstrate their solidarity with the great American nation which became the standard-bearer of the fight for freedom and justice everywhere and for ever. This chance should be given to them by enabling them to form an army of Palestinian and stateless Jews, who will fight side by side with the American people and her allied nations.

Many American strategists and many of America's most far-seeing statesmen are already convinced of the rightness of this plan and have endorsed it. Secretary of War Stimson has wired to the inaugural session of this Committee the following encouraging and inspiring words:

"Free men everywhere are arming for the defense of democracy. I send my best wishes for the success of your movement."

A powerful and courageous army ready to give its life for the ideals that mark the Allied cause lies waiting to be born.

The Committee asks that men and women of all creeds come to its aid by a determined effort in the creation of this first great modern Jewish Army.

With your help and cooperation the cause of the Jewish Army will be victorious. It will be victorious not only in the interest of the Jewish people but also in the interest of world democracy. Because ours is a struggle for right and justice—and right and justice are indivisible—they should be for all and everywhere.

COMMITTEE FOR A JEWISH ARMY

NATIONAL HEADQUARTERS

285 Madison Avenue   New York, N. Y.

LEx. 2-7646

Washington Office: Willard Hotel

REGIONAL OFFICES:

Philadelphia, 716 Walnut St.
Chicago,   139 No. Clark St.

HELP MAKE THE JEWISH ARMY A REALITY NOW!

FOR SALE to Humanity
70,000 Jews
Guaranteed Human Beings at $50 a Piece

Roumania is tired of killing Jews. It has killed one hundred thousand of them in two years. Roumania will now give Jews away practically for nothing.

SEVENTY THOUSAND JEWS ARE WAITING DEATH IN ROUMANIAN CONCENTRATION CAMPS:

Roumania Will Give These 70,000 Jews to the Four Freedoms for 20,000 Lei ($50) a Piece. This Sum Covers All Transportation expenses.

To The FOUR FREEDOMS
Care United Nations' Leaders.   February 16, 1943

My Dear Noble State of Mind:

I know you are very busy, too busy perhaps to read the story on the left hand side of this page.

For that reason I am writing an ad. Ads are easier and quicker to read than stories.

Your admirer,

Ben Hecht

RUMANIA WILLING TO TRANSFER 70,000 JEWS TO PALESTINE

Loss of Faith in Germany's Victory Seen in Rumanian Proposal

Newspaper reports from London reveal that the Rumanian Government has proposed to the United Nations to transfer 70,000 Rumanian Jews from Trans-Dniestria to any refuge that will be assigned by the Allies.

This proposal was made through the medium of neutral diplomats. According to the reports, the Rumanian proposal implies that the Rumanian Government is ready to release the Jews from Trans-Dniestria in Rumanian ships which would be permitted to display the insignia of the Vatican to insure safe passage.

The Jews would be first transferred under the supervision of ecclesastic dignitaries in Bucharest, the capital of Rumania, where special accommodations will be made for them until the evacuation.

It is also reported that the Bishop of Bucharest and the Papal Nuncio will be in charge of the arrangements to well as the supervision of the transfer from Bucharest to the place of destination.

According to the proposal the Rumanian Government would levy a tax of 20,000 lei on each refugee to cover traveling expenses.

Although the Rumanian Government is ready to release the Jews from Trans-Dniestria to any place that will be selected by the Allies, it suggests, nevertheless, that the most convenient destination would be Palestine because of shipping facilities. Other destinations will create a serious shipping problem.

Political observers in London believe that the Rumanian suggestion is proof that German power and prestige in the Balkans are declining and there is a rising confidence in the victory of the United Nations.

But some officials, it is reported, in analyzing this plan intimated complications and difficulties. First, they think there is danger in receiving such a large number of refugees at one time because there is the possibility that spies may be among them. Secondly, they think that the arrival of the Jewish refugees in Palestine may have deplorable effect upon the Arabs of this country and possibly those of neighboring countries.

The influential Manchester Guardian in discussing the general Jewish situation editorially, on Feb. 9, said:

"The Jews only symbolise what Hitler might do to the British if he gets the chance. If the refugees were British, American or Russian, the United Nations would be up and doing something despite all difficulties."

ROUMANIA OFFERS TO DELIVER THESE 70,000 ALIVE TO PALESTINE

Attention Four Freedoms !!!
NO SPIES WERE FOUND AMONG THE 300,000 JEWS WHO CAME TO PALESTINE SINCE HITLER ASSUMED POWER IN GERMANY
THERE WILL BE NO SPIES SMUGGLED IN AMONG THESE JEWS.
(IF THERE ARE YOU CAN SHOOT THEM)

Attention Humanity !!!
PALESTINE'S ARABS WILL NOT BE ANNOYED BY THE ARRIVAL OF 70,000 JEWS THE ONLY ARABS WHO WILL BE ANNOYED ARE THE ARAB LEADERS WHO ARE IN BERLIN AND THEIR SPIES IN PALESTINE.

Attention America !!!
THE GREAT ROUMANIAN BARGAIN IS FOR THIS MONTH ONLY!
IT IS AN UNPRECEDENTED OFFER!
SEVENTY THOUSAND SOULS AT $50 A PIECE!
The Doors of Roumania Are Open! Act Now!

The four million Jews of Nazi-held Europe can be saved from the fate of their two million brothers already exterminated.

The Germans have dared to undertake this process of annihilation because they knew that the Jews are defenseless and forgotten.

The great, humanitarian people of the United States and Great Britain must be made aware of the facts.

To that end the Committee for a Jewish Army of stateless and Palestinian Jews has launched an intensive campaign to arouse the conscience of humanity and to demand that something be done NOW, WHILE THERE IS STILL TIME, to save the remaining Jews of Europe.

The principal demand of the Committee is that the United Nations immediately appoint an inter-governmental committee to formulate ways and means of stopping this wholesale slaughter of human beings.

You are part of the collective conscience of America; this conscience has never been found wanting. Join in this fight! You can help spread this message to your friends. You can write to your Congressmen. You can make contributions for the further distribution of messages like these to kill the people of the United States. In this way, you, with the force of your indignation, of your wrath, and of your action, you can help save European Jewry!

Committee for a Jewish Army
of Stateless and Palestinian Jews

National Headquarters • New York, 535 Fifth Ave. • Murray Hill 2-7237

I want to support your campaign to save European Jewry by action—not pity, and to help publicize your messages through the press, the radio and public meetings throughout the country. I am glad to enclose my check in the amount of

$ ....

Name ....

Address ....

PLEASE MAKE YOUR CHECK PAYABLE TO THE COMMITTEE FOR A JEWISH ARMY OF STATELESS AND PALESTINIAN JEWS, 535 FIFTH AVE., N. Y. C.

To those of my people who fight for the right to die with their boots on — my pride, my love, my devotion...

New York Dec. 1943.

"We shall no longer witness with pity alone..."

We All Stand Before the Bar of Humanity, History and God

We will all be judged bloodguilty if we do not create the machinery to save the Jewish People of Europe

GOVERNMENTAL AGENCY PREREQUISITE FOR ACTION

During the Quebec Conference, this Committee dared to address a vehement plea to the President and the British Prime Minister, drawing their attention to the national disaster of the Jewish people of Europe.

This Committee did so because it was convinced that 2,000,000 dead and 5,000,000 doomed deserve their attention even, and especially, when plans of a global character are discussed and elaborated.

It did so because the situation, in which a whole people is being put to death and yet being ignored and forgotten, is intolerable.

It did so because the human mind cannot conceive any longer the United Nations being in constant cooperation—with their general staffs, their post-war planners, their economic councils, their relief organizations—and for the tortured Jews not a single idea, not one concrete program, not an official body appointed to act.

The Jewish people of Europe is still caught between the hammer of the enemy's brutality and the anvil of democracy's indifference.

In this respect, the very influential and liberal English newspaper, the Manchester Guardian has written: "If the victims were British, American or Russian, the United Nations would be up and doing something despite all difficulties."

This people cannot wait until victory is won because there is real danger that when the United Nations Armies will triumphantly march into the liberated countries of the European continent, there will be no more Jews—there will be only corpses—a continental cemetery. For the Germans have sworn to exterminate the whole Jewish people before their own doom.

The Jewish People Can Be Saved

Therefore the Emergency Committee to Save the Jewish People of Europe addressed its plea to the President and to the Prime Minister. They did so in fulfilling a mandate they received from the Emergency Conference held lately in New York City where recognized experts on international, economic and immigration questions formulated practical plans of salvation.

These experts, representative of a cross section of public opinion, came to the conclusion that the Jewish people of Europe can be saved—must be saved now, though the task is difficult.

They came to the conclusion that a prerequisite of any action must be the immediate creation of a specific agency specially charged with the task of saving the Jews of Europe.

The Least the United Nations Could Do

What less could be done for a whole people in agony and torture than to appoint a few men, with compassion in their hearts and knowledge and experience, for the task of saving countless human lives. Even an agency to save European treasures of art was created recently. Such a step is commendable. It shows the deep concern of the United Nations Governments toward the problems of culture and civilization. But should it not at least show equal concern for an old and ancient people who gave to the world the fundamentals of its Christian civilization, the Magna Charta of Justice—the Bible—and to every generation some of its most outstanding thinkers, writers, scholars and artists? A governmental agency with the task of dealing with the problems of saving the Jewish people of Europe is the least the United Nations can do.

Winding up its appeal, in Quebec, the Emergency Committee expressed the following plea:

"The supreme leaders of world democracy and champions of Four Freedoms—President Roosevelt and Prime Minister Churchill—are the last hope of the doomed Jewish people of Europe.

"In this exalting hour, when the victorious American and British armies are poised to strike at the continent of Europe and the onslaught of the United Nationals is proving irresistible, we appeal to you, Mr. President and Mr. Prime Minister, to lead the moral offensive against this cold-blooded massacre as you have led the military offensive against brutal aggression.

"One word from you, Mr. President and Mr. Prime Minister, and a machinery of immediate action—a specific governmental agency to deal with the saving of the millions of Jews caught in a death trap—will be created.

"One word from you and the fate of multitudes will be affected.

"The destiny of a great and ancient people rests in your hands.

"History awaits your answer. For, as the Archbishop of Canterbury declared in the British Parliament, "We all stand before the bar of history, humanity and God."

Good and decent people of America, the role of leader has fallen to you. The eyes of the world's oppressed and heavy-laden are on you. From this nation, free and mighty, the world expects the moral leadership for liberation. The time for action cannot be postponed any longer.

You Must Act Now and With Determination

To secure effective and speedy government action, a vast nation-wide campaign must be organized; a truly democratic government acts under the pressure of an enlightened and aroused public opinion.

The United Nations passed from a defensive to an offensive strategy because you wanted so.

The United Nations recognized, though with limitations, the French Committee for National Liberation, because you wanted it so.

The Governments will act in the direction to save the Jewish people of Europe if you will express your will with determination.

This Is What You Could Do

Demand from your government the immediate creation of an Agency to Save the Jewish People of Europe. Write to your Senator and Congressman; ask them to support our campaign, so vital for the moral victory of democracy and so essential for the future of a decent world.

In order to carry out our tremendous task without a waste of time, considerable funds are required. We appeal to you to assist us with your generous contribution in order to enable us to carry out our work in Washington, London and other Allied Countries—where our committees or our representatives function.

Our Co-Chairman, Congressman Will Rogers Jr., is in London on a special mission of our Committee. He is seeking the co-operation of the British Government for the great humanitarian campaign so that our two great democracies can act simultaneously.

Similar delegations will be dispatched to Palestine and Turkey.

We are trying to do our duty.   Do your share too.

Realistic Possibilities of Saving the Jewish People of Europe

Digest of program adopted at the Emergency Conference.

The Emergency Committee to Save the Jewish People of Europe is an outgrowth of the Emergency Conference which convened in New York, July 20th to 25th. The members of this Committee have pledged themselves to remain on the scene until their task is achieved and to urge the Governments of the United States and the United Nations to carry out the following plans worked out by the Conference:

1. To create an official agency specifically charged with the task of saving the Jewish People of Europe. This agency to be initiated by the United States and the United Nations to be invited to participate in the agency when organized.

2. To seek guarantees from the Axis satellite countries, through the International Red Cross, Neutral Countries or the Vatican to insure Jews the same treatment given to other nationals.

3. To demand relief from starvation and disease in Axis-held territory by distributing food and medical supplies under the supervision of the International Red Cross, following the precedent established in feeding the starving people of Greece.

4. To bring pressure on Axis-held territory through the intermediary of the International Red Cross, Neutral Governments or the Vatican to permit Jews to leave Axis-controlled territories.

5. To urge Neutral Countries—Sweden, Ireland, Portugal, Spain, Switzerland and Turkey—to grant the Jewish people temporary asylum. The United Nations to be called upon to feed and clothe these refugees and arrange for return to their homelands, as soon as safety permits.

6. To urge that foreign exchange controls of the governments of the United Nations be operated to such manner as to make possible financial assistance to Jewish refugees in non-belligerent territory.

7. To convince the governments of the United Nations that they should grant temporary asylum and transit to territory under their control to Jews who cannot be accommodated in non-belligerent countries, with the understanding that these refugees will have no claim to permanent residence.

8. To concentrate particularly on admitting European Jews to Palestine, because of its proximity and the fact that evacuation can be accomplished without diverting shipping space. In Palestine the Jews will be received not as refugee burdens of war but welcomed as brothers.

9. To ask neutral countries to grant transit facilities to all Jewish people passing from Axis-controlled lands to any United Nations territory, regardless of whether the persons involved be refugees, immigrants or repatriates.

10. To use every available means of transportation to rescue the Jewish people.

  a) By rail and road into Turkey and from Turkey to Palestine and other Allied territory.

  b) By rail and road into Spain, Sweden and Switzerland.

  c) Neutral shipping lying idle in United Nations ports, can bring 50,000 persons per month to safety. Other idle tonnage of neutral registry can transport many additional thousands.

11. To inform all Axis and satellite governments that they will be held strictly accountable for the death, through murder, torture, deportation, starvation or denial of medical aid, of all Jews in their territories. To warn them further, in line with the announced policy of the United Nations, through the means of radio, leaflets, etc., that just reprisals will be initiated against them immediately for all atrocities and crimes committed against the Jews as well as any other defenseless civilian people.

12. To urge that 100,000 stateless Jews outside of the United States who are not being used for military service, together with the 23,000 in the Jewish Palestinian military force, be employed specifically in such reprisals as well as in the most dangerous military operations against the Axis in general.

EMERGENCY COMMITTEE TO SAVE THE JEWISH PEOPLE OF EUROPE

One East Forty-fourth Street, New York City

Suite 701   MUrray Hill 2-7237

Executive Board

Co-Chairmen:

Peter H. Bergson   Ben Hecht   Rep. Will Rogers, Jr.
Louis Brumfield   Dr. Max Lerner   Madame Sigrid Undset

Vice-Chairmen:

Dean Alfange   Dr. A. Hadani   Fletcher Pratt
William S. Bennet   Prof. Francis McMahon   Lisa Sergio
Konrad Bercovici   Dean George W. Matheson   Rep. Andrew L. Somers
Jo Davidson   Herbert S. Moore   Dr. Maurice Willis
Oscar Ekrhorn

Treasurer: Mrs. John Gunther

Members:

Stella Adler   Nathan G. Horvitz   Victor M. Ratto
Al Bauer   E. Jabotinsky   Curt Reiss
Y. Ben-Ami   Rose Krause   K. Shridharani
A. Ben-Eliezer   Emil Ludwig   Johan Smertenko
M. Bezdin   Paul Longgel   Arthur Szyk
Rabbi Philip D. Bookstaber   Laurence Lipton   Irving Talmi
Bishop James A. Cannon, Jr.   Emil Ludwig   Thomas J. Watson
Lester Cohen   S. Merlin   Gabriel Wechsler
Rep. Samuel Dickstein   Michael Potter   Alex Wйll

EMERGENCY COMMITTEE
TO SAVE THE JEWISH PEOPLE OF EUROPE
1 East 44th Street   New York 17, N. Y.

Gentlemen: I hereby add my voice to your efforts to secure United Nations' action to save the Jewish People of Europe. In order to enable you to carry out your tremendous task, I enclose my contribution of $_____

Name _____

Address _____

Make checks payable to Mrs. JOHN GUNTHER, Treasurer.

My Uncle Abraham Reports...

By Ben Hecht

I have an Uncle who is a Ghost.

But, he is no ordinary Ghost like so many dead uncles.

He was elected last April by the Two Million Jews who have been murdered by the Germans to be their World Delegate.

Wherever there are Conferences on how to make the World a Better Place, maybe, my Uncle Abraham appears and sits on the window sill and takes notes.

That's how he happened to be in Moscow a few weeks ago.

My Uncle Abraham sat on the window sill of the Kremlin and listened with great excitement, to one of the Finest Conferences he has ever attended since he has been a World Delegate.

He heard every word that Eden, Molotov and Hull spoke.

Last night my Uncle Abraham was back in a Certain Place where the Two Million murdered Jews meet. It is the Jewish Underground. Only Ghosts belong to it.

When the Two Million Souls had assembled, my Uncle Abraham arose and made his report to them as World Delegate.

"Dishonored dead," said my Uncle Abraham, "Fellow Corpses, and Ghosts from All Over. Of the Moscow Conference I have this to report. The Conference made a promise that the world was going to punish the Germans for murdering all the different peoples of Europe—Czechs, Greeks, Serbs, Russians, French hostages, Polish officers, Cretan peasants. Only we were not mentioned. In this Conference, which named everyone, only the Jew had no name. He had no face. He was like a hole in Europe on which nobody looked."

A Ghost from the Lime Kilns of Warsaw spoke.

"Why is this?" asked this Ghost, "why is it that we who are dead are without a Name in the Conferences of Fine People?"

"This I do not know," said my Uncle Abraham, "I can only report what exists. Jews do not exist, even when they are dead. In the Kremlin in Moscow, in the White House in Washington, in the Downing Street Building in London where I have sat on the window sills, I have never heard our name. The people who live in those buildings—Stalin, Roosevelt and Churchill—do not speak of us. Why, I don't know. We were not allowed by the Germans to stay alive. We are not allowed by the Four Freedoms to be dead."

A Woman Ghost from the Dynamite Dumps of Odessa spoke.

"If they didn't mention the two million murdered Jews in the Conference, isn't that bad for four million who are still alive? The Germans will think that when they kill Jews, Stalin, Roosevelt and Churchill pretend nothing is happening."

And from the Two Million Ghosts came a great cry.

"Why is this silence? Why don't they speak of Us?"

My Uncle Abraham raised his hand.

"Little Children," my Uncle Abraham spoke: "Be patient. We will be dead a long time. Yesterday when we were killed we were changed from Nobodies to Nobodies. Today, on our Jewish tomb, there is not the Star of David, there is an Asterisk. But, who knows, maybe Tomorrow—!"

This ended the Meeting of the Jewish Underground.

My Uncle Abraham has gone to the White House in Washington. He is sitting on the windowsill two feet away from Mr. Roosevelt. But he has left his notebook behind.

* * * *

★ ★ ★ ★

HELP Prevent 4,000,000 People from Becoming Ghosts

There are four million Jews still alive in Europe.

They can be saved. Experts agree on that.

Sweden and Denmark have just proved it by saving 6,000 Jews in a few days.

This Committee considers it a sacred duty to do all humanly possible to save them.

Our offices and representatives in Washington and in London, in Palestine and in Turkey, are steadily working in this direction, trying to get large-scale government action. This action will have to express itself in the creation of an Intergovernmental Agency to save the Jewish people of Europe and in declaring the doors of Palestine and other countries under United Nations control open for escaping Jews. For, it is now strictly a race for time against death.

Every day that passes dooms thousands who can be saved.

This Committee is asking the American people for a half million dollars with which it hopes—and believes—results can be secured effecting the rescue of the four million martyred Jews in Europe.

We need your financial help immediately. By your support will be determined the speed, scope and affectiveness of our work to save the Jewish people of Europe.

Emergency Committee to Save the Jewish People of Europe

One East Forty-fourth Street, New York 17, N. Y.   MUrray Hill 2-7237

--[**By a ruling of the Treasury Department,**]--
[**contributions to this Committee are tax exempt**]

EMERGENCY COMMITTEE
TO SAVE THE JEWISH PEOPLE OF EUROPE
1 East 44th Street, New York 17, N. Y.

I hereby join your efforts to obtain immediate United Nations action to save the Jewish people of Europe. I enclose my contribution to enable you to carry out this tremendous task in the sum of

$_____

NAME_____

ADDRESS_____

Please make checks payable to Mrs. JOHN GUNTHER, Treasurer

New Palestine Group Formed --Zionist Chiefs Oppose It

Washington Bureau Special to The Post

By CHARLES VAN DEVANDER
Post Staff Correspondent

Washington, May 19 — Announcement by a group of seven Palestinian Jews that they have organized as the "Hebrew Committee of National Liberation" and intend to seek recognition of the United Nations today was met by a storm of protests from Zionist leaders.

Chairman of the new committee is Peter H. Bergson, a 34-year-old Palestine national who previously has been active in organizing the American Friends of a Jewish Palestine, the Committee for a Jewish Army, and the Emergency Committee to Save the Jewish People of Europe.

Bergson disclosed the formation of the "Hebrew Committee of National Liberation" at a press conference in a newly acquired building on Washington's "Embassy Row" which Bergson referred to as the committee's "embassy." A Jewish and an American flag flew over the entrance of the building, which is as yet unfurnished.

Seek Place at Peace Table

Bergson said his committee would seek recognition from the Allied governments as spokesman for the "Hebrew Nation" and that it would request membership on the War Crimes Commission, United Nations Relief and Rehabilitation Administration and other United Nations' bodies, as well as a seat, eventually at the peace table.

Dr. Leon Feuer, Washington director of the American Zionist Emergency Council, which is jointly headed by Dr. Stephen S. Wise of New York and Dr. Abba Hillel Silver of Cleveland and speaks for all major Zionist groups in the U. S., promptly denounced the new Bergson venture as "a brazen fraud," and said the committee consisted of "half a dozen adventurers from Palestine with no standing, no credentials, no mandate from anyone."

Sponsors of the committee, he declared, have "thrived on publicity tricks" in their earlier organizations, which he asserted have had "one common feature—

PETER H. BERGSON
Heads "Liberation Group"

a persistent request for contributions."

Dr. Nahum Godmann, Washington representative of the Jewish Agency for Palestine and of the World Zionist Organization, said: "The attempt of a few persons, who have come from Palestine without any authority, without having been delegated by any group in Palestine, having played no role whatever in Jewish life in Palestine or elsewhere, to proclaim themselves as the 'trustees of the Hebrew Nation's interests' is an act which, I am sure, will be rejected by all sections of the Jewish people as a fraud."

Fear Harmful Result

His statement included a warning to "well-meaning friends" among non-Jewish groups not to be "fooled" by the claims of the new committee. Any aid extended to it, Dr. Goldmann said, would weaken the prestige and influence of the Jewish organizations "charged with the complex and responsible task of building the Jewish homeland," and would result in doing harm, instead of good, to the Jewish people.

The new organization was similarly denounced by the administrative committee of the American Jewish Conference, which said that the leaders of the "Hebrew Committee of National Lib-

eration" were linked with an "extremist clique" which had been outlawed in Palestine because of its "anti-democratic and terroristic tactics."

The new organization's program, the statement said, was intended to divide and disrupt the Jewish people and to destroy existing agencies for establishment of a national home in Palestine. Co-chairmen of the AJC Interim Committee are Israel Goldstein, Rabbi Wise and Henry Monsky of Omaha.

Seek Seat at Peace Table

Undisturbed by the furore he was causing among virtually all established Jewish organizations, Bergson told 25 reporters at his "embassy" press conference that they were witnessing the "rebirth" of the Hebrew Nation after 18 centuries with his committee as the temporary custodian of its interests.

Bergson claimed no specific mandate, but said his committee represents the interests of "members of the Hebrew Nation," whom he defined as the Palestine Jews and those living in the Axis and occupied countries.

"I consider the Palestine Jews, who are dominated by the British, as absolutely not free to speak for themselves and absolutely not free to act for themselves," he said in reply to a question.

Plans to Sell Bonds

The committee hopes to finance its activities by selling interest bearing "Free Palestine" bonds as an obligation of the Hebrew Nation, he said, mentioning $1,000,000 as the desired amount for the first issue. Asked whether the Treasury Dept. had given permission for sale of such bonds, he replied: "Not yet." Bergson added that the committee had paid $65,000 for its "embassy," which was formerly occupied by the Iranian government. The money was contributed by "friends."

Members of the National Liberation Committee, in addition to Bergson, are Arieh Ben Elizer, Theodore Bennahum, Pinhas Delougaz, Jeremiah Helpern, Eri Jabotinsky and Samuel Merlin. Jabotinsky is the son of Vladimir Jabotinsky, one of the early pioneers of Zionist.

CHAPTER FIVE

THE HOSKINS AFFAIR

U ntil the creation of Israel in 1948, the Jews were at the mercy of other nations. But America, despite widespread, often virulent anti-Semitism, was not eastern Europe; and American Jews during World War II were far from being "powerless," as apologists for the Zionist and Jewish establishment have declared.

It was true that Jews were underrepresented in government – there were only seven Jewish congressmen, for example, at a time when Jews constituted a much larger percentage of the United States population than they do today.[1] And the Jews who formed a major part of FDR's braintrust felt themselves in a tenuous position and never raised delicate subjects – such as the rescue of European Jews – with their patrician boss. But those who maintain that American Jews were completely powerless in the wartime era usually choose to ignore a chapter in the history of those years, the Hoskins affair, which shows that American Jews could and did exert power when they mobilized their resources.

In 1943, the establishment Zionists, anti- and non-Zionist Jews, and the Bergsonites, all pulling in different directions, managed to torpedo a sinister attempt by the State Department to issue a Joint Declaration with the British that would disavow commitment to a Jewish state in Palestine, and prevent freedom of expression to a minority in the United States. The proposal, all but forgotten by historians (especially those interested in maintaining the myth of powerlessness), incredibly enough, had the backing of Roosevelt and Churchill. Sir Isaiah Berlin, commenting forty years after witnessing the affair as an official at the British embassy in Washington, believed the Hoskins proposal would have been "a terrible blow" to the Zionist cause.[2]

In the Hoskins affair, a real threat to the future Jewish state arose, and, for various reasons, American Jews displayed the very strength they are said to have lacked when it came to the matter of mobilizing for a rescue campaign.

Lieutenant-Colonel Harold Boies Hoskins, an Arabist in the Office of Strategic Services – the precursor of the CIA – became Roosevelt's special Near East envoy after he predicted in a January 23, 1943 report from Cairo, that there would be bloody fighting at any moment between the Zionists and Arabs in Palestine which would have "domestic repercussions" in Britain and the United States, as well as inflame the entire Moslem world "from Casablanca to Calcutta." In the report to Undersecretary of State Welles, Hoskins said that "in venturing any comments on the complicated Arab-Jewish problem, I realize I am moving into deep waters."[3] But they were not unfamiliar waters, and Hoskins had a definite point of view.

Hoskins, the son of American Protestant missionaries, was born in Beirut in 1895 and spent his boyhood in Lebanon and Syria, where he learned fluent Arabic and became permanently imbued with the idea of a Greater Syria, which included the territory of Palestine. He was educated at a private boarding school and at Princeton, where he graduated with honors. He and his wealthy family were closely connected to the virulently anti-Zionist American University of Beirut; and another family member worked for the Arabian American Oil Co. In World War I, he served as a second lieutenant in the Marine Corps. In the twenties, Hoskins became an executive for the textile giant Cannon Mills, and maintained a home in Manhattan's elegant Sutton Place and a summer residence in Millbrook, a community notorious for its exclusion of Jews. In 1941, he became attached to the State Department "for special political assignments in Washington and in [the] Middle East,"[4] a euphemism for intelligence work. He remained an OSS high-flyer throughout the war years. In June 1942, he was assigned by Assistant Secretary of State G. Howland Shaw "to obtain information regarding foreign groups, their proposed organization and their membership." He was also attached to Assistant Secretary Berle, the same official who always put on an amiable face when he met with Peter Bergson, but who all the while was writing reports to Welles complaining that "the Committee for a Jewish Army has been besieging the White House."[5]

Hoskins felt at home in the anti-Zionist atmosphere of the State Department, and for its part, the Near East Division felt he was a kindred spirit. Hoskins also worked closely with Wallace Murray, perhaps the most vehement opponent of Zionism in the State Department. On June 2, 1942, Murray sent the Secretary of State a draft letter to the President, approved by Hoskins, which said that "the agitation for the formation of a Jewish army in Palestine is having such alarming effects in the Near and Middle East that I am impelled to draw your attention to the matter."[6] Murray, basing his assessment on reports by Hoskins and others, said it was "clear" that Palestine could not be used as a base of operations against the Axis. Murray condemned the Bergsonites' full-page ads and other "widely publicized" activities, saying that it had helped the Axis to win over Moslem support.[7]

In November 1942, Hoskins went to Cairo to conduct a survey for the Joint Chiefs of Staff and to build an intelligence network (or "friendly contacts" as the OSS called it) in the Arab world. FDR himself, and Secretary Hull, asked U.S. officials to facilitate Hoskins' mission.[8]

Hoskins traveled to his old stomping grounds, and assessed the Middle East situation through the partisan lens of his particular background. In his January 1943 message to Welles, Hoskins said that Zionist officials of the Jewish Agency in Jerusalem were trying "to goad Palestinian Arabs" into breaking the informal truce that had been in effect since the beginning of the war.[9] He proposed a joint declaration of Britain and the U.S. that would rule out British or American military support for the Jews if the neighboring Arab states invaded Palestine. In order to appear "even-handed" he also stated that the Allies should not give military support to the Arab side, either. (In the same report, he recognized that the Jews would not be strong enough to ward off the Arab attack.) In addition to this initial broaching of the idea of a joint statement on Palestine, he also proposed that Emir Abdullah of Trans-Jordan and other moderate Arab nationalists be brought to the United States, in order to make the Arab case before the American public that "Palestine is not an uninhabited area into which several million Jews from Europe can at [the] end of [the] war be dropped."[10]

Hoskins developed his ideas for a Joint Declaration and drew up his final report. Secretary Hull, on April 20, 1943, sent FDR a summary of the Hoskins report on the Near East, suggesting that if FDR agreed, the declaration could be discussed first with the British, and then "with other United Nations."[11]

The proposed declaration would have foreclosed public debate and all lobbying related to the Palestine question until the war's end. The report urged that any eventual agreement on Palestine be contingent on Arab consent – otherwise,

Hoskins maintained, civil war would erupt, endangering the entire Allied war effort.

Hoskins said that the Arabs would break the informal truce that had existed in Palestine since the outbreak of the war in 1939 because they felt "that the Zionists, by continuing a world-wide propaganda [campaign] for a Jewish state in Palestine, have not kept their part of the bargain." He said that Arab fears of American support "for political Zionism with its proposed Jewish State and Jewish Army in Palestine... is now extending to the further fear of American support for the penetration of Jewish people into Syria and other neighboring Arab areas, once Palestine has been fully populated."[12] He also wrote (perhaps ingenuously) that the Jews of Syria and Iraq and other countries probably would be slaughtered as soon as fighting broke out.[13]

In warning of the effects of the Arab-Jewish conflict on the United States, the unorthodox OSS agent said that "our domestic disunity is aggravated by dissension among American citizens of various foreign-born groups and increasing conflicts among various Jewish groups, as well as increasing anti-Semitism."[14] The conflict he was probably referring to was the increasingly bitter campaign led by Stephen Wise, Nahum Goldmann and others against the Bergsonites. And Hoskins understood that, "An unfortunate effect for the Jews themselves has resulted from mixing together two problems that should be kept quite separate. Support for all-out aid to persecuted Jews in Europe, on which there can be no difference of opinion, should not be diminished by tying it up with the extremely controversial proposal to establish a Jewish political state in Palestine."[15] He had learned much from his earlier OSS assignment, under State Department cover, to study "foreign groups."

Hoskins maintained that the proposed Allied statement would ease the tension in the Near East and constitute the military equivalent of at least several divisions that would have to be pulled out of the war. His full proposal said that additional divisions would be needed in Palestine unless Zionist agitation, especially the campaign for a Jewish army, was muffled immediately. His report agreed with the British view, as well as the general assessment in the State Department, that there would be an Arab uprising if Jewish refugees were allowed sanctuary in North Africa or Palestine. His vision of the post-war Middle East was clearly dominated by his Greater Syria ideas, although he shrouded his language in diplomatic niceties. Hoskins proposed that the status quo be maintained in the existing Palestine population – the figures he gave were one million Arabs and one-half million Jews – who would form a bi-national state (obviously dominated by its Arab majority) within a "Levant Federation. This independent Levant Federation would be formed by the re-uniting of Lebanon, Syria, Palestine and Trans-Jordan that, prior to their dismemberment after the last war, had for years been one natural economic and political unit."[16]

In the Hoskins universe, there would be no Jewish state in Palestine, only, perhaps, in some other place, "possibly northern Cirenaica [sic], which is now virtually uninhabited." (Cyrenaica is a stretch of the Sahara which is today part of northern Libya.)[17]

The actual declaration Hoskins proposed consisted of only two paragraphs:

> The United Nations, having in mind the terms of their Declaration of January 1, 1942, are agreed that while public discussions on controversial international questions are in general desirable, in order to promote an informed public opinion and clarification of the issues involved, it is undesirable that special viewpoints should be pressed while the war is in progress to such a degree as to create undue anxieties among United Nations and other friendly governments and people.
>
> In this connection, the United Nations have taken note of public discussions and activities of a political nature relating to Palestine and consider that it would be helpful to the war effort if these were to cease. Accordingly, the United Nations declare it to be their view that no decision altering the basic situation of Palestine should be considered until after the conclusion of the war. When the matter is considered, both Arabs and Jews should be fully consulted and their agreement sought.[18]

The State Department's Wallace Murray, head of the Near East desk, who was considered the most intransigent foe of Zionism in the government, tried to get Secretary of State Cordell Hull and Undersecretary Sumner Welles to accept a draft of the joint declaration based on Hoskins' report, which would then be sent on to FDR for his final approval. But, according to an August 1943 report to the British Foreign Office written by Isaiah Berlin, Murray was initially rebuffed.

Berlin, one of the leading intellectuals of modern times, chronicled the Hoskins affair just after it ended and the declaration was rejected. Angus Malcolm of the Foreign Office had requested the report from Berlin, who was stationed at the British embassy in Washington (he was formally attached to the Ministry of Information, but was, in his own words, "a reporter of opinion" and an eloquent one at that.)[19]

A principal source for the report was Nahum Goldmann, who was in a particularly expansive mood when he came to see Berlin at the British embassy. Berlin went into great detail in the report to the Foreign Office "because it is an absolutely clinical case of how things are done in Washington nowadays."[20]

(Although this fascinating August 9, 1943, seven-page document is referred to here as "the Berlin report," Sir Isaiah today points out that instances of anti-Zionist language in the document, FO 371/35037 xc/a/049358, were added to his original report and in no way reflected his views. Fellow British officials were well aware of his Zionist sympathies. "The interpolator of the damning passages was... the late Sir Michael Wright," whose anti-Zionism was well-known).[21] The document, which, as it says on its frontispiece, "sets out the background of the (apparently) final abandonment of the joint Anglo-United States statement on Palestine, and gives an account of Zionist agitation on the subject,"[22] presents the fullest contemporary account of the events surrounding the Hoskins affair, even though some of the story was unclear or missed entirely.

Zionists of all stripes knew that Murray was "the enemy," but establishment Zionist leaders had always been very careful not to cross swords with him. They frequently consulted Murray, and sought his advice in the summer of 1943 on whether or not to hold the American Jewish Conference, for instance. When Nahum Goldmann asked him if it was "all right to hold it," Murray said that there would be no objection if the Zionist-dominated conference "behaved with tact."[23]

Both Secretary Hull (whose wife was Jewish) and Undersecretary Welles were generally considered to be out of step with the rest of the State Department on "the Jewish question." Hull was worried about offending American Jewry, and was "almost neurotically sensitive to criticism in the obscurest journals," Berlin commented in his report, citing the New York newspaper *PM*, whose contributors included Ben Hecht, Max Lerner, and I.F. Stone. But in fact, Hull in 1942 had already sought an anti-Zionist declaration, and had obtained War Department support, principally from G-2 intelligence division head George Strong. But Strong's statement was toned down considerably by higher ups.[24] The War Department would also play a role in grounding the Hoskins plan.

Hoskins' proposal for a joint declaration got significant backing after similar recommendations were made on May 5, 1943, by another anti-Zionist FDR emissary, General Patrick Hurley of Army Intelligence. FDR knew all about Hoskins' Middle East reports and his proposal, and was enthusiastic – the

President liked Hoskins personally, and the OSS man and fellow Ivy Leaguer frequently dropped in for lunch and a chat with the Roosevelts.[25]

The British, who at first reacted rather coldly to the American agent's initiative, were now also pressing for a joint declaration, which coincided with their intention of continuing the 1939 White Paper policy, freezing any prospect of a Jewish state in Palestine (although the actual declaration did not positively exclude this option in the future). Isaiah Berlin, in hindsight four decades after the event, said that the declaration "would have inflicted great damage on Zionist activity" and was clearly conceived "in the spirit of the White Paper," which had virtually closed the gates of Palestine to Jewish immigration on the eve of the war.[26]

"Churchill's name would certainly have shaken the American Jewish community (not to speak of the Jews in the British Commonwealth), but Roosevelt's much more violently," according to Berlin, because "Roosevelt was at the time a great Jewish hero in America and the entire free world; a statement made on his authority that Zionism was doing harm to the war effort would have produced a deep trauma: Jewish loyalties would have come into conflict with those to America...."[27]

In any case, it would have been a devastating blow – and that is how it was perceived by the Zionists in the summer of 1943. Although no one outside the government had actually *seen* the Hoskins report, information had been leaked to the Zionists that the declaration was imminent; and they were in a panic.

In July 1943, FDR instructed his top Jewish aide, Judge Samuel Rosenman, to call a meeting in New York of Jewish leaders and to "sell" them on the necessity of the joint statement on Palestine. Upon hearing of the proposed declaration, Rabbi Wise rushed to see the President. However, he afterwards gave conflicting and jumbled accounts of what had happened – Isaiah Berlin conjectured in his August report that this was because "Stephen Wise is really getting very gaga."[28]

Besides speaking to Goldmann about the affair, Berlin also interviewed Rosenman before reporting back to the Foreign Office on how the Hoskins report and the joint declaration came to be shelved shortly after FDR had received them so enthusiastically.

Rosenman told Berlin that when Rabbi Wise went to see FDR about the affair, the President replied that "a statement was coming out and a very good one too, but perfectly innocuous from the point of view of the Zionists." The President then told Rosenman to allay Jewish anxieties. "Rosenman did as instructed and, naturally enough, his report of what was coming, instead of allaying, blew the lid off in Zionist circles, and Goldman [sic] came rushing to see me to ask if anything could be done to stop the declaration," Berlin wrote.[29]

Comments on Berlin's lengthy report were scrawled by four Foreign Office officials. The first, by H.M. Eyres, said: "This is a fascinating story, and rather ominous as showing just what Jewish influence in the U.S. can achieve. I think we have heard the last of the Palestine declaration."[30] Despite the anti-Semitic tone of his official's comment, it was an accurate appraisal – the declaration would not be taken off the shelf, and American Jews could and did exercise power, when it was in their own interest to do so.

Berlin's report said that even anti-Zionist Jews in official Washington were upset about the proposed declaration, fearing that "the Zionists would inevitably issue a shriek,"[31] and the ensuing public controversy would be bad publicity for American Jews, whether Zionists or not. Berlin's report (rather, the report altered by Wright or some other anti-Zionist official, though signed by Berlin) said that the joint declaration should have been issued immediately. "Both William Hayter [an embassy colleague of Berlin's] and I thought that... delay would automatically invite intrigue. We were, therefore, somewhat dismayed to learn that the statement had been postponed in order to get the War Department to vet it and if necessary strengthen it."[32] The delay gave the Zionists a chance to mobilize, and "terrific lobbying followed."[33]

Rabbi Wise, after talking with Rosenman about what both men regarded as the disruptive activities of the Bergsonites, telephoned Peter Bergson in Washington and asked him to attend a meeting in New York of a small group of Zionist leaders.[34]

According to the Berlin report to the Foreign Office, Rosenman "went to New York to persuade Wise to stop Jewish Army advertisements etc., in return for suppression of the statement. Wise pointed out, quite justly, that he had no control over the Jewish Army people, but that he would see what could be done."[35]

At the meeting, Wise reprimanded the young Palestinian, charging that the Jewish Army Committee was endangering the entire Zionist movement. Wise spoke animatedly and angrily, saying that FDR had just told him about a forthcoming "change of policy" on Palestine, and had threatened that if the Bergson group's inflammatory propaganda were not curtailed immediately, he would take away the tax exemption status of all Zionist organizations in the United States. Wise warned that the President might even go further. He said that FDR had told him that a change in policy was in the works and that the Hoskins report predicted that ten Allied divisions would be needed to put down an Arab uprising that would result from all the Zionist agitation.[36]

Bergson remained suspicious of Wise and was not certain that the rabbi had met directly with FDR on the matter; Wise sometimes would relate conversations with one of FDR's Jewish aides, like Rosenman or David Niles, to direct conversations with the President.[37] Wise berated Bergson, as he had done in the past, for being an "unappointed" spokesman for half a million Palestinian Jews, while he, Wise, was "responsible for five million American Jews" who were endangered by the Bergson group's propaganda campaign. "Mi samcha?" Wise asked in a phrase from the Hebrew Bible – "Who appointed you?" (Wise, who was far from being a savant in Torah and Talmud, may very well not have realized whom he was quoting: an arrogant, rebellious biblical Jew, who chided Moses for protesting the beating of a fellow Israelite – Exodus, Chapter II, verse 14). Bergson answered that he and his colleagues had appointed themselves to do something to save their people, that there was a vacuum that had to be filled. Wise stared into the young man's cold-blue eyes with the contempt of a man who for long had felt himself omnipotent – Wise had gone so far as to essentially change the Sabbath from Saturday to Sunday; the day when he chose to deliver his sermons at the Free Synagogue.

Wise shook his imposing leonine head at the troublemaker, perhaps blaming him entirely for the potentially disastrous declaration, which, he said, FDR had told him would be released soon, though he did not know exactly when.[38]

Bergson realized that Wise had not made the story up out of whole cloth, and that a major event with harmful implications was indeed taking place. Bergson responded that he would act immediately and bring the matter before the leadership of his committee.

Wise probably did see FDR, in person, about the matter, although he may indeed have been informed earlier of the President's position regarding the Bergsonites' agitation. Wise wrote to Chaim Weizmann and said that FDR had told him on July 22 that he was upset by one of the Bergson group's statements and that he wanted to put an end to the activities of the vocal and irritating group.[39] (Wise's conflicting accounts and dates of his meeting with FDR, noted by Berlin at the time, have made an exact chronology of the events difficult to reconstruct.)

Once again it became evident that the quite legitimate fear of an anti-Semitic backlash in America preoccupied the thoughts of the Jewish establishment. Now that it was apparent that the Bergsonites had aroused the powers that be with their vigorous propaganda campaign, the primary goal for the establishment Zionists became the silencing of the militants, whether or not they were the leading activists on behalf of the Jews in Europe.

Bergson, immediately after his meeting with Wise, contacted his friend Senator Johnson, chairman of the Senate Military Affairs Committee and national chairman of the Committee for a Jewish Army, to find out what he knew of the Hoskins report. Johnson was puzzled, no one in the government had told him anything about it. He said he would check it out right away.[40] Meanwhile, Bergson coincidentally heard Hoskins' name mentioned by Congressman Will Rogers, Jr., who said that the colonel had recently spoken to a group of Republican senators about his report and the proposed declaration. Bergson called Johnson again and told the Colorado Democrat what he had heard, adding that it seemed strange to him that the report should be treated "as a partisan issue." Johnson was furious and whipped off a letter to Chief of Staff George Marshall demanding an immediate inquiry into Hoskins' activities.[41]

After Johnson finally obtained a copy of the report, he told Bergson that the recommendations in it were based purely on opinion, that there was no substantiation for the OSS man's assessments of a possible Arab revolt.[42] Johnson was not alone in this opinion. I.F. Stone, the left-wing journalist, would write in *The Nation* a few months later that Hoskins was "politically a Syrian nationalist" who had given FDR alarmist reports.[43]

On July 13, 1943, General Marshall replied to Senator Johnson's letter. He stated that "the War Department did not authorize the appearance of this officer before members of the Senate to discuss problems of the Near East," and that steps would be taken to "prevent a recurrence of unauthorized activities by Lt. Col. Hoskins."[44] The Bergsonites felt that this "reprimand" went a long way toward discrediting Hoskins, but they had no idea how many other fronts were opening against Colonel Hoskins.

The establishment Zionists, meanwhile, had approached Treasury Secretary Morgenthau. Morgenthau had been "inexpressibly shocked" by the ferocious language of the draft declaration and said that he would do his best to stop it.[45] He defended the right of all Zionists, including the Bergson group, to freedom of speech, adding that if Britain was anxious about the security situation in Palestine (British officials in the Middle East shared Hoskins' visions), then they should ask the U.S. for more troops "and not seek to deprive U.S. citizens of their constitutional liberties... never before had any such attempt been made to silence a minority of citizens," Morgenthau was quoted as saying.[46] (He apparently either overlooked or ignored the fact that the attempt to gag Zionists in America was not initiated by the British, but by Hoskins of the OSS and the State Department, and by his sponsor, President Roosevelt.)[47]

Other pressure against the issuing of the declaration was brought to bear by journalist Herbert Bayard Swope, a Jewish assimilationist antagonistic to Zionism, who argued that publication of the declaration would set off the riots in Palestine that the document ostensibly aimed to prevent.[48] The Jews would inevitably be blamed for the ensuing bloodshed and the obstruction of the Allies' war effort, and an anti-Jewish backlash in America would not discriminate between Zionists and non-Zionists. All the Jews, even the most assimilated and upper-crust, would suffer. Rosenman, too, felt that the Hoskins' proposal was dynamite, although he apparently did not bring up his reservations with FDR directly.

Swope took up the matter with his close friend, Bernard Baruch, the financier and "adviser to presidents." Baruch was a non-Zionist who was worried that anything said about Jews at that moment would increase American anti-Semitism.[49] The financier discussed the proposed declaration with his old friend, Secretary Hull, while Swope, Morgenthau, Felix Frankfurter and Senator Johnson, mostly working through separate channels, got the War Department to agree that it was unwise to proceed further with the joint declaration.[50] War Secretary Stimson, who had been a supporter of the Jewish Army Committee almost from its inception and did not want to see the Bergsonites muffled, was provided with anti-Hoskins ammunition in the form of Chief of Staff Marshall's July 13 reprimand of the colonel. Nor was Stimson likely to ignore Senate Armed Forces Committee Chairman Johnson's opposition to the joint declaration.

A Swope or a Rosenman or a Morgenthau, like Rabbi Wise, could not be considered "powerless" Jews – at least not when the issue appeared certain to affect American Jewry itself. In the weeks following the liquidation of the Warsaw Ghetto, they acted forcefully and effectively on behalf of the "threatened" Jews of America. A "pincer movement by Messrs. Baruch and Morgenthau (who don't, in fact, get on with each other at all well) had its effect," Berlin wrote.[51]

On August 6, 1943, Hull wrote Rosenman that Stimson had informed him on the previous day that the War Department woud not support the Hoskins proposal, and "that settled it so far as the State Department is concerned."[52] Hull, at this point, apparently had lost interest in pursuing the declaration. That same day, the story was leaked to newspaper columnist Drew Pearson. Berlin conjectured that either Welles or Swope had given the full story to Pearson, but, he said in his report of three days later, "the Zionists say the Jewish Army people (their regular scapegoat and alibi) told P."[53] Over forty years later, Berlin would say that it may never be known who managed to torpedo the declaration, "nor does it matter – there was some Esther involved in averting that particular act of Haman-Hoskins."[54] Berlin met Hoskins for the first time a month or so after the declaration was shelved, at the home of an anti-Zionist embassy colleague. "Hoskins launched a diatribe against the Zionist intrigues which had scotched his excellent plan, which he described to me – Joint Declaration and all. I told him what I thought of his plan and his motives, and the likely consequences. We began to argue, it ended in a violent row, I think the worst row I have ever had with anyone, and finally he left in a state of great anger. He told one of my friends, a British official... that I was a Zionist agent and that he would try to convey to the British Embassy that they should get rid of me. For all I know he may have tried to do this, but I heard nothing of it, although our common friend could never understand why Hoskins conceived such hatred for me. It was, in fact, reciprocated."[55]

No single group or individual was responsible for thwarting Hoskins' effort. The Bergsonites deluded themselves in believing that they alone had totally discredited the colonel and brought about the demise of the declaration. They were oblivious to the concerted effort by the big guns of the American Jewish establishment, including especially key members of FDR's "Jewish circle," to sink the joint declaration.

One can only speculate on the dynamics of Roosevelt's decision to let the Hoskins proposal die. Stimson's veto would not be enough to kill the declaration if FDR was really intent on issuing it. Perhaps the President realized that he was facing, for the first time, united Jewish and Zionist opposition representing the entire spectrum: Morgenthau, Baruch, Wise, Goldmann, Swope, Frankfurter and Rosenman, suddenly in the same company with the clamorous Bergson group they, like FDR, regarded as a loose cannon. All these Jews would be in open revolt if the joint declaration were forced through. Stimson's negative response provided the perfect excuse for backing out – not only for Hull, but for FDR as well. The "united front" – united on a matter of secondary importance when compared to the rescue issue – had won.[56]

In Berlin's altered report to the Foreign Office, the narrator writes: "I rather get the impression (from Rosenman at second hand) that the President was a trifle nettled by all this Jewish barrage – after all, what it comes to is the triumph of the Zionist lobby... I do not know what moral should be drawn from all this, except that the Zionist lobby seems strong enough to achieve at any rate short lived triumphs, and this fact should be taken into consideration. It is a melancholy thing that on the one occasion when the Eastern Department of the S.D. [State Department], which, as you know, has not been too friendly to H.M.G. [His Majesty's Government], in the past, had seemed to wish to do something for us they should have failed so ignominiously. Nor will this make Hoskins' task any easier, but that looks hopeless in any case."[57]

Hoskins himself appeared to be in hot water because of General Marshall's reprimand and Senator Johnson's antipathy. But he had powerful friends and secret mandates, and his actions in the late summer of 1943 may simply have been diversionary – he may still have been in charge of the OSS investigation of "foreign bodies" in the United States. Toward the denouement of the affair, Peter Bergson was taken aback when Col. Hoskins called on him at the committee's Washington headquarters on Fifteenth Street. Hoskins asked Bergson, a foreigner, to help arrange a meeting with the irate Senator Johnson.[58] Bergson was unaware of Hoskins' OSS background, or that some U.S. intelligence and State Department officials suspected that the Bergsonites were a pro-Nazi front.[59] Perhaps Hoskins was only "sniffing around," or perhaps he genuinely needed to assuage Johnson or thought this was the best way to do it. Bergson called Senator Johnson, but the Armed Forces Committee chairman refused to meet with Hoskins, saying that he was nothing more than a propagandist.[60]

But Hoskins' career was far from over. He still had easy access to the White House, and FDR sent him on further missions to the Middle East, mainly for important talks in Saudi Arabia with King Ibn Saud. Hoskins continued to do all he could to prevent a Jewish state from rising in Palestine.[61]

Although the joint Anglo-American declaration was permanently shelved, there were periodic reports throughout 1943 that it would be revitalized. According to one historian, "the fate of the joint Anglo-American statement did not alter the perspective of the two governments vis-a-vis Palestine. Moreover, the democracies' efforts to quiet discussion on Palestine faithfully mirrored their silence about the rescue of European Jewry and Palestine Jewry's war contribution."[62]

The Hoskins affair proved to be a significant event in Jewish history, although to date it has all but been ignored by scholars.[63] A close examination of the affair contradicts the argument that the Jews and Zionists in America were too weak to influence the government or that their position was too tenuous for them to lobby fiercely for rescue of European Jews. Though Isaiah Berlin had noted in his August 9, 1943, report that American Jews were far from powerless, forty years later he would say that he had not realized just how strong American Jewry really was: "I also underestimated, at times, as it turned out, Jewish influence on American opinion at such crucial times as 1944-1945."[64] Berlin came to realize that Jews in Hungary, Rumania, Yugoslavia could have been saved: "Jewish pressure in the U.S. – especially by eminent Jews... might have worked. Such pressure did not occur on a sufficient scale, for fear, I suppose, of rocking the military boat: such attitudes have occurred before and after... humanity, courage and persistence are always in short supply."[65] During the war years, Berlin thought that Nahum Goldmann and company were correct in believing that Bergson's activities were likely to irritate or alienate important American individuals and groups, whose support they regarded as crucial to the fulfillment of Zionist aims. "I admit I did not give much thought to the rights and wrongs of the matter," he said in retrospect.[66]

The rescue issue itself was never mentioned in the various correspondence and reports concerning the Hoskins affair. The different groups – the Bergsonites, the establishment Zionists and important anti- or non-Zionist figures, each for its own reasons – were unified in opposition to the proposals made by Hoskins. They showed formidable strength in defeating plans favored by FDR, the British and most of the State Department hierarchy. No similar effort was made – except by the Bergson group – to lobby so massively for the rescue of Jews. It remained a question of priorities: the Bergsonites, after the last months of 1942, put rescue first, Palestine second. The Zionists openly admitted, even at the height of the Holocaust, that Palestine should be "first and foremost" on the agenda, as Dr. Israel Goldstein, a Wise ally, put it in a statement at the establishment's American Jewish Conference, held a month after the Hoskins affair ended.[67]

Colonel Hoskins himself faded from the spotlight after his dramatic Middle East missions in 1942-1944. Eventually, he left intelligence work to pursue his State Department career, becoming director of the department's Foreign Service Institute from 1955 to 1961, training a new generation of diplomats. Later, not surprisingly, he became a Middle East consultant to Standard Oil of New Jersey. When he died in April 1977, the *New York Times* in its long obituary never mentioned the historic report which bore his name and which, but for the lobbying efforts of American Jewish leaders, almost became Allied policy.

CHAPTER SIX

JEW AGAINST JEW

Two days before Yom Kippur, the Day of Atonement, on October 6, 1943, some five hundred black-garbed Orthodox rabbis marched from Union Station to the Capitol in Washington, calling for action to save European Jews. The well-publicized march was organized by the Bergson group with the cooperation of the Union of Orthodox Rabbis of the United States and Canada, and the Union of Grand Rabbis. The Orthodox Jews had adopted the committee's program urging creation of a special U.S. government agency to "rescue the remnant of Israel" from Nazi satellites, as the rabbis' spokesman told network radio and newsreel reporters. The Bergsonites had encapsulated their idea in the form of a Rescue Resolution which the committee's supporters had just brought before Congress, and hoped the march would boost its chances.[1]

Jewish congressmen, led by Sol Bloom, the former Yiddish comic who headed the House Foreign Affairs Committee, had tried to dissuade the rabbis from participating in the march. But when Bloom added that it would be undignified for such an un-American looking group to march in Washington, it only reinforced the rabbis' resolve to take part.[2]

A guard of honor, comprised of veterans of the World War I Jewish Legion, accompanied the solemn procession through the streets of the capital. They were not received by the President "because of pressure of other business," as FDR's secretary, Marvin McIntyre, put it.[3]

In fact, Roosevelt was annoyed by the march and made it a point to rebuff them – one newspaper reported a "chilly reception at the White House."[4] Just as the rabbis converged on the White House, FDR ducked out to attend the dedication of four bombers for a Yugoslav combat, the "other business" referred to by McIntyre.[5] FDR's top Jewish aide and speechwriter, Judge Rosenman, the man who had coined the phrase "New Deal," advised the President that the Orthodox rabbis were "not your kind of Jews," and told Zionist leaders, in turn, that the President was "much displeased" by the march organized by Bergson.[6]

The rabbis got a relatively warm reception on Capitol Hill, however, where they were met by Vice President Henry Wallace and most leaders of Congress, who heard their appeal for a U.S. rescue agency as the Bergson group had proposed. Wallace accepted a petition on this issue, signed by half a million Americans. *Time* Magazine said that the vice president "squirmed through a diplomatically minimum answer." Senator William Langer gave a speech on the steps of the Capitol in which he condemned United States inaction, epitomized by the empty promises of the Bermuda Conference held six months earlier.[7] He noted that Sweden had just taken in thousands of Jews from Denmark, and asked why Britain couldn't open Palestine to thousands of others. He assailed the executive branch of the U.S. government: "Normally, it would have been the job of the government to show itself alert to this tragedy; but when a government neglects a duty, it is the job of the legislature in a democracy to remind it of that duty."[8]

The march of the rabbis, though not as highly publicized as the Bergson *We Will Never Die* pageant, was a page-one story or picture item in several major American newspapers, and some, such as the Hearst papers and the *New York Post,* showed support for a special rescue agency.[9] The march succeeded in at least reminding the politicians of the critical moral question they should be facing.

But the mainstream Zionists were appalled by the march. Perhaps one underlying reason was that Agudas Israel, the main organizational arm of Orthodox Jewry, was anti-Zionist – the ultra-Orthodox believed only the Messiah could return the Jews to Zion and rule over them. This did not deter the Bergson Zionists from working with the "black coats" on what should have been, for all Jews, a non-political, strictly humanitarian issue: rescue. At the same moment that the Orthodox rabbis were demanding rescue, the major Zionist groups led by Reform rabbis – Wise, Silver, Israel Goldstein – were launching a crusade against the 1939 White Paper, demanding open immigration to Palestine.[10]

Wise and Goldmann and their lieutenants may have also genuinely believed that the Bergsonites were really only interested in furthering the cause of the Revisionists or of the Irgun (which was virtually non-existent from 1941 to the end of 1943). "These are the enemies of Zionism," a Wise aide, Rabbi Morton Berman, informed a member of his congregation who had become active in the Chicago chapter of the Bergson committee.[11] But what really accounted for the extreme acrimony and the intensity of the establishment's attacks was the classic struggle over power, a Freudian conflict between fathers and sons, kings and princes. "Zionist records reveal that the number-one concern was the fear that the Bergsonites could build an effective rival Zionist organization... To read through the archives and publications of American Jewish organizations of the period is to journey through a landscape of continual fighting."[12]

The American Zionist Emergency Council devised a strategy of frequent phone calls, visits and letters to prominent Bergson supporters to woo them away from the "impostors," and were partially successful in their time-consuming efforts. As one Bergson volunteer would recall years later, the establishment constantly "challenged our right to speak and to exist."[13] This was true of the non-Zionist establishment as well. The American Jewish Committee, in letters to its members, termed the Bergson group's ads tasteless and "embarrassing to Jews." It sent a standard letter to anyone inquiring about the Bergsonites: "The efforts which these people proposed to make for the rescue of Jews... cannot be a duplication of efforts already made and being made by organizations which are recognized as representing the Jewish community of America."[14] But the record shows that this was simply not true: the Bergsonites were the only organization pushing for a rescue agency. The leaders of the mainstream organizations were either not interested or openly antagonistic.

On the day of the rabbis' march, Wise and Goldmann met with Breckinridge Long and excoriated the Bergson group as "a body composed of a lot of persons, many of whom were not Jews" and who did not represent "Jewish thinking" in America.[15] That same month, Wise's American Jewish Conference set up a committee under I.L. Kenan to prepare a public statement "exposing" and condemning the Bergsonites – the statement was released to the press two months later, at the most crucial stage of the Emergency Committee's fight for the Rescue Resolution.[16] The Conference's committee, and an earlier body set up by the Emergency Council for Zionist Affairs to counter the Bergson threat, added to the flood of thousands of letters which the various organizations sent out attacking the Bergsonites. Chief coordinator for the anti-Bergson campaign was Judge Louis Levinthal, of the Zionist Organization of America (ZOA). "It was Levinthal's domain – that's why Wise didn't sign the letters," according to Wise aide Rabbi

Morton Berman.[17] By November 1943, the establishment had succeeded in getting forty-six of the rabbis who had taken part in the march to disavow their support for Bergson and the Rescue Resolution.[18]

In January 1943, the Zionists' organ, *New Palestine*, published a message from Levinthal calling on all Zionists to refrain from aiding the Bergson group. The core group of Palestinians, he said, were Irgunists: "As you know, the Irgun is the extreme wing of the Revisionist Party, which seceded from the World Zionist Organization several years ago." He condemned the fact that many of the committee's sponsors were "non-Jews and non-Zionists," who, presumably, were only interested in saving Jewish lives and would not further the Zionist goal of a commonwealth in Palestine.[19]

Bergson and his colleagues were demonized because their roots were in the Jabotinsky movement, which liberal, labor-oriented Zionists despised. There was no recognition of the fact that the Bergsonites' rescue proposals had nothing to do with Irgun (moribund at the time) or Revisionist ideology, or anything other than the basic Jewish injunction to save life. This was not an issue of left or right, Weizmann or Jabotinsky, Reform versus Orthodox. But Jewish leaders like Wise, who considered themselves liberal, progressive people, were the most dogmatic when it came to the Bergsonites, perhaps because of a basic uncertainty about their Jewishness in American life, their simultaneous pursuit of Zionist and assimilationist goals. "The solutions provided by the liberal Jewish world have failed to reach the depths of the problem," wrote Protestant theologian Reinhold Niebuhr in 1942, as he speculated on why the liberal world, Jewish and gentile, did not face squarely the peril of European Jews.[20] Niebuhr, who consistently lent his name to Bergson group statements, clearly saw this flaw in the actions of those who subscribe to a humanist, progressive philosophy – the often grating declarations of the Bergson group had obviously touched a raw nerve. As one scholar of Jewish organizations in the Holocaust era put it: "Certainly one of the shortcomings of American Jewish organizations was that they refused to recognize that, even if Bergson had ulterior motives for his activities, his organization was accomplishing things that they were not doing and added greatly to the total rescue movement in the United States."[21]

Soon after the March of the Rabbis, Nahum Goldmann and Isaiah Berlin discussed the irritating affair in one of their meetings at the British embassy. Goldmann recounted a conversation with Judge Rosenman, who had told him that "The

President had been much displeased by the March of the Rabbis instigated by the notorious Bergson."[22] FDR had used language on the morning of the march which, according to Berlin, "would have pleased Hitler himself." Goldmann told Berlin that the President had asked whether anything could be done "to liquidate Bergson" since he was, after all, a British (Palestinian) subject.[23]

Goldmann also reported that the Zionists were fed up with Bergson's "antics" and that "they had persuaded Senator Johnson as well as Max Lerner... to resign from his [Bergson's] Committee, but as a counter coup" Bergson had engineered the resolution in Congress to create a special government body to help save Jews in Nazi-dominated countries. Goldmann told Berlin that he thought the special agency idea was "a grotesque suggestion which annoyed the President."[24]

Goldmann's penchant for hyperbole was well known, although it was not remarked upon in Berlin's report to the Foreign Office. Senator Johnson did not resign from the Bergson group, though Lerner did. The statement that FDR had said he wanted Bergson "liquidated" must be treated skeptically. As Berlin noted, the expression would have been worthy of the Nazis. But it was Goldmann himself who was prone to use the word "liquidate" when he reported on the Bergsonites or corresponded with foes of the group.[25]

An illuminating aspect of Berlin's report on his long conversation with Goldmann – dialogue between two East European-born Jews in November 1943, at the height of the Holocaust – is what is not mentioned: the ongoing extermination, and possibilities of rescue. The discussion revolved around Palestine and internecine rivalries among the Zionists. This was not the exception but the rule, as can be seen in the memoranda of conversations between Zionist leaders and State Department officials, for example, throughout the entire period from 1942 until Germany's defeat. For the mainstream Zionists, the preoccupation with Palestine, the post-war situation and "the Bergson problem" was almost total. On the rare occasions when the extermination was mentioned. it was incidental, almost as an afterthought. The obsession with Palestine had precluded the conducting of a politics of rescue. As Goldmann said at a May 3, 1943, meeting of the establishment's Emergency Committee for Zionist Affairs (a telling title in itself), "There is not enough manpower to engage in two campaigns."[26]

Once the systematic nature of the genocide was made widely known in November 1942, the Palestinian-led Bergsonites, though they too were Zionists by any definition, tabled the Palestine issue, which could not be solved during the war in any case. Instead, throughout 1943, they set for themselves one goal: to make the rescue of Jews a top priority, and to force the U.S. to create the vehicle for saving lives. The March of the Rabbis was a key element in rallying public opinion to the cause. The march helped shape congressional opinion and added to the momentum being built up in Congress for the Rescue Resolution sponsored by Bergson supporters.

All the while, Bergson, seeking Jewish and Zionist unity on a crucial issue, tried to make peace with the mainstream leaders. He and other committee members negotiated with Judge Levinthal in November 1943, seeking some form of cooperation with the establishment, which continued to rebuff him. Samuel Merlin, Bergson's closest aide, disagreed with his colleagues' efforts at unity, believing it was futile. "But Peter thought it worthwhile... at least from a tactical point of view."[28]

The benefits of unity were unclear. Had the October demonstration been sponsored by Wise and Silver, the two feuding Reform rabbis who led American Jewry, five thousand rabbis might have marched instead of five hundred, including Roosevelt's "kind of Jews"; and the President would have had to swallow his distaste and to meet with them. Instead, Zionist leaders campaigned against Bergson, as well as each other. Silver had humiliated Wise at the American Jewish Conference a few weeks before the March of the Rabbis. Over the next year they would exchange charges of "dictatorship." Silver also would explode at Nahum Goldmann's personal diplomacy – the two men loathed each other.[29]

In the history of "official" Zionism, the March of the Rabbis, the only such demonstration by American Jews calling for an agency of rescue, was an incident to be deplored. "It was not Mr. Roosevelt only who was moved to fury by such antics," Sir Isaiah Berlin said in a major address at the Hebrew University in Jerusalem in 1972. Berlin termed it the "notorious" march of the rabbis, an example of "excess of zeal or disregard for the truth or... breaking the rules of politically decent conduct."[30] (Twelve years later, Berlin was far less dismissive of the rabbis' march and the Bergsonite record.)[31]

The Zionist and Jewish establishment assailed such tactics as the march on Washington, even though no one else had brought the issue of the extermination to the doorstep of the government, which obviously had to be prodded into doing something. John Pehle, a top Treasury official who took a pro-Jewish stand against the State Department and served as the first director of the rescue agency FDR finally set up, claimed that "Only when the matter [of rescue] was brought to the President forcefully did Roosevelt act."[32]

But the establishment phones were tied up. The pressure was not on Washington, but on prominent supporters of Bergson's Emergency Committee to Save the Jewish People of Europe, who were urged to leave the ranks of "the upstarts." Just as the momentum for the Rescue Resolution got moving, Max Lerner admitted in a phone conversation with Bergson that he could not stand up to the pressure from the mainstream Zionists. Bergson responded, sardonically, "What about the Jews, Max Lerner?", echoing the title of Lerner's powerful *PM* article asking FDR the same question. Lerner huffed, "I don't have to take that from you."[33]

In the program of genocide, the Nazis were stymied in instances where the leaders of a country, or significant sectors of the population, refused to participate in rounding up Jews. Most of the Jews of Italy, Bulgaria and Finland, for example, were saved. The only country in which the population as a whole rallied around the rescue effort was Denmark. The Danes spontaneously acted to protect the country's Jews, smuggling them out in boats to neutral Sweden in early October 1943.

Even Hitler's allies, in varying degrees, resisted the Final Solution. But in significant ways the Allies, and the Jewish leadership in the free world, failed to differentiate between the Nazis and their satellites. This attitude, which continued even after the tide of war had turned and the satellites scrambled to make deals, frustrated attempts to rescue hundreds of thousands of Jews.

Early in the war, the Rumanians tried to outdo the Nazis in the brutality of their mass slaughter of Jews.[34] Of 130,000 Jews in occupied Transnistria – an area of the Ukraine that the Nazis had given to their Rumanian allies – 60,000 were butchered and their bodies burned. But after Stanlingrad, in the winter of 1942-43, Rumania was willing to "sell" Jews, in defiance of Hitler's wishes. Rumanian dictator Ion Antonescu made an offer: If world Jewish organizations would pay the expenses, he would allow the surviving 70,000 Jews interned in Transnistria to be transferred to any refuge selected by the allies. News reports of the offer reached London in early February 1943, and political observers suggested that the proposal was proof that German power in the Balkans was waning. In a dispatch on February 13, C.L. Sulzberger of the *New York Times* reported that the Rumanians had figured the cost of transport to Palestine would be about $130 per refugee. But, as events would show, the Allies viewed the release of large numbers of Jews "as a threat, not an opportunity."[35]

The Zionists and the British government knew about the offer much earlier, U.S. officials would learn. A Jewish official had told the Foreign Office of the Rumanian offer a month before.[36] Apparently, they had sat on the news and not brought it to the attention of top American government leaders.

The Bergson group's response, on the other hand, was immediate. Ben Hecht wrote the copy for a huge ad that ran in the *New York Times* and other major newspapers three days after Sulzberger's story, under a banner that screamed: "FOR SALE to Humanity 70,000 Jews." The subhead read: "Guaranteed Human Beings at $50 a Piece." The ad demanded immediate action, saying that "the great Rumanian bargain is for this month only!... The Doors of Rumania Are Open! Act Now!" The February 13 news story was printed in full, alongside an open letter from Hecht to Allied leaders, saying "I know you are very busy, too busy perhaps to read the story on the left hand side of this page. For that reason I am writing an ad. Ads are easier and quicker to read than stories." The ad also stated that "the principal demand of the Committee is that the United Nations immediately appoint an inter-governmental committee to formulate ways and means of stopping this wholesale slaughter of human beings." As in all Bergson group ads, a coupon appeared at the bottom of the page asking for financial support of the "campaign to save European Jews by action – not pity, and to help publicize" the committee's message through the media. It was in no way implied that any contributions would be used to pay the ransom money the Rumanians were demanding.[37]

Rabbi Wise immediately issued a statement attacking the ad and the Bergson committee, saying that there had been no "official" confirmation of any such offer and calling the ad a "hoax." Wise had accepted the State Department line as set forth by Welles in its immediate reaction to the report: "This story is without foundation... the probable actual source is the German propaganda machine..." The Zionist press assailed Hecht as a sensation-monger and termed the ad "abominable." Wise wrote to his friend, the Christian cleric Reverend John Holmes, that the offer was a "swindle" on the part of Rumania and a hoax on the part of Hecht. In any case, the rabbi said, "We could not afford to pay a penny to Rumania." Chaim Weizmann also thought the offer might be a "trap" by the enemy in an attempt to embarrass the United Nations, while the Jewish Agency denied the existence of the offer altogether.[38]

The Bergsonites were baffled by the denials and the secrecy, especially after Bergson phoned Assistant Secretary of State Berle, who unofficially confirmed the

Rumanian offer.[39] The Bergsonites decided to press on with follow-up ads, signed by Senator Johnson, in the *New York Herald Tribune* and other major newspapers, reiterating the demands for Allied action on the Rumanian proposal and on the establishment of a special rescue agency. Johnson noted that there had been tremendous public response to the ad a week earlier. "We have stirred public opinion," and mass demonstrations were being organized all over the country, the senator said. "It matters little whether the Rumanian proposal has been officially presented or not... it is imperative on the part of the United Nations governments to state that their ears are open for such proposals."[40]

Six weeks after the Sulzberger report and almost three months after the Zionists first learned of the Rumanian offer, the State Department officially confirmed its authenticity to Wise, but he never issued a retraction of his attacks on the Bergson group's original "70,000 souls for sale" message. "His original condemnation helped kill all response to our ad," wrote Yitshaq Ben-Ami.[41]

Wise's initial negative reaction to paying ransom for the 70,000 was in character; such deals were routinely denounced as dastardly attempts at "blackmail." As evidenced by his autobiography, the rabbi was no Falstaff – honor was more important than life: "The honor of Israel, the values of civilization, the ideals of mankind are even more precious than life itself," he wrote. He could not countenance any deals with the forces of evil, not for the "security of some Jews through the shame of all Jews."[42] Such remarks were made before the extermination began, but even Wise's most fervent admirers criticize the way he dismissed the Rumanian offer as a fraud. Biographer Melvin Urofsky does it quietly, in a footnote, saying that "Wise should have known better," since the report came to him from his own, trusted World Jewish Congress representative in Geneva, Gerhart Riegner, who cabled the information to Wise on January 21, 1943. Wise's denial of the deal is attributed by his biographer to the bitter campaign the Zionists were waging against the Bergson group. If this assessment is correct, it is the most damning indictment imaginable of "the voice that spoke for justice."[43] Another reason for Wise's calumny and then his long silence was, his biographer speculates, "partly because he recognized that nothing could be done without government approval of a license to export money."[44]

In fact, Wise simply thought that "Perhaps we are asking [Allied leaders] more than we should..."[45] The *Manchester Guardian,* on the other hand, editorialized that if the 70,000 had been British, American or Russian, "the United Nations would be up and doing something despite all difficulties."[46] But the Jewish leaders, in the ensuing months, compounded their sins, maintaining a policy of silence and wasting many precious months in fruitless negotiations with recalcitrant U.S. officials. They never voiced a public complaint about the State Department's refusal to approve the depositing of funds in a blocked account in Switzerland – one which the Rumanians would not have been able to touch until after the war.

It is a truism that there are times when "quiet diplomacy" is the best course to follow, and other times when a proper balance between public activity and behind-the-scenes efforts is essential. But Bergson and his supporters, including key senators like Johnson, had no doubt that the Rumanian offer should be shouted from the rooftops and not allowed to die on a State Department shelf.

By July 1943, five months after the Bergson group's ad brought the offer into the open, Wise, through quiet diplomacy, had managed to get government authorization for the transfer of only $25,000. The State Department obstructed him all along the way. Although Wise had never been sanguine about raising the required sums, he was still upset about the department's perfidious ways, and he registered a complaint with Roosevelt, who met with him on July 22. FDR, according to Wise, was quite open to suggestions about cutting through the red tape surrounding the transfer of funds. "Stephen, why don't you go ahead and do it?" the President reportedly said.[47]

At one stage, the Treasury Department was brought into the negotiations to arrange for the license to release the initial $25,000 payment, and this led to a feud between Morgenthau's men and the State Department, a conflict of policy and moral attitudes regarding the refugees. The State Department's main worry about the Rumanian deal was that it might be the first wave in a flood of Jewish refugees who would inundate America. During the earlier period, when the Rumanians were butchering tens of thousands of Jews in Transnistria, the department's Cavendish Cannon warned that a migration of Rumanian Jews would "open the question of similar treatment for Jews in Hungary... So far as I know, we are not ready to tackle the whole Jewish problem"[48]

The British held a similar view. The Foreign Office, in a February 26, 1943, telegram to the embassy in Washington, said that if the deal went through it would result in "Germany and her satellites... unloading, at a given price, all their unwanted nationals on overseas countries." When Foreign Minister Anthony Eden met Roosevelt and Hull in March 1943, Eden said that if they rescued the Transnistria Jews, "the Jews of the world will want us to make similar offers in Poland and Germany."[49] In December 1943, ten months after the offer had been confirmed and more than four months after Wise met Roosevelt about the Transnistria Jews, Britain presented to the State Department its final judgment on the rescue project: the Foreign Office was "concerned with the difficulty of disposing of any considerable number of Jews." Morgenthau called the British message "a satanic combination of British chill and diplomatic double-talk, cold and correct, and adding up to a sentence of death."[50]

Wise, by refusing to wage a public campaign on behalf of the Jews in Rumania, contributed to the disaster. Yet he never expressed self-criticism about his handling of the affair. In his autobiography, he reserved his curse for the main culprits: "Let history record for all time that were it not for State Department and Foreign Office bungling and callousness, thousands of lives might have been saved."[51] No reference was made to his own suppression of news of the Rumanian ransom offer, or his vindictive campaign against those who did go public, just as he similarly avoided mentioning his own physical weakness during this period: it was a closely held secret that Wise suffered from polyerythemia, a blood disease that had sapped his energies for years.[52]

Wise knew from the moment the drama unfolded that the State Department was a terrible obstacle. It was not that he was unconcerned about saving Jews: unlike Goldmann or Silver, he was considered by many to be a warm, passionate person – but not passionate enough. Bergson, decades later, would say that Wise, in reaction to the extermination, should have rent his clothes in mourning, called emergency meetings, done everything in his power to effect a rescue of his brethren. But he did not.[53] He was trapped in petty egotism and in the traditional role of the court Jew, working behind the scenes and imagining himself far more important than he was. It was not a question of malice, but of character weakness, the romance of power and poor political judgment: what he thought was his greatest asset, his tie with the President, was in fact his Achilles' heel.

Throughout the Transnistria affair, the official Zionists by and large carried on business as usual. Wise did, in response to the Transnistria news, help organize, in March 1943, a Joint Emergency Committee on European Jewish Affairs. Although this body held mass rallies to influence Anglo-American refugee policy, they were polite affairs which kept Transnistria in the closet. The new committee was made up of eight major Jewish organizations, Zionist and non-Zionist, but when the Jewish Army Committee asked to join, the Bergsonites were rebuffed.[54]

The establishment leaders, meanwhile, remained impervious to criticism, what little of it there was. One of the few Jewish newspapers that seemed to notice, the

Philadelphia *Jewish Exponent*, condemned the leadership for its part in the conspiracy of silence and for failing to arouse the rank and file. What American Jews needed, the newspaper said, was "flaming indictments" instead of polite phrases.[55] But the indictments issued by the establishment were saved for the renegades who were trying to create a movement to mobilize the U.S. government into action. The core group of Palestinians remained "revisionist fascists" or "Irgunists" in the eyes of Wise and Goldmann. And in the paranoic universe of Wise's friend, J. Edgar Hoover, they were transformed into "a group of thoroughly disreputable Communist Zionists."[56]

Collusion with sympathetic officials – whether they were enemies of Zionism or not – was a continuing process. On May 29, 1943, Chaim Weizmann, staying at the St. Regis Hotel on Fifth Avenue, sent a letter to Wise's office a few blocks away, thanking the rabbi for keeping him posted on the Bergson group's advertisements and other activities. Weizmann said that it must be made perfectly clear to American as well as British government officials that the establishment Zionists had nothing to do with the radical approach of the Bergsonites and that they had "no control over these people either."[57]

Stephen Wise was astonished and appalled by the inroads made by the Bergson group, and resented the attractiveness of the young Palestinians. But Wise apparently respected the fact that Bergson came from the leading rabbinical family in the Jewish world, that he was a kind of maverick prince. Wise once asked Rabbi Berman, his young disciple, if he had ever met Bergson and if so, what did he think of him. "I think he's a gentleman," Berman replied. "Well, of course he's that," Wise said, "he's from our finest rabbinical family."[58] But this grudging respect may have only fueled Wise's hatred for Bergson. He, too, came from a distinguished rabbinical clan, and he was a snob about it, but his family did not have the stature of the Kooks.[59] Both men were the sons of Orthodox rabbis. One became a founder of the Reform movement and an apostle of Herzl and Weizmann, while the other was a secularist apostle of Herzl and Jabotinsky, and later, advocate of a post-Zionist philosophy. Their conflict undoubtedly was far deeper than a generational difference, a clash of personalities, or a struggle for power. But Bergson, in the name of Jewish unity, chose not to fight Wise (although he did attempt on one occasion in early 1944 to strike back, following Wise's attempts to subvert the Rescue Resolution).

Wise evidently grew obsessive in his drive to crush what he perceived as an impudent and dangerous young man. Yet in thousands of Wise's letters that have been preserved, and in his voluminous orations, he did not mention the actual name Peter Bergson even once, and made only a few passing or vague references to the committee, or to its other leaders such as Ben Hecht. Nowhere does he refer to the mammoth campaign he orchestrated against the Bergsonites. Wise's first biographer, his Christian friend Carl Hermann Voss, said in a letter to the author that he had "pored over the papers and letters of Stephen Wise for many years and found no reference to Peter Bergson."[60]

A pattern of "historical amnesia" concerning the name of Wise's young rival would emerge again in the rabbi's testimony in December 1943 before the House Foreign Affairs Committee. The Bergsonites were always called "them" or "that group."[61] In the same month, Wise wrote to Interior Secretary Harold Ickes criticizing his decision to head the Washington division of "that group" – the Emergency Committee to Save the Jewish People of Europe. Ignoring the non-sectarian nature of the committee, Wise wrote, in his invariably windy prose: "I do not like to speak ill to you... concerning a group of Jews, but I am under the inexorable necessity of saying to you that the time will come and come soon, when you will find it necessary to withdraw from this irresponsible group which exists and obtains funds through being permitted to use the names of non-Jews like yourself..."[62]

Ickes, at a lunch with Congressman Will Rogers, Jr., told him that he was perfectly satisfied with the Bergson committee, despite Wise's "great fuss about this" and his suggestions that they were financial adventurers.[63] Later, at a meeting with Bergson, Ickes said that he did not like Wise's implied threats, adding that he had sent him a sharp reply assuring the rabbi that he could take care of himself.[64]

Official Washington was aware of Ickes' strong support for the committee. On one occasion, Morgenthau aide John Pehle told the Treasury secretary that Bergson "has only been over here three or four years and he gets tremendous public support. People like Ickes have backed him all the way through on this Emergency Committee."[65]

Almost without exception, all of the prominent personalities who supported the Bergson group and its goals came under the kind of intense pressure that Ickes experienced. For various reasons, several committee members or participants in committee activities – like Max Lerner, Pierre van Paassen, and actor Edward G. Robinson – had caved in to the Zionist pressure. Robinson, who had appeared in *We Will Never Die*, left when he was told that the group's efforts on behalf of

European Jewry were only a smokescreen for the Palestinian terrorist underground.[66]

But most of the well-known personalities who were active with the committee remained fiercely loyal, and resentful of the multi-pronged offensive staged by the establishment in its attempts to discredit the Bergsonites. The committee as a whole, and the "nuisance diplomat," Bergson himself, did not believe that they should respond to the attacks, holding that the eternal "war between the Jews" should not be waged while the Germans engaged in exterminating European Jewry.[67]

Within the establishment, the fighting between the rival camps of Rabbi Abba Hillel Silver and David Ben-Gurion, on the one hand, and Rabbi Wise, Nahum Goldmann and Chaim Weizmann, on the other, remained vicious and debilitating. Wise's American Zionist Emergency Council "seemed to be expending more of its energies attacking Bergson than supporting Zionism. And across Washington from Silver's headquarters were other Zionist activists who frankly wondered where all the commotion was leading."[68]

Silver was the most abrasive of the American Zionist leaders – not at all like Wise, who could turn on the charm. Silver was not obsessed by the Bergsonites. On the contrary, he picked up some of their positions on issues other than rescue. Alexander (Hadani) Rafaeli of the Bergson group met with Silver at the end of 1942. "He told us we were on the right track on the Jewish Army issue," Rafaeli reported. "He was encouraging, but not wholeheartedly for us."[69]

Goldmann, on the other hand, appeared to share Wise's preoccupations. During one of Goldmann's regular meetings to discuss the Bergson group with U.S. officials, he told Treasury Secretary Morgenthau that the committee's attempts to raise money were part of a gigantic swindle.[70] (Thirty-five years later, Goldmann would perform a complete turnabout, telling documentary filmmaker Laurence Jarvik that the Bergson group "did a very good job." He said that he fought them only because "they were very anti-government."[71]

Peter Bergson met with Goldmann in November 1943 to try to persuade him to help – or at least not to undermine – the Rescue Resolution that had just been introduced into Congress. The official Zionists opposed the Bergson group's initiative because the resolution, which called for the creation of a special rescue agency and implementation of a plan to save the surviving Jews of Europe, did not mention Palestine as the destination of those who would be saved. The two Jews, both born in the Baltic states, walked around Capitol Hill conversing in Hebrew and English, arguing amiably about the conflicting priorities of Jews and Zionists. Goldmann told Bergson that the resolution would never have been introduced, that it would cause nothing but damage, and that it would not pass anyway. He did not indicate why he was so sure of this. Bergson at this time still had no idea of the extent of the behind-the-scenes lobbying by Goldmann and Wise to sabotage the bill in the House.[72]

Goldmann, like Wise and Silver, was locked into their ideology and persisted to the end of the war in continually making the question of rescue contingent on the Palestine issue. The Bergson group's proposals to designate Palestine a temporary shelter – refugees would not be allowed to stay there after the war – was rejected scornfully. In September 1944, Goldmann told U.S. officials that yet another congressional resolution sponsored by the Bergson group, calling for a temporary shelter in Palestine, was an "idiotic plan," nothing more than a publicity-seeking ploy. He boasted that the bill would be killed in committee, and that the official Zionists had already arranged this with the chairmen of the two Foreign Affairs Committees, Senator Tom Connolly and Congressman Sol Bloom.[73]

Goldmann's vision was beclouded by his immense self-esteem – he never tired of trumpeting his connections with the rich, the powerful, and the famous. He apparently had little patience for routine activities such as delving into rescue possibilities once the tide of war had turned against Hitler, but he did have time for one mundane task: a good part of Goldmann's time was spent composing scores of letters warning congressmen, foreign diplomats and prominent personalities that the Bergson group was nothing more than a "fraud," as he informed Senator James Mead. In a May 19, 1944, letter to Morgenthau aide Henrietta Klotz, Goldmann wrote: "Everything must be done to liquidate the Bergsonites."[74]

On that same day, May 19, Goldmann – in at least the third such meeting in ten days – told State Department officials that American Jewish leaders were "distressed" that Bergson was "received in high places and given facilities by the government."[75] Goldmann said that he could not understand why the government did not either deport Bergson or draft him. Then came the capper: Goldmann declared that Rabbi Wise "regarded Bergson equally as great an enemy of the Jews as Hitler."[76] It was an extraordinary performance by the representative of the Jewish Agency in Palestine and the World Jewish Congress, in front of the very people who were blocking rescue of Jews. Goldmann's statement linking Hitler and Bergson may have been typically hyperbolic, but it is illuminating, nevertheless. It reveals the depth of fears of anti-Semitism engulfing the Jewish leadership, and the strategy the leadership was willing to adopt to discredit Bergson.

Goldmann's correspondence that May and June reflected the obsession he shared with Wise. As usual, he never mentioned the situation in Europe, where, in the month of May 1944, some 200,000 Jews were being shipped to death camps in Poland from two of the six deportation zones Adolf Eichmann had designated in Hungary.[77] Goldmann was preoccupied writing individual letters to every ambassador in Washington – the longest to Soviet Ambassador Andrei Gromyko – warning them about the Bergsonites, insisting that they did not represent the Hebrew nation and were nothing but swindlers.[78]

Goldmann was just one of several commanders in the Zionist offensive against the Bergson group, which lasted from 1941 to 1948. In November 1943, at the peak of the European extermination, the Zionist Organization of America's Louis Levinthal issued another in a series of broadsides against "Jewish dissenters." Judge Levinthal, whom Rabbi Morton Berman described as the field-marshal of the anti-Bergson campaign, did not mention Bergson by name. He simply lamented the fact "that we still have among us a handful of Jews who, oblivious to immediate, pressing needs, prefer to argue about theories and definitions." The immediate pressing need he referred to was not rescue. Rescue was not mentioned in this long Credo of an American Zionist. What was needed was "pragmatic realism," as the pamphlet was entitled. He waxed poetic about the development of Jewish Palestine, urging American Zionists to concentrate on one issue and one issue only: "Prepare for the Post-War Period."[79] At the same time, Levinthal's organization continued to send out mass mailings, as well as hundreds of individual letters, attacking the Bergson group and urging its supporters to withdraw.

Leon Feuer, an Ohio Zionist rabbi and a Reform movement follower of Rabbi Silver's, went to Washington at the end of 1943 and was among the middle rank of officials charged with dealing with the "most troublesome problems" that faced the Zionists outside Europe – Peter Bergson – "a personable young man who was in the country illegally," Feuer claimed in a memoir. "Some discreet inquiries suggested that he was being sheltered from deportation by a highly-placed personage, there being good reason to believe that this was Eleanor Roosevelt." Feuer, who also modestly claimed to have founded the Jewish Lobby, experienced several other hallucinations as well: He described Bergson, Merlin, and their colleagues as wearing "black shirts and black boots" at their press conferences.

(The meticulous Bergson always wore business suits and ties; while the frumpish, pipe-smoking Merlin would have looked ridiculous indeed in the fascist clothing Feuer has assigned him).[80]

But Feuer, in his 1976 article, attempted to distance himself from his superiors in the wartime Zionist organizations, averring that he was not one of those who sent regular reports on the Bergsonites to the FBI and other government agencies. He said that the reason he did not "turn Bergson in" was because the young man was "a fellow Jew."[81]

In early December 1943, Bergson met with Rabbi Wise at the Zionist offices in Manhattan to appeal for his support of the pending Rescue Resolution. As on previous occasions (such as during the Hoskins affair five months earlier), Wise asked him, "Whom do you represent?" Bergson replied that neither the Hebrew people in occupied Palestine, nor those in Europe, were in a position to choose their representatives freely, "so we represent our consciences. We admit being self-appointed. In an emergency you have to do that. The minute there will be Palestinian sovereignty, I'll be there in some capacity, as a citizen, while you, Rabbi Wise, will be here as an American clergyman of the Jewish faith and a member of the Democratic Party, and Rabbi Silver will remain here as an American clergyman of [the] Jewish faith and a member of the Republican Party."[82]

It was a correct assumption: few of the American Zionist leaders ever conceived of actually going to live in Palestine.

Although Bergson was well aware of the fact that Wise was working against him personally, as well as against the group as a whole, he still had no idea of the extent of the campaign: connivance with officials in the Justice and State Departments, and the FBI; the imputations fed to reporters as fact; or the attempts to have the Palestinians deported and sent to a British prison camp. Wise, a central figure in the plotting, was possessed of a distorted sense of reality and could not conceive himself capable of any wrongdoing. On December 30, 1943, the rabbi told Congressman Bloom that the Bergson group's activities were all part of an "evil and wretched plot..."[83] When Wise met Morgenthau aide John Pehle in New York, he spoke of Bergson in violent terms. Wise had told his family that if he were found dead in an alley one night, they would know who had done it. "He seriously felt that Bergson might kill him," Pehle reported to the Treasury secretary.[84]

CHAPTER SEVEN

BLOOMSDAY

It was impossible to save any significant number of European Jews as soon as "the Jewish problem" was relegated to one of Breckinridge Long's State Department fiefdoms, and by early 1943, this had become increasingly apparent to Jewish leaders and a growing number of government officials outside "Foggy Bottom." The Bergson group pushed forcefully for a new, special agency to bypass the State Department, an emergency governmental unit whose only task would be to save European Jews who had managed to escape the German extermination machine. The proposed agency would be backed up by executive powers and funds; would be free of the fossilized bureaucracy in Washington; and perhaps most important, beyond the reach of the cool anti-Semitism of bluebloods like Long. The Bergson campaign for a special agency, and the concurrent actions of Treasury officials who had been awakened to the State Department's deliberate policy to block rescue, led directly to President Roosevelt's establishment of the War Refugee Board in January 1944. It proved to be the Bergson group's most tangible achievement, but the establishment Zionists, whose efforts were spent trying to block the Rescue Resolution, would claim all the credit for the WRB's creation.

Over three months after the Bergsonites' proposal for a special agency was first made in a public forum, at the Emergency Conference in July 1943, the committee succeeded in getting resolutions calling for such an agency introduced in both houses of Congress, and organized sufficient support to ensure its success.

In the Senate on November 9, 1943, the bipartisan Resolution 203 was introduced by three Bergson group activists: Senators Guy Gillette of Iowa, Elbert

Thomas of Utah, and Edwin Johnson of Colorado. They had the active backing of big state Senators Robert Taft of Ohio, Homer Ferguson of Michigan, Joseph Guffey of Pennsylvania, and Sheridan Downey of California.[1] Taft and U.S. Solicitor-General Fowler Harper, another Bergson group activist, helped draft the resolution, which declared that Congress "recommends and urges the creation by the President of a commission of diplomatic, economic and military experts to formulate a plan of immediate action designed to save the surviving Jewish people of Europe from extinction at the hands of Nazi Germany.[2]

House Resolutions 350 and 352 were introduced by Rep. Will Rogers, Jr., and Rep. Joseph C. Baldwin the same day. The Emergency Committee launched the Rescue Resolution with a press conference, in which they declared that the first priority of the proposed new agency should be to set up transit camps in neutral countries, including Turkey, Spain, Switzerland and Sweden. The refugees could be moved later to Palestine or some other United Nations territory.[3]

In the days leading up to the introduction of the Rescue Resolution, the Bergsonites intensified their newspaper ad campaign, attacking the Roosevelt administration for not including the protest of extermination of the Jews on the lengthy agenda of the Allies' Moscow Conference, which warned the Nazis against atrocities directed at other peoples.[4] "My Uncle Abraham Reports" was the title of Ben Hecht's bitter message which appeared in the *Washington Post*, the *New York Times*, and other major newspapers between November 5 and 22.[5] In the ad, he lashed out at Stalin, Roosevelt and Churchill for ignoring the death of millions of Jews. The Moscow Conference "made a promise that the world was going to punish the Germans for murdering all the different peoples of Europe – Czechs, Greeks, Serbs, Russians, French hostages, Polish officers, Cretan peasants. Only we were not mentioned." Hecht put the Ghost of his "Uncle Abraham" in the White House, hinting that he would haunt Roosevelt for his inaction.

FDR was disturbed by the Bergsonite ads, and felt the "Uncle Abraham" one had hit below the belt. He was also aware of the Emergency Committee's efforts in Congress. On November 10, 1943, a day after the committee's press conference and the introduction of the Rescue Resolution, he met with Undersecretary of State Edward Stettinius, who had replaced Welles in September, and finally suggested that more could be done for the Jews. His suggestions closely paralleled those presented on the previous day by the Bergson group. "This marked Roosevelt's first initiative to help the stricken Jews. Apparently, the Emergency Committee had forced the issue on the President."[6]

The State Department denigrated the idea of a special rescue agency. In mid-October 1943, Breckinridge Long sent a memorandum to Judge Rosenman concerning a conversation with Bergson, in which Long had declared that such an agency would be superfluous, since there was a section of the State Department's Visa Division "which devoted its entire attention to the refugee problem."[7]

Long's opposition was to be expected, but what surprised many of the resolution's congressional supporters was the hostile reaction of the major Zionist and Jewish organizations (as in the case of the March of the Rabbis, only the Agudas Israel group of Orthodox Jews, and the Union of Orthodox Rabbis of the U.S. and Canada, lent their backing to the Bergsonites).[8] Wise, Silver, Goldmann and other Zionist leaders all were against the Rescue Resolution, although they could not publicly oppose a step directed at saving Jews.[9] Their antagonism was aroused, ostensibly, because the resolution did not make the Palestine question part of the rescue issue. This was done purposefully by the Bergsonites, who feared the resolution would never pass if the two issues were mixed together. But the real reason for the establishment's antipathy was that the Jewish leaders feared the Bergsonites would gain considerable prestige and attract growing support if the resolution succeeded. The long campaign to discredit the Bergsonites had some effect, but it was obvious that a new offensive would be necessary. So the organization leaders set in motion a plan to launch a public attack on the Bergsonites *and* their resolution at the moment when its fate would be hanging in the balance.[10] They also continued to lobby legislators to defeat the resolution.

On the day that the Senate Foreign Relations Committee was to vote on the Rescue Resolution, one of Senator Gillette's colleagues told him: "I wish these damned Jews would make up their minds what they want. I could not get inside the committee room without being buttonholed out here in the corridor by representatives who said that the Jewish people of America did not want the passage of this resolution."[11]

Inside the committee room, Senator Thomas, a Mormon who was close to Bergson personally, waited for the right moment – when chairman Tom Connally, a foe of the Bergsonites, was absent – to push through the resolution. It passed unanimously.[12] But in the House, Sol Bloom, the pro-Zionist chairman of the Foreign Relations Committee, maneuvered to bottle up the resolution.

Bloom's opposition was in character with his past record on issues related to rescue. In 1939, at a time when the Nazis were not yet committed to the Final Solution and were allowing Jews to leave Germany, the New York Democrat had buried a rescue plan submitted by the HIAS organization (Hebrew Immigrant Aid Society) because he agreed with his friend "Breck" Long that German "spies" would be among the Jewish refugees.[13]

Bloom's appointment as a U.S. delegate to the Bermuda Conference had shocked and disturbed many Jewish leaders because it was widely known that the Yiddish-speaking former vaudevillian was a State Department stooge, who constantly downplayed or ignored reports of the extermination and who refused to liberalize immigration laws.[14] In his 1948 autobiography, Bloom rationalized the Bermuda Conference's failure to mention "a particular group" (the Jews) at the very apex of the extermination, claiming that it might have led to "intensified persecutions" – a mind-boggling hypothesis.[15]

Bloom and Wise were friendly, though Wise had been among the Jewish leaders who protested against the appointment of Bloom to the Bermuda delegation, and had referred to him as "the State Department's Jew." Long came to Bloom's defense during the furor over Bermuda, saying that he was "representative of America."[16]

Wise, Long and Peter Bergson would all appear before Chairman Bloom's committee during the dramatic hearings on the "Establishment of a Commission to Effectuate the Rescue of the Jewish People of Europe," which began at 10:30 A.M. on Friday, November 19, 1943, and concluded on December 2.[17]

Bergson, who appeared before the panel at the first, second and final sessions, stirred Sol Bloom's deepest emotions, and the congressman would become intent on destroying the young Palestinian. Other members of the Bergson group to testify included Dean Alfange, co-chairman of the Emergency Committee; publisher William B. Ziff; journalist Herbert S. Moore; committee treasurer Frances Gunther; Congressman Rogers; and Senator Johnson. Mayor Fiorello LaGuardia, who had been active at the Emergency Conference, also testified on behalf of the Bergsonites.

In his opening testimony, Bergson recounted the August 12, 1943, meeting between Secretary of State Hull, Breckinridge Long and members of the Emergency Committee, who presented their concrete plan for a special rescue agency to the U.S. government. Bergson said that there had not been any action on the proposals, although "we kept at it." Congressman Andrew Schiffler asked him if negotiations with the State Department were still going on.

"I presume yes, if one can call them negotiations," Bergson answered. "We actually are in a position of people who plead. We come to the State Department and bang and knock and ask for things. Sometimes we get answers, sometimes we do not."

"The difficulty," he said, "was that the State Department and we spoke on two different subjects. We have come to plead and discuss possibilities for the rescue of four million Jews inside Europe, and the State Department told us what they were doing about refugees who are outside Europe."[18]

Congressman (later senator) Karl Mundt rushed to the defense of the State Department, as he would throughout the hearings.[19] But Rep. Joseph Clark Baldwin, one of the sponsors of the resolution, reminded the panel and the audience that the proposal was the "first concrete, practical suggestion, perhaps, that has been made," and that it was imperative to obtain temporary shelter for the endangered Jews.[20]

Chairman Bloom, reacting to the adverse criticism directed against him for opposing measures that would help the Jews, constantly defended himself, the State Department, and his congressional colleagues, telling Bergson, "So I want to impress you, sir, that we are not idle here. We are doing everything that we possibly can."[21]

In general, there were no indifferent reactions to the charismatic young Bergson – he either won a large measure of respect and loyalty, or drew an inordinate amount of fire. Bloom, stung by the Bergson group's attacks on the Bermuda Conference, alternately badgered Bergson about being an alien, nit-picked about language, or assumed a haughty tone, while losing no opportunity to praise himself for the "achievements" at Bermuda: 22,000 refugees in Spain [who had been out of the Nazis' reach] had received help from the Allies, Bloom enthused.[22] This was a paltry achievement by any standard, and it had nothing to do with the hearings at hand. The sponsors of the Rescue Resolution, and the members of the Emergency Committee to Save the Jewish People of Europe, were not interested in obtaining help for refugees; they wanted to *create* refugees, to get Jews out of the countries under Nazi control, Jews who were not fleeing hardship, but extermination. This point was made repeatedly by Bergson and other committee members who testified. But the inarticulate, muddled chairman was on a different wave-length altogether. Harping again on the 22,000 who were helped in neutral Spain, Bloom said: "...Mexico has been very nice. A lot of countries have been very nice. Most of them have been nice where they were able to take them in, just the same as the United States, but they have laws and different things that they must conform to."[23]

The chairman did not regard the Bergson group so kindly. He was livid over the use of the word "force" in a lengthy telegram that the Emergency Committee had sent to its supporters on November 13 and which "fell" into his hands; and he would take up hours of the hearings expressing his pique. The telegram, written by Alexander Rafaeli (Hadani), one of the Palestinian core group, listed the committee's recent activities and asked for funds to help carry on its projects, such as: the tribute to Denmark and Sweden for rescuing Danish Jewry; the Week of Compassion in which 6,000 churches took part; a mass petition movement; protest rallies against the Allies' Moscow Declaration for omitting mention of the Jewish disaster while listing all other Nazi crimes; and finally, the introduction of the Rescue Resolution. It also implied that a good part of the contributions the committee received were used to maintain several of its offices abroad which were involved in rescue-related work. Bergson and other committee members later conceded that this was an unfortunate distortion. The telegram was signed by co-chairmen Dean Alfange and Sigrid Undset, the Nobel laureate.[24]

Rafaeli had included the sentence, "Imperative to mobilize public opinion throughout the country to force passage resolution..." And Bloom castigated the Emergency Committee for daring to imply that Congress could be "forced" to pass anything. Alfange, who had opened the testimony, disavowed the use of the word and apologized profusely. But the hornet remained in Bloom's bonnet throughout the hearings. He grilled Bergson about it, and Bergson, bending over backwards to try to mollify the chairman of the powerful House committee, replied that the word was indeed totally inappropriate, "and the committee is willing to apologize for using the word 'force'; it should have said 'secure passage of the resolution.'"[25]

When Bloom continued to fasten on this irrelevancy, Bergson appealed to him to "refrain from adding injury." Bergson said that he could not understand how Bloom could go off on tangents just because "a certain word in the telegram drew your attention the wrong way."[26]

Congressman Robert Chiperfield, probably unaware of the underlying causes of Chairman Bloom's antipathy, commented that "every congressman receives many telegrams stronger than these words..." Rep. J. William Fulbright also could not fathom what all the fuss was about, and Rep. W.O. Burgin wondered, "Is this an investigation or a hearing on the resolution?" He was baffled by Bloom's obsessional concern with the use of the word "force."

Bloom switched back and forth between questions about the telegram and personal queries about Bergson. Distrust of foreigners was at its apex in the United

States at this time, and Bloom was well aware of it – he was, after all, one of the worst obstacles in the way of refugees clamoring to get into the United States. He and Mundt exploited the fear of aliens (the stock-in-trade of the State Department and the patriotic right), fastening on the fact that Bergson, who was not an American, had the audacity to try to influence U.S. governmental policy. Bloom's attack echoed that of his friend and colleague at Bermuda, Senator Lucas, who had vilified Bergson from the Senate floor in May.

> Chairman Bloom: Now. will you tell the committee where you were born?
> Mr. Bergson: Does this make any connection, Mr. Chairman?
> Chairman Bloom: We should like to know. You are being examined. You have placed the committee and the Congress of the United States in a position where you are sending out telegrams stating that it is necessary to force the Congress of the United States to pass legislation and asking people to send funds, so that you may force the Congress of the United States to pass legislation.
> Mr. Bergson: I repeat again, Mr. Chairman –
> Chairman Bloom: Do you object to saying where you were born?
> Mr. Bergson: Not at all.
> Chairman Bloom: What country are you a citizen of?
> Mr. Bergson: Not at all; as a matter of fact, I could, if you insist, give you quite a story.[28]

Bloom had evidently been briefed by Jewish establishment foes of the Bergson group, or by Long, or both, about the efforts to have Bergson deported. At the time of the testimony, the State Department, prodded by the official Zionists and perhaps by Roosevelt administration officials as well, was making inquiries about the possibility of deporting Bergson and other Palestinian members of the Emergency Committee.[29] Bloom, after accusing Bergson and Alfange of "betraying" an executive session of the House committee, returned to the third degree, oblivious to the seriousness of the issue his committee was supposed to be addressing.

> Chairman Bloom: ...How long have you been in this country, Mr. Bergson?
> Mr. Bergson: I will try, if you insist, Mr. Chairman, to give you a short biography of myself.

Chairman Bloom: Will you kindly answer the question? We shall get your
biography in the way the committee would like to get it. How long have
you been in this country?

Mr. Bergson: About three years.

Chairman Bloom: Where did you come from?

Mr. Bergson: I came here from London.

Chairman Bloom: Where were you before you went to London?

Mr. Bergson: I was in Warsaw.

Chairman Bloom: What kind of passport are you traveling on?

Mr. Bergson: A Palestinian passport.

Chairman Bloom: You came here as a visitor three years ago?

Mr. Bergson: Right.

Chairman Bloom: The time has been extended?

Mr. Bergson: Well, I have a very long dossier of correspondence with the State
Department –

Chairman Bloom: Are you legally in this country today?

Mr. Bergson: To my knowledge, yes.

Chairman Bloom: Do you not know?

Mr. Bergson: No, no.

Chairman Bloom: You do not know whether you are here legally?

Mr. Bergson: No, because I have submitted some papers –

Chairman Bloom: That is all right. You do not know whether you are here
legally?

Mr. Bergson: Is this an investigation of me –

Chairman Bloom: This is an investigation –

Mr. Bergson: Or is this an investigation by the House committee to save the
Jews of Europe?[30]

When the hearings were finally turned back to the extermination of the Jews,
Bergson used the example of Bulgaria, one of the Axis satellites, to make his case
for the Rescue Resolution.

Bulgaria, for various reasons, had resisted Nazi demands to whip its Jews to the
death camps in Poland. The allies had missed an opportunity to transfer these Jews
to safety in Turkey. Bergson said that pressure could still be brought to bear on
Bulgaria, a Nazi satellite, through a special agency such as the one proposed in the
Rescue Resolution.[31] (Less than a year later, this is exactly what happened. The

Bulgarians negotiated the evacuation of its Jews with the special agency, the War Refugee Board, and the Russian invasion of Bulgaria in September 1944 guaranteed that Bulgaria's 50,000 Jews would be spared.) "The objective of this resolution," Bergson said, "as I see it, as a man who is interested in results, is to form a procedure to solve what the President calls a ways and means difficulty... The resolution speaks of one thing, and that is to form a certain body which is able to take charge" of the rescue problem.[32]

Bloom, after another round of interrogating Bergson about his background and fund-raising activities (Bergson informed the congressmen that he got a spartan $45-a-week salary and did not take expenses), returned to his theme that everything possible was being done for the Jews of Europe and that there was no need to do more.[33] He remained blind to the fact that this was not a refugee problem, but a question of rescue.

> Chairman Bloom: Mr. Bergson, is it not a fact that the intergovernmental committee that has been functioning now, and reorganized with offices in London, is doing just the same work – the same kind of work – as any committee that could be organized today or appointed today would have to do?
>
> Mr. Bergson: Mr. Chairman, this is what I termed before "a tragic misunderstanding." There is a difference of a full 100 per cent... I say that not only is there no similarity, there is contradiction.[34]

By calling it a "misunderstanding," Bergson was being polite. Bloom's position was simply iniquitous. The Intergovernmental Committee on Refugees that Bloom was referring to was set up in 1938 at the Evian Conference, a debacle that was the precedent for Bermuda. After the war started, the agency was virtually dormant. Its only activity was to encourage Poles to stay in Poland and not become refugees. For the Jews, such a request was obscene: they had to be helped to flee occupied Europe and *become* refugees, Bergson explained.[35]

Congressman Mundt did not care for the fact that the Rescue Resolution specified Jews. "We ought to take care of people of all races, religions and colors," the right-wing legislator preached, adding later that Breckinridge Long and the State Department had done "a perfectly grand job." Mundt asked Bergson why the resolution's sponsors did not subscribe to his ecumenism and broaden their call.[36]

Bergson responded, "Very fortunately for humanity, there is no other people in Europe who are being exterminated... The Nazis are not trying to exterminate the Greeks; the Nazis are not trying to exterminate the Czechs."[37]

But Mundt persisted throughout the hearings in his effort to have the word "Jew" stricken from the resolution, and made his proposal in a suggested amendment. Bloom, who had helped keep the word "Jew" out of the Bermuda Conference, naturally agreed with Mundt. The chairman thought the South Dakota congressman's amendment "would be a better way of doing it, so as to include everyone and not call especial attention to the Jews."[38]

This reflected the general position of the State Department and the British government. Jews should not be singled out in discussing the "refugee" problem, just as the Jews had not been included in the lengthy list of peoples referred to in the recent Moscow Declaration on German atrocities, the refugee conferences, or other Allied forums.[39]

Bergson explained that there was a *specific* Jewish problem in Europe, and that nothing had been done "because the problem has not yet been recognized. This resolution is the first time."[40]

Once again, the identity issue had emerged as a roadblock to rescue. Mundt wanted to know, "When does a Pole become a Jew or a Jew a Pole?"[41]

The Jews of Poland were classified by the Poles as a national minority, Bergson explained, their status was not to be confused with the situation of Jews in America, for example. Sol Bloom was an American of Jewish extraction. But in Poland, the Jews were separate from the Poles; the Germans had made that clearer than ever. The Rescue Resolution was the first attempt to spell out the fact that the Jews, who were not even mentioned by the Allies because they were categorized as "Germans" or "Poles," were Hitler's number-one victims, deserving of a special effort to save them.[42]

Bergson said that the Emergency Committee's purpose was to wake up America to the greatest crime in history against a segment of humanity. Asked if passage of the resolution would "give tremendous impetus to your movement" (a question reflecting the main concern of the official Zionists), Bergson answered: "...the passage of the resolution is at the present moment the reason for our existence. We exist in order to save the Jews of Europe. Today the biggest thing that is being done in which the Jews of Europe can have some hope is this resolution...."[43]

Bergson told the panel that the Palestine question was extraneous to the resolution. He voiced his disagreement on this point with the establishment

Zionists and the Revisionist Zionists, including William Ziff, an Emergency Committee supporter who had testified earlier.[44] Rabbi Wise's American Jewish Conference was enraged that the Bergsonites did not mention the Palestine issue in the Rescue Resolution. But Bergson was a realist. The U.S. could not slap its British ally in the face in the middle of the war – the resolution would not stand a chance if it also tried to address the Palestine question. The official Zionists, however, were incapable of dividing rescue from the issue of the national homeland.

Bloom, who thought of himself as a staunch Zionist and a friend of Stephen Wise, questioned Bergson about the goals of the mainstream Jewish and Zionist organizations, prefacing his queries by declaring: "I want to say for the record that I have been contributing to Palestine for 65 years. That is a long time to be contributing to one charity." After a cat-and-mouse game over whether Wise's organizations were doing what the Bergsonites were doing, and an exasperated reaction by Bergson, Bloom exploded: "You may think this is a joke, Mr. Bergson, it is not a joke. The chair would like to get an answer, yes or not. Is Dr. Wise's organization and are the other organizations trying to do the same as your organization is doing?"[45]

"No," Bergson answered, "Dr. Wise's organization was formed in 1918... They are interested in what is happening over in Europe, but they were formed for a different purpose."[46] Bloom, between his diatribes and self-justifications, paid scant attention to the issue at hand, but Bergson kept his cool. He stated flatly that his only purpose in life was to generate help for his people. But the dimunitive chairman was certain that the official Zionists – Dr. Wise, Dr. Goldmann and Dr. Goldstein – were right, that Bergson was nothing more than a crook or a revolutionary.

When Rabbi Wise was called before the microphones, he was treated with the utmost deference by Chairman Bloom, who told him, "Take all the time you want." Wise introduced himself as a co-chairman of the American Jewish Conference, "which is not an unauthorized, irresponsible" body like "the other small group of American Jews." Although it was obvious to everyone whom he was talking about, Wise employed his familiar tactic – throughout his testimony, the leader of American Jewry never referred directly to the Bergson group, never dignified them with a name. He would only refer to "this group," or "several handfuls" of Jews and Christians, which cast aspersions on the "responsible, authorized, organized Jews of America."[47]

Wise said that there were no disagreements among the major Jewish organizations about the Rescue Resolution, that they were in favor of anything that might help. The Zionists, he said, were not at all opposed to the resolution, but they wanted to amend the measure. He said that two years previously, on Labor Day 1941, he had "called together the Jews of America," and that the Jewish organizations for the next eighteen months, until the founding of the American Jewish Conference, "worked on the problem of rescuing Jews." So no one could doubt his credentials, unlike that of "the others." "I represent the American Jewish Conference, made up of the great Jewish organizations, and we are not prepared to give our approval to the rashly written and rashly published advertisements asking for help and simultaneously always asking for money, for which, as far as I know, there has not been, up to today and, I venture to predict, there never will be, an accounting in any sense worthy of the name."[48]

Wise characterized the Rescue Resolution as "inadequate" because it did not mention Palestine as the destination of the Jews who were to be saved. He castigated Congressman Will Rogers, Jr., for excluding from the measure mention of Palestine, where "600,000 colonists... have performed miracles in developing a Jewish national home out of the arid deserts... In that country Jews will find not only a refuge but a permanent home."[49] He said that inclusion of Palestine in the resolution "would morally help." The thick-tongued, barely literate Bloom cheered him along, saying: "If the committee will permit the chairman at this time to ask the doctor a question, I think it would be very interesting and informative to the committee if you would just give us a short picture of what Palestine is and what they have done in this location, so as to show that they could be absorbed if they get in there. I mean, to show that it is not just a village that we are going into as refugees."[50]

As Wise droned on in his long discourse about Palestine and its history, the more attentive congressmen, who had just been told how American Jews like Wise were Americans, might have become confused. For Wise spoke in the "Zionist We." He said, "we have a great philharmonic orchestra" in Palestine; and he recounted a conversation with "Mayor Disenbach" (he meant Dizengoff of Tel Aviv) about how many oranges "we are going to export." The American rabbi was unaware of the identity questions raised by the Zionist We: "We have never seized an acre of land" from the Arabs, he said. "The Arabs and the Jews get along beautifully together. There is no ill will... We have paid largely to the Arabs for every dunam of land we have secured." His account must have sounded even stranger to the

Palestinian Jews whom Wise was campaigning against; one could hardly imagine a wider cultural chasm than the one between them and Wise.[51]

At the end of Dr. Wise's description of Jewish settlement in Palestine, Rep. Herman Everharter dutifully praised the eloquent rabbi and noted that he represented sixty-five impressive organizations, but nevertheless questioned the advisability of combining the Palestine issue with "the present and immediate necessity of rescuing the Jews."[52] Obviously, behind the politeness, Everharter could not understand how the Zionists could so callously jeopardize passage of the resolution. Wise insisted that members of his umbrella organization were "unanimous" on getting the resolution amended to include Palestine.

Will Rogers, Jr., in an exchange with Wise, said he doubted the wisdom of injecting the "acrimonious Palestine question into a resolution specifically involving the rescue issue." The Bergsonites were at least as devoted as Wise in their desire for an independent national home in Palestine, but in late 1943, in the midst of the Holocaust, it was not the right time to hold up the possibility of a sustained rescue effort for the sake of additional demands that would not be met.[53]

But Wise could not countenance such realism. The exclusion of the Palestine issue from the resolution "is one thing I cannot understand," Wise said. He assailed once again "the group which you [Rogers] represent," implying that it solicited money under false pretenses.[54]

Rogers reiterated his view that getting the people out was one question. "Where they go is another... the question of getting them out, that is the purpose to be undertaken by this resolution, as I think my co-sponsor Mr. Baldwin has previously said. It is to have no connection with Palestine. And in my opinion it would be unwise to inject that into a question of relief."

Chairman Bloom asked, "Do you want to answer that, Dr. Wise?" Rabbi Wise replied, sniffily: 'I don't care to answer it."[55]

(Wise's *idée fixe* was shared by his disciples, including the editors of the American Jewish Congress' organ, *Congress Weekly*, which soon after the hearings praised the testimony of the organization's founder, saying that Wise had used the hearings to "lift the discussion from the plane of abstract plans to the most immediate practical measures of rescue, and in the first place to the opening of Palestine.")[56]

Toward the end of the hearings, Breckinridge Long testified in a closed session. He claimed that 580,000 refugees had been taken in by the U.S. in the ten years since Hitler's rise to power. But his figures were a total fabrication. (After part of his testimony was published, three Jewish organizations released figures that ranged between 138,000 and 166,843. These statistics were never officially challenged, though they showed that Long had tripled the number of refugees who entered the U.S. between 1933 and 1943. Long's testimony was also attacked in *The New Republic*, and the *New York Post* called it "false and distorted." In Congress. Rep. Emanuel Celler said that Long should resign, and that he was either "woefully lacking in knowledge" or "did not tell the truth."[57]

When Rep. Will Rogers asked Long if it were possible to get people out of the Nazi satellite countries, he replied, "They are not permitted by the German army."[58] If this were true, then there would have been no need for a rescue resolution, since there would be no one to rescue. But Long knew it was a lie, pronounced while half-hearted negotiations dragged on over the lives of 70,000 Jews in Transnistria, whose fate had been in Long's hands for eleven months.

Long was totally opposed to the resolution, although he could not say so openly in his testimony. He could only hint that Jewish pressure groups in the United States had actually hampered rescue operations and exaggerated the sufferings of the Jews, and to state that the State Department was doing everything humanly possible to help the Jews. (A month before the hearings, Long had sent his memorandum to Judge Rosenman opposing a special agency to save Jews.)[59]

Chairman Bloom and Karl Mundt continually complimented Long during his testimony on the grand job that the State Department was doing. "I thoroughly appreciate your testimony," Mundt said, "and I think it has given a rather complete rejoinder to the implications of earlier witnesses that the Bermuda conference was ineffectual."[60] Mundt referred to the resolution as "this hot poker on the table," and said "we must dispose of it in the most diplomatic and effective manner. Simply to pass it as such, I infer from what you [Long] stated earlier, might be considered a criticism of the efforts which have been made to date." He then asked Long what he thought of his idea to amend the resolution, to take the focus off the Jews and to include "all refugees and persecuted peoples." Mundt did not want to single out any group of people. "It seems to me," he said, "that that would be treading a pretty dangerous path. It is sort of doing the Hitler thing in reverse."[61]

Long said that this was the State Department's position all along, "but the situation has come to a state of publicity today where I think the Jewish interests have emphasized the fate of the Jews as such."[62] But it would be "very dangerous to vote it down, very unwise," Long said. "I think this is a very important moment in the history of this refugee movement, and I think the Jewish people are looking forward to this action and the decision of the committee, and I think that if entirely negative action were taken here, it would be misconstrued and might react against the Jewish people under German control."[63] Long knew very well what he was talking about. The Nazis for years had gotten the message from the State Department and the Foreign Office that nobody wanted the Jews, and nothing would be done for them.

On the last day of the hearings, Senator Johnson appeared before the House committee and read a cable from the Chief Rabbi of Palestine, Yitzhak Herzog, who condemned those who could have helped the Jews but did not. "Let them confess with Joseph's brothers of old, 'Verily we are guilty concerning our brother in that we saw the anguish of his soul when he besought us and we would not hear.'"[64]

Chairman Bloom thought the message "very inspiring."[65]

Bloom suppressed the minutes of the hearings on the Rescue Resolution by declaring them secret executive sessions. Consequently, they were not released until 1976.[66]

In the weeks following the hearings, the Bergson group publicly criticized both Bloom and Long. Long was assailed in full-page advertisements for befogging the issues, for implying that the Jews who might be rescued would seek refuge in the United States, and for ignoring more accessible temporary havens under Allied control, such as Cyprus, Palestine and North Africa, as well as Turkey and other neutral countries in Europe.[67]

Bloom continued to keep the resolution bottled up in his committee, preventing it from coming to a vote. The hearings in themselves were part of the obstacle course he constructed – the Senate committee had not needed any hearings to determine that a special rescue commission was vital. The Bergsonites lashed out at Bloom as a "party to the conspiracy of silence about the catastrophe that has befallen your brothers... We would not be happy in your place, Mr. Bloom. We would have nightmares; our ears would be split by the cries of all the Jews who have perished since Bermuda; and we would feel blood, Jewish blood on our hands."[68]

After this, Bloom rededicated himself to getting Peter Bergson expelled from the country, pressing for investigations of Bergson and the committee by government agencies and the press. Bloom's autobiography, however, contains not a word of any of this. The debate on the Rescue Resolution and the Bergson group do not exist, just as they are not mentioned in Stephen Wise's autobiography or other writings.[69]

Zionists like Dr. Israel Goldstein, who with Wise and Silver led the American Jewish Conference's Interim Committee, had once criticized Sol Bloom's performance and his role in blocking rescue. But because Bloom was a Zionist and had performed manfully in battling the Bergsonites, all was forgiven. A few months after the hearings, a grove was planted in Bloom's name in Palestine, and, in June 1944, the official Zionists held a gala testimonial dinner for him at the Commodore Hotel in Manhattan. After Bloom's re-election in November of that year, Rabbi Goldstein declared that Bloom's espousal of the Zionist goal "had lifted the hearts and hopes of the Jewish people everywhere."[70]

Except, of course, in Europe.

CHAPTER EIGHT

AN AGENCY OF RESCUE

In the last week of December 1943, in the midst of the campaign to get the Rescue Resolution passed in Congress, Rabbi Wise's organizations stepped up their offensive against the Bergson group, condemning the Emergency Committee as a front for the Irgun, creating rumors of financial irregularities, and issuing a long report on the committee's "attempt to establish a front against the Jewish Agency." A statement was published in the *New York Times* that the Bergsonites did nothing but cause discord "resulting frequently in a disservice to the cause they had assumed to represent," and informing the State Department and the American people of the Jewish establishment's disapproval of the committee's ads and other activities. The press release said that the Rescue Resolution was "in complete disregard of the rescue plans that authorized Jewish organizations were pressing in Washington." The attack, by casting the resolution's supporters in so unfavorable a light, certainly did not help the cause of rescue legislation. But what the public did not know was that the so-called rescue plan the American Jewish Conference was "pressing" in Washington – devised by Sol Bloom and State Department officials in a last-ditch effort to undermine the Rescue Resolution – was for the creation of a commission that would be under the State Department's thumb.[1]

The gentile members of the Emergency Committee reacted immediately to the Zionists' charges that they were Bergson dupes misled by "clever press agentry." They called the establishment organizations statement "a tragic error on the part of those who took upon themselves the responsibility of such vindictive action."[2]

The stepped-up attacks were in part an act of revenge – the Bergson group had to be punished for its success in creating the national debate about rescue. Breckinridge Long remarked in his diary that the World Jewish Congress was "provoked because the 'Emergency Committee' had stolen its thunder."[3]

The attacks were unrelenting. On January 7, 1944, the Zionist organ *New Palestine* published a long statement saying that the Bergsonites did not have a mandate or constituency and did not cooperate with the Zionists, but engaged in "sporadic and sensational competitive activities." The journal questioned the Emergency Committee's fund-raising and condemned its prominent supporters for backing the wrong horse. It assailed the Rescue Resolution because it was "confined solely to an American effort," and because "the issue... of Palestine has been specifically avoided." That same day, Wise's *Congress Weekly*, organ of the American Jewish Congress, heaped scorn on the Bergsonites for appealing for Christian support: "Any fly-by-night organization composed of a few energetic individuals can persuade these good people to give their names to the cause of saving the Jewish millions of Europe from extermination." The official Zionists never approved of the committee's non-sectarian orientation, or such activities as the Week of Compassion and Prayer in which 6,000 churches took part. "Bergson's non-sectarian and non-partisan stance," writes Israeli historian Zvi Ganin, "contrasted with the Zionist practice of separating Jews and Christians."[4]

A week later, the American Jewish Conference issued another broadside condemning the leaders of the Bergson group as "opportunists" who represented a small political party "whose only purpose was to spread chaos and demoralization in Jewish life."[5] The umbrella organization lashed out at the Bergsonites for such "separatist activities" as holding the Emergency Conference a month ahead of the August 1943 American Jewish Conference. Since the Bergsonites were ostracized and their overtures rejected, condemning them for holding a separate meeting was "patently unfair," according to a scholar generally critical of the Bergson group.[6]

As the Rescue Resolution and the Emergency Committee came under a hail of attacks, Bergson made a vain attempt to win support from the anti-Zionist elite of U.S. Jewry, the American Jewish Committee. He wrote to its president, Judge Proskauer, on December 31 and lamented the fact that some Jewish leaders, at the moment of greatest emergency and catastrophe for the Jewish People, thought it more important to fight among themselves, and to attack the non-sectarian and non-partisan Emergency Committee. "We must keep before us just one grim fact – we must rescue Jews who are about to die. If they are allowed to die, their blood will be on our hands, for there can be no greater sin against God or man than to permit divergence of opinion on internal political questions among Jewish-American groups to affect the rescue of millions of Jews in Europe."[7]

Bergson had met with Proskauer a few weeks earlier, having been summoned to an urgent meeting at the judge's home by a leader of the American Jewish Congress. Both organizations were upset about the Bergson group's intention to run an ad in the *New York Times* containing Ben Hecht's "Ballad of the Doomed Jews," which concluded with the fear that the Christian world would be *judenrein* by Christmas. Proskauer was in a panic and said that the message would cause pogroms in America.[8]

Bergson relented, saying that one more ad was not important, but that unified action was. In exchange for his promise to delay the ad, representatives of the major American Jewish organizations met with the Emergency Committee. The meeting broke up, however, when the establishment organizations would not agree on the formation of a new umbrella group of Jewish and non-Jewish organizations which would have one goal: to push the Rescue Resolution through Congress, to pressure the government to take action to save Jews.

Ben Hecht was furious with his friend about the postponement of the advertisement, feeling that it was a waste of time to keep trying to make peace with the establishment groups. When the ad finally ran, a few weeks later, it precipitated no pogroms.[9]

The number, frequency and intensity of the attacks against the Bergsonites must have seemed staggering to anyone who was aware that rescue was being impeded by "petty rivalries in the face of a historic disaster," as Zionist journalist Hayim Greenberg wrote in a New York Yiddish paper. Greenberg condemned both the Zionist and the assimilationist Jewish organizations as bankrupt, vacuous and dull.[10]

Nevertheless, there were a few isolated voices from organized Jewry who defended the Bergson group. Rabbi Eliezer Silver, president of the American Union of Orthodox Rabbis, vehemently objected to the slur campaign conducted by the Reform rabbinical organizations, on the grounds that such slander is a violation of Jewish law. Bergson also received support from Jews on the other side of the religious spectrum. On January 21, 1944, *The Reconstructionist*, organ of the most liberal stream of Judaism, noted that the Bergson group, although under constant attack, had "filled a vacuum created by many years of ineffective activity on the part of Zionist bodies and philanthropic organizations."[11]

Rabbi Meir Berlin, leader of the major Zionist religious party, World Mizrachi, assailed the leaders of the World Jewish Congress and the Zionist Organization of America for obstructing the Bergson group's important efforts to awaken Americans to the need for rescue. As in the case with the anti-Zionist Orthodox, Berlin saw in this not a question about Zionism, but about the holiest imperative in Judaism, *pikuah nefesh*, the saving of life. Berlin called a press conference in Jerusalem in June 1944, just after he returned to Palestine from a trip to the United States, and assailed Wise, Goldmann and Bloom for their destructive attitudes. Six months earlier, Congressman Bloom, upon hearing that the Orthodox Zionists were supporting the Rescue Resolution, had telephoned Rabbi Berlin. Bloom explained to him how the establishment Zionists were against the resolution, and asked him if he thought all "this noise" was helping Zionism. Berlin told him he thought "it would help a lot."[12]

But prominent personalities were not the only people constantly being lobbied by establishment Zionists to disavow the Bergsonites. Helen Brown Sherman, who was active in the Bergson movement's Chicago office and later in the committee's public relations effort on Capitol Hill, cited an example of the everyday pressure experienced by hundreds of committee members and supporters.

On a visit to her family in Seattle, Washington, she attempted to help the cause by obtaining a full-page story in the *Post-Intelligencer*. Her mother, who had long been an active member of the Hadassah women's organization, which had the largest membership of all Zionist groups, was told that she should stop her daughter's work – otherwise she would be forced to resign her position in another Zionist organization, Youth Aliyah, which sent young people to Palestine. Later, when the Bergson group's local representative tried to hire a hall for guest speakers, the local branches of the Zionist organizations saw to it that the hall would no longer be available to them, and the meeting had to be cancelled.[13]

The British, too, continued to monitor all Bergson group activities closely, obtaining much of their information from the official Zionists. On January 5, 1944, in a confidential Foreign Office message, a British Refugee Department official discussed the Senate Foreign Relations Committee's unanimous passage of the Rescue Resolution and its likely prospects in the House. A.W.G. Randall's report to Sir Herbert Emerson said that "these resolutions owe their inspiration to the various Revisionist [sic] Zionist committees organized by Peter Bergson, and are disapproved by the Orthodox Zionists almost as strongly as by the State Department."[14]

Three weeks after the Senate panel's approval of the resolution and while it lay bottled up in the House, matters were brought to a head by a small group of gentile U.S. government officials, who demanded that the President take rescue action independent of the obstructionist State Department.

For months, Treasury officials had been upset by the State Department's foot-dragging on Rumania's offer to sell 70,000 Jews, and had kept careful records on the interdepartmental negotiations. Finally, an outraged John Pehle, head of the Treasury's Foreign Funds Control, told Breckinridge Long that he must not continue to hold up the project. The Treasury's Randolph Paul and Josiah DuBois, Jr., were equally irate over Long's ongoing sabotage. They, like Oscar Cox of the Foreign Economic Administration, were in close touch with the Bergson group and favored the immediate setting up of a special rescue agency as the only solution. On January 13, 1944, DuBois, Pehle and Paul collected the evidence and took their report on "The Acquiescence of This Government in the Murder of the Jews" to their boss, Henry Morgenthau, Jr. The report said that as one of the greatest crimes in history continued unabated, "State Department officials have not only failed to use the Governmental machinery at their disposal to rescue the Jews from Hitler, but have even gone so far as to use this Government machinery to prevent the rescue of these Jews." The report cited the Bermuda conference, and Long's "disclosures" of what happened there in his testimony at Bloom's hearings on the Rescue Resolution. The report praised those who had introduced the Rescue Resolution, and said the whole situation could be best summed up in one sentence in which the Senate Foreign Relations Committee recommended passage of the resolution: "We have talked; we have sympathized; we have expressed our horror; the time to act is long past due."[15]

Morgenthau knew his aides were not exaggerating in unfolding the State Department's complicity in the Nazis' crimes – everyone knew where Breck Long stood. But the highly cautious Treasury secretary felt he could not go to FDR with only a condemnation and no program of action. His aides, all intimately familiar with the provisions of the Rescue Resolution, told Morgenthau that they had a "specific proposal," but he did not even inquire what it was. They gave him more details about the resolution being discussed in Congress and the press.[16] Morgenthau aide Ansel Luxford informed him that the measure had passed in the Senate committee but that Congressman Bloom was doing everything possible to block it in the House. Luxford and Cox explained to Morgenthau that Bloom had been a delegate at the disastrous Bermuda Conference and now took "a personal emotional interest in the thing" to the extent that he was covering up for Long and for the State Department.[17]

As Arthur Morse noted in *While Six Million Died*, "It is one of the fascinating paradoxes of the era that it was necessary for the non-Jewish members of [Morgenthau's] staff to awaken him to the interminable delays in the rescue of the Jews." DuBois, who prepared the report to Morgenthau in collaboration with Pehle and Paul, threatened to quit the Treasury if the Treasury secretary did not go to FDR to demand action, and call a press conference "and rip the lid off the entire State Department refugee scandal."[18]

Until January 1944, Morgenthau, scion of a leading American Jewish family, was not different from other members of Roosevelt's Jewish circle, none of whom dared to challenge FDR's virtual indifference to the fate of European Jewry. Roosevelt was like a god to American Jews in general. They felt that they had a friend in the White House, and they did not want to alienate him. Rabbi Wise always approached him on tenterhooks, and actually apologized for bringing up the Holocaust. Even the maverick Peter Bergson subscribed to the myth that Roosevelt's heart was in the right place and that he was simply being undermined by the State Department. He felt that it was unreasonable to expect FDR to react more strongly to the extermination of the Jews than did his Jewish advisors.[19]

Morgenthau knew that the only way to get to Roosevelt was on a political level. He realized immediately that the Rescue Resolution, about which he knew little until his aides briefed him, was the strongest point he had with FDR: The Congress was about to do something, and he could legitimately advise Roosevelt to move very fast and beat Congress to the punch. The President had to be made aware of the threat posed by the Rescue Resolution. It was political dynamite that had bipartisan support but would help Republicans the most; and this point was driven home to Morgenthau by Cox: "Look at the guys who introduced this resolution in the Senate – Gillette, Taft, Ferguson – and those fellows aren't on the President's team."[20]

The Bergson group had been in touch with the Treasury officials for months, raising their consciousness about the circumstances contributing to the Jewish tragedy, and suggesting what course of action should be taken. Bergson, Merlin and other Emergency Committee members met regularly with DuBois, Pehle, and Luxford, and on occasion with Cox. They believed it was essential to take up their rescue plans with whoever would listen. For example, after a lunch with Cox on September 14, 1943, Bergson sent him the findings and recommendations of the

Emergency Committee, with the blueprint for a new governmental body specifically charged with the task of saving Jews.[21] The Bergsonites cultivated any government official who they thought could help the cause, and they felt the Treasury men could bring them closer to Morgenthau and perhaps the President himself. Bergson and DuBois eventually became good friends, with Bergson and his girl friend, Betty Keane Caplan, frequently visiting the DuBois family at their home in Camden, New Jersey.[22]

On January 15, 1943, Morgenthau, Pehle and Paul went to FDR with their "Personal Report to the President," a slightly toned down version of the report to Morgenthau detailing the "utter failure" of State Department officials to help Europe's Jews. John Pehle, in a memorandum for the files written that same day, reported that FDR "listened attentively and seemed to grasp the significance of the various points." The President agreed that some effective action could be taken and referred in particular to the movement of Jews through Rumania into Bulgaria and out through Turkey. According to Pehle's account, FDR was well aware that these channels were wide open, and in fact, these were exactly the avenues of rescue that the Bergsonites had been pointing to in their ads.[23] That same week, the last in the Bergson group's long series of full-page statements regarding the need for a rescue agency appeared in *The Nation* and *The New Republic*, urging a letter and cable campaign to spur Congress to pass the Rescue Resolution.[24] But the Emergency Committee's campaign had already paid off.

On January 17, a day after the Treasury officials met with FDR, Morgenthau, at the President's suggestion, met with Judge Rosenman and Undersecretary Stettinius, who was about to replace Hull. Stettinius read a draft of the Executive Order that would create the War Refugee Board five days later, and said, "I think it's wonderful."[25]

On January 22, Roosevelt signed Executive Order No. 9417 establishing a presidential agency for saving Jews and officially titled the War Refugee Board. The order declared that the special agency would carry out the government's policy "to take all measures within its power to rescue the victims of enemy oppression." The WRB was mandated to develop plans and take measures for the rescue, transportation, maintenance and relief of the Nazis' principal victims and to establish "havens of temporary refuge" for them. The State, War and Treasury departments were ordered to execute all of the WRB's requests.[26]

The board's representatives were given extraordinary powers to cut red tape and get around the Trading with the Enemy Act. Pehle, Morgenthau's brilliant young aide, was appointed the agency's first executive director. The Bergsonites had worked hard to get Pehle appointed. Several months later, Ansel Luxford told Morgenthau that he thought they had influenced FDR's choice, but this was only conjecture.[27]

The State Department, smarting under the order, was instructed to appoint special envoys with diplomatic status to be stationed in areas where it was possible to help the refugees. The WRB was also authorized to work with envoys from neutral countries. One of these diplomats was Raoul Wallenberg of Sweden, the extraordinarily courageous man who would save tens of thousands of Jews in Hungary. Wallenberg, the thirty-two-year-old scion of a famous Swedish banking dynasty, was given the necessary diplomatic cover through the board. The WRB orchestrated the operation by providing documents and other support; financing was provided by the Joint Distribution Committee (JDC).[28]

Wallenberg used both legal and forged documents, bribery and other methods that had been scoffed at by State Department and British Foreign Office officials. In recent years, though Wallenberg's heroic work has finally been recognized, the fact that it was the WRB that got him there, and that this was just an indication of what could have been done, has been overlooked. The creation of the WRB was of great historic importance since, for the first time, the force and prestige of the U.S. government were directed toward efforts to save the Jews.

The Emergency Committee had pushed so hard for the special presidential agency in the belief that the saving of Jews should become an Allied war aim, that this was not merely "a Jewish issue," but a basic concern for humanity. Therefore, the U.S. government as a whole should have paid for this governmental body. But once the agency was created, the Jewish establishment rushed in. In Bergsonite eyes, Jewish organizations feared an anti-Semitic backlash among American taxpayers who might resent their money being used to save European Jews. Using a clause in the Executive Order which allowed for private contributions, the Jewish organizations stepped in to pay for virtually all of the WRB's expenses. The Bergson group considered this endowment – some $20 million – to constitute a harmful restriction on the WRB's mandate. In financing the board, the Jewish groups detracted from the WRB's standing and hampered the scope of its activities.[29]

However, there is evidence that the Jewish organizations did recognize the need to press the government for financing, but that John Pehle felt Congress would not appropriate rescue funds.[30] The Bergsonites, though, were certain that the WRB could have worked on a much grander scale had more presidential funds (Roosevelt had $50 million at his immediate disposal) been used.

The board was financed mainly by the JDC (the "Joint"), the aid arm of the American Jewish Committee, which spent $15 million on WRB projects. From 1942, the JDC had been the only Jewish organization to engage in life-saving efforts in the field, and the often heroic work of its staff in Europe is the one bright spot for organized American Jewry during the war.[31]

Within weeks of the WRB's establishment, the agency, which never had more than thirty employees in Washington, saved hundreds of Jews in Greece who, because of the board's intervention, were shipped to neutral Spain instead of to the extermination center at Auschwitz. Thousands of other Jews were rescued in the Balkans. It became immediately apparent that many thousands of other Jews – perhaps hundreds of thousands – could have been saved if the State Department, the Foreign Office, and Zionist leaders had not for so long dismissed the possibility of dealing directly with certain of the Devil's helpers. According to the board's official history, "Lesser German officials were bribed. False identification papers were supplied... Border officials were bribed to pass refugees... Tens of thousands were rescued from the Nazis by these clandestine means."[32]

A month after the board's creation, the Emergency Committee, in ads in *The Nation* and *The New Republic*, hailed FDR's action and the appointment of Pehle, and noted that the WRB's establishment had attained two priorities for rescue: for the first time, bringing a halt to the extermination had become a primary war aim; and a powerful new agency had been empowered to implement a rescue program. But while praising the U.S. government's decision to meet Hitler's challenge on the question of Jewish survival, the Bergsonites noted that other Allied governments must also cooperate. Now was the time to open the gates to Palestine, and for Britain to end its discriminatory White Paper policy. The committee urged a new campaign to rouse public opinion in the U.S. to influence "this great and gallant ally" to lift its curbs on the entry of Jews into Palestine, and quoted the Archbishop of Canterbury, who, in calling for action to save Jews, said: "We all stand before the bar of history, of humanity and of God."[33]

But the British were not only disinterested in opening the gates to Palestine, they were also opposed to the very creation of the WRB and to its methods. Falling back on the old argument that allowing any transfer of funds provided the enemy with foreign exchange with which to prolong the war, London opposed U.S. rescue efforts. It was clearly an unwarranted fear, since no direct ransom to the enemy was permitted, and most of the ransom money dispensed by the WRB "went into the hands and private hoards of individual border guards."[34]

Months before the board was set up, it had proven impossible to transfer a mere $25,000 down-payment for 70,000 Jews in Transnistria, most of whom consequently perished. Now, however, such financial transactions could not be so easily blocked by State Department officials – but they still tried. Of the three government departments which were ordered to do the WRB's bidding, only the Treasury cooperated fully. The State Department's main liaison with the WRB, George Warren, "did little to counteract the opposition to the board that prevailed among the department's middle-level officials. The way was left open for them to interfere with its activities."[35]

In addition to rescue efforts, the War Refugee Board was also able to influence Allied policy on punishment of the Nazi murderers. The board, under the prodding of the Bergson group, which worked closely with WRB officials, moved to win recognition of the Jews of Axis countries as a separate national entity. Previously, the United Nations War Crimes Commission had argued that there was no precedent under international law for including as a war crime an act committed by a nation against its own subjects, or citizens of aligned nations. The WRB's position was finally incorporated into the UN program for punishment of war criminals.[36]

In the introduction to the War Refugee Board's official history, the crucial role played by the Bergsonites' Rescue Resolution in bringing about the creation of the board is recognized and acknowledged.[37] The press at the time also noted the connection between the Gillette-Rogers resolution – which was pre-empted by FDR's action – and the setting up of the board. This was no small matter, for the establishment of the WRB would be regarded by some historians as "a major event in the history of the war" because it was the one and only step taken by any of the Allies to thwart Hitler's extermination plan.[38]

The non-Jewish press saw the obvious connection between the Rescue Resolution and Roosevelt's establishment of the WRB, but the Zionist and Jewish press "preferred not to notice the link."[39] On January 24, 1944, the *Christian Science Monitor* stated that FDR's move two days earlier "is the outcome of pressure brought to bear by the Emergency Committee to Save the Jewish People of Europe, a group made up of both Jews and non-Jews that has been active in the capital in recent months."[40] The editor of the *New York Post*, Theodore Thackery, wrote to

Peter Bergson to praise his efforts: "I think your activities in this country for the past two years have resulted in the one effective step taken thus far to break through the dyke of indifference, intolerance, suspicion and opposition." Roy Howard, the publisher of the Scripps-Howard newspaper chain, said that his newspapers would continue to assist the Emergency Committee "not only because of admitted worthiness of your cause, but because of our belief that the methods you are apparently determined to employ are the most apt to be productive."[41]

Interior Secretary Ickes, in congratulating the Emergency Committee, noted that it had "kept itself free from collateral entanglements and has concentrated on the creation of an official agency to do this job." And the *Washington Post*, which had often been hostile to the Bergson group, said in a January 25 editorial that the Committee's "industrious spadework" had contributed greatly: "...the Committee is likewise entitled to credit for the President's forehanded move."[42]

But the Zionist leadership and the organizations making up the American Jewish Conference, which had either bitterly opposed the Rescue Resolution or refused to endorse it, now totally ignored the Bergson group's contribution and tried to claim the credit for themselves.

The American Jewish Conference's "Committee on Jewish Rescue," set up in late summer 1943, did not get beyond the talking stage until January 1944, when it decided it would engage in political and social work to promote rescue. Yet, just a few days after deciding what its aims were, this committee issued a press release congratulating FDR for establishing the WRB and claiming, unblushingly, that *it* was responsible, that "The Conference's Commission of Rescue had asked the government to establish this interdepartmental board... and representatives of the commission have been negotiating with government officials to that end for some time."[43]

While the Jewish establishment was ludicrously patting itself on the back, the government officials responsible for moving Roosevelt were quite clear about who deserved credit for the WRB. On March 8, a few weeks after the agency was set up, Pehle, DuBois and another Treasury aide met with Morgenthau to discuss how to present FDR with the suggestion of a temporary shelter in Palestine for the refugees, an idea that Bergson's Emergency Committee had been urging for nine months. In the conversation, the Treasury secretary credited the Bergson group for getting "the President really to act on this thing – we are talking here among ourselves..." Morgenthau, speaking "a little bit more frank," referred to "the

Resolution in the House and in the Senate by which we forced the President to appoint" a rescue agency.[44]

Pehle acknowledged "public pressure too" for FDR's action. DuBois, who was denounced as a "Jew" by State Department officials, told Morgenthau: "It was more because of what you did than anything else." The Treasury secretary replied, "I had something to do with it, granted, but the tide was running with me... I think that six months before I couldn't have done it. Now, what I am leading up to is this: I am just wondering who the crowd is that got the thing that far?" Pehle answered that the tide was created by "the Emergency Committee: Peter Bergson and his group."[45]

Morgenthau then suggested that the Bergson group could also push through a resolution for temporary shelters. But Pehle recalled the bitter struggle the Bergson group had just been through – Congressman Bloom's attempts to bury the Rescue Resolution, and Wise's divisive campaign – and said that there would be too much opposition.[46]

Despite repeated warnings from Jewish establishment figures such as Nahum Goldmann that they should have nothing to do with the Bergson group, Pehle, DuBois and others involved in the WRB chose to work closely with the outcasts. On several occasions, the WRB officials told Bergson and Merlin that they were under constant pressure from Wise, as well as from the non-Zionist establishment, to disavow the committee. They felt that these leaders of American Jewry were impairing WRB operations by taking up so much valuable time in what appeared to be an exercise in fratricide. At a New York reception in May 1944 for Ira Hirschmann – a department store executive and vice-chairman of the Emergency Committee, who was picked as the WRB's man in Turkey at the urging of the Bergsonites – Pehle said that in a democracy, the government does what public opinion wants it to do, and that was why the Emergency Committee's efforts were so important. A simple truth, but one that seemed to escape the Zionist and Jewish establishment.[47]

The issue of who deserves credit for bringing about creation of the WRB seems minor indeed when compared to the question of what a more powerful agency could have done, and how many more lives could have been saved if the agency had been created six months earlier, at the time when the Emergency Conference was held, with its focus on this issue. According to the WRB's Final Summary Report in May 1945, some 50,000 Jews were ransomed; and in recent years, some historians – David Wyman for one – credit the agency, despite its many shortcomings, with saving a total of up to 200,000 lives.[48]

"In the last analysis," Wyman concluded in *The Abandonment of the Jews*, "the WRB's greatest weakness was that it came into existence too late. Virtually everyone close to the rescue issue thought that the board could have achieved far more had it been formed a year, or even several months, earlier."[49] One can only speculate on how many more lives might have been saved if the Zionist establishment had put aside the issue of post-war Palestine for a few months, in order to work with the non-Zionist Jewish establishment, and even with the despised Bergsonites. DuBois and Pehle, the two key U.S. officials who did the most to implement the Emergency Committee's call for a special rescue agency, would, years later, lament the fact that the WRB was too little, too late. The WRB "did a fair amount," DuBois would say, but by the time it was created, "it was too damned late to do too much."[50]

Throughout the Holocaust years, Wise and his lieutenants moved at an agonizingly slow pace as they pursued a policy of hushed diplomacy. In any case, it was not their all-consuming interest. According to Sir Isaiah Berlin, what divided Weizmann and his followers, Wise and Goldmann, from activists like Ben-Gurion and Silver and from "Revisionists and their proto-Irgun allies" was Weizmann's persistent belief in "patient diplomacy," a policy Berlin applauded. "Marches, petitions, resolutions, advertisements in the press with signatures of prominent persons, fiery philippics – all this might impress the Jews, it would not succeed in moving Washington," Berlin said in 1972 at The Hebrew University in Jerusalem. But precisely the opposite was true. The Jews were not impressed; Washington, in establishing the War Refugee Board, had indeed been moved, albeit ever so slightly, by public pressure alone.[51]

In the months following the creation of the WRB, Morgenthau and his aides frequently discussed Peter Bergson and the committee he headed. Morgenthau wanted to know, "What is our contact with him and what are we doing with him and what is he doing with us."[52]

Luxford told Morgenthau that he knew Bergson personally and spoke highly of him. He compared the twenty-nine-year-old leader to De Gaulle, and praised the committee's work. DuBois agreed. "They certainly made a contribution toward the establishment of the Board," he said. Pehle added: "Even the people who hate them agree they made a substantial contribution in stirring up public opinion here."[53]

Luxford said it was generally acknowledged that the Bergson group had made the extermination of European Jewry a problem for all Americans, not just Jews. Pehle expressed amazement that the establishment leaders were as concerned about the inroads Bergson was making as they were about the Holocaust. "I have had a stream of people from various Jewish organizational groups, who, as you know, feel as violently about this as they do about anything else." Pehle said that Congressman Bloom had advised him to look at Bergson's "record" at the State Department, where a dossier was kept on the young Palestinian.[54]

Ansel Luxford felt Bergson was fighting the good fight, but that he would fail, and might even be assassinated. "I wouldn't be surprised to see Bergson a martyr, if anybody is a martyr. You can talk about Wise," he said, referring to a remark by Pehle that the rabbi, the king of American Jewry, suspected Bergson was out to kill him; "I think the feeling is so strong in this issue that I wouldn't be surprised to see Bergson killed." Pehle concurred: "They are certainly out to get him."[55]

When Morgenthau asked who was after Bergson, another aide said that it was most Jewish organizations; Luxford added that it was the bitterest feud imaginable. Like Pehle, Luxford was amazed that the major Jewish organizations were focused on the Bergson group and neglecting the issue that should have commanded their undivided attention. "Every organization, I sometimes think, is more interested in their fight with some other organization than they are with the objective of saving Jews."[56]

Morgenthau ordered further sessions to discuss Bergson and his activities. "This is important," he said, "because that fellow is important." Upon hearing that Felix Frankfurter had hailed the work of the WRB, Morgenthau commented on the array of "Jewish power" backing the special agency: "We have Justice Frankfurter, Rosenman and Bergson! That is quite a combination."[57]

But while Morgenthau was acknowledging Bergson's contributions to the Jewish cause, and putting him in the company of the two most important Jews (other than himself) in the U.S. government, the Zionist establishment continued its long and unrelenting campaign to destroy the Bergson group and all its works. The attacks in the press and the poison letter campaign would continue unabated throughout 1944 and 1945, as did the efforts to inform on Bergson to various government agencies, including the FBI, and the attempts to have him deported. Committee member Yitshaq Ben-Ami, for example, was the subject of seven different reports by FBI agents. In May 1943, the Justice Department asked J. Edgar Hoover to "obtain the assistance of the British authorities" in Palestine to investigate Bergson and the other Palestinian Jews. In August 1943, Secretary of State Hull was inspired – perhaps by the Zionists, or by Roosevelt, the British, his own officials, or all of the above – to ask Attorney General Francis Biddle if the Palestinian committee members were registered as foreign agents, and if not, why? And in a May 9, 1943, meeting between Nahum Goldmann and the State Department's Gordon Merriam, chief of the Near East Division, Goldmann said that "Bergson and his group were perpetuating a gigantic hoax" on the Jewish community, and demanded to know why the government did not "deport or draft" the Palestinians. In mid-May 1944, at the same time the Nazis started shipping half a million Jews from Hungary to the death camps, Goldmann warned John Pehle that if he did not disavow the Bergson group, the World Jewish Congress would denounce the WRB.[58]

Sol Bloom worked especially hard to get rid of Bergson, and the powerful congressman regularly kept Zionist leaders like Rabbi Israel Goldstein informed of his progress. On one occasion in February 1944, Bloom chastised Dr. Goldstein for having been in contact with Samuel Merlin; on another occasion, Bloom sent him a photostat of a letter from Merlin to a prominent Jew (whose name has been blackened out) decrying the vicious attacks on the Bergsonites.[59]

A U.S. government office memorandum in March 1945 reported that there were moves afoot in high official circles to deport Bergson, and quoted Congressman Bloom as having said that unless this were done, Bergson would "eventually provoke antagonism among the citizens of the United States" and cause "anti-Semitic pogroms."[60] This was exactly the line followed by Stephen Wise, who seemed to think that the threat of anti-Semitism in America was as great as Hitler's threat to European Jews. Today, such convoluted thinking may appear inconceivable. But men like Bloom and Wise and Goldmann were incapable of confronting the reality: that the State Department and FDR would do nothing for the Jews unless there was enormous public pressure to do so, and that the loathsome Bergsonites had mastered the methods for whipping up the necessary support.[61]

Instead, the official Zionists shared a community of interest with the State Department and the British in their opposition to the Bergson group, and this was why they cooperated in the attempts to have Peter Bergson deported to a prison camp in Palestine. The Jewish Agency's office in Washington, headed by Goldmann, traded information with the British embassy about the common struggle. In an August 8, 1945, letter, British embassy official A.H. Tandy thanked Mrs. Miriam

Taub Cohen, Goldmann's aide, for her endeavors and related that "Bergson has been given until November to leave the country."[62]

In the press, the fiercest Zionist-inspired attack on the Bergson group appeared in a series of articles in the *Washington Post* in the first week of October 1944.[63] The series apparently was ordered by publisher Eugene Meyer himself, one of the leading assimilationist Jews in America, but whose Christian wife had been a supporter of the Bergsonites. The Zionist organization leaders had implored Meyer to do something about the committee and to run Bergson out of town, because his activism, they said, constituted a threat to all American Jewry. In the past, the non-Zionist Meyer had not been averse to appealing to FDR for increased immigration to Palestine. When the Zionists convinced him that Bergson would cause pogroms in America, the publisher acted.[64]

The *Post*, then a far cry from the newspaper it later became, based the series heavily on innuendo and on information from Rabbi Wise and Congressman Bloom; it clearly violated standard journalistic norms. Even at the time, it was considered libelous, and Bergson committee activist Prof. Fowler Harper, the U.S. Solicitor General, urged Peter Bergson to sue.[65]

The first headline, on October 3, read: "Bergson Admits $1,000,000 Fund Raised, Vague on Its Use." The article, by reporters Gloria Lubar and Edward F. van der Veen dripped with venom about the "self-styled" and "boastful" leader of the movement, whose "voice cracks or squeaks when he gets excited."

The reporters derided the committee's activities, past and present, quoting sources in "reputable Jewish national organizations" (headed by Wise), who said, "The public might be interested in knowing just how much has been collected and what disposition was made of the money. To date, Bergson has made no such accounting." If the reporters had bothered to check, they would have found that this statement was a calumny, since the committee's books were open to all, and had been carefully inspected by independent accountants, as well as the Internal Revenue Service. The article went on to explore Bergson's draft status in depth, quoting British officials who were upset that Bergson "has not yet enlisted," an argument that played on the notion that Jews were draft dodgers. It also quoted American Jewish Conference sources who said that the Bergsonites used names in their ads without permission. Old enemies, like Senator Lucas, and former supporters, like Pierre van Paassen, were also quoted.[66]

In the second article, on October 4, Sol Bloom's comments were showcased under a headline that read: "Bergson Admits His Committee Has No Right to Collect Funds."[67] Bloom, the man who, along with Breckinridge Long, was most responsible for blocking rescue or shelter for European Jews, said that "no authorized Jewish agency approves of the methods adopted by Bergson and his groups." Bloom condemned the committee's "lobbying and high pressuring," and exhibited the Emergency Committee telegram of the year before with the infamous phrase "force passage of a resolution" which had so excited Chairman Bloom during his House committee's hearings. "If that isn't high pressuring and lobbying, I would like to know what is," said Bloom, who went on to boast to the reporters, inaccurately, that it was he who had put a spoke in Bergson's wheel:

> Bloom recalled Bergson's appearance before the House Foreign Affairs Committee last fall: "I asked him if he had come into this country legally," the Congressman said.
>
> "I don't know," Bergson told me.
>
> "What the hell do you mean you don't know?" I thundered.
>
> Chuckling, the Congressman added, "It's the first time I ever remember swearing at a committee hearing."[68]

Prof. Harper, who was dean of Yale Law School until taking over at the Interior Department's law division, immediately wrote a scathing letter to the newspaper, assailing the series as "vicious," unsubstantiated and unwarranted. Harper reminded Eugene Meyer that Mrs. Meyer, at a meeting with Bergson at the home of Oscar Chapman of Interior, had "displayed a great deal of enthusiasm and provided much inspiration for the program there outlined." He avowed that he had personally drafted the Rescue Resolution and a subsequent resolution to admit Jewish refugees to the U.S., and had spoken for the Bergson group in thirty-five weekly radio programs over Meyer's WLNX station. "I know personally that anyone can examine the books of this association, and I find them in perfect order." In light of the *Post*'s previous favorable editorial comments on the work of the committee, he simply could not understand what motivated the attack. Harper did not mention the obvious – that the people who had pressed for the series were also the two reporters' main sources.[69]

In one of the few instances of a Bergson group response to the ongoing attacks initiated by the official Zionists, Bergson held a press conference and wrote a letter to the newspaper to protest the series.[70] He charged that reporter van der Veen had never met him, let alone interviewed him, as he had appeared to have done; the quotes, in fact, were culled from press conferences or reports in other newspapers. Bergson said that he had spoken with Lubar, but that she did not report on anything they had discussed. He added that he had not raised a million dollars, that his own salary was now $75 a week (up from $45 in 1943) and his bank balance was $100, and that the committee could not afford to be anything but open and explicit "in the face of watchful public opinion and bitter opposition." In his October 10 letter to the newspaper, Bergson, condemning the "quiet diplomacy" of court Jews, wrote that the committee had abolished "the old, bankrupt and undignified system of subjecting the Hebrew people to back-door pleas before subaltern or high government officials," taking instead a "revolutionary" path.[71]

Much of the *Post* series was devoted to claims that there was an almost total misuse of the names of prominent people in the Bergson group's newspaper advertisements. In his reply to the newspaper's charges, Bergson pointed out that Meyer had published many of the ads over the last two years with the signatures of hundreds of high officials who lived in Washington and that none of them had registered a complaint.

Ten days after the series began, the *Washington Post* admitted it had erred and ran a long editorial recanting most of the charges. It also gave the Bergson group space on page one to present its side of the story. The newspaper credited the Bergsonites with bringing about creation of the WRB – just as it had done editorially nine months earlier.[72] In the series, the two reporters said in a throw-away paragraph: "The spade work for creation of the WRB had long been carried on by Jews and gentiles of other organizations in no way connected with the Bergson committee. The culmination of the [rescue] resolution was the result of the combined effort of all these organizations."[73] Since the reporters cited no evidence for this extraordinary contention, and no source, it was obvious where it came from – they were simply repeating the Zionist line. The people who had initiated the *Post* series and provided the reporters with their "scoop" were the same ones who had opposed the Rescue Resolution, yet who nevertheless claimed all credit for creation of the WRB.

The October 13 editorial said it clearly: The Emergency Committee to Save the Jewish People of Europe, "under the active leadership of Mr. Bergson, played a great part in developing public and congressional opinion in support of the Gillette resolution, which resulted in the establishment of the War Refugee Board by executive order of the President... The War Refugee Board, as we have hitherto said, is a very necessary agent in saving the Jewish refugees from the Nazi fiends." The recanting editorial said that there were no question marks about the committee's use of funds: "In this respect our news stories may have given a misleading impression... as if the money had been improperly collected." But it also reiterated that the official Zionists opposed the group and that it "had no mandate" from either right or left – as Wise constantly said – in the political life of Palestine. The editorial went on to conclude that "the Bergson group would contend that the previously established [Jewish] organizations have not been persistent and energetic enough in prosecuting the cause of the refugee Jews. The successful campaigning of the Emergency Committee at least to some extent seems to substantiate this contention." The Bergson group may have been a "duplicate" of the established organization, but it was far more effective in fighting for the cause of rescue, the editors said.[74]

For obvious reasons, the Zionists did not include this editorial, or mention the fact that the IRS had found the committee's books in perfect order, when they circulated tens of thousands of copies of the original *Post* series to Jewish organization members and backers of the Bergsonites. This resulted in a serious weakening of support for the Bergson group.[75]

In an unsigned letter, dated November 16, 1944, from the Jewish Agency's office in Washington to Arthur Lourie, of the American Zionist Emergency Council in New York, the writer (presumably Nahum Goldmann, who was in charge of the office) said that he had just spoken about the *Washington Post* series to "our friend IB." This was, perhaps, Zionist leader Rabbi Isadore Breslau. IB, the conspiratorial letter said, had told the writer that the *Post* was "much disaffected" by the fact that there was not enough vocal Zionist support after the anti-Bergson articles had appeared, while in contrast, the newspaper was being deluged by letters supporting Bergson. (In the third article of the series, the two reporters led with the statement: "Nationwide repudiations of Peter H. Bergson and his numerous committees continued to flow into The Post last night.") IB told the letter writer that because there was no popular support for the articles, "the Post is thoroughly irritated and not likely to render a Zionist service again."[76]

Goldmann, in another letter – this one signed – congratulated Eugene Meyer for the series of articles, which "have done much to enlighten the public and to stop the activities of a group which could only create confusion and misunderstanding."

The Jewish Agency had also officially thanked Meyer on October 12, a day before the editorial, in a letter to the publisher from Miriam Taub Cohen.[77]

Bergson himself seemed to be unfazed by the personal focus of the attacks, although he realized how injurious the series was to the movement. Before the *Washington Post* series, Victor Riesel, in a *New York Post* profile of Bergson, noted that the "sensitive intellectual" leader remained "unruffled" by the attacks led by Wise, Goldmann, Goldstein, Henry Monsky, Judge Levinthal and others.[78] But the *Washington Post* series undermined the Bergson group's broad-based support and constituted a severe blow. The Zionist leadership smelled blood, and pressed on for government or police action against the activists, who were alternately styled as con men, spies, clowns and fascist terrorists.

The only time the Bergsonites tried to respond in kind to the continuing attacks was in June 1944, when several committee members filed a rabbinical court slander suit against Wise for having obstructed the Rescue Resolution and libeling Bergson. They were encouraged to do so by Orthodox rabbis, who were shocked by the attacks instigated by Reform rabbis on a group devoted to the cause of saving Jewish lives. The Jewish press and Wise's defenders would term the move "a cheap publicity stunt." Wise called the Bergson group's statements about him "moral blackmail." In the end, nothing came of the suit, which proved embarrassing and ill-advised – Wise was unassailable.[79]

In general, however, the committee adhered to its deliberate policy of not responding to the attacks. According to Samuel Merlin, the committee activists felt that had they responded they would have had "precious little time to do anything else." Merlin said he was "saddened by what preoccupied these people at a time of total disaster for their kin in Europe. I couldn't understand what caused this fury of hatred, and why it took on such irrational proportions."[80]

Despite the attacks, the committee had made the extermination a major issue for Americans, and had concentrated their efforts on the powerful U.S. officials who were the main obstacles to rescue. By January 1944, FDR's old friend Breck Long was virtually *persona non grata* at the White House – the fire he drew had made him a political liability. The isolated State Department official confided his hurt in his diary, and wrote that the creation of the WRB was superfluous: "What they can do that I have not done I cannot imagine." But he thought it a clever political ploy by FDR because four million New York Jews "feel themselves related to the refugees," and the creation of the board might pacify them in the election year.[81] Morgenthau, too, had recognized that FDR would only act if there was a political payoff, or to prevent a political setback. The threat over the President's head did not emanate from the Jewish and Zionist leadership, but from the grass-roots movement spearheaded by the small group of young Palestinians who were trying to revolutionize American Jewry while awakening the conscience of the entire American nation.

CHAPTER NINE

THE SURVIVORS AND THE HEBREW NATION

Bringing about the WRB's establishment was an achievement of historic importance, but the agency was not the answer the Bergsonites were praying for. DuBois and Pehle had concurred with the Bergson group: It was too little, too late. However, for the Bergsonites there was no choice but to accept it, to work through the board, and to try to move on. Now, the Bergson group gradually shifted its emphasis to the struggle for Hebrew independence in Palestine.

In the view of the Bergsonites, the stateless Jews of Europe and the Jews of Palestine constituted the nascent Hebrew nation. The word "Hebrew" was often used by Jewish political activists in the years before the accepted term became "Israeli" as a way of stressing the national rather than the religious aspect of the Jews.[1] What the Bergson group now undertook was to update the Zionism of their mentor, Jabotinsky, to think deeply about the implications for the entire Jewish People of an independent state in Palestine, and to act as a sort of temporary representative, a *locum tenens*, for the Palestinian and stateless European Jews.

The Bergsonites, whose political Zionist outlook had been transformed by their exposure to the pluralism of America and by the trauma and lessons of the Holocaust, maintained that there was a basic difference between Jews who chose Palestine as their home and Jews who chose, for example, America. All Jews had a *right* to belong to the emerging Hebrew nation-state, but not a *duty* to belong. The Bergson group felt that clarifying this question of national identity would expedite independence, and redefine the Jewish People. In holding this view, they were already heretics in the eyes of classical Zionists.

The underground liberation movement in Palestine which had sent Bergson, Ben-Ami, Rafaeli, Eri Jabotinsky, Ben-Eliezer, Merlin and others on missions to help save European Jews was left in ruins by the Stern-Raziel split and the realities of the world war; but the Irgun was revitalized towards the end of 1943 with the goal of intensifying pressure on the British to open the gates of Palestine.

The committee sent Arye Ben-Eliezer back to Palestine, where he helped choose a new Irgun commander, a recent arrival from Poland named Menachem Begin. Ben-Eliezer, who had come to America a year before Bergson, had worked assiduously for the committee as it evolved over the years, traveling frequently across the country to help set up and nurture Bergsonite branches in several major cities. A handsome, soft-spoken man with dark eyes, he was once chased from the Chicago train depot by movie fans who thought he was Charles Boyer. Although he was an effective speaker and a key member of the committee's "cabinet," he was pleased to be back home. Begin made him his top aide in charge of political affairs.

In Palestine, the wartime truce with the British was over – it was now felt that there was no choice but armed struggle against London's White Paper policy. (In April 1944, Ben-Eliezer was captured by the British and imprisoned in a detention camp in the Horn of Africa, where he remained until escaping four years later with Yitzhak Shamir, Begin's eventual successor as prime minister of Israel. Soon after independence, he became deputy speaker of the First Knesset).[2]

As the underground's revolt against the British gained momentum, the Bergsonites in America were coming to the conclusion that they needed a new organizational structure to meet the demands of the changing political situation. The core group in the spring of 1944 was down to Bergson, Merlin and Eri Jabotinsky. Ben-Ami, who had run the New York office, and Rafaeli/Hadani had joined the U.S. army in September 1943.

They had all worked very well together, despite occasional bridling over the fact that the head of the unit, Bergson, was the youngest among them. The disagreements were mostly over tactics and style. Ben-Ami had been critical of Bergson's arrogance when dealing with the "little people" in the organization, for example. But there were no major policy differences until 1947. The Palestinians still acted as a military unit, and Peter Bergson was undisputedly the man in charge.

For three years, Rafaeli, a debonair, Heidelberg-educated man, had criss-crossed the country on behalf of the committee, and was considered a top organizer on the grass-roots level. He set up and ran the Chicago office, and worked at a furious pace during the campaign to push the Rescue Resolution through Congress. Merlin remained in charge of administration, while Bergson was still the man in front, commuting between New York and Washington and concentrating on political affairs. None of them would marry during their busy years in the Bergson group, but Merlin, as well as Bergson, met their future wives in the course of their efforts. By mid-1944, Betty Keane Caplan had become a publicist for the committee in Washington, and Merlin met Winona Weber, his future wife, that same year, after she began as a volunteer in the Chicago office.

It was a dedicated, collegial group, but Bergson's friends as well as his enemies agreed that it was he who remained the moving spirit, the focus, the spokesman, the captivator. His energy and inventiveness were inexhaustible; he was, in essence, a revolutionary devoted to his cause, and this totally secular scion of the Kook rabbinical dynasty was possessed by a religious intensity in the matter of saving Jewish lives.[3]

In deciding upon a new course in the wake of the establishment of the WRB, Bergson, Merlin, Eri Jabotinsky and their colleagues created a new committee, patterned after the committees of national liberation of the various occupied countries, such as the French Committee for National Liberation.

The Hebrew Committee of National Liberation (HCNL) was officially launched by Bergson in Washington on May 18, 1944. The new body had several aims: It would continue to agitate for the rescue of the surviving Hebrew remnant in Europe, and in the Bergson tradition, it would orchestrate a dramatic public campaign – this time, to back the Irgun's struggle against Britain's leaders, who were unmoved by the Holocaust and refused to modify immigration policy.[4]

In effect, the Bergson committee saw itself as the representative of the Hebrew (Israeli) nation, a nation that still had no territory of its own. The question the official Zionists had long and improperly raised in regard to the Bergson group now took on a certain legitimacy. For it was not immediately clear if the Bergson group was representing itself only, or the Irgun underground, or both – in any case, it could not claim to represent more than a small minority of Palestinian Jews. Yet it aspired to speak for the entire "Hebrew nation," to be something of an alternative Jewish Agency. Bergson, though he never thought of himself as a revolutionary, had something of the young Bolshevik in him, seeing himself and his well-organized small band as a vanguard that could help bring about the goal of the Zionist revolution, an independent Jewish state in Palestine. But the revolt was that of the Hebrew nation against a colonial power, not a revolution against a social system.[5]

In the transition from the Emergency Committee to the Hebrew Committee and in the aftermath of the WRB's creation, the Bergsonites now gradually divided their focus between the rescue issue and solutions for the post-war period, while the official Zionists' attention still remained almost exclusively on the post-war questions. The Zionists were speaking of a Jewish state, or commonwealth, but did not weigh what would happen to the Jewish People as a whole once the state came into being – an oversight with deep implications for future generations.

In announcing the formation of the HCNL, Bergson declared that what was happening to the Jews of Europe was the culmination of centuries of oppression and persecution, of ghettos, pogroms, economic strangulation, and endless humiliation and insult. "The Hebrew nation can no longer endure the status quo," he said. In a letter to Secretary of State Hull informing him about the new committee, Bergson spelled out the group's definition of the term "Hebrew nation" as those Hebrews already in Palestine and those in occupied Europe: "It is essential to maintain the clear distinction between Hebrews, who are people belonging to a specific national and political entity – the Hebrew Nation – and the 'Jewish People,' which is a religious and ethnic entity. 'Jewish people' can be Americans, Russians, Britons, etc. Hebrews can be but one thing – *Hebrews*." (Again, if the word Israeli is substituted for Hebrew, it clarifies what the Bergsonites were talking about, namely, the difference between Israelis and Jews.)[6]

The Hebrew Committee, chaired by Bergson, included Merlin as secretary-general; Eri Jabotinsky; Aryeh Ben-Eliezer (in name only, since he had just been taken prisoner by the British in Palestine); Prof. Pierre Delougez, a Palestinian archeologist who taught at the University of Chicago; Palestinian businessman Theodore Bennahum; and Jeremiah Helpern, a former naval captain who had been close to Ze'ev Jabotinsky. The Bergson core group also set up a parallel mass organization for its American supporters – the American League for a Free Palestine, headed by Senator Gillette, who had been co-chairman of the Emergency Committee. This body, whose executive board included Ben Hecht, Louis Bromfield, Congressmen Will Rogers, Jr., and Andrew Somers, also took over the Emergency Committee's functions, sponsoring full-page ads that demanded such moves as the setting up of emergency rescue shelters in Palestine. Its formation was in keeping with the Bergson group's distinction between Hebrews – future Israelis – and American Jews and their gentile supporters.[7]

The succession of committees during the Bergson group's eight years in America was sometimes confusing, especially since there was much overlapping. The original Committee for a Jewish Army, for example, was still not dissolved when the Emergency Committee to Save the Jewish People of Europe was formed at the July 1943 Emergency Conference. Ben Hecht once remarked that every time he turned around, Bergson had created another committee. The playwright and journalist could not abide the long titles; they sounded too complicated or slightly pompous to him. But Bergson was a stickler for "getting it right" and weighed every word in the verbose titles.[8]

Critics of the Bergson group (for instance, the *Washington Post* which followed the official Zionist line in attacking "the maze" of Bergsonite organizations) refused to recognize the legitimate reasons for the changing of the primary goals, for adapting to the quickly changing realities of history; and a good number of people assumed that the Zionists were right in saying that it was all a dance of the seven veils. But the transition from Jewish army, to Emergency rescue, to Hebrew liberation seemed perfectly logical to most of the Bergsonites' supporters. Ben Hecht, in welcoming creation of the Hebrew Committee, wired Bergson: "The Jewish cause has been too long under the domination of people like Stephen Wise and his fellow Jewish fossils. What the Jews need most is a high wind to blow these ossified politicos out of their places. They are the dust that has gathered over a lost cause." And Congressman Rogers, praising Bergson's "unquestioned integrity, tireless energy and dynamic leadership," predicted that the young Palestinian would become a leading figure in the post-war world.[9]

The creation of the HCNL, not surprisingly, prompted a new wave of outrage in the organized American Jewish community. As Josiah DuBois noted in a conversation with Morgenthau, the Jewish press now not only continued to ignore the extermination, but even the Palestine question was bumped off the front pages to make room for attacks on the Bergson group.[10]

Nahum Goldmann called the HCNL a "fraud." Leon Feuer of the American Zionist Emergency Council said, "Every movement has its lunatic fringe." Wise's lieutenant, Meir Grossman, used the rabbi's favorite description, "hoax," and said the Bergsonites were "a bunch of clowns," and Dr. Israel Goldstein in the *Washington Post* called it "buffoonery and comic opera drollery... Here is truly a case of a self-appointed group of four or five irresponsible young men who have assumed the role of Don Quixote and Pancho setting forth singlehandedly" to re-establish Hebrew self-determination.[11]

Labor Zionist Marie Syrkin, daughter of a founder of left-wing Zionism, Nahum Syrkin, added the epithet "charlatans" to the chorus, but at least she delved a bit deeper into the subject: Syrkin, who would remain an intellectual leader for the next forty years (a Zionism, like Goldmann's, that did not include living in the Zionist state), wrote that the Bergsonite ideology stressing the difference between the Jewish religion and the Hebrew nation was based upon a cunning appraisal of the fact that most American Jews, assimilationists, were terrified of accusations of dual loyalty.[12]

The latest Zionist assault against what they perceived as a direct attempt by the Bergsonites to wrest control of the world Zionist movement resulted in a serious setback for the Bergson group. As historian David Wyman put it, "The rush of animosity took a heavy toll on Bergsonite rescue activities... The Emergency Committee did not go under. But never again was it as effective as it had been before."[13]

The Hebrew Committee bought the palatial former Iranian embassy building on embassy row in Washington for $63,000, hoisted a blue and white flag with a Star of David, and became the "Hebrew Embassy" on Massachusetts Avenue – at a time when the official Jewish Agency of Palestine maintained only a small office in the capital. Indeed, it must have seemed a quixotic enterprise, and not only to the majority Zionists. After all, there was no "Hebrew nation" in the eyes of Americans. The Allies all had refused to recognize a Hebrew nation. The Bergson group believed it could change this perception through public relations, and in so doing, to clarify the difference between Jews in free countries and the Jews of Palestine and stateless Jews.

In mounting a new propaganda campaign for a nation-state in Palestine, the committee published a magazine, *The Answer*, fortnightly, held rallies and congresses across the country, staged press conferences and pageants, and continued its high-powered lobbying tactics in the corridors of power.

Millions of European Jews were dead, and more were still to die. Their murder was expedited by the fact that they had no country of their own. The survivors could no longer be considered Germans, Poles or Rumanians; and in Palestine, under the terms set out by the White Paper, half a million Jews had no hope for sovereignty. The HCNL made it clear that American Jews did not belong to this Hebrew nation unless they chose to emigrate. During the first press conference in the reception hall of the ornate four-story embassy, Bergson declared that American

Jews "are Americans of Hebrew descent... adherents of the Jewish religion. They do not belong to the renascent Hebrew nation any more than the Hon. Justice Frank Murphy 'belongs' to the Irish nation or General William Knudsen 'belongs' to the Danish nation... 'Hebrews' and 'Jews' are not synonymous terms." In *The Answer*, Bergson wrote that the U.S. government would never really listen to Stephen Wise on the Palestine question because an "American rabbi" had no right or authority to speak for Jews of other countries.[14]

The Bergson group had begun to differentiate between American Jewry and the "Hebrew nation" three years earlier. When the United States entered the war, it had become necessary for the Committee for a Jewish Army to lengthen its name in order to specify that it was not for American Jews – who would serve in the U.S. army – but for Palestinian and Stateless European Jews. Now, more than ever, it seemed clear to them that the Allies' failure to recognize the dispossessed Jews of Europe as a nation had encouraged the genocide. In major international conferences from 1938 to 1946 and in official pronouncements, the Allies used the euphemism "refugee" (or "persecuted minorities" or "unfortunate people"); the word "Jew" seemed to have been taboo. In a brief presidential message from the White House in March 1944 marking the first anniversary of the Warsaw Ghetto uprising, the word "Jews" was not even mentioned.[15]

The "refugee" designation obfuscated the real issue and restricted action. It was part of deliberate Allied policy. This was true at the Evian Conference in January 1942, where the mass murder of Jews was not included in the Allies list of crimes against civilian populations; the Bermuda Conference in the spring of 1943; and at the Moscow Conference in November 1943, where atrocities against the Jews of Poland were described as "slaughter inflicted upon the Polish people" – even though the Poles themselves (and of course, the Germans) regarded the Jews as a separate nation.

The Bergsonites insisted all along that the Allied policy was tantamount to giving the Germans *carte blanche* to continue their extermination campaign. The Germans characterized the Jews as a diabolical enemy nation, while the Allies refused to grant a national identity to the stateless Jews.

The Bergson group also found it appalling that Jewish, and especially Zionist, organizations did not focus on the question of the national identity of the Jewish victims of Nazism or press an indifferent Roosevelt even to recognize that it was the Jews who were being exterminated, not "humanity" or "refugees."[16]

The activists in the Bergson group were also upset by the name War "Refugee" Board, but voiced only mild criticism in public because it might have harmed the WRB. The establishment organizations, on the other hand, welcomed the fact that the word Jew, or Jewish, did not appear in the name of the special agency set up to save Jews. They still believed it would create an anti-Semitic firestorm in America if the saving of Jews were to become a war aim, or if American taxpayers had to foot the bill for rescue operations. But behind this fear was the general lack of understanding of the difference between an American Jew, whose nationality is American, and Polish or Russian Jews, who were never regarded as members of the Polish or Russian nations by those governments, and who, for the most part, did not regard themselves as such. As a result, American Jewish leaders were paralyzed by fear that they would be accused of dual loyalties.

For the Bergson group, by contrast, the identity question – the differences between Hebrews and Jews (Israelis and Jews in post-1948 terms) – was to become a major programmatic issue in the years leading up to the creation of the state.

In September 1944, the United Nations' forty-four members did not include a government or organization to represent either the Jews of Palestine or Germany's Jewish victims in Eastern and Central Europe. Toward the war's end, the UN Relief and Rehabilitation Administration, in keeping with the Moscow Declaration, shipped surviving Jews back to their former homes in Germany and Poland, on the theory that they were nationals of those states. The Jews were carted back to countries where they were not wanted, where their families had been murdered and their property stolen. In 1946, Jews who were returned to Poland were greeted by bloody pogroms, and many survivors of the Holocaust were massacred by their former neighbors.

The Hebrew Committee sent a delegation to lobby for its program at the UNRRA conference in Montreal in the fall of 1944, where they persuaded the Cuban representative, Gustavo Gutierrez, to propose that "the Hebrews of Europe be recognized as a nation," but the move was rejected by a large majority. In November 1944, following a WRB report on the Auschwitz extermination camp, Peter Bergson demanded that the Hebrew people be represented on the War Crimes Commission of the United Nations, but this, too, was to no avail.[17]

Between November 1942 and March 1944, the Bergson group never mentioned the Irgun in its propaganda campaign for the saving of Jewish lives. The leaders, all of whom had been committed Irgunists, believed there was no room for partisan

Jewish-Zionist politics during the gravest emergency that ever confronted the Jewish people. But now, as the Hebrew Committee, the Bergson group reverted to a position of support for the Irgun and the national liberation movement in Palestine. Bergson himself, however, did not regard his group as an arm of the military organization but as an independent auxiliary, a parallel group.[18]

Ben Hecht, for one, felt much more at home working in support of the Irgun in its struggle against the British. He had a romantic, naive vision of the Irgunists as "new Jews," unfrightened and heroic. This would eventually lead him to the use of some tasteless, excessive language in full-page ads that appeared to celebrate violence.[19] Rallies were held, for instance, on behalf of a "24-year-old Hebrew patriot," Mattityahu Shmuelevitz, whom the British had sentenced to death for shooting at a policeman. (He missed. Thirty-five years later, Shmuelevitz would hold a senior position in the Israeli government under Begin.)[20]

The official Zionists immediately put pressure on the government to register Bergson and his colleagues as foreign agents, something the Bergsonites welcomed, since this would have meant some form of recognition of the existence of a Hebrew nation. The HCNL said it considered itself as an agent in the United States for the interests of a nation abroad, but maintained that its officers took orders from no one, following their own consciences. (In fact, Bergson did not seek clearance from Begin for any of their activities.) Finally, in July 1944, the Justice Department accepted their claim and registered the group as agents of the Hebrew nation, a disagreeable development for the Zionists after all.[21]

By then, the committee's headquarters had already taken on the full trappings of a diplomatic mission. Committee members converted the innumerable rooms of the historic mansion at 2315 Massachusetts Avenue into offices, reception rooms and sleeping quarters. A press photograph released by the HCNL showed Bergson, Merlin and Bennahum discussing some issue on a garden path next to the embassy's ivy-covered facade. Bergson's future wife, Betty Keane Caplan, who was writing for *The Answer*, in addition to her office and public relations duties, gave a gushing description of the stately mansion's spiraling marble staircase and elegant French windows.[22]

But the Hebrew embassy was not just window dressing. "There was tremendous activity in and around the embassy, with lectures, discussions, receptions for diplomats and congressmen," recalled lawyer Charles E. Stein, who was a high school student in Washington when he joined the office staff as a volunteer. He worked in the mail room and in the archives under Betty Keane Caplan. He felt that the embassy was "the only Zionist show in town – no one else seemed to be doing anything about the Holocaust. These people had real expertise in public relations... they struck the right chords, and generated an enormous amount of activity."[23]

To Stein and other volunteers, Peter Bergson was a heroic figure, a mercurial and mysterious Hebrew messenger whom they idolized. "Bergson and the other Palestinians seemed like King Arthur's knights. There was something noble about the way they acted and what they were doing."

Like the embassy, the committee's New York offices, behind frosted doors on West 45th Street, were also buzzing, with a bank of desks occupied by advertising experts, journalists, secretaries and scholars. Most of the editorial staff of *The Answer* worked under Merlin in the Manhattan offices. There was a dedicated staff on subsistence salaries, and many volunteers, such as Alex Wilf, who gave up his home and business to work for the cause. One successful magazine and book editor, Harry Louis Selden, took a six-month leave from his lucrative job and, at Bergson's suggestion, came to work for the committee full time for one dollar a year.

"The six months stretched into five years," Selden recalled a generation later. He greatly admired Bergson's "genius and ingenuity," and never regretted his commitment. "I backed all but the most extravagantly irresponsible proposals, and performed some other useful functions: I wrote articles and memorandums for dissemination; I edited the copious materials we produced; I talked on the radio and to meetings; and I held seminars. But most of all, I think, I served as a balance wheel. The people engaged in the work – volunteer and paid – were of varied characters and temperaments. Many, though their intentions were good, fell (like myself) below Peter's expectations; and though Peter was, in the ordinary course, the soul of kindness, he was sometimes less than tolerant of inadequacy or inferiority and, under stress, was sometimes less than kind in his reactions to them. Understanding this, I was generally able to soothe injured feelings and smooth ruffled feathers."[24]

Selden, who regarded the Palestinians as disciplined and loyal to each other, always considered himself an outsider, which he was content to remain. Although he knew there were differences among them (especially in the post-war period), and between them and Begin's staff, "I did not probe and I was not informed. I was not happy that these differences existed, but I could not have presumed to adjudicate." According to Selden, the continual and often vicious establishment attacks on the committee and on Bergson personally did have an effect on Bergson, "but he did not let it show, which is one of the reasons Ben Hecht found him indomitable. What the assaults did was to spur him on, as it did the rest of us..."[25]

Selden, like all those who joined the Bergson group, regularly received letters and phone calls from prominent Jews pointing out that he had been "taken in by charlatans." He had met Rabbi Wise on several occasions, and the contrast with the idealistic Palestinians seemed to him quite stark. Wise gave an impression of pomposity and arrogance, while the young Palestinians, Selden felt, were hard-working altruists, devoted to the cause of rescue and revival. The distinction drawn by Bergson between "Hebrew" and "Jew" made complete sense to Selden, who consciously chose to remain an American Jew, and not to join the Hebrew-Israeli nation.[26]

The Hebrew Committee took as its motto a line from Thomas Jefferson: "Resistance to tyranny is obedience to God," and vowed to force the British to open the gates of Palestine to the hundreds of thousands of Jews still imperiled in Hungary in the last months of the war.[27] The HCNL and its American support group, led by persons like Gillette and Selden, continually sought co-belligerent status for the Hebrew nation, held rallies and conferences on the situation of the surviving Jews, pressed for more congressional resolutions, and worked with the WRB in the drive for creation of temporary shelters in neutral countries. Still, the committee's campaign for rescue, in the wake of the WRB's establishment, was only an echo compared to the Bergsonites' work leading up to the Rescue Resolution. A second Emergency Conference to Save the Jewish People of Europe, held at the Hotel Commodore in New York on August 7-8, 1944, had nowhere near the impact of the first conference held in the pre-WRB era,[28] though large-scale action by the allied governments was still awaited.

One of the WRB's major efforts was to seek temporary havens for the rescued victims of the Germans; in this matter, the Bergsonites continued to work as closely as possible with the board. Peter Bergson was "an unofficial but ubiquitous presence in the WRB," and his "influence was pervasive." It was clear to the board's members that their activities in 1944 and 1945 paralleled suggestions which the Emergency Committee had formulated in mid-1943.[29]

The mainstream Zionists had also included proposals for temporary shelters in their programs, but little pressure was applied, and the idea of establishing temporary shelters in Palestine was summarily dismissed. In a speech at the American Jewish Conference in 1943, Rabbi Abba Hillel Silver had mocked those who sought a way around British objections by asking for only temporary shelter in Palestine. "Are we to ask merely for the right of asylum in our historic home... Is this Jewish statesmanship? Is this Jewish vision, courage, faith?"[30]

All along, the attitude exemplified by Silver's remarks had been a basic point of divergence between the Bergsonites and the establishment. "What Bergson and the WRB staff had in common was that both gave rescue priority," according to one student of the WRB. Palestine was an issue of extreme importance, but during the war, it could only be thought of as a possible site for refugee camps. Doctrinaire Zionists could not face this reality.[31]

Bergson wrote to Lord Halifax, the British ambassador, pleading that the contention between Britain and the Jewish People over Palestine be set aside in the emergency, and urging that temporary camps be established there. It was an appeal to recognize the moral and legal rights of the surviving Jews of Europe to emigrate to Palestine before the German extermination machine devoured them. After the war, Bergson wrote, the refugees would be sent elsewhere. It was a call for a compromise "which will not decide anything for the future, nor affect the present status of men or territories, but will merely keep human beings alive." Of course, the letter went unanswered – the British did not once respond to the hundreds of letters and telegrams that came from the Bergsonites and their supporters, since the group was considered affiliated with the Irgun, an enemy body.[32]

Meanwhile, the WRB asked for and obtained UNRRA help in finding other temporary shelters, maintaining them and arranging transportation. Thousands of rescued Jews were brought from Europe to UNRRA camps in the Middle East and North Africa. But the board was continually confronted by roadblocks set up by State Department officials, who deliberately delayed coordination with the British to establish a camp at Cyrenaica on the coast of North Africa. One department official sneered that the Jews were trying to take over the functions of the State Department.[33]

In theory, the best shelter was America itself – the "haven of the oppressed." But Roosevelt and the State Department disdained the idea of bringing rescued Jews to the U.S. for the duration of the war. The Bergson group pressed for a change in the government's attitude; and Josiah DuBois went so far as to suggest to Pehle and Morgenthau that the Jews could at least be treated as POWs and interned in the United States.[34]

FDR finally appeared to relent on the idea of temporary shelters in June 1944, when he established the Emergency Refugee Shelter at Fort Ontario, Oswego, New

York. One thousand stateless Jews who had fled Germany, Austria and the Balkans to Southern Italy were brought to the United States outside the immigration laws that had been so strictly upheld by Long, Bloom, and others. Roosevelt, in advising Congress of his action, specified that the one thousand Jews would be held under "appropriate security restrictions until they could be returned to their homelands" after the war.[35]

The refugees themselves recognized that the Bergsonites were among the first to promote the idea of temporary havens in the United States and were the most persistent in pressing for it, with a nationwide drive and advertising campaign, and pro-haven editorials and articles in many newspapers, including all of the Hearst chain. In addition, Gillette had introduced a resolution to the Senate calling for temporary havens on Ellis Island and elsewhere in the U.S. John Pehle at the WRB and Morgenthau discussed plans for emergency shelters with the President, and Pehle reported that he was "very favorably disposed." When FDR's order brought one thousand Jews to the Oswego shelter, the refugees thanked not only the President and the WRB, but the Bergson group as well. "God be with you," their telegram to the Bergsonites began, "Blessed be those who assist you in your holy work for the salvation of the remnants of Israel."[36]

Roosevelt's Oswego action proved to be only a token gesture, aimed at defusing criticism of his own attitude toward admitting Jews – even temporarily – into the United States. "We do not need any more free ports at the present time," FDR said.[37] The Bergson group had loudly hailed Roosevelt for Oswego, and never attacked him for not following up on the highly publicized, but superficial humanitarian move.

The official Zionists rarely gave positive endorsements to suggestions for temporary havens because Palestine remained their all-consuming passion. The Bergson group fought a losing battle against both the British and the Zionists to establish transit camps in Palestine for Hungarian Jews who would soon be shipped to the death camps.

From a logistical point of view, Palestine was the perfect location for emergency shelter. It could be reached by land route from the Balkans; thus no crucial shipping would have to be diverted. and the Jewish community in Palestine clamored for an opportunity to shelter and feed their tormented kin. The Bergson group, in August 1944, said that "in order to avoid political controversies, the Jews saved from the Nazis would be admitted to Palestine only on a temporary basis" – a treasonous view in the minds of a Wise or a Silver, who still regarded rescue a secondary issue. "Despite a distinct decline in activity during 1944, the Bergsonite Emergency Committee continued as the leading force in building pressures for rescue," according to historian Wyman. But there was no satisfaction whatsoever to be gained; only death lay down the road.[38]

In the months before March 1944, when the Nazis occupied their erstwhile satellite, Hungary, dictator Miklos von Horthy officially informed the British that the Jews in Hungary could leave if they were granted visas to Palestine. In May, two months after the Germans marched into Hungary, Adolf Eichmann, in charge of the logistics of extermination, promised to suspend deportations of Jews from Hungary to Auschwitz and to sell one million Jews in exchange for 10,000 trucks, and sizable quantities of soap, coffee and cocoa. It was believed that SS chief Heinrich Himmler, who was known to be seeking a "separate peace," was behind the proposal. The offer was made to a Zionist relief official in Budapest, Joel Brand, who was sent to Istanbul to meet with Jewish Agency officials. But British officials blocked Brand's mission on the grounds that there could be no dealing with the Nazis – even though it was apparent that Eichmann's demands could be regarded as an invitation for negotiations, and that some arrangement could have been worked out that would not in any way help the German war effort.[39]

Brand was held in Cairo for three months under orders of the top-ranking British official in the Middle East, Lord Moyne. Jewish Agency leaders, Pehle, Morgenthau, the WRB's Ira Hirschmann and others, supported continuing negotiations, but the British were implacably opposed. In Washington, in the first week of June, Lord Halifax delivered an aide-memoire to the State Department which said: "Implied suggestion that we should accept responsibility for maintenance of additional million persons is equivalent to asking the Allies to suspend essential military operations." It was tantamount to a mass death sentence, and the Soviets concurred.[40]

The United States had informed the Soviet Union of the offer and had given assurances that no deal would be struck that might split the Allies (Eichmann had said that the trucks would be used only against the Russians). The Soviet reaction in mid-June was to demand an end to any negotiations.[41]

The Zionist leaders were "far from apathetic about the slaughter in Hungary. But they committed their resources to the Palestine-commonwealth resolution introduced in Congress in January 1944." Wise, Silver and Goldmann were busy elsewhere, so "the responsibility for pressing the rescue issue fell to a second level of leaders in the World Jewish Congress and in the faltering American Jewish Conference... they took little action." But the establishment did hold a mass demonstration in New York on July 31, calling for immediate implementation of von Horthy's offer.[42]

Wise, busy with the Palestine question, did not get a response out of FDR until October 25, 1944. The President cryptically wrote the rabbi, "We are doing something about it." Ten weeks later, on Jan. 8, 1945, Wise finally got around to raising the issue again. In a letter to David Niles, the White House liaison and a personal friend, Wise said: "I haven't troubled you with the details of the fight [to save Hungarian Jews], which has been as nasty as can be."[43]

The Bergson group continued to try to keep the plight of the Jews in Hungary before the public eye. On July 9, 1944, the Bergsonites sponsored special services in Hungarian churches throughout the United States. The services were recorded by the Office of War Information and broadcast to the people of Hungary. William Randolph Hearst once again lent editorial support to the Bergson campaign, while friends of the committee in Congress – Gillette, Ferguson, Somers, Baldwin, Taft, Lane, Scott, Murray, Thomas – introduced resolutions urging the President to press Britain to allow Hungarian Jews temporary refuge in Palestine. (The handful of Jewish congressmen, however, did nothing to further the resolutions. In fact, four of the seven Jews summoned Bergson to a House hearing room, where Samuel Dickstein of New York threatened him with immediate deportation if he continued to lead a vocal campaign for rescue.)[44]

Bergson, in a cable to Prime Minister Churchill on July 9, 1944, pleaded for temporary shelters to save the remaining Jews of Hungary: "...if His Majesty's government persistently refuses this time too to establish emergency refugee shelters in Palestine, it will be conclusive proof of its indifference to plight and agony of martyred Hebrew people in Europe."[45] To the British, Bergson was an outlaw, unworthy of any reply, but it was doubtful whether the British would have been moved by imprecations from any quarter.

At a press conference on July 30, Bergson tried again, reiterating his group's position that, in order to overcome Britain's White Paper policy, Hungarian Jews be admitted only temporarily to the Holy Land, on the Oswego pattern. Palestine itself was of secondary importance at this moment in history, "only one thing... is paramount: the rescue of human lives," he said. The British would not have to pay for the operation – funds would be provided by the WRB, the Jews of Palestine and relief organizations. Bergson said that if the British refused to establish the emergency shelters, the Colonial Office would "actually share the guilt of the murder of Hebrews in Europe in the event the deportations from Hungary to Poland are resumed."[46]

By July 7, 1944, Eichmann had already deported 400,000 of the one million Jews in Hungary. But even under Nazi guns, thousands of other Jews were being saved, due to the works of the War Refugee Board and its heroic emissary in Budapest, Raoul Wallenberg. The WRB gave the situation in Hungary top priority, and took a position on temporary shelters that paralleled that of the Bergsonites. The Bergson group presented the government with a petition signed by half a million Americans – a tremendous effort for that time – asking immediate support of the bipartisan congressional resolution that called on FDR to urge the British to issue temporary visas to the Jews in Hungary. But, in the face of Zionist and State Department opposition, the proposal collapsed.[47]

In September 1944, during one of Nahum Goldmann's visits to the State Department, the Zionist leader said that the Palestine-shelters resolution was nothing but a gimmick for self-promotion of the Bergson group, and termed the plan "absurd." He assured the State Department officials that the Zionists had already made certain that Congressman Bloom and Senator Connolly – the respective chairmen of the House and Senate Foreign Relations Committees – would kill the resolution in committee. "...the Zionists strenuously opposed any plan to send Jews to Palestine with the understanding that they might have to leave after the war. Such a concession legitimized by the approval of Congress, might establish a precedent that could impair the Jewish claim to Palestine." Once again, there was a stark difference of perception between the small group of Palestinians who had come out of the Jabotinsky movement and establishment Zionists, as represented by Wise, Goldmann and Silver.[48]

Britain recognized that Palestine was ideal as a haven – but not for Jews. Since 1939, the British had admitted tens of thousands of Poles, Greeks, Yugoslavs and others to temporary shelter in the League of Nations mandated territory. But when it came to the Jews, the White Paper policy prevailed, and the British continued to maintain that there would be an Arab revolt if Jews were allowed even temporary asylum in Palestine. There was evidence of this: The leader of Palestine's Arabs, Amin el-Husseini, the Mufti of Jerusalem, was a guest of Hitler's in Nazi Europe, working closely with the SS, and envisaging a "final solution" for the Jews of Palestine.[49]

The British were not about to make an exception for the Jews of Hungary. What would they do with a million Jews? In any case, Britain could point to the support it was getting on the temporary-haven issue from the Zionists themselves. There were only a few voices in the wilderness calling for pragmatism and sanity in the face of this inhumanity.

The behavior of the leaders of the Jewish community in Palestine in reaction to the Holocaust is beyond the scope of this book, but in the briefest terms, it can be said that, even though the circumstances were different, their behavior mirrored that of the Zionist leadership in America. The leadership of that community – of the *Yishuv* – was not in a position to launch any kind of major effort on behalf of European Jews – they had no autonomy, let alone ships (as has often been pointed out), nor did they have the potential to do what American Jewish and Zionist leaders could have done. In the first years of the war, they were directly threatened by Rommel's advancing troops. Even so, they did little to effect rescue; in some cases, they were opposed to any outcry whatsoever.

It was apparent that there were basic conflicts between Jewish interests and Zionist interests. For example, in January 1943, soon after Rabbi Wise had released the figure of two million dead, Dov Joseph, a key Jewish Agency figure in Palestine, advised against publicizing the death toll, since it might weaken the Zionist claim for a Jewish state. Joseph's reasoning was that the enemies of Zionism would say that there were now too few Jews left to make good the claim for a large territory. Most important, the Jewish Agency leaders did not instruct their people in the United States to put rescue at the top of the agenda.[50]

When the Bergson group sent Eri Jabotinsky to Turkey in April 1944 to help rescue Jews from the Balkans, he met constant interference from Jewish Agency representatives there, as well as from British and U.S. officials, including Ira Hirschmann. His experience rescuing refugees in 1938-1941 was for nought; Jewish Agency envoy Ehud Avriel, and Nahum Goldmann, pressured the Turks to expel him. He was put on a train for Palestine, where the British arrested him.[51]

Israeli historians have shown that rescue was a secondary issue, not only for Ben-Gurion, Weizmann, Shertok and other labor Zionists, who chose not to spur American Zionists to press for rescue action, but also for the underground Zionists led by Menachem Begin. The Irgun never showed much interest in the Bergson group's efforts to mobilize public opinion for a rescue effort. Begin makes no mention of their campaign when he refers to Bergson and the committee in passing in his memoir of the period.[52]

In later years, Begin's aides, such as Haim Landau, would denigrate the work of the Bergson group, saying that "they were going to fancy cocktail parties in Manhattan while we were fighting the British."[53] There was a certain truth to that. The Bergsonites were not living the underground realities of Palestine. But the charge obscured the real issue: No other group in the Jewish world outside occupied Europe was doing as much as the Bergsonites to awaken the world to the realities of the extermination, and to the possibilities of rescuing the surviving remnant of European Jewry, not even those fighting for the establishment of a Jewish homeland.

CHAPTER TEN

A FLAG IS BORN

In the struggle against the British occupation of Palestine, the Bergson group was politically the most radical among Zionist groups in the United States, both in its demands and in the style of its campaign. In the course of its militant drive backing the liberation movement in Palestine, the Bergson group provided a new and unique twist in the history of the Zionist movement: At the height of the struggle for national fulfillment, the Bergsonites were already thinking in terms of post-Zionism.

The outlines of Peter Bergson's post-Zionist analysis were contained in a long letter he wrote to Chaim Weizmann in April 1945. Weizmann, as head of the World Zionist movement, presumed to speak for the interests of all of world Jewry. Bergson, in his unabashed style, started out his letter by reminding Weizmann that American Jews "wish to remain Americans" – a profanity to doctrinaire Zionists then and now. He said that they could not be called Hebrews – Israelis – but are Americans of Hebrew extraction. "Like all Americans, they have a national extraction (Hebrew) quite apart from and in addition to their religious affiliation, which is Jewish... Rabbi Wise is an American who practices the Jewish religion."[1]

He said that the extermination had completely altered the position of the Jews in the world and the future existence of the state that would arise in Palestine. The key to the situation, he said, was the problem of the surviving European Jews, which depended on resolution of the Palestine question. He believed that the British would not relax their restrictions on immigration of Jews and that Palestine's fate would be sealed if the survivors were not "repatriated."[2]

The Bergsonites wanted the Zionist leadership to initiate a unilateral political action which would culminate in a declaration of independence of the "Hebrew Republic of Palestine." It was precisely the kind of policy Ben-Gurion, Weizmann's "radical" rival, would adopt in the spring of 1948.[3]

Bergson's letter, written in the last month of the war, also referred to the Allies' continued refusal to recognize the Hebrew nation – that is, Palestinian and stateless European Jews – and said that the results of the confusion about the Jews' national status were "four million dead... The results were refusal to recognize their murder as a war crime. The results are refusal by UNRRA to give one loaf of bread to the 400,000 surviving, starving Hebrews in Rumania whom it insists on treating on the same footing as it treats their Rumanian murderers."[4]

Bergson quoted an American statesman who had told him, "the Jews must make up their mind what they are." This was the crux of the problem. Bergson took the position that Palestine should be "a free state and not a 'Jewish state.'" The Hebrew nation would inhabit Palestine along with minority populations, which would be integrated with full rights in a democratic society.

Bergson expressed faith in the young generation in Palestine, both his generation and the one growing up, and asked why their interests should be in the hands of American and British Zionists. He pointed out the errors of his own movement in demanding a "Jewish army" instead of a "Hebrew army," explaining that his committee over a period of four years had outgrown old notions and had learned from experience in a rapidly changing world. He called on the Jewish Agency and its governing arm, the *Vaad Leumi* (National Committee), to reconstitute themselves into a provisional government. Jews of other nations, like America and Britain, would not be included. He said the Hebrew Committee would acquiesce to any decisions made by that provisional government. Bergson also lamented the continuing offensive against his group by the Zionist and Jewish organizations, and noted that the committee had refrained from launching a counter-attack, despite the "sins and crimes" and the "hysterical mud-slinging" to which it had been subjected. The bid to deport the young Palestinians had failed, and the Hebrew flag was still waving over the Hebrew Embassy on Massachusetts Avenue.[5]

Weizmann ignored the Bergson letter. To Weizmann, as to the British, a reply would be tantamount to dealing with the enemy. The "Bergson problem" was a matter for low-level Zionist functionaries to contend with, and the mud-slinging campaign continued unabated.[6]

The Morgenthau Diary shows that Bergson's concerns as expressed to Weizmann were of importance to American Jews, such as Morgenthau himself. The Treasury secretary, in May 1944, showed that he was disturbed by the questions the young Palestinian was raising, primarily with the issue of Jewish identity that Bergson outlined in his letter to Weizmann. When Morgenthau told his aides that he thought it unfortunate that Bergson had set himself up in Washington as "representing the Hebrews of Europe and Palestine," Luxford said that Bergson was doing just what De Gaulle had done with the Free French. Morgenthau replied, somewhat defensively, "Yes, but I don't happen to think the Jews are a race. I think it is a religion... I happen to think of myself as an American citizen of the Jewish faith." Luxford answered: "Bergson agrees with you a hundred per cent."[7]

As stated in Bergson's letter to Weizmann, the Hebrew Committee was pressing for the establishment of a provisional government. This was a new element in the struggle for a state in Palestine. Even as the Jewish Agency, on May 27, 1945, petitioned the British government to declare Palestine a Jewish state, its officials actually believed that independence was decades away. When David Ben-Gurion did make the move for independence three years later, he had to fight massive internal opposition, led by the followers of Weizmann. The threat that the "Jabotinsky people" would set up a provisional government pushed Ben-Gurion to act against those who opposed taking immediate steps. Ben-Gurion had no faith in American Zionist and Jewish leaders or in Weizmann and Wise's "patient diplomacy" and felt, as did the Bergson group, that the Jewish masses and public opinion must be mobilized.[8]

In May 1945, the revitalized Irgun in Palestine ostensibly followed the line set forth by the self-styled political arm – the Hebrew Committee – and urged the establishment of a provisional government that would lead the "revolution" against the British and set up a legislature to "draft a constitution for the Hebrew Republic," as Menachem Begin wrote in *The Revolt*.[9]

Yet Begin himself was remote from the programs and ideas of the Bergson group. Although he never issued a public statement disowning the Bergsonites, Begin was against the "Hebrew nation" concept, and he felt that the political struggle being led by Bergson thousands of miles from the realities of Palestine was a minor sideshow compared to the armed struggle against the British. Begin feared that an Irgun initiative to set up a provisional government if the Labor Zionists did not do so would lead to civil war. In 1945, this appraisal was undoubtedly right and Bergson was wrong.[10]

Begin's Irgun remained in conflict with the American committee over the question of priorities. The Bergson group's budget was devoted to political propaganda activities, and Bergson had insisted on keeping a certain distance from the Irgun, especially during the time of the Emergency Committee to Save the Jewish People of Europe, when a completely non-partisan stance was vital. After the Bergson group evolved into the Hebrew Committee, its links with the Irgun became much stronger. Yitshaq Ben-Ami believed that the work of the Bergsonites in support of the Irgun struggle from 1945 until independence was a great success, much more successful than the rescue campaign which culminated in the creation of the WRB. "We gave the Irgun fight in Israel the political background, the political tone, the political meaning" that made the Irgun's military actions acceptable to many Americans. "I would say (and can quote Begin) that to a very large extent the fact that neither the British nor the Jewish Agency crushed the Irgun fight is due to our campaign in the United States, and this probably was the most successful effort on our part."[11]

But the differences over policy were becoming sharper. Throughout the years 1944-48, Begin continued to insist that the armed struggle was all-important and that funds should not be diverted to political activities. He met with Ben-Ami, who journeyed to Palestine in October 1945, and although he acknowledged the Bergson group's political and public opinion successes, he demanded that the funds they raised be used exclusively for the Irgun's military efforts. Ben-Ami (who would remain a Begin supporter over the years) agreed with "The Commander," that the Bergson group "was developing an over-emphasis on the political and symbolic aspects of the struggle, ironically tilting backwards towards Jabotinsky's old political Zionism when the time for it was past."[12]

But Samuel Merlin, Jabotinsky's former secretary and Bergson's chief lieutenant, saw it differently. "The Irgun in Palestine took pride in and credit for our work but was totally schizophrenic about us," he recalled. "They would say, 'Who needs ads and propaganda? We need every penny here because we deal in blood, not words.' They sent separate emissaries to the U.S., and there was a tremendous strain in relations between us. Peter thought that we had to ignore Begin, tell him he's wrong, a provincial, an instrument of the Jewish Agency, that we have to do what we think is necessary... Peter behaved as if he didn't care if there would be a break or not."[13]

One of those emissaries was Shmuel Katz, a member of Begin's high command. Katz, who was in close contact with the Hebrew Committee, said he was "filled with admiration for what the Bergson group had achieved in America and believed that we had a common objective," but he deplored the committee's philosophy because of "the unnecessary antagonisms it aroused."[14]

Ironically, at the same time that Begin complained that the Irgun received no funds from the Bergson group, and while the Zionists were saying the committee raised money under false pretenses, J. Edgar Hoover was investigating Zionist charges that most of the Hebrew Committee's funds were being funneled to the "pistol-packing Irgun" by the small group of "adventurists" who led the HCNL.[15] In truth, the committee was spending the money it raised on efforts to bring refugees from Europe to Palestine through the British blockade, and continuing its mass appeals, pageants and lobbying efforts, with the aim of achieving national recognition. The Bergsonites believed that armed struggle in Palestine would be fruitless unless it was accompanied by an effective propaganda and political campaign.

For Bergson, more than for any of his colleagues, independence from the Irgun was crucial because of the role he wanted the committee to fulfill in defining what he frequently referred to as the "human boundaries" of the new state. According to Bergson's post-Zionist vision, the creation of the new state would mean the end of Zionism with all its trappings. The Zionist organizations, claiming to give political representation to all the Jews of the world, would cease to exist. The process of normalization, as his mentor Jabotinsky had envisioned, would begin. The Jews of the new republic would fashion a modern democratic, secular state, with state and religion separated on the American model. Jews outside the new state would have religious ethnic or cultural ties to Israel; but politically, they would be entirely separate.[16]

Although they sometimes paid lip service to these ideas, Begin and other Irgun leaders would remain traditional Zionists, believing, like Ben-Gurion, Weizmann or Golda Meir, in the political unity of the Jews of the world.

In late April 1945, Peter Bergson led a delegation of six HCNL members to seek representation at the assembly convening in San Francisco to establish the United Nations. He sought representation for the Palestinians and stateless European Jews. In effect this meant no role (unless they immigrated to Palestine) for Rabbi Wise or Rabbi Goldstein, Zionist Americans who attended the UN founding conference as outsiders, like Bergson, and representatives of other Jewish organizations. Rabbi Goldstein, who was one of those rare American Zionists who eventually did immigrate to Israel, wrote that it soon became evident at the conference that there would be no hearing for the Jewish People. "They had no status there," he said, adding that it was "a humiliating experience."[17]

Also working the corridors of the assembly was Eliahu Epstein (later Elath), representing the Jewish Agency. Epstein, who would become Israel's first ambassador to the United States, spoke at a San Francisco gathering of local Zionist and Jewish organization leaders. He was taken aback by the vocal support expressed there for the Bergson group, and he would report later to his superiors that "There is little doubt that dissident groups in the United States have apparently gained some hold on Jewish opinion... I have been told that Bergson and his associates have succeeded in attracting to their cause groups of people who have previously been indifferent to Zionism and non-Jews of high social and political position."[18] In public, however, he followed the pattern set over the previous four years by Wise, Goldmann and their associates, holding the Bergsonites up to ridicule, and pretending that they were no more than bothersome gnats. Elath told his audiences that the Bergson group "made some noise like skilled circus people, but no one took them seriously."[19]

What infuriated the Zionists most of all was that journalists paid as much attention to the Bergson group at the UN assembly as to the Jewish Agency. In San Francisco, both Wise and Bergson were staying at the St. Francis Hotel, and on one occasion ran into each other in the lobby. To Bergson's surprise, the aging, ailing Zionist leader (who once thought Bergson was plotting to kill him) invited Bergson to a Saturday service at Temple Emmanuel, the main Reform synagogue of San Francisco's highly assimilated Jewish community. Bergson, who did not feel kindly disposed to Wise – and undoubtedly did not trust him – said that although he drove a car on the Sabbath, he did not think his father, Rabbi Dov Kook, would approve of his driving to a synagogue for Sabbath services.[20]

In the end, neither the Agency nor the Hebrew Committee was accorded any recognition by the UN. But the HCNL, through the Yugoslavian government, did succeed in getting the Mufti's name on the UN's list of war criminals (The Mufti was responsible for the SS Moslem legion in Yugoslavia, which had taken part in the slaughter of Yugoslavian, as well as Jewish, civilians. In spite of this, the British and French allowed the Mufti to escape to refuge in Egypt.)[21]

While the British continued to treat the Mufti as a privileged person, Eri Jabotinsky and scores of other Palestinian Jews were being held at Acre Fortress. At a New York press conference, Merlin said that Jabotinsky's only crime was to try to save Jews who were about to be exterminated in the last weeks of the war. Congressman Andrew Somers reminded the House that Jabotinsky had been sent to Turkey with "full approval of the President's War Refugee Board" in an army plane provided by the State Department. Ben Hecht wrote an open letter in *The New Republic* demanding to know the grounds for Eri's arrest, but the British did not reply. Under the Prevention of Crime Ordinance, the British mandatory regime in Palestine could incarcerate anyone for up to a year without any charges or any access to legal defense. Charges were brought against Jabotinsky – the British asserted that he was linked to the assassination of Lord Moyne on November 6, 1944, in Cairo, an act carried out by the Stern group. But the British finally succumbed to congressional pressure and released Jabotinsky, who rejoined his colleagues in the U.S.[22]

At the end of the war, about 700,000 European Jews who had survived the extermination machine were human driftwood in the rubble of Central and Eastern Europe; and some 100,000 "displaced persons," or DPs – yet another euphemism for Jews – were in camps. They did not want to return to Germany or Poland; almost all wanted to settle in Palestine and nowhere else. Never was the need for the return to Zion more clear.

The Bergson group focused its energies on the issue of the DPs, and on May 15, 1945, Rep. Somers, an Irish-American who had been one of the Bergson group's staunchest friends over the years, introduced a congressional resolution that provided for recognition of the "Hebrew nation" and for national rights for the Jewish survivors in Europe. But the resolution was blocked in the Senate after Zionist leaders pressured Senator James Murray of Montana to withdraw his co-sponsorship of the measure.[23]

However, the committee's campaign for recognition of the "Hebrew nation" did have an effect on U.S. policymakers, as did Rabbi Silver's increasing agitation for a "Jewish state" in Palestine.

A month after the war ended, President Truman appointed University of Pennsylvania Law School dean Earl G. Harrison to inquire into the situation of the "displaced persons." In August, Harrison submitted a report urging that Jews be recognized as Jews and not as members of the nationalities among whom they had lived before the war. This was the essence of what the Bergson group had been talking about for years. The DPs "want to be evacuated to Palestine now, just as other national groups are being repatriated to their homes," Harrison wrote. He recommended that the British be asked to admit 100,000 survivors to Palestine, and Truman specifically requested this from the British. Harrison had reported to Truman after seeing the shocking conditions at the DP camps: "We appear to be treating the Jews as the Nazis treated them, except that we do not exterminate them"[24]

On September 21, 1945, Truman summoned three Bergson group partisans – Guy Gillette, and Senators Warren Magnuson and Owen Brewster – to tell them of the Harrison report, to express his personal concern about the plight of the refugees, and to brief them on negotiations with the British, who were adamantly opposed to bringing the survivors to Palestine.[25]

Truman told the three men that he had forwarded the report to the British and had asked Prime Minister Clement Attlee and Foreign Secretary Ernest Bevin to issue the DPs immigration certificates to Palestine. Truman added that Attlee had told him that the whole Middle East might be "set aflame" if the DPs were allowed into Palestine. Gillette leaked the news to the press, which had important consequences in forcing Truman's hand because of domestic political considerations.[26] This was the intention of the Bergsonites, who were fully aware of the importance of the DP issue in local elections that November, especially in New York. The story of Truman's letter to Attlee, and the fact that the Bergson group leaked it, infuriated both the British Labor government and the establishment Zionists. Truman's move on behalf of the DPs made the Zionists feel that they had been circumvented.[27]

There had been debate within the Bergson group about what position to take regarding the DPs. As during the Holocaust, it was a question of choosing to emphasize a humanitarian issue over the question of Palestine. The Bergsonites thought that the British would allow the 100,000 to enter Palestine as a humanitarian gesture if enough noise was made, but they were fully aware that this would set back the national liberation movement because it would take the pressure off the British on the question of independence. The opinion that prevailed was that the well-being of the survivors was the first priority.[28]

In reaction to Truman's initiative, Bevin issued a proposal for an Anglo-American Enquiry Commission into the DP situation and the Palestine question in general. Bergson thought that this was nothing more than a British ploy to ignore Harrison's harrowing report and to sidestep the issue of what to do with the survivors of Hitler's death camps. The official Zionists shared this skepticism of Bevin's intentions.[29]

The Bergson group, in opposing Bevin's proposal, intensified its campaign demanding admission of the 100,000 Jews to Palestine. The group's effort apparently had its effect on the Foreign Minister. On October 12, 1945, Bevin wrote to Lord Halifax in Washington that the public campaign being waged in New York had destroyed the "reasonable atmosphere." He was convinced that Truman had only supported the demand for immigration certificates for the DPs because of the New York Jewish vote, and he intimated as much to Weizmann on October 10.[30]

The leak of the story and the fuss raised by the Bergsonites helped to harden Bevin's heart and his obstinacy proved to be a great gift to the cause of the Jews; for there is a direct line between Bevin's intransigence on the DP issue and the creation of the state of Israel thirty months later, as has been pointed out by politicians and scholars alike. What has not been duly recognized is the part played by the Bergson group in bringing about these reactions.

On November 15, a Bergson group mission to Britain, led by Gillette, Somers, Fowler Harper and J. David Stern, publisher of the *Philadelphia Record*, met with Bevin and obtained his agreement that the committee of inquiry would issue interim reports on the DPs which could be acted upon immediately. It was a big concession for Bevin, who two days earlier had made his notorious remark that the Jewish "race" was pushing to get at "the head of the queue," and advised the Jews to disappear as a people – to assimilate or risk another Hitler.[31]

The only time that the mainstream Zionists agreed to work with the Bergson group for a common goal was on a joint congressional resolution which commended Truman's interest in solving the problem of the 100,000 refugees and urged the Palestine Mandatory Power to allow the entry of Jews, who would help establish a democratic commonwealth. The resolution was adopted by the two houses on December 17 and 19, 1945. Not coincidentally, this was the same period when the Haganah and the Irgun cooperated in military actions against the British in Palestine.[32]

Later in December, publisher Stern represented the Bergsonites in a second meeting with Truman, who also met separately with Zionist leader Weizmann and assimilationist leader Lessing Rosenwald of the American Council for Judaism. Stern reported that Truman was opposed to setting up a state in Palestine "based on Judaism, for the same reason that he would be opposed to basing it on the Moslem religion or the Baptist denomination." He was against a "theocracy," but favored making Palestine a haven for the Jews.[33]

Other prominent Americans, including Jews, were disturbed by the religious-national aspects of a Jewish state and what it implied for American Jews. One of the most important was Arthur Hays Sulzberger, the publisher of the *New York Times* and the most powerful pro-assimilationist Jew in America. He met with Peter Bergson several times between the end of 1945 and June 1946. In their first encounter, Bergson declared that Sulzberger was an American of Hebrew descent and Jewish religion, while he, Bergson, was a Hebrew who sought freedom for his country: Palestine. As long as Bergson did not have his country, both he and Sulzberger would remain two Jews in the perception of others, with the distinction between their nationalities obscured.[34]

Sulzberger, averring that he was not an actual member of Rosenwald's assimilationist council, said that the Bergson group's position was closer to his own – there was a common interest in promoting the separation of religion and nationality.[35] He had visited Palestine in 1937, where Zionist zealots had informed him that he was a "foreigner in America." He came away with the realization that he was a Jew by religion, while the Palestinians were Jews by nationality. This distinction was of the utmost importance to him.[36]

At their first meeting, Bergson told Sulzberger that the *Times* had generally been unfair to the movement – there had been a period when the newspaper even refused to print the committee's ads – and that the group deserved a hearing.[37]

The publisher arranged a lunch at the *Times* for Gillette, Bergson and Prof. Johan Smertenko with half a dozen members of the editorial board, and Jerusalem correspondent Clifton Daniel. Sulzberger opened the luncheon by saying that the anti-Zionist *Times* had decided to give editorial support to the Hebrew Committee on its distinction between Hebrew nationality and the Jewish religion. Former senator Gillette, who had turned down a high-paying job in business to become full-time chairman of the committee's affiliate, the American League for a Free Palestine, delivered the first speech. He expressed his anger and disillusionment over the treatment he personally had been subjected to at the hands of the major Zionist and Jewish organizations. His remarks were well-received, up until a one-line *faux pas*: "A free Palestine will deepen the roots of American Jews in the United States." Sulzberger interrupted him: "I don't know when your ancestors came to America, Senator, but mine came in the seventeenth century, and my roots in America are deep enough."[38]

That was the last the committee saw of Sulzberger. A year later, Ben Hecht would deliver a tirade against the publisher of the *Times*, saying he was a Jew whose reaction to being turned away by a hotel in Florida was to try all the harder to be accepted by gentile society. In a speech at a Hotel Astor dinner on April 27, 1947, Hecht attacked "a white Christmas named Arthur Sulzberger" whose actions "among the Anglo-Saxons set a new spectacle in Jewish history."[39]

By the time the Anglo-American Commission of Enquiry got under way in January 1946, the DPs' desperation and their desire to emigrate to Palestine had become the central issue in the debate over a Jewish state. The pressure throughout the fall had been significant. In September, the British had reacted to the "mounting agitation in the United States" by drawing up an interim policy statement before the imminent end of the five-year immigration quotas set by the 1939 White Paper. The statement called for maintaining the monthly quota of 1,500 Jews.[40]

The Anglo-American Commission was chaired by Britain's Sir John Singleton and America's Judge Joseph Hutcheson, and included a brilliant young Laborite, Richard H.S. Crossman, who was pro-Zionist. It convened in Washington in January and continued later in Europe, Jerusalem and Arab countries.

When Peter Bergson appeared before the commissioners, he attempted to explain the necessity for separating Jewish nationality and religion and to clarify the confusion over Jewish identity. In a highly-charged atmosphere, in which survivors of the extermination were being intercepted by the British as "illegal" immigrants to Palestine, Bergson assured the commissioners that he would not make any demands or insist on "any extreme sorts of deeds." But as a man identified by some as "a well-known terrorist," he came under sharp questioning, especially by the British members of the panel.[41]

Bergson had become, at age thirty-one, a polished and articulate man who exuded leadership qualities. Although "the movement" dominated his thoughts and the presence he put forward, Peter Bergson had a definite taste for the high life that America offered. But in his appearance before the commission, he did not refer to the six years he had lived in America. He was still a citizen of Jerusalem. "I came here to try and describe to you our minimum requirements for survival and a free and dignified life," he began, and then tried to convey what it meant to be a Hebrew – an Israeli. "I am a Hebrew – a person who has no other national allegiance except that of the Hebrew nation... I live in Jerusalem. There are all sorts of people living around me. What I am looking for is not a political formula which sounds very good in Washington, but I am looking for a workable way of life which will make it possible to get up in the morning peacefully, go to work, and come home at night."[42] Bergson outlined the historical, political, ethnic and moral links to the territory of the Hebrew people, defining what would shortly be called the Israeli nation.

He explained the difference between the Hebrew (of Palestine and the DP camps) and the Zionists of America, who were not members of this Israeli nation, unless their feet were to carry them to Zion. The "National Home for the Jewish People," as the Mandate preamble termed it, would not include every Jew the world over, but only those who chose to go there, where their nationality would be Hebrew – Israeli – and their religion, for those who practiced it, Jewish. Religion and nationality would no longer be combined – Jews of other nations accepted the nationality of these nations, so there could be no political meaning to their being Jewish, but only religious, cultural or ethnic identity. Bergson said that the ancient Hebrew nation was a theocracy, based on the unification of religion and nationality, and he quoted Webster's entry on theocracy, which gives as the prime example "the Hebrew Commonwealth before it became a kingdom."[43]

Why was this important? Bergson said that if the human boundaries had been taken into account in the return of the Hebrews to their ancestral homeland, the tragic events surrounding that return could have been alleviated, and "a great deal of human blood would have been spared." The Hebrew Committee did not believe that the people put into the furnaces of the death camps were "Germans" – they had been denationalized. "They are not Poles, they are not Rumanians or Hungarians – they are Hebrews." Yet this Hebrew nation lived in a world where its very existence was debated. The Hebrew Committee, Bergson continued, wanted to end that era: "We exist. We are here. The Hebrews are a nation as real as any other in the world."[44]

Bergson's argument focused on the identity question. "Here I am, an individual, standing before you. What am I? Well, you say, 'He is a Jew.' What do you mean?... Being a Jew, what is my position in the world? What is my relationship to human society? In simple terms, what nation do I belong to? I say I am a Hebrew. My allegiance is to the Hebrew nation. My country is Palestine."[45]

In his testimony (which filled thirty pages of transcript), Bergson also discussed a wide range of other questions related to Palestine, the refugees and the Arabs. He said that Hebrew independence should in no way be at the expense of another people, but he did not recognize the legitimacy of Palestinian Arab nationalism – a view he would one day change. The committee's program, based on separation of religion and nationality, would enable Palestinian Arabs to enjoy equality as citizens of the republic.

The extent of the confusion about Jews of the world and the budding Israeli nation was exemplified by Judge Hutcheson's questioning of Bergson. "What country did you come from?" he asked. "From Russia," Bergson replied. An hour later, the judge showed how this bothered him, and why he could not readily relate to the concept of an independent state for Israelis. "Are you a Russian Jew?" he asked. Bergson did not explain that Jabotinsky, Ahad Ha'am, Weizmann, Joseph Trumpeldor, Berl Katznelson, Ben-Gurion, Golda Meyerson (Meir) and countless other Zionists had been born in Russia or its satellite states, and that the Russians and Poles regarded the Jews as a separate nationality. It was a concept foreign to Americans, and Hutcheson could not grasp it. "I am a Palestinian," Bergson told him, "I was born in Lithuania. I was a refugee at the age of four. I went to Russia, and from Russia to Palestine at the age of eleven. With all due respect and admiration for the Russians, I don't consider myself a Russian any more than you do."[46]

When Britain's Justice Singleton suggested that Bergson go to Palestine ahead of the commission to arrange testimony by Hebrew Committee members interned by the British, Bergson responded that if he went to Palestine and said what he had said in Washington, he would be in a British concentration camp the next morning. The experience of Eri Jabotinsky and Aryeh Ben-Eliezer – the latter was still in a prison camp – was ample evidence of this. In addition, it was obvious that Bergson would have been arrested as soon as he set foot in Palestine, since the British Mandate authorities had put a bounty on his head. Singleton, taken aback, commented: "I didn't know you were concerned in the matter." Bergson, concluding his testimony, replied, "I am very much concerned, Sir. It is my life."[47]

The Anglo-American commission issued its report on May 1, 1946. While rejecting independence, it recommended that the 100,000 DPs be allowed to immigrate to Palestine and that the long ban on Jewish land purchases be lifted; in effect, it proposed abrogation of the White Paper. The critical but basically pro-British recommendations were turned down by Attlee and Bevin – the latter refused even to meet with the commissioners his own government had appointed. American members of the commission, such as lawyer Bartley Crum, were "deeply shocked" by the British government's "indecent and inhuman actions."[48]

Britain's repudiation of its pledge to allow the DPs into Palestine if the commission recommended it "incensed American public opinion" and endangered the granting of an urgently needed $375 billion U.S. loan. New York Mayor La Guardia told an audience of 45,000 that if Britain wanted credit, the best way to get it was to show it knew how to keep its word. The contentious debate in Congress inflamed British hostility to Zionist aspirations. Bergson, at a HCNL press conference in Washington, attacked the "practiced imperialists" of Britain and their apologists who asked the Hebrew nation "to sympathize with the terrible plight of the British Empire, which would collapse if it lost the tiny land that was entrusted to its tender mercies."[49]

At another press conference on August 15, 1946, Bergson, displaying an increasing anger and stridency, blasted the Jewish Agency for "cowardice" vis-a-vis the British, and stated that the agency was an obsolete body "dominated by Englishmen like Weizmann" and in no way represented "the Hebrew people." He styled them as "collaborators and quislings" who had no plans to actually live in Palestine, the "Hebrew-national territory from time immemorial, by the will of God and under the law of nations."[50]

In his book on the Anglo-American commission, *Palestine Mission: A Personal Record*, commissioner Richard Crossman described "young Peter Bergson" as appearing "more like a Russian university student than a terrorist, the sole spokesman in Washington of the Irgun, a skeleton which the orthodox Zionists obvious thought should have remained in the cupboard." Crossman, as a Weizmann supporter, was critical of Ben-Gurion and contemptuous of the more radical Zionists in general. He believed that the "high-powered American propaganda" spearheaded by the Bergsonites increased the pervasive British hostility to Zionism. But Crossman acknowledged being influenced by Bergson's testimony and came to believe that the 600,000 Jews of Palestine had become "the nucleus of what Bergson, in his evidence, called the new Hebrew nation."[51]

In the years leading up to Israel's independence, Bergson remained one of the most controversial figures in the Jewish world – not only because of his heretical ideas on post-Zionism, but also because the Bergsonites were usually a step ahead of everyone else with the audacious campaign in support of the independence struggle. Long before the mainstream Zionists dared to speak of it, the Bergsonites were championing the idea of a declaration of independence. They were doing it with the same flare for agitprop and publicity that they had shown over the years in the committee's various incarnations.

Theater remained an integral element in the group's overall propaganda efforts, guided by Hecht and by Stella Adler, the tall and beautiful member of one of America's great theatrical families. Adler, an actress, stage director and acting teacher, who had brought Stanislavky's "Method" to America, remained one of the most active members of the Bergson group from 1942 until its dissolution in 1948. She drew many prominent people to the committee, and her Manhattan home buzzed with activity.[52] When Ben Hecht wrote a play for the committee about the extermination of the Jews in Europe and the emerging Hebrew nation in Palestine, one of Adler's students, Marlon Brando, was cast in a leading role, alongside Paul Muni. Hecht's play, A Flag is Born, opened at the Alvin Theater on Broadway on September 5, 1946.

The play, like its predecessor pageant, We Will Never Die, attracted many Broadway personalities to the cause of Hebrew liberation. They generally worked "for scale," and Brando, who was becoming a well-known actor, joined the company for $48 a week. He shared with his Jewish friends, like Adler, Muni and Paul Henreid, the excitement over the growing movement for the creation of Israel. A Flag Is Born brought home the plight of the Jewish survivors trying to get to Palestine, and it was an instant success, drawing overflow audiences in New York for several weeks before moving on to other cities. In Baltimore, the committee paid for a special train to bring hundreds of congressmen, government officials and prominent Americans like Eleanor Roosevelt to see the pageant, which depicted DPs trying to get to Palestine, but being barred by the British. The central character, David, played by Brando, decides to commit suicide, but his hand is stayed by a dramatic light from the right of the stage, the playing of "Hatikva" ("The Hope," Israel's future anthem), and three Hebrew soldiers, representing the Haganah, Irgun and Stern group. The soldiers beckon to him: "We're waiting for you, David." They tell him that they fight "in the streets of Jerusalem... in the hills of Lebanon, in the deserts of Judea... We battle the English, the sly and powerful English. We speak to them in a new Jewish language, the language of guns... We promise to wrest our homeland out of British claws."[53]

Hecht's nationalistic pageant once again aroused the ire of the British and of the establishment Zionists. The London Evening Standard assailed the fact that thousands of people were flocking to theaters "to see the most virulent anti-British play ever staged in the United States." Judah Magnes, president of The Hebrew University of Jerusalem and a leader of the extreme dovish wing of the Zionist movement (he had been one of the only Zionists acceptable to Col. Hoskins), wrote to Mrs. Roosevelt to protest against her support of a play in which there was an appeal to support the armed struggle in Palestine: "Are you in favor of supplying money and arms for the terrorists... who are poisoning the minds and souls of the younger generation?" Magnes asked.[54]

Hecht told reporters that the play netted $1 million; and the profits from *A Flag Is Born* were used to buy and outfit a ship to carry refugees to Palestine. The play was also succcessful with the DPs themselves, who staged it in a British detention camp in Cyprus. The committee's ship, reputedly the former private yacht of the Krupp family, was renamed the *SS Ben Hecht*. When Hecht was asked to comment on an official British message to the State Department protesting against the raising of funds for "illegal" immigration, he gave a Runyonesque retort: "Britain may be able to patrol the Mediterranean, but she cannot patrol Broadway."[55]

The propaganda and fund-raising successes of the Bergson group spurred Ben-Gurion to set up the American arm of the Haganah in July 1946 to raise money for arms and ships. It became known as the "Sonneborn Institute," named after Rudolf Sonneborn, the oil and chemical magnate who was Ben-Gurion's main fund-raiser in America. The new organization was "especially concerned about the flamboyant advertising of a razzle-dazzle organization calling itself the American League for a Free Palestine," according to a chronicler of the institute's history. Because the Bergson group was attracting thousands of Americans, the institute decided to do exactly what the Bergsonites were doing: It published a newspaper, held press conferences, rounded up its own celebrities and staged mass meetings. But "it never made as much of a splash as the American League."[56]

Bergson himself remained an outlaw not only to establishment Zionists but to the British as well. The *New York Herald Tribune* correspondent in Jerusalem, Homer Bigart, reported in December 1946 that the censors stopped "all stories from America referring to the activities of Peter Bergson, leader of the Zionist faction in the United States sympathetic to terrorists." Around the same time, the Haganah's clandestine radio in Palestine stepped up its attacks on the Bergsonites. A woman announcer, reiterating the line formulated by Rabbi Wise and Nahum Goldmann, said that the Bergson group had not brought a single Jew to Palestine and called Peter Bergson "a false prophet spreading phoney gospel." The Bergsonites were labeled "enemies of the Jewish people."[57]

Bergson's reaction to the broadcast was recorded by the *New York Times*: "When the shouting and the shooting is over, it will be possible to judge who is a false prophet." He condemned the latest attack as part of the Jewish Agency's "bitter and unscrupulous fight" against the Hebrew Committee and its support groups.[58]

One mainstream Zionist who dissented from the attacks on Bergson was Gershon Agronsky (Agron), the American-born founder and editor of *The Palestine Post* (the *Jerusalem Post* after independence), and later, mayor of Jerusalem. Agronsky tried to run an editorial criticizing those who were still trying to have Bergson deported from the United States. The British censors killed the editorial, but Agronsky sent a copy to Harry Louis Selden for the record. It is an important document because it shows that independent thinkers in the establishment Zionist camp refused to accept the shibboleths of the leadership, and it recognized Bergson's unique contribution to Jewish history:

> Throughout the war years Peter Bergson played an important national role in the United States. Backed by no official authority, and thanks only to his energy, application, natural talent and faith, he succeeded in drawing the attention of extensive circles in the United States to our problem. He was the first to conduct propaganda on a large scale hitherto unknown to Jewish endeavor anywhere in the world for the creation of a Jewish Army to make war on the Nazi regime. He succeeded in attracting many friends to this idea not only in America but also in Britain. The creation of the Jewish Brigade [a few months before the war ended] owes much to his efforts. He was the first to try to influence the U.S. Government to tackle the question of Jewish refugees, and was the man who broke down the wall of silence that surrounded the annihilation of the Jews of Europe. He was the first to bring to the fore in the United States the question of representation of the Hebrew nation in international deliberations and showed the way to activity in this direction. With his political sense and his dynamic personality which impressed all those who came into contact with him – Jews as well as gentiles – he knew how to overcome the many difficulties that beset him in his work. The Jewish People is very poor in forces endowed with the courage to stand guard over its interests. It would indeed be a pity if for formal reasons, Peter Bergson's work in the United States should at this decisive hour cease.[59]

But in the eyes of the official Zionist leadership, Bergson was the false prophet whose "dangerous" organizations were as threatening to Zionist goals as were the terrorist underground groups inside Palestine. The Zionists in late 1946 were particularly upset by Bergson's call for a provisional government, especially after the French government allowed Bergson's HCNL, the political organization associated with the Irgun, to set up a preliminary government-in-exile in Paris. The French had given the Hebrew Committee more than just another base of operations. The committee had won support for the struggle against the British from Premier Leon Blum and Foreign Minister Georges Bidault, both of whom met with Merlin. The French newspapers, including *Le Monde*, were full of praise for the armed liberation struggle in Palestine. There had, in fact, been ongoing contact between the Hebrew Committee of National Liberation and De Gaulle's French Committee of National Liberation during the last year of the war, and the Gaullists would remain strong supporters of the HCNL until Israel's independence in May 1948.[60]

CHAPTER ELEVEN

TO NATIONHOOD

In late December 1946, immediately after the French had made their anti-British decision to back the Hebrew Committee, Bergson left the United States for Paris to lay the foundations of the government-in-exile. "Bergson Leaves, Vowing Revolution," read the *New York Post* headline on December 27, 1946. Bergson had told a Washington press conference on the previous day that the "revolutionary government" would coordinate underground fighting and "transform the present sporadic struggle in Palestine into a full-fledged active force for national liberation."[1]

The government-in-exile proposal went far beyond agitprop. To many at the time, it appeared to be nothing more than a stunt by a group of self-proclaimed "leaders." But the events in Palestine were moving so fast and in such a way as to make the idea of a provisional government suddenly seem more realistic – something the Yishuv as a whole should proclaim. But disputes between the HCNL and the Irgun over the question of timing would soon escalate. Ben-Ami, for one, foresaw rocky times ahead trying to reconcile Begin's beliefs in the supremacy of armed struggle and the views of Bergson and Eri Jabotinsky that the political course would bring the greatest results. There was, as well, increasing tension among the original members of the "cut-off battalion." Ben-Ami bridled under Bergson's leadership and his often brash demeanor. A good deal of personal resentment had built up since the mid-thirties, when the younger man, Bergson, was made Ben-Ami's superior in the Irgun. Merlin, meanwhile, who always had had a love-hate relationship with Bergson, angrily rejected some of Bergson's suggestions regarding issues such as the mooted partition of Palestine.

Bergson chaired a meeting of the HCNL in which he proposed supporting the mainstream Zionists on partition, and a majority voted with him and against Merlin: The committee would welcome creation of a Jewish state in a small part of the mandated territory, while at the same time reiterating, in a *pro forma* way, the maximalist position that all of Palestine – both sides of the Jordan – belonged to the Israeli nation that was about to be declared. At one point, Merlin, a hawk on this issue, threatened to resign.

Bergson's "Israeli arrogance" and vanity undoubtedly increased along with his success over the years. He was idolized by many of the volunteers and supporters of the Bergson group, and *The Answer* sometimes took a hagiographic view of him, as exemplified by one caption under a Bergson photograph: "The foremost statesman and diplomat of contemporary Hebrew history." His self-confidence was undoubtedly fed by the many prominent personalities who, like writer Arthur Koestler, felt that he was "a dynamic and original personality." He was still the "star" of the Bergson group, even though some people felt he was simply too brainy for his own good.[2]

At a farewell party in Manhattan on the evening before he left for Paris, Bergson told two hundred guests that "We Hebrews are very much in the position of America in 1776... This is the beginning of a national revolution, and the British have never yet won a revolution." (One of the slogans frequently used by the American League was: "It is 1776 in Palestine.")[3]

Shortly after his arrival in Paris, Bergson helped recruit former leaders of the French Resistance and leading intellectuals to the Hebrew liberation movement. Headquarters had been set up by Merlin, Rafaeli, Eri Jabotinsky and others in a large dwellng at 18 Avenue de Messine, where they promoted the planned provisional government. The group, which was bolstered by Irgunists such as Eliahu Lankin, who had just escaped from British detention in Eritrea, put out a French-language version of *The Answer* – *La Riposte* – and won the active support of Jean-Paul Sartre, Simone de Beauvoir and Paul Eluard. A French League for a Free Palestine was set up on the American model and would remain active until Israel's independence was achieved.[4]

Bergson thought that the proposed government-in-exile could win recognition from some Latin American governments, such as Guatemala and Uruguay, and he made significant progress toward this goal. On March 7, 1947, Zionist diplomat Eliahu (Epstein) Elath reported to the Jewish Agency on Bergson's success with French intellectuals, influential persons in the French government, and Gaullists "who identified with Hebrew National Liberation because of the nature of their own struggle." Elath was miffed because Premier Blum had met with Merlin; and parliamentarian Edgar Faure, the future premier, not only came out in support of the Hebrew Committee's program but became an activist as well. Elath reported that Bergson was becoming a major threat to the Zionist movement and a challenge to the Jewish Agency in many capitals of the world. In the United States, the American Jewish Conference, which declared that it had "exposed" Bergson in December 1943, warned in December 1946 in its official organ, *The Record*, that Bergsonism cannot be dismissed as by-play and buffoonery." A threat to their monopoly on power was no longer just an occasion for derision.[5]

The British, meanwhile, sought to have Bergson expelled from France on the grounds that he was traveling under false papers. But the French government's support continued unabated, and later included large supplies of arms for the Irgun's fight in Palestine.[6]

From January 1947 until May 1948, Bergson divided his time equally between France and the United States. Soon after he first arrived, he traveled to Nuremberg, Germany, at the invitation of Josiah DuBois, to witness the trial of Nazi war criminals. He used the opportunity to help get 700 DPs onto the *Ben Hecht*.[7]

Despite the strong support from the French government, the Hebrew Committee's plans for a provisional government never materialized because of Menachem Begin, who had at first agreed and then backed out of an official proclamation of a government-in-exile. As Ben-Ami would put it, "bitterness" crept into the dialogue between the Irgun command and Bergson and Eri Jabotinsky; a final split was inevitable.[8]

The Bergson group's French connection remained strong until the independence struggle was won, and not only in the supply of arms. The Hebrew Committee got the French government to agree to give assistance and asylum to Aryeh Ben-Eliezer, who had escaped from British detention. The committee arranged for a French aircraft carrier to bring him from Djibouti, on the Horn of Africa, to France. (As a courtesy, the French also took along his fellow escapee, Yitzhak Shamir, although he was not connected to the Bergsonites.)

While Begin and his command showed continuing ambivalence towards the Bergson group, the mainstream Zionists kept up their long battle against the "careerist adventurers." The Hebrew Committee was assailed in December 1946 by the Twenty-Second Zionist Congress meeting in Basel, which issued a resolution that said: "By drawing meaningless and misleading distinctions, such as between

Jews and Hebrews, they confuse and distort the issues of the Jewish national cause." (Bergson would have it the other way around: By ignoring or obfuscating the differences between Israelis and Jews, Zionists were confusing and distorting the crucial issues.)[9]

To outsiders, the Irgun and the Bergson group in its last phase appeared to merge. Thus, in March 1947, Moshe Shertok reported to the Jewish Agency "on the increased activities of the Bergson group in support of the Irgun's armed insurrection."[10]

On February 28, 1947, the Bergson group's *S.S. Ben Hecht* sailed from Port du Bouc near Marseilles and headed for Palestine with about 700 passengers and an American crew. The 700 were assembled by Bergson and Avraham Stavsky, the man who had been accused but acquitted of the 1933 murder of labor Zionist leader Chaim Arlosoroff. The group included camp survivors and Jewish refugees from Poland, Shanghai, Tunisia, France and Russia who dreamed of return to the national home. The voyage was not kept secret – on the contrary, the committee intended for the British to intercept the ship and arrest its American crew. The action would then be challenged in the courts of Palestine and the United States, with the intent of setting off a public storm. The passengers and crew had been instructed to engage in only passive resistance when stopped by the British.[11]

There were doubts within the Bergson group about committing so much of the committee's meager budget on this project instead of leaving it up to the Haganah to break the British blockade, and the Irgun was against the project, wanting the money to be spent on arms, instead.[12] Bergson himself was sensitive to the establishment's charge that the Bergson group had not physically brought any European Jews to the shores of Palestine – the fact that the Bergsonites had contributed greatly to the creation of the WRB, which saved thousands of Jews, seemed too abstract to him.[13] So once again, Bergson did not do what The Commander, Begin, wanted him to do.

On March 8, 1947, two British destroyers intercepted the *Ben Hecht* and interned the DPs. The seizure of the ship created the expected storm in the media and in Congress; and after the House of Representatives condemned the seizure, the British released the American crew. The *Ben Hecht* sailors received an official City Hall welcome in Manhattan on April 17, while thousands of young people mobilized by the Bergson group picketed the British Consulate. At a banquet, Hecht vowed to raise enough money to buy more ships; and hundreds of American sailors swamped the committee's offices volunteering to defy the British blockade.[14]

Two months later, the Bergson group created another furor with the publication of Ben Hecht's maledictory "Letter to the Terrorists of Palestine," which appeared in full-page ads in the *New York Herald Tribune* and the *New York Post*. The offending lines read: "Every time you blow up a British arsenal or wreck a British jail, or send a British railroad train sky high, or rob a British bank, or let go with your guns and bombs at the British betrayers and invaders of your homeland, the Jews of America make a little holiday in their hearts. Not all the Jews, of course."[15]

In early May, a few days before the advertisement was to run, Merlin told Bergson, who had just returned from Paris, that he was disturbed by Hecht's tone and thought they should not run the ad. Bergson, who was usually prudent about the committee's messages, thought it read well and saw nothing wrong with it – he came to regret it much later, and then only because it was "bad propaganda." Bergson was never rubbed the wrong way or embarrassed by Hecht's overexuberance, his tasteless romanticizing of violence. His friend's Jewish macho seemed defensible to him at a time when millions of Jews were being slaughtered, or when the British put survivors of Hitler's death camps into post-war concentration camps.[16]

Hecht, aged fifty-two in 1947, brimmed with pride over every Irgun action, and it became his all-consuming interest. He was appalled by the labor Zionists, who betrayed Irgun hide-outs to British intelligence, and he regarded Ben-Gurion as a "stool-pigeon." Hecht railed against the labeling of the Irgun as "terrorists" when they were, in his eyes, "fighters" (a semantic battle the Irgun lost), although he said the epithet was correct in one sense: the Irgun would succeed in terrorizing the British out of Palestine.[17]

After "Letter to the Terrorists" ran for a second time, the British issued a formal protest to the U.S. government, and the issue was debated in the House of Commons. Hecht paid dearly for the ads: he would be officially boycotted by the British for years to come, and many of his old films were banned. Hecht, presaging the Hollywood Ten, was forced to write under a pen name at a fraction of the sums he once received as Hollywood's number-one scriptwriter.[18]

The controversy over Hecht's "Letter" led to a statement by President Truman in June 1947, urging every citizen and resident in the United States to refrain from activities that might inflame passions in Palestine. A handful of journalists came to Hecht's defense, including columnists Walter Winchell and Leonard Lyons. In

Palestine, the Jewish Agency welcomed Truman's appeal, while the Irgun hinted darkly that Washington was more interested in Arab oil than in Jewish freedom.[19]

Neither the public nor the mainstream Zionists were unaware that while the committee's ads were extolling the Irgun's exploits in Palestine, the squabble over funds between the two groups had intensified. At the same time, the differences over a provisional government grew more acute. Begin sent an angry letter to the HCNL rejecting outright the proposal for a provisional government, saying that "to rush such a political decision will be to destroy the edifice before it is built." Then Begin appeared to change his mind once again after the UN decision in November 1947 to partition Palestine. At that time, Begin threatened Ben-Gurion that if he did not set up a provisional government, the Irgun would.[20]

The Bergson group, with its unorthodox methods – and in an as yet unrecognized way – had been charting the course for what would soon come about: the sudden "bursting forth" of Israel.[21] All along the way, Ben-Gurion and his American followers had been forced to become more militant because of the Bergson group's successes in propaganda, fund-raising and lobbying. Abba Hillel Silver, for one, admired the Bergsonites' activism, and his hand "was repeatedly forced by the brash and unabashed public relations campaigns of the imaginative renegade, Peter Bergson."[22] In the same vein, Ben-Gurion took an increasingly more radical route away from the gradualism of Weizmann and Wise. In 1948, he would finally recognize the need for speedily declaring independence. It seems clear today that the Begin-Bergson threat played a major role in bringing about his action. Ben-Gurion pushed the idea in the face of intense opposition from Shertok (Sharett), Goldmann and others. He knew it was essential to do so in the light of U.S. backtracking from the UN partition decision and the momentum of events in Palestine.[23]

Throughout the summer and fall of 1947, the Hebrew Committee focused on prompting its three-point program to solve the "Palestinian problem" (as it was called then): repatriation of surviving European Jews, resistance to British occupation, and establishment of the Hebrew Republic of Palestine.

The Bergsonites also continued to hammer away at the difference between the national and religious identity of the Jews, which they believed had become an urgent issue, now that independence was approaching. In a statement issued on December 15, 1947, following the UN decision on partition, the committee outlined its program for the coming "post-Zionist" era, a phrase the Bergsonites were now using to sharpen differences with the Zionists. The statement, entitled "A 'Jewish State' or the Hebrew Republic of Palestine," declared that the UN decision meant that certain questions could no longer be ignored: Would it be a religious, a theocratic state, as its name implied? Would the Jewish government represent the Jews of the world? Would all the Jews eventually move to the "Jewish state," or would they belong to a special international nation? If the new state did not belong to the "Jewish nation," then to what nation did it belong?[24]

According to the Bergsonites, the answer was that the new state belonged to the Hebrew nation ("Israeli" was to replace "Hebrew" six months later, with the birth of the state). In a remarkably prescient demographic forecast, they saw the nation as comprising some three million people: the 600,000 Palestinian Jews, the displaced Jews of Europe, and the Jews of the Middle East "who need Palestine to live in and want to belong to it." The other ten million Jews of the world, the statement continued, did not intend to move to Palestine and therefore "belonged" to other nations.[25] By contrast, the Zionists defined the nation as thirteen million Jews – all the Jews of all the nations.

In its statement, the Hebrew Committee paid homage to the great achievements of Zionism and the leading role played by the practical Zionists in building Palestine; but it attacked the Jewish Agency as "an archaic body that insists on perpetuating 'the Jews' as a unique entity," thus eternalizing anti-Semitism and contradicting the very basis of Zionism. To the Bergsonites, Zionism still meant the normalization of the Jewish People. By perpetuating the unique status of the Jews in the world, the Bergsonites maintained, the Zionists were ignoring Herzl and Jabotinsky.[26]

Days after the statement, Peter Bergson was deposed as leader of the Hebrew Committee (he took a euphemistic "leave of absence"), the result of almost two years of struggling with the Irgun. Ben-Ami, Rafaeli (Hadani) and the Irgunists in Palestine felt that it was pointless and counterproductive to try and separate Jewish nationality and Jewish religion because they were so intertwined. Bergson's struggle was a lost cause, and this was a great loss for the nation, Rafaeli felt. "Peter was like Begin in a lot of ways – had he a different way of saying things, he would have been one of Israel's leaders. But Peter was too bohemian, concentrating on artists and journalists."[27]

The split was never announced publicly, and there was never a formal change. But Bergson had his priorities, and Begin had his. In the last six months of the Bergson group's activities, its erstwhile chairman remained active in such efforts as promoting the George Washington Legion to fight in Palestine (patterned after the Lincoln Brigade of the Spanish civil war), and buying and outfitting a ship to carry arms and immigrants from Europe to Palestine. In Paris, Bergson, in negotiations with the French government, obtained $5 million worth of arms to be brought to Palestine by an ex-U.S. Navy vessel which the HCNL and the American League had acquired. There was a crisis atmosphere in Palestine between the Haganah and the Irgun underground on the eve of decision – but the arms were desperately needed by the Jews in the face of all-out war against the Arab world. The ship was called the *Altalena*, after Jabotinsky's pen-name. That name would ring forever in Israel's history.[28]

Just as Independence was finally achieved on May 15, 1948, Peter Bergson dropped his alias, and Hillel Kook returned home that day for the first time since he had left on a "short" Irgun mission to Jabotinsky in September 1937. The special plane that brought him (along with other leaders of the Hebrew Committee, the Irgun, and journalist Arthur Koestler) was almost shot down by Haganah anti-aircraft guns at Sde Dov airport, as it landed minutes after an Egyptian bombing run. The new state was in obvious trouble.

The arms on the *Altalena*, en route to the state of Israel from France, were of vital importance to Palestinian Jews who were desperate for weapons in the face of overwhelming odds. But unity among the Jews was a chimerical notion, as had been shown by the Zionist reaction to the Holocaust. Both Menachem Begin and David Ben-Gurion, stubborn and self-righteous men, were responsible for a squabble over the arms on the *Altalena* which led to a murderous attack on the ship by the Haganah in June 1948. The events are a story of confusion and hysteria, on both the Irgun and the government sides. In any case, Kook, who was on the beach as the ship headed for Kfar Vitkin, told Ben-Ami, "It will end badly," and it did.[29]

The new army of Israel opened fire on the ship, at Ben-Gurion's order, as it headed to Tel Aviv, where a full, final assault was launched by Yigael Yadin, Yigal Allon and Yitzhak Rabin. Stavsky and about forty others were killed. Merlin, sitting next to the ship's radio shack, was shot in the leg. The wounded jumped into the Mediterranean and were still fired upon. Begin, who had boarded the ship at Kfar Vitkin, and the captain, Monroe Fine, got off just as the remaining arms exploded. Kook was arrested on the Kfar Vitkin beach, and Ben-Gurion announced that "Peter Bergson-Kook is already under arrest as a draft evader. What happens endangers our war effort... this is an attempt... to murder the state."[30]

For a few days, it looked like civil war would erupt, but the situation calmed down a week later, and the renewal of Arab attacks put an end to the internal dissension.

Several of the Irgun leaders were detained at various kibbutzim, and were moved around for security reasons. While Kook was being held at Kibbutz Gan Shmuel, affiliated to the then pro-Stalinist Mapam Party, there was a plot to assassinate him, according to journalist Shlomo Nakdimon, author of a pro-Begin book about the *Altalena*.[31] However, a senior Haganah officer, Bezalel Lev, refused to go along with the plot, and Kook's life was spared. The order to save him may have come from Reuven Shiloach, founder of the Shin Bet, the Israeli secret service, whose father was a rabbi and close friend of the Kook family. Kook was finally released on August 27, 1948.[32]

Kook, although not a member of the new Herut party which Menachem Begin set up – and still antagonistic toward The Commander – agreed to run near the top of its list for the Constituent Assembly, a body which was supposed to deal with fundamental questions and definitions created by the revolutionary change in Jewish existence. The organizations Kook had set up in America were now obsolete, and he was a man who took post-Zionism seriously. The only place where debate would matter would be Israel's constitutional convention. The Hebrew Committee and the American League were disbanded. It was probably the only time in Jewish history that a major organization retired from the field after its stated goals had been accomplished.

Kook, Eri Jabotinsky, Merlin and Aryeh Ben-Eliezer were elected to the Constituent Assembly, the first independent Jewish legislative body set up in two thousand years.[33] But Kook was to be profoundly disappointed.

Under Israel's Declaration of Independence, the Constituent Assembly was mandated to lay the foundations of the new state and to set down its laws in a constitutional framework. But the enterprise lasted only one day. Before it had begun to deal with any of the basic issues, the Ben-Gurion government transformed the Assembly into the First Knesset – it was as if America's Constitutional Convention had metamorphosed into the U.S. Congress in a single day, skipping the "formalities" of laying out a structure for the new nation.[34]

As maverick Labor Party Knesset member Shulamit Aloni would remark thirty years later, the only one who seemed to notice what was happening that day was Hillel Kook, who cried out in the chamber that a "putsch" had taken place. There was no attempt to deal with the basics, to transform the old abnormal Jewish existence to a normal national existence. A classic dishonesty developed from Day One because the Assembly did not deal with the structure of the Israeli republic and its relationship to the religion, to Jews outside Israel, as well as to non-Jews inside the country.[35]

Kook had sought debate on the whole complex of ideas developed by the Bergson group during their experience in America: the political composition of the Israeli nation (Kook grudgingly conceded that the term "Hebrew" was a lost cause), separation of religion and nationality, and constitutional laws that would have allowed Arabs to become part of the Israeli nation – not just residents with the right to vote. All these, he believed, were crucial identity issues that could not be suppressed forever.

Menachem Begin never openly attacked Kook, Eri Jabotinsky, and their ideas, even after the split that had been growing for so long finally developed into a complete break. By 1950, both Kook and Jabotinsky, neither of whom felt they were politicians, had little in common with Begin's Herut party. Merlin, on the other hand, became Herut secretary-general, while Ben-Eliezer became Herut's deputy speaker of the Knesset. But Merlin also grew disillusioned and eventually resigned from the party.

Alexander Rafaeli, looking back on those days a generation later, said he greatly regretted that Kook, because of his differences with Begin, was lost as a potential leader of Israel. He believed that Kook's negative attitude toward Begin was influenced by Eri, Kook's closest friend. "The whole Jabotinsky family hated Begin. The Jabotinskys were also fanatically anti-religious, and Eri was close to Hillel on this."[36]

But Rafaeli, like others, apparently misinterpreted Kook's position on separating Judaism from the Jewish nationality, assuming it meant that Rav Kook's nephew was anti-religious. This was anything but the case. Kook held that the religion was seriously damaged by Israel's mixing of state and religion, as well as religion and nationality. In his view, separation would purify the religion, and make it more honest.

Ironically, the man who skillfully focused a nation's conscience on the most momentous occurrence of the modern age was not able to communicate to his own countrymen the urgency of his continuing concerns for the fate of the Jewish People and of the Jewish State.

A POLITICAL EPILOGUE

Hillel Kook has once again become a member of a "cut-off battalion," a battalion of one.

In 1951, given all the acrimony and the impossibility of accomplishing anything in an Israel divided between ideologues like Ben-Gurion and Begin, Kook decided to wait for a few years until a "new generation" emerged from the desert and there was a change in what he thought was Israel's stifling ghetto atmosphere. Kook chose temporary exile and left Israel with his wife Betty (whom he had married in 1950) and their baby daughter, Astra. He had no money and no profession, but within a few years in America and Cuba, he made a small fortune in commodity trading, oil and Wall Street finance. Years later, he would say that he had made the wrong choice. After the First Knesset, he would never enter politics again.

In 1964, Betty died after a long battle with cancer, and four years later, Kook, at age fifty-three, retired from business and brought Astra and his second daughter, Rebecca, home to Israel. In 1975, he married an Israeli of the new generation, Nili Haskell. In recent years, Kook has lived in retirement in Kfar Shmaryahu, a wealthy suburb of Tel Aviv. From time to time, his name has cropped up in the Israeli media as journalists and scholars interviewed him about his activities in America during the 1940s. The bearded, impeccably dressed Kook looks every inch the elder statesman, a Trotsky in Mexico whose brilliant theories have been filed away, a Jabotinsky with no following.

He is not enthusiastic about biography or to talk about his life. Kook never saved his letters or documents (although he did finance Merlin's thirty-year-long project of assembling thousands of important papers at the Institute for Mediterranean Affairs, which are now at Yale University). Although he is cooperative and answers questions about the past, he makes it clear that he is not interested in rehashing the arguments about the Jewish and Zionist leadership and their lack of requisite response to the destruction of the European Jews. What interests him far more is the situation of Israel and world Jewry today. The extermination of over five million Jews and how it occurred is a part of history that must never be forgotten; but it is Israel's future that worries him – and he sees great danger ahead. His analysis of the cause of the malady is unique, out of synch with conventional opinions about Zionism and Jews.

Kook sometimes shocks his interlocutors with his blunt and provocative way of saying things, as when he declares that Israel has not yet recognized itself and that this is the crux of the country's problems. What he means is that Zionism, which was supposed to bring about the normalization of the Jewish People as a means of solving the Jewish problem, has instead perpetuated the anomalous status of the Jews in the world. Israel fails to delineate between itself as a nation-state and the Jews of other nations. In his view, the "putsch" that transformed the Constituent Assembly into the First Knesset was not simply a momentary lapse. Ben-Gurion skipped more than one step.

He believes that the failure of the Jews of Israel to deal with what he calls "the fundamentals" has led to the current situation of an Israel that on one hand claims all the rights and privileges of a sovereign nation, but on the other hand has not yet lived up to the responsibilities of that sovereignty. Sometimes he will express his deep disappointment with the continuing situation by saying that Israel is "a Jewish ghetto with a modern army" (a phrase other mavericks, such as Ezer Weizman, have adopted).

Such words tend to repel and shock, but behind them is a provocative, coldly realistic analysis that Kook has clung to all these years. The ideas are essentially the same that he and his closest colleagues developed during their experience in America in the 1940s. What he was saying then, and feels is equally true today, was that Zionism's success in creating the State of Israel meant a profound revolution in the situation of the Jews, and that the Zionist leadership, just as it demanded recognition and support from the world, had a responsibility to deal with the political consequences of a sovereign state. Primary among those responsibilities was to define the demographic boundaries of the state – not only the geographical boundaries, but the human boundaries, as well. That is precisely what the Constituent Assembly was supposed to do.

In Kook's view (in the tradition of classical political Zionism), the creation of the state was to rectify the abnormal situation of the Jews as an international people without a country of its own. Now that the Jews who needed it had a country, that abnormality had to be ended. What Kook and his committee had said over forty years ago was that the Jews could not have their cake and eat it too – they could not claim the privileges and rights of a sovereign nation, yet at the same time continue to perpetuate the Jews as a unique-international people.

Kook believes that this is exactly what has happened. The State of Israel was declared in 1948, yet the leaders of the country and of the Zionist movement continue as if Israel had never been established: Zionist congresses are held every four years, as if the Zionist goal had not been achieved. These congresses pretend to represent the Jews of the world in a political sense, thus perpetuating the confusion in the world about just what Israel is supposed to be. This failure to make distinctions between the Jews of Israel and Jews of other nationalities is not simply an abstract concern but has practical consequences for world Jewry, the Jews of Israel, and the Arabs of Israel.

Kook says that the foremost question to be confronted is not "Who is a Jew?" but "Who is an Israeli?" and "What is the Israeli nation?" He says that once the state was created, there could no longer be any national content in the word "Jew." After 1948, one could be a Jew by religion or culture or ethnic identity. However, for Jewish nationality, there was no longer a "Jewish nation," but an Israeli nation. Yet the doctrinaire Zionists did not and do not recognize this. They believe that Zionism is "a continuing revolution" whose work "is never concluded," as former president Yitzhak Navon has written.[1]

Kook's ideas should not be confused with those of the so-called Canaanites, a moribund movement that once appealed to a segment of Israel's intelligentsia. Kook disdains Canaanite beliefs that they are not Jews, that the nation that evolved in Israel is a new nation. His beliefs are quite the opposite. He has said, "We are Jews... the Israeli nation is the political heir of the Jewish nation."

Although he is still a secular person, Kook remains a believer, one who could bring himself back to observance only once the religion and the nationality are separated. Many members of his family are leading Orthodox rabbis in Israel, in the Kook tradition. Despite the fact that he does not keep a kosher home or otherwise observe the religion, the family honors the aging maverick as a *Tzadik*, a righteous man who saved Jewish lives.

Kook's views on the Diaspora are sacrilegious to Zionists who contend that there is still an Exile, even though there is a state. They see a Jewish nation of thirteen million; he sees an Israeli nation that is already there (Jews in lands of distress, as was the case in Soviet Russia, he regarded as captive Israelis).

Zionists, from writer A. B. Yehoshua on the left to former Stern group leader Israel Eldad on the right, give credence to Kook's ideas when they maintain that the Diaspora is sick, that American Jews are not really Americans but Jews in exile, that Israel is only a state and not a nation.

Golda Meir, in an address in Washington to the Conference of Presidents of Major American Jewish Organizations on November 2, 1973, repeated what she had recently told Israeli soldiers who had just fought the Yom Kippur War, that the whole thing – Israel itself – was not really worth it if it was for "only" three million Jews. She stressed what she called "the unity and identification and oneness between you and us," in the spirit of the Zionist motto: "We Are One." What this represents is obfuscation of the question of political loyalty: Zionists like Ariel Sharon, for example, maintain that the Jews of England and the Jews of Argentina should not have fought each other in the Falklands war, because all Jews everywhere belong to the Jewish nation. Kook believes this dogma is the Achilles heel of the Jews of the world.

The Jews of America have chosen America as their nation. An American Jew can support Israel, or identify with it, but his political identity is American, not Jewish. And American Jews are not "sick exiles," as Zionist ideologues would have it. The Israeli government's information service makes films depicting American Jewry as miserable, decadent, frightened, pompous or pitiful. A recent propaganda film, "Quest for Identity," featured a dynamic Zionist American rabbi, whipping off his glasses and proclaiming passionately, "Israel does not belong to the *Israelis*! Israel belongs to the JEWISH PEOPLE!"

All Jews do have religious or emotional or historical ties to Israel, and Kook is far from being opposed to their coming to live there. But it is a choice, not a *duty*. The Jewish nation concept is a big lie, and an injurious one. Sharon's attitude can only feed anti-Semitism. And to say, as then president Navon did during an official visit to the United States in January 1983, that American Jews do not really belong to America, shows unconcern for those Jews who choose not to become Israelis – or Hebrews, as Kook called them long ago.

To Kook, the conditions for peace and security for Israel cannot come into being until the basic issue is resolved. If the Jewish religion and Israeli nationality are separated, aims become clearer. Israel accepts itself as a nation that does not include the Jews of other nations. Until that recognition of the Israeli nation comes, there cannot be true acceptance of non-Jews. Israeli Arabs carry identity cards that say they are not members of the Israeli nation. Under the word "Nationality" appears the designation "Arab." Israeli Jews are also deprived of Israeli nationality, for their nationality, as in the former totalitarian Soviet Union, is called "Jewish."

As long as this situation continues to exist, non-Jews will not be able to participate fully in the Israeli nation, the fact that they can vote notwithstanding. They cannot be equal as long as they are identified as belonging to another nation – they are another *people*, not another nation. For Kook, it is not a quixotic pursuit to aim for separation of religion and nationality, to clear up the confusion over Israel's human boundaries.

If the basic issue is confronted, he believes, normalization can at last become a reality. Israel will no longer see itself as an exclusivist "Jewish state" which is only a bridgehead for the rest of world Jewry. A major psychological obstacle to Middle East peace will be removed.

But Kook is very much a voice in the wilderness. Although there has been growing attention to his ideas in the media and in university forums, he has remained for the most part a "one-man alternative," as Israeli journalist Doron Rosenblum termed him in a profile in *Ha'aretz*.

It has been a long wait for normalization, and Kook is prone to despair. He believes he is a failure. But the man who was called Peter Bergson, though old and ailing, has not given up all hope that his ideas will one day take hold. He keeps coming back to his mentor Jabotinsky's one-word definition of Zionism – "normalcy" – a basic change in the existence of the Jews.

In a January 8, 1982, interview (with this writer) for the *Jerusalem Post*, Kook spoke directly on the issues of the Palestinians, identity and religion, and relations between Israel and the United States:

The Palestinians – "The Palestinian problem has to be faced squarely and realistically. There is a Palestinian people. I see no reason to continue claiming that there is no such people. At the same time, Israel claims that there is a Jordanian people, when in fact there isn't. There is a Jordanian state and a Palestinian people.

"Jordan, formerly Transjordan, is part of Palestine. We can reach peace with the Palestinians first of all by recognizing them unilaterally as people and offering to partition the historic Mandatory Palestine between the two peoples occupying it. It is in our national interest to do so.

"The Israel government should launch an energetic peace offensive towards the Palestinians, recognizing their existence as a people. That's what they want, that's what we don't do. After the recognition, Israel should endeavor to convene a peace conference which would work from the premise that in the territory of Palestine there are two nation-states – Israel and Palestine, which is now called Jordan. The peace conference should aim to transform the conflict into a boundary dispute between the nations. They would negotiate a settlement over the disputed territory that changed hands in the war of 1967.

"I think it's a disaster to equate the Palestinians with the PLO. The PLO has only attained its political power because we don't give the Palestinians an alternative.

"In order to achieve a settlement there can only be two entities. There's no room in the territory of Palestine for three states. Which is easiest: to eliminate Israel, to destroy all the Palestinians, or to change the name of Jordan? Hussein himself, in an interview with *Nouvel Observateur* in July 1967, launched a trial balloon. He said, 'I'm thinking of abolishing the monarchy, or changing the name of my country to Palestine and becoming its first president.'

"When the Kingdom of Transjordan was established in 1946 – not in 1922, as some people think – King Abdullah wanted to call it the Kingdom of Palestine, but the British wouldn't let him.

"A Palestinian state on the West Bank alone wouldn't solve the problem but only exacerbate it. It doesn't bother me if the Palestinians get a state 'on Both Sides of the Jordan' [Jabotinsky's song of that title claimed both banks for the Jews], including part of a demilitarized West Bank, so that Israel can have a secure, viable national existence on one side of the river.

"I believe we can achieve peace between us. I'm even utopian enough to believe that somewhere along the road we can be allies."

Identity and religion – "No one confuses the words Christian and Christianity with the word American. In Israel, people are confused about the word Jewish – it's a Jewish nation and a Jewish religion.

"Israel is not a Jewish community with an army but a nation-state which has to update itself. And while the majority of its people are Jews by religion, we have to provide full equality for Israeli nationals who are Moslems or Christians.

"I'm an Israeli national by right and by choice, and anyone who says it's my duty to be an Israeli I regard as an enemy, trying to deprive me of my rights. Kissinger and the Lubavitcher Rebbe are American by choice.

"There is no exile. The exile ended on May 14, 1948, when Israel was established and the Jews of the world knew its gates were open. The fact that in the thirty-fourth year of Israel's existence we talk about the *Galut* [Diaspora] and exile is part of the general confusion which dominates our political life.

"You cannot force Israeli national allegiance upon the Jews of the world.

"In 1945, when the UN was created, the Hebrew Committee sent a delegation to ask for membership for the Hebrew – the Israeli – nation. The Jewish Agency sought recognition of the Jewish People. There were Jewish delegates in twenty of the fifty delegations there. On behalf of which Jewish nation was the Agency speaking? This is not a quibble.

"The question of Gush Emunim ['Block of the Faithful,' made up primarily of super-nationalist religious Israelis] relates to basic issues of identity. If Israel is a Jewish theocratic religious state, then you have no choice but to abide by the rules of religion – as Professor Yeshayahu Leibowitz says, Jews have no rights, they have only duties. The Jewish religion is not exactly a democratic manifesto – it just tells you what to do, it doesn't tell you what your rights are.

"We cannot for long have a state without defining politically the nation it belongs to – Israel belongs to the Israeli nation, and it's time for that nation to be recognized by a constitutional law. The present confusion between messianic Zionist myth and a modern nation-state surrounded by enemies and misunderstood by the world undermines the position of Jews everywhere and constitutes a mortal danger to the Israeli people and their republic.

"A major example of the confusion in American-Jewish relations with Israel is the fact that the two main Jewish denominations in the U.S. [Reform and Conservative Judaism] are not legally recognized in Israel.

"If we had a plebiscite on our national and religious identities, most people would not want a theocracy. They accept it de facto."

The U.S. and Israel – "Most American Jews are unorganized; the vast majority of them are pro-Israel, just as most American non-Jews are pro-Israel. I think a great deal of the Jewish support for Israel is because of the non-Jewish support.

"Israelis not only are confused about their own identity but also about American-Jewish identity. American Jews are proud of their ancestry, but they are Americans, just like other Americans who are Catholic or of Greek ancestry.

"There is a very serious erosion in U.S.-Israeli relations that has been going on since the 1973 war. Fortunately, the political system in America works very slowly – to the average American, Israel is not a burning issue. But it is becoming one...

"God forbid that we wait until the day when the American Jews have to choose sides."

AFTERWORD
HISTORICAL AMNESIA AND JEWISH COVENTRY

❝ When the Historian of the future assembles the bleak record of our days, he will find two things unbelievable: first, the crime itself; second the reaction of the world to that crime," Chaim Weizmann prophesied in a speech at Madison Square Garden on March 1, 1943. Weizmann was speaking on a rare occasion – a mass meeting held by the establishment Zionists specifically to protest against the indifference surrounding the Holocaust.[1]

Evidently, Weizmann, who was a giant of the Jewish cause in so many ways, did not imagine that one day the conduct of the Zionist and Jewish leadership in the free world would also be weighed and found wanting, that it would be shown that the American State Department and the British Foreign Office were not alone in their obstruction of efforts to save hundreds of thousands who might have been saved. The difference was that Zionist obstruction was not deliberate – that of the State Department and the Foreign Office was infinitely worse. Nevertheless, the hubris and duplicity of the Zionist leadership compounded the tragedy, and fed the belief that Jews are basically self-destructive.

For many years, the activities of Hillel Kook and the Bergson group of the 1940s were almost totally ignored by historians. While there were critical studies detailing the inaction of the State Department and President Roosevelt, there was little scholarly effort to examine the activities of the Jewish community and the Bergson group. In recent years this has changed, and younger scholars have started to get the skeleton out of the closet.

Nevertheless, recent attempts to address these questions about what was done, and what was not done, have come under attack from defenders of the wartime Jewish establishment. The charge of "Revisionist history" has been levelled against those who have dared to explore the possibility that thousands could have been saved had the Jewish leadership acted more forcefully. It has been alleged that journalistic sensation mongers and "predators of history," flocking together with "guilt-ridden Jews," are embarked on a destructive campaign to rewrite history, that it is simply "fashionable" to attack any establishment.[2]

But the real disservice to the cause of truthful historiography is when highly reputable scholars ignore vast areas of primary material in order to protect their thesis, or to support a political line or, worse, a personal whim. In disregarding the evidence, these scholars develop a kind of historical amnesia. Sometimes they really do forget. How else can one explain the deliberate distortions of the Bergson group's role in the creation of the War Refugee Board by generally respected historians such as Lucy Dawidowicz and Bernard Wasserstein?

Prof. Dawidowicz, widely acclaimed for her book *The War Against the Jews*, has elsewhere propounded the theory that Hitler's war against the Jewish People was so relentless, and that Jews everywhere were so powerless, that any attempt to criticize Jewish behavior during those horrible times is *ipso facto* a way of blaming the victims. During recent years, she has focused on the Bergson group, repeating many of the accusations of forty years ago and maintaining that it is all a part of a sinister plot to rewrite history. But in making her case, she sharply contradicts her own writings. In a 1962 *Commentary* piece she wrote that the Bergson group's "only achievement" was the creation of the WRB, but that this meant little since the board did nothing at all; but then, twenty years later in the *New York Times*, she contended that the Bergsonites really had nothing to do with the WRB, which, it turns out, did accomplish something after all.[3]

Further, in 1982, Dawidowicz wrote glowingly of the Bergson group in the *American Jewish Year Book*, saying that they had achieved a "stunning success" in mobilizing prominent Americans on the issue of the Holocaust, that they "electrified the American public by their tactics", and that the Bergsonites "were probably the most potent influence, seconded by Henry Morgenthau's staff in the Treasury Department, in Roosevelt's creation of the War Refugee Board in January 1944." But then, in yet another turnabout a few months later, she attacked the Bergson group in a *Commentary* article, in which she suddenly discovered that Bergsonites had nothing to do with the WRB whatsoever, that it was all the work of Oscar Cox, a Morgenthau aide, who somehow had singlehandedly brought it about. In addition, she also coupled the Bergson group with the lunatic left as enemies of the Jewish People.[4]

In a September 1983 exchange of letters in *Commentary* in response to her article, Dawidowicz defended this pirouette style of history by asserting that she was not being fickle: "Further research and new evidence led me to a more accurate rendering of the past than the one I wrote when I relied more fully upon Messrs. Bergson and Merlin for their version of the event."[5] In other words, she'd been taken in. But was there no Rescue Resolution, no congressional hearings, no storm in the media, no editorials in the major newspapers about what the Bergsonites had done to create the climate for FDR's move?

A researcher can and should undergo a change of mind in the light of new evidence. But too often, what is claimed to be "new evidence" – in this case, the Cox connection – is neither new nor evidence, but an attempt to find support for a preconceived thesis. It becomes a vehicle for by-passing the main body of facts. Rare is the purely objective writer, journalist or historian. Editing skills make it easy to manipulate readers; playing with the focus distorts the rest of the picture – undoubtedly, my own, purposefully narrow focus on the Bergsonites has created inevitable distortions. But at least such "overcompensation" as there may be is meant to counterbalance the mostly negative images of the Bergson group found in the work of defenders of the wartime Zionist establishment.

Cox did, in fact, contribute to the establishment of a special rescue agency. But to compare the massive Bergsonite public and private campaign to the sporadic efforts of Cox is ludicrous. The real evidence, from the Morgenthau Diary to the newspapers of the day to the transcripts of Chairman Bloom's hearings to the testimony of central figures in the story like Josiah DuBois and John Pehle, is simply ignored. Dawidowicz's evidence turns out to be an attempt to credit anyone but the hateful "Irgunists," as she calls them, with bringing about the creation of the War Refugee Board. It is itself revisionist history *par excellence*.

Dawidowicz, repeating verbatim the Zionist-inspired libels of forty years ago, also claimed that the Bergson group raised money under false pretenses and that they "never rendered an accounting of the money they raised." In fact, as has been shown, their books were always open for public inspection and were audited by the Internal Revenue Service. The Solicitor General of the U.S. vouched for the honesty and openness of the Bergsonites with whom he worked; and the reputation of committee treasurer Frances Gunther, a journalist and wife of writer John Gunther, was beyond reproach.[6]

Similarly, Dawidowicz charged that Bergson's only motive in staging the 1943 Emergency Conference to Save the Jewish People of Europe was to create "another in a series of Irgun fronts" to raise money for arms to fight the British. This is unscholarly, not to say cynical and slanderous. In the summer of 1943, there was no Irgun to speak of. No money at all went to the Irgun during the war, and, as we have seen, this was a major source of contention between the Irgun and the Bergson group. To say that Bergson was only interested in exploiting the Holocaust in order to buy arms is beyond slanderous; it's positively macabre.[7]

"When historians knowingly or unknowingly omit from their historical writing an account of any given course of events, those events disappear from history," Dawidowicz wrote in *The Holocaust and the Historians*, a book in which she tried to deal with the mystery of why mainstream historians have belittled or overlooked the extermination. She also argues that Holocaust historians themselves are handicapped because subjects such as Jewish resistance, or collaboration, or the Zionist attitude toward rescue, are emotional dynamite. It is to belabor the obvious to point out that these same emotional factors may apply to Dawidowicz and other Jewish historians in writing about the Bergson group, or in ignoring their existence altogether.[8]

Thus, British pro-Zionist historian Bernard Wasserstein can write a lengthy article entitled "The Myth of 'Jewish Silence,'" in which he accepts uncritically Rabbi Wise's contention that Zionist leaders "working behind the scenes" inspired FDR to create the WRB, and never once mention the Bergson group or the Rescue Resolution by name. Is it possible that he erases the Bergsonites from history – in the spirit of Wise – because he does not approve of them?[9]

The historian's ethical standards and moral concepts weigh heavily in his or her reflections on persons and events. But what becomes of history when the historian's predilections or prejudices cause him to censor, repress or excise events altogether? Dawidowicz writes 10,000 words in the *New York Times* on American Jews and the Holocaust, in which she excoriates Senator Guy Gillette as nothing more than an anti-British former isolationist, yet never mentions the Rescue Resolution which he co-sponsored. Apparently, she cannot abide the thought that gentiles like Gillette could have been genuinely concerned with the fate of European Jews, and can only ascribe ulterior motives to their activities. Gillette's support of and devotion to the Bergson group was not engendered by an "anti-British attitude." He was, as historian David Wyman, a non-Jew, has pointed out, "one of the few political leaders who worked hard to save European Jews." But in the Jewish world, schools and museums and streets are named after Wise and Goldmann; Sol Bloom is memorialized by a forest in Zion; Gillette, however, is remembered only as "an isolationist."[10]

Another gentile political leader who worked closely with the Bergson group was Paul O'Dwyer of New York. In response to the Dawidowicz broadside in *The Times*, O'Dwyer wrote this testimonial to the Emergency Committee: "Their public advertising was direct, forceful and effective, and I joined in the movement," which had "struck a responsive chord in many hearts, including mine... It attracted many non-Jews like myself. We were working members of committees which Ms. Dawidowicz charges were 'names adorning the letterheads'... I can bear witness that the implication is a gross untruth."[11]

In a March 1982 exchange in the Zionist monthly magazine, *Midstream*, about the continuing controversy over the Bergson group, Israeli political scientist Charles S. Liebman wrote that scholars should no longer view Jewish history "through the prism of Zionist ideology; nor are Zionist figures, Labor Zionists at that, automatically right and non-labor Zionists or even non-Zionists automatically wrong." He concluded that the ideology of the wartime Zionist leaders often blinded them to the reality of the situation during this period: ...their Zionist commitment did diminish their efforts on behalf of world Jewry."[12]

Nevertheless, defenders of the establishment continue to raise red-herrings to dismiss criticism, saying that only "guilt-ridden Jews" could possibly conclude that not enough was done. One Jewish organization official accused a *Midstream* book reviewer of trying to blame the leaders of American Jewry for the Holocaust itself.[13] Stephen Wise biographer Melvin Urofsky claims that the critical scholars are simply possessed by the *"angst"* of "Holocaust guilt." Marie Syrkin (who buried the 1942 Bund report in the back pages of her Zionist journal) terms it "necrophilic digging into the guilt of the victims" – as if Wise, Silver, Bloom, Goldmann, *et al.*, were victims. Wasserstein, in his "Myth" article, says that the accusations are "well-calculated to appeal to the mixture of historical ignorance and guilt complex... It's all a total fabrication with no basis in reality."[14]

In her *New York Times* article, Lucy Dawidowicz concluded that the wartime Jewish and Zionist leadership did *everything* short of committing suicide, but that "rescuing the Jews of Europe was an unachievable task." That was certainly true for the Jews of Poland or in the Ukraine, but it was not at all true for the Jews of

Hungary and Rumania, for example. Dawidowicz herself says that the WRB "distinguished itself by rescuing Jews from those places where rescue was possible." How, then, can she conclude in the same article that Jews could not have been saved? Her conclusion is not only contradictory, it is also invidious. Tens of thousands of Jews *were* saved by the WRB and its emissaries.[15]

Although the congressional Rescue Resolution has virtually disappeared in the historical accounts offered by Dawidowicz, Wasserstein and others, neutral scholars believe it deserves more than a mention. In 1976, as part of historical series to commemorate America's bicentennial, the U.S. Government Printing Office issued transcripts from the history-making House Foreign Relations Committee hearings on the Rescue Resolution. The editors, historians from the University of Pittsburgh, apparently did not share the handicaps or carry the heavy luggage of right-wing or left-wing Zionists, or anti-Zionists. Their introduction to the transcripts tells the whole tale;

> News of the extermination of European Jews began to filter in from various sources to the State Department beginning in mid-1942. It has been conclusively established that an effort was made to suppress this information, and later to limit its distribution to a very small number of individuals.
>
> As the horrifying details of the "final solution" became known, Jewish organizations in the U.S. strove to come to grips with the unfavorable atmosphere towards efforts at rescue. The established Jewish leadership of the country, however, as represented by Rabbi Stephen Wise, leader of the American Jewish Conference, was reluctant to antagonize the Roosevelt administration... But the issue was felt by many to be too important to be treated in a spirit of compromise... Peter Bergson and Samuel Merlin... organized a number of public committees throughout the U.S. Their vigorous propaganda campaign succeeded in attracting the support of a large number of Senators, Representatives, university professors and public personalities by the end of 1943. It was this pressure which resulted in House Resolution 350 and 352 and led to the Congressional hearings of November 1943.
>
> The conflict between Bergson's ECSJPE and the mainstream Jewish organizations represented by Rabbi Wise became apparent during the hearings... as well as in criticism of inaction levelled against House Foreign Affairs Committee Chairman Sol Bloom and at the State Department....
>
> House Resolutions 350 and 352 were never passed, but the hearings and the resulting debate in the media led to the formation of the WRB by President Roosevelt on January 22, 1944.[16]

The purposeful historical amnesia that affects certain scholars is by no means a phenomenon confined to historians, as evidenced by the fact that Rabbi Wise and/or his aides "sanitized" the papers he left to posterity. Consequently, the massive, eight-year-long campaign waged against the Bergsonites does not exist in Wise's papers housed at the American Jewish Historical Society. A shameful chapter in Jewish history simply did a disappearing act. According to the archive's librarian and executive editor, Nathan Kaganoff (responding to the author's requests for Wise material, the existence of which being documented elsewhere), "it seems... the material you are looking for has not survived in the Wise papers." If Wise himself did not get rid of what must have been at least an occasional reference to matters which had obsessed him for years, then it was done later for him. "I understand that the synagogue [Wise's Free Synagogue] itself hired someone to eliminate a good deal of material," the archivist stated.[17]

Wise's malady also affected the Menachem Begin school of history, as well as the mainstream Zionist school. Begin referred to the entire Bergson group campaign in but a few sentences and a footnote, albeit a positive one. Begin said at a public meeting a few years before becoming prime minister that he believed wartime Zionist leaders had done everything possible to save European Jews; he used the argument that the Jews had no navy. In essence, he agreed with the position of Dawidowicz, Wasserstein, Urofsky and company, ignoring the fact that the issue was to get the U.S. government to do something. The U.S. did have a navy, one that brought hundreds of thousands of German and Italian POWs to detention camps in America. If the WRB had been set up a few months earlier, if Roosevelt had been pressured to make Oswego the rule rather than the single exception, those ships, or others, could have been filled with Jews who were otherwise doomed.[18]

The Israeli-produced *Encyclopaedia Judaica* provides other kinds of historical distortions. It includes a long and laudatory entry about Sol Bloom, ignoring the fact that almost the entire American Jewish leadership – and not just the Bergsonites – considered him to be a State Department "flunky," a handmaiden to the Holocaust whose obstruction of Jewish rescue was second only to that of Breckinridge Long. Yet Bloom, because of his Zionism, is accorded as much space in the encyclopedia's 1975 edition as Menachem Begin. There is no individual entry for Peter Bergson in the encyclopedia (a project begun by Nahum Goldmann), nor is there an entry for any of Bergson's committees, next to nothing about their work in America, good or bad, and nothing at all about the War Refugee Board.

Excommunication, one concludes, is the price for battling the establishment: a Jewish Coventry. It does not seem to matter that the issue was the saving of human life. Even when a committee activist like Arthur Szyk is profiled, not a word is mentioned about his years of passionate involvement with the Bergsonites.

In her writings, Lucy Dawidowicz has cited Cicero's homily that the historian's first law is never to utter an untruth, and the second is that he suppress nothing that *is* true. Yet nowhere in her various treatments of the rescue issue does she mention what has been shown to be the intense "dirty tricks" campaign that consumed so much of Wise's and Goldmann's time while millions screamed for help.[19]

Bernard Wasserstein, following the oddly deterministic line advanced by Dawidowicz and others, states categorically that there was never a chance for rescue, that nothing could have been done to save more of the Jews. He terms any criticism of the wartime leadership – criticism that has come from highly respected historians like Wyman and Saul Friedman – as part of "Begin's plot." In *Midstream*, Israeli Prof. Michael J. Cohen, who has written widely-praised histories of Palestine during and after the war, refuted Wasserstein's views:

> It seems to me that Wasserstein... himself falling into the same partisanship of which he accuses his debaters, is particularly niggardly in respect of Peter Bergson. It is hardly disputable that Bergson's revolutionary methods... not only made the American public and administration aware of the 'Jewish problem,' but indeed caused a flurry of diplomatic feathers to fly as far afield as London, Baghdad and Damascus. That the Jewish establishment did not link up with Bergson, or at least adopt his methods, was of course a matter of internal Jewish politics... That Bergson has never been given due credit is also a matter of internal politics, this time in the writing of history.[20]

Cohen wondered how Wasserstein could "possibly state categorically that more could not have been done, or that any additional pressure would not in any case have moved the Allies." He also attacked the notion of utter "powerlessness" of the wartime American Jewish community.[21]

When it was in their interests, the Jewish and Zionist leadership showed that they were anything but powerless, as the Hoskins affair shows. Both the Bergsonites and the establishment leaders, working independently, succeeded in getting the Joint U.S.-British Declaration shelved. They showed great strength in influencing American policy, as disappointed British officials ruefully noted. Yet this seminal affair goes unrecorded in the works of the establishment's apologists.

Wasserstein, in stating that the American Jews were powerless, attacked Bergson's "hysterical campaigns": "Newspaper advertisements may have been irritating to Stephen Wise... but they were not marches on Washington. How many such marches did the Wise or Irgunist groups organize?"[22] The answer: The Bergson group organized one; the Zionist establishment organized none.

Lucy Dawidowicz may contend that the accusations against Wise, Goldmann and other Zionist leaders are "laughable and outrageous," but to anyone who investigates the matter, even superficially, the evidence is staggering, and it is *her* contentions that appear to be outrageous. And not just concerning the war against the Bergsonites. For even an historian in basic agreement with her – Israeli Prof. Yehuda Bauer – writes that toward war's end, American Jews were coming to see the elementary truth that with more money, more could have been done to save lives.[23]

Philosopher of history Sir Isaiah Berlin, who witnessed these events from his perch at the British embassy in Washington, says today that deals with Nazi satellites might have worked, "And this was not attempted." Jewish pressure in the U.S. "did not occur on a sufficient scale, for fear, I suppose, of rocking the military boat: such attitudes have occurred before and after... humanity, courage and persistence are always in short supply." One wonders how Berlin, as late as 1972, could have criticized "the notorious Bergson," who was long on just those rare qualities the historian cited.[24]

There are those who say it is too simplistic to assess the traumatic events of forty years ago with the benefit of hindsight. Zionist writer Marie Syrkin criticizes those who apply the "activist standards of the 1960s" to the situation of the wartime Jewish and Zionist leadership, besieged by anti-Semites.[25] But despite the oft-mentioned constraints and pressures of the period, these leaders did exercise free will – Wise and Goldmann were not members of a *Judenrat*, besieged by Nazis. Is it then hindsight to judge them? As Isaiah Berlin has written concerning the judging of historical personalities, "Our situations may differ from theirs, but not always so widely as to make all comparisons unfair."[26]

Historians face the awesome task of disentangling a complex network of "facts" to get at a small part of the truth. No matter how difficult, there must be a place for moral judgments, for deciding who are the heroes and who are the villains. To quote Berlin again: "...it becomes the business of historians to investigate who wanted what, and when, and where, in what way; how many men avoided or pursued this or that goal, and with what intensity."[27] Stephen Wise did not pursue the goal of a rescue agency; Peter Bergson did. The WRB was not created out of FDR's *tabula rasa*. Two months before the formation of the agency, Judge Rosenman, Nahum Goldmann – even Roosevelt himself – thought the idea ludicrous. In the campaign for a special rescue agency, the Bergson group proved in yet another way that American Jews were not powerless, despite the impotence of establishment organization leaders. To "forget" or totally dismiss the Bergsonite contribution is to favor deceit.

In the end, the politicans who make their careers in Jewish organizations did great damage to the Jewish People, while the Bergson group was piercing the silence around the extermination, transforming the face of Jewish politics, and bringing the requisite pressure to bear on an (at best) indifferent FDR. If the establishment organizations had done as much, hundreds of thousands more lives might have been saved.

As Prof. Cohen wrote in *Midstream*, "...let us not cover up the inhibitions of the Jews, or their inability to comprehend the magnitude and nature of the crime in progress, with platitudes about there being no viable option available. No one can be sure that mass protests would have brought policy changes, but it seems quite evident that there existed a moral obligaiton to at least try."[28]

The crux of the matter is that the establishment leaders basically did not try. The Bergson group's records "remain today as the best proof that American Jews did care about the European co-religionists, and did try desperately to rescue them," as one student of organized American Jewry has written.[29]

In 1962, fifteen years after Rabbi Wise's death, Stephen Wise Road was dedicated in Jerusalem. Rabbi Nelson Glueck, president of Hebrew Union College in New York, hailed Wise as the "Champion of God," a man of "unflinching moral bravery," a kind of Messiah in Europe's concentration camps.[30] Wise, the glory of his times, left his name behind him, while others have no memorial. They are perished, as if they had never been. Peter Bergson's deeds are still being obliterated by those who have become practised in the art of historical amnesia.

The historian looks backward, to paraphrase a Nietzschean maxim, and eventually, all too often, he also *believes* backward.

NOTES

1. *The Making of a Hebrew Revolutionary*

1. At some time in the distant past, the Kook family name had been Yoffee. Nahum Kook – Rapoport interview, Sept. 16, 1982.

2. Rav Kook's only son, Zvi, Hillel's first cousin, would become head of the Rav Kook Institute in Jerusalem and mentor of *Gush Emunim* ("bloc of the faithful"), the spearhead of Israel's post-1967 Messianic nationalist movement.

3. Nahum Kook – Rapoport interview, ibid.

4. See the works of Simon Dubnow and M. Tchernikover; also *Pogromchik: The assassination of Simon Petlura*, Saul S. Friedman, Hart Publishing Co., 1976. Another interesting account of the pogroms in the Ukraine can be found in *The Unknown Revolution*, an anarchist classic written by Voline (V.M. Eichenbaum), published in 1955 by London's Freedom Press.

5. Journalist Victor Riesel, in a July 11, 1944, *New York Post Magazine* profile of Peter Bergson, wrote that the Ukrainian pogrom "seared" Kook's mind. (Copies of all documents at the Institute for Mediterranean Affairs are also part of the Palestine Statehood Committee Papers archived at the Sterling Library of Yale University.)

6. Nahum and Herzl Kook both became doctors. Hillel was the only maverick among Rebecca Kook's sons.

7. Arthur Hertzberg in *The Zionist Idea* (p. 417) writes that because Rav Kook believed he was living in the Messianic era, "He could therefore both seriously prepare himself for future office as priest of the restored cult in the Temple in Jerusalem and accept all builders of Palestine, heretics included...."

8. Hegel's classic definition of freedom.

9. Jerusalem, Safed and Tiberias are the other three cities holy to the Jews. The Jewish quarter in Arab Hebron was near the Machpelah cave, traditional burial site of Abraham, Isaac and Jacob, and of the Matriarchs other than Rebecca.

10. Lord Josiah Wedgwood, namesake of the eighteenth century potter who founded the family business, favored the more radical nationalist brand of Zionism and was a fervent spokesman for Zionism in the House of Lords, until his death during World War II.

11. In the propaganda battle between the pro-Zionist and pro-Arab sides, the 1929 events are often described either as "the massacres" or "the riots," or, alternately, "the national uprising" of 1929.

12. The word "Hebrew" was considered an elevated, prouder appellation than "Jew" until it was superseded by "Israeli" with the coming of the state.

13. The fraternities were patterned after German and American models, including some fencing, drinking and hazing.

14. Batya Kook – Rapoport interview, Oct. 5, 1982.

15. The "Bet" was to differentiate it from the original Haganah, "Aleph."

16. Betar is, in addition to the name of an ancient Judean-Roman battlesite, an acronym from Brit Trumpeldor, the Trumpeldor League, named after Jabotinsky's friend and hero of the early Zionist settlers.

17. There were about 500 students at Hebrew University in 1932.

18. A rough translation of Stern's lyrics (the music was composed by his girl friend, Roni, whom he later married):

> Unknown soldiers we were
> without uniforms;
> Around us, horror and the
> shadow of death;
> We've all been mobilized,
> for the rest of our lives;
> From this formation,
> only death liberates.
>
> In these red days
> of pogroms and
> black nights of despair,
> in the cities and villages
> we shall raise our flag proclaiming:
> Defense and Conquest!
> We were not whipped into
> mobilization like a pack of slaves
> in order to spill our blood in foreign lands;
> It's our will to be forever free;
> Our dream is to die for our nation.

If we shall fall in the streets
and the houses and will be buried
quietly at night, in our place
will come thousands of others
to defend and guard forever;
The bereaved mothers
who have lost their sons
and the blood of innocent babes
will be like cement
with which to glue our
bodies – bricks – which
we'll use to build our homeland.

19. Levine, p. 108. The Hebrew press deplored the incident and said that the students had used "Nazi tactics."

20. Tehomi asked Kook to become involved in the Boycott Committee in 1934.

21. Hillel Kook does not recall the exact words of his uncle's appeal. Two years earlier, in 1933, Rav Kook took an unpopular, "pro-Jabotinsky" stand in the Arlosoroff murder case, saying that the accusation by labor Zionists that Revisionists had murdered the Jewish Agency leader was a calumny.

22. "My father obviously knew and silently approved of Hillel's activities," according to Nahum Kook (Sept. 16, 1982 interview).

23. Amikam – Rapoport interview, Jan. 28, 1983. Amikam later joined the Stern group and was among those held soon after Israel's independence for the murder of UN envoy Count Bernadotte. He later became a leading right-wing journalist.

24. Alexander Rafaeli – Rapoport interview, Nov. 26, 1982. Rafaeli would later become one of the core group of Palestinians to serve under Kook's command in the U.S.

25. Jabotinsky gave a full account in his book *The Story of the Jewish Legion*, New York, 1945.

26. Trumpeldor entered the Zionist pantheon for his defense of the Tel Hai settlement in 1920 against Arab marauders. The mortally wounded hero's last words, the story goes, were: "Never mind. It is good to die for our fatherland." Avraham Stern's "our dream is to die for our nation" is quite a different sentiment.

27. Samuel Merlin, formerly Jabotinsky's secretary and later right-hand man to Peter Bergson in the U.S., characterized Jabotinsky thusly. Merlin – Rapoport interview, Sept. 10, 1982.

28. See Schechtman, *Fighter and Prophet*. Jabotinsky's only son, Eri, would soon become Hillel Kook's closest friend, and eventually his fellow rebel in the First Knesset.

29. Ben-Ami, *Years of Wrath, Days of Glory*, pp. 102-103.

30. Shoshana Raziel – Rapoport interview, Oct. 28, 1982. Her general bitterness, and her animosity towards Hillel Kook, increased as the years went by. She and other members of *Brit Habiryonim* would claim that Kook, on orders from Raziel and

Stern, backed out of a role as getaway driver in a September 12, 1937, bank robbery. But Kook was already in Poland at that time.

Haim Dviri, one of the *Brit Habiryonim* men caught and imprisoned for the robbery, said in an interview (Dviri – Rapoport, Nov. 18, 1982) that Kook and the rest of the Irgun High Command were against the robbery because they were engaged in an internal struggle against an outsider, Colonel Robert Bitker, whom the Revisionists tried to install as head of the Irgun. Bitker, a Russian Jew from Shanghai, knew nothing of Palestine and could not speak Hebrew. He favored robbing banks (in the tradition of Russian revolutionaries) to finance the underground. The young Irgun leaders were not opposed to this in principle, but wanted only to get rid of Bitker, and he was soon ousted.

31. The Canaanites identified with the ancient inhabitants of Palestine and disavowed "Jewishness." It was never a major movement. Kook's later ideas about separating Jewish nationality and religion have nothing in common with the Canaanites, and Kook was entirely opposed to their philosophy.

32. Hertzberg, *The Zionist Idea*, pp. 559ff.

33. Weizmann's "Dust" remark, ibid., p. 588, and *Kongresszeitung 1937*, Twentieth Zionist Congress, Zurich, Aug. 4, 1937.

34. Ironically, Walter Laqueur, in his *History of Zionism* (page 551) would refer to Kook as "a young Palestinian revisionist leader." The often intense rivalries between the Irgun and the Revisionists and the Revisionist youth organization Betar are generally ignored. One of the young local Betar officers Kook met in Poland was Menachem Begin, the future Irgun leader who one day would erase the Revisionists from the map.

35. Merlin interview, ibid.

36. In his February 1937 appearance before the Peel Commission, Jabotinsky praised the Polish government for helping bring notice to the world that it was "humanity's duty" to provide a territorial home for the Jewish People. *The Zionist Idea*, p. 560.

37. Ironically, the Palestine Liberation Organization would one day adopt an emblem along almost exactly the same lines: a rifle held in a hand superimposed over a map of both Israel and Jordan – Mandate Palestine. The political party founded by Rabbi Meir Kahane in Israel took its name from half of the Irgun slogan, Kach ("thus").

38. Stavsky had been tried, and was acquitted, of the 1933 murder of the brilliant young labor Zionist leader Chaim Arlosoroff, a watershed affair in relations between the two main camps of Zionism. A commission appointed by Menachem Begin fifty years after the murder also found no evidence that Stavsky was involved.

39. Yitshaq Ben-Ami in his memoir gives an account of the "swashbuckling" Galili's exploits. *Years of Wrath, Days of Glory*, pp. 122f.

40. His original mission on behalf of the Irgun High Command, supposed to last a few weeks, lasted a decade.

41. The figures vary widely, in accordance with the ideological predilections of the writer. Ben-Ami (ibid., pp. 253ff) gives the high figure. Yehuda Bauer, an historian

unfriendly to the Irgunists, offers the low figure in *American Jewry and the Holocaust*, pp. 130ff, and incorrectly gives grudging credit solely to "the Revisionists."

42. Ben-Ami on behalf of the Irgun dealt directly with Eichmann and his superiors in the months before the war (ibid., pp. 147ff). In March 1939, Chaim Weizmann discouraged Robert de Rothschild from contributing to the Irgun immigration effort, saying that it was wrong to deal with the devil (ibid., p. 209).

43. The Irgunists could have bought a seaworthy ship, the *S.S. Pilsudski*, which could carry 10,000 passengers, but they could not come up with the $25,000 because the Rothschilds heeded Weizmann's warning (ibid, p. 211).

44. Katznelson, a former follower of Ahimeir, became an Irgun member. The immigration coordinator was based in Warsaw.

45. On Wise and Montor, see Ben-Ami, ibid., pp. 211, 267, 320. Montor's four-page letter was dated Feb. 1, 1940.

46. House of Commons debate – *Hansards*, April 26, 1939.

47. Lourie document PRO FO 371/2400/2829.

48. For accounts of the *S.S. St. Louis* affair, see Saul Friedman's *No Haven for the Oppressed* and Yehuda Bauer's *My Brother's Keeper.*

49. *No Haven for the Oppressed*, ibid., p. 98.

50. Ibid.

51. Schechtman, ibid. pp. 481-482.

---

2. The Right to Fight: The Idea of a Jewish Army

1. Merlin – Rapoport interview, Sept. 10, 1982. Kook – Rapoport interviews, July 1982.

2. Ben-Ami, *Years of Wrath, Days of Glory*, p. 237.

3. Ibid.

4. Ibid., p. 238.

5. Eventually, about 30,000 Palestinian Jews managed to serve with British forces.

6. Levine, *David Raziel, the Man and His Times*, p. 294. The quote is by Shalom Rosenfeld, an underground member who eventually became editor of the daily *Ma'ariv* newspaper and one of Israel's most prominent journalists. Kook knew Raziel and Stern too well to idealize either of them.

7. Schechtman, *Fighter and Prophet*, p. 460.

8. Ben-Ami letter to Rapoport, Feb. 17, 1984. Also Schechtman, vol. II, p. 392.

9. Ben-Ami, *Years of Wrath, Days of Glory*, p. 224.

10. Ibid., p. 319.

11. Ibid., p. 255 and p. 319.

12. The forerunner of the United Jewish Appeal.

13. The Feb. 11, 1940, letter to Rabbi Baruch E. Rabinowitz is in the Palestine Statehood Committee papers at Yale University.

14. Foreign Office 371-25241/12.

15. Jabotinsky's unfinished book was published posthumously in 1942, with an introduction by Pierre van Paassen.

16. Urofsky, *A Voice That Spoke for Justice*, p. 312; and Ben-Ami, op. cit., p. 243.

17. Berlin – Rapoport interview, op. cit. Kook – Rapoport interviews, op. cit. Merlin, who had become very close to Stern in Poland, had been greatly upset about the way Raziel, in frequent letters to Stern in 1939, reproached and threatened him. Merlin also did not like the way Stern treated Raziel's closest friend, Kook. Stern, part of the Irgun high command, pulled rank on Kook/Bergson – ostensibly the Irgun's chief emissary abroad – whenever possible.

18. Ben-Ami letter to Rapoport, op. cit.

19. Ibid. "Hardly any funds were raised" in the U.S. for the immigration effort, "and from this viewpoint undoubtedly we failed."

20. Kook-Rapoport interviews, op. cit. The core of the Bergson group was often referred to as "the Palestinians."

21. Merlin had never lived in Palestine, but the Hebrew-speaking former secretary to Jabotinsky was regarded by his colleagues as a *landsmann*.

22. Ben-Ami letter, op. cit., and his memoirs, p. 242.

23. Rafaeli – Rapoport interview, Nov. 15, 1982. Merlin – Rapoport interview, op. cit. "We functioned as a military unit."

24. Merlin – Rapoport op. cit. Later, Merlin and Bergson moved to an apartment on Central Park South.

25. Zar, *Rescue and Liberation*, p. 20.

26. Lookstein, *American Jewry's Public Response to the Holocaust 1938-1944*, p. 70.

27. Silver Shirts, Gallup Poll, in Friedman, *No Haven for the Oppressed*, p. 174.

28. Ibid., pp. 46-47.

29. Goldstein – Rapoport interview, Jan. 12, 1983.

30. Bauer, *American Jewry and the Holocaust*, p. 123.

31. Ganin, *Truman, American Jewry and Israel*, p. 4.

32. Arendt, *The Jew as Pariah*, p. 150. According to Hannah Arendt, "the only important issue in a war against Hitler was a Jewish army."

33. Merlin – Rapoport interview, op. cit.

34. Young-Bruehl, *Hannah Arendt, For Love of the World*, p. 174. Arendt was enthusiastic over the public support the Bergson group was whipping up, and she attended the group's meetings until she "realized," according to her biographer, that the committee was "a Revisionist front." This was a falsehood used by the establishment Zionists to discredit the Bergsonites.

35. Kook – Rapoport interviews, op. cit. Ben-Ami memoirs, p. 245.

36. Young-Bruehl, op. cit. The mainstream Zionists, in Arendt's view, reflected "the old mentality of enslaved people... Only through the pressure of Jews throughout the world was the Zionist organization driven to ask for a Jewish army."

37. Kook – Rapoport interviews, op. cit.

38. Palestine Statehood Committee Papers, Dec. 4, 1941.

39. Kook – Rapoport interviews, op. cit.

40. Palestine Statehood Committee Papers, Jan. 17, 1942. Knox also said that "In Palestine Hitler faces the wrath of the people he has starved and tortured and degraded – Jews, over half a million strong."

41. *Congressional Record*, Nov. 28, 1941.

42. Ibid., April 16, 1942.

43. *New York Times*, Jan. 5, 1942.

44. Merlin – Rapoport interview, op. cit.

45. Zar, op. cit., p. 39.

46. Edwin Johnson File, Institute of Mediterranean Affairs.

47. Halifax, in Cohen, *Palestine: Retreat from the Mandate*, p. 119.

48. Ibid.

49. Arendt, op. cit.

3. *The Front Page*

1. Ben Hecht, *A Child of the Century*, pp. 515ff.

2. Ibid.

3. Ibid.

4. Hecht's line from *We Will Never Die*.

5. Hecht, *A Child of the Century*, pp. 515ff.

6. According to biographer Justin Kaplan, in a Sept. 19, 1983, letter to the author, the whole business of Chaplin's Jewishness "is very murky" and compounded by Chaplin's "refusal ever to deny publicly that he was Jewish."

7. Patterson's best-known book was *Man-Eaters of Tsavo*.

8. Hecht, *A Child of the Century*, pp. 515ff.

9. Kook – Rapoport interviews, July 1982.

10. Hecht's identification was already expressed in the title of his article in the newspaper *PM*, "My Tribe is Israel."

11. Hecht, *A Child of the Century*, pp. 515ff. Louis Bromfield had what one of his biographers called a Midwesterner's attitude towards Jews, stereotyped and vague,

believing them to be mysterious and unknowable. Despite the pressure from some of his Jewish friends, like Ferber, he remained a committee activist for years.

12. Hecht, *A Child of the Century*, pp. 515ff.

13. Ibid.

14. Szyk, *The Answer*, August 1944.

15. Ibid. Szyk was eventually acclaimed as one of the greatest of Jewish artists, but his long and strong association with the Bergson group would be ignored – see, for example, the biographical entry on him in the *Encyclopaedia Judaica*.

16. Ickes, however, was never as active as Rogers, Gillette, Johnson or other officials involved in the Bergson cause.

17. Truman to Somers, Jewish Army File, Jabotinsky Institute, Tel Aviv.

18. At a time when Rommel was pummeling the British, in February 1942, a full-page committee ad in the *Philadelphia Record* (Feb. 10, 1942) said: "200,000 men to ask the right to fight for a free world... They wait only on the British government's 'Yes.'"

19. Flanagan's letter, Jewish Army File, Jabotinsky Institute.

20. de Haas and Hitte letters, Jewish Army File, Jabotinsky Institute.

21. Stella Adler letter to author, Feb. 7, 1986.

22. Kollek on Rose, *The Jerusalem Post*, Feb. 11, 1966.

23. Gillette's speech, Aug. 1, 1946, Gillette File, Institute of Mediterranean Affairs, New York.

24. Unpublished article/interview by Charley J. Levine, 1974.

25. Merlin letter to author, Feb. 4, 1984; Merlin – Rapoport interviews, Sept. 1982.

26. Ibid.

27. The latter characterization was that of Lucy Dawidowicz, *New York Times Magazine*, April 18, 1982.

28. Urofsky, *A Voice That Spoke for Justice*, pp. 107, 162.

29. Ibid., pp. 43, 292.

30. Ibid., p. 304.

31. Ibid., pp. 247, 256, 289, 25.

32. Wise's showmanship is described by Ira Hirschman, *Caution to the Wind*.

33. Documenting the extent of this collusion is difficult, since Wise's papers have been "sanitized" on matters relating to the Bergson group, and the parties involved tried to keep to a minimum written correspondence about their campaign against Bergson. But sufficient evidence survives.

34. Goldmann, *The Jewish Paradox*, pp. 42, 30.

35. Ibid., p. 31.

36. Wise's FBI files obtained by author under FOIPA request 240, 668.

37. Hoover to New York office, Aug. 9, 1941, 100-24701.

38. *Jewish Frontier*, March 1942.

39. Urofsky, op. cit., p. 336.

40. Wise, *Personal Letters*, p. 266.

41. Weisgal quoted in Urofsky, op. cit., p. 332.

42. Neumann, *In the Arena*, p. 187.

43. Wasserstein, *Britain and the Jews of Europe*, pp. 145-146; and Ben-Ami, *Years of Wrath, Days of Glory*, p. 269.

44. According to Chaim Pozner's widow, Gini, Arthur Sommer was the source of the information (Pozner – Rapoport interview, Jan. 20, 1983). Sommer, an economist attached to Hitler's headquarters, gave the information to his former professor at Heidelberg, Edgar Salin. It eventually got to Riegner through Pozner. To his dismay, Pozner found that the Zionists in Palestine to whom he reported did not believe his report of the "Final Solution."

45. Urofsky, op. cit., pp. 319ff.

46. State Dept. memo 862.40 16/23333 Aug. 13, 1942.

47. Dawidowicz, op. cit.

48. *The Warsaw Diary of Chaim A. Kaplan*, p. 347. The diary was discovered a generation after the ghetto was liquidated.

49. Wiesel, "Telling the Tale," *Dimensions in Judaism*, spring 1968.

50. *New York Times*, Nov. 25, 1942, p. 10. Even the *Palestine Post* in Jerusalem played down the Wise press conference – it, too, tacked on his information to the report from London, although it put it on page one.

51. Hecht, *A Child of the Century*, pp. 515ff.

52. Bergson/Kook only learned of this dossier a generation later. Kook – Rapoport interviews, op. cit.

53. Ibid.

54. *New York Times*, Nov. 30, 1942.

55. *New York Times*, Dec. 7, 1942.

56. Wise, quoted by Dawidowicz, op. cit.

57. Dawidowicz, *Commentary*, June 1983.

58. Urofsky, op. cit., p. 322.

59. Ibid. Others who subscribed to the "powerlessness" theory include Wasserstein and Dawidowicz.

60. Wise to FDR cited in Friedman, *No Haven for the Oppressed*, p. 139.

61. Bauer, op. cit., p. 191.

62. Friedman, op. cit. p. 141.

63. Friedman, op. cit., p. 139.

64. Ben-Ami letter to author, Feb. 7, 1984.

65. FDR's quotes in Matzozsky, "An Episode: Roosevelt and the Mass Killing," *Midstream*, Aug/Sept 1980; and in Lookstein, *American Jewry's Public Response*, etc., p. 175.

66. Urofsky, op. cit., pp. 322, 327.

67. *American Mercury*, Feb. 1943, pp. 194-203. *Readers' Digest*, Feb. 1943, pp. 107-110.

68. Urofsky, ibid.

69. *New York Times*, Dec. 7, 1942.

70. Landon in Zar's *Rescue and Liberation*, p. 30.

71. Hecht, op. cit., p. 577.

72. Meeting cited by Merlin, *Commentary*, Sept. 1983.

73. Hecht, ibid.

74. Voss, *Servant of the People*, p. 258.

75. Hecht, op. cit., p. 564.

76. Weizmann quoted in Laqueur, *History of Zionism*, p. 551.

77. Hecht, op. cit., pp. 564-576.

78. Ibid.; and *New York American*, Mar. 10, 1943.

79. Peck, "The Campaign for an American Response to the Nazi Holocaust (1943-1945)," *Journal of Contemporary History*, v. 15, 1980.

80. Eleanor Roosevelt quoted in Ben-Ami, op. cit., p. 286.

81. Johnson's speech in *New York Times*, March 10, 1943.

82. Ben-Ami, op. cit., p. 325.

83. Dawidowicz, *New York Times Magazine*, Apr. 18., 1982. See also her *War Against the Jews*, p. 335.

84. Ibid., *New York Times Magazine*.

85. Reams and other anti-Jewish State Department functionaries have been profiled in Arthur Morse's groundbreaking *While Six Million Died*, in Friedman's *No Haven for the Oppressed*, and in Wyman's *The Abandonment of the Jews*. The remark about Sol Bloom was made many years after these events by his colleague in the House, Emanuel Celler, in Laurence Jarvik's documentary film *Who Shall Live and Who Shall Die*. The characterization of Lucas is in Friedman's book, p. 162.

86. *Foreign Relations of the United States*, 1943, v. 1, pp. 148, 151. *Kansas City Star*, Apr. 19, 1943.

87. Morse, op. cit., p. 47.

88. Isaiah Berlin spoke mockingly of Bloom in his despatches from Washington to the Foreign Office, e.g., F0371/35041/xc/a/047702.

89. Kook – Rapoport interviews, op. cit.

90. *The War Diary of Breckinridge Long*, April 20, 1943. Some defenders of the Zionist establishment, such as Marie Syrkin, have cited this passage as proof of the great work of the establishment Zionist leaders – making the same mistake Long did, by

associating, for example, Rabbi Wise with the Bergsonite Senator Johnson and the inflammatory full-page ads.

91. Wise to Welles, Apr. 4, 1943, State Dept. file 548. G1/38.

92. Memo of phone conversation, Long and FDR, Mar. 19, 1943, B. Long papers; Long also cited in Friedman, op. cit., p. 172.

93. *Foreign Relations of the United States*, 1943, v. 1, pp. 157-161; v. 1, p. 179, 307-325.

94. Ibid., pp. 173-174.

95. Urofsky, op. cit., p. 329.

96. Minutes of Apr. 18, 1943, meeting, American Jewish Committee Archives.

97. Ad in *New York Times*, May 5, 1943.

98. Ibid.

99. Friedman, op. cit., p. 182.

100. Ibid.; and Ben-Ami, op. cit., p. 290.

101. Ibid.

102. Kook – Rapoport interview, op. cit.

103. *Harold Ickes Diary*, Library of Congress, Oct. 31, 1943.

104. Ibid.

105. Charley Levine, op. cit.

106. It was not an easy task, given the hostility of the British Foreign Office and the State Department, as well as the general suspicion of foreigners fostered by men like Senator Lucas, or Congressman Martin Dies of the House Un-American Activities Committee. Assistant Secretary Long continued to rationalize his barring of Jewish refugees with the absurd contention that many Nazi spies might be among the Jewish refugees. Another State Department immigration official who worked against the Bergson group's proposals, George Warren, believed this argument to the end of his life. In 1978, he said: "I know of only one refugee who got in [to the U.S.] through presidential order, a man from Czechoslovakia, and when he went back after the war, he was a Communist – so you see..." Jarvik film, op. cit.]

107. I.S.A. Weizmann Files 105/1/4.

4. *The Emergency*

1. Alexander Rafaeli – Rapoport interview, Nov. 29, 1983. The special agency was Bergson's idea, according to Rafaeli and others.

2. Wyman, *The Abandonment of the Jews*, p. 183.

3. Minutes of American Emergency Committee for Zionist Affairs, May 3, 1943; Zionist Archives.

4. *New York Times*, Mar. 10, 1943.

5. Welles to Taylor, June 23, 1943; Myron C. Taylor Papers, Box 5, Correspondence 1938-1954. Tucker in Wyman, op. cit., p. 144.

6. Morgenthau Diary, Book 6881, pp. 47-67.

7. *The Answer*, 8/44, pp. 6-14. Hearst's flagship, the *San Francisco Examiner*, frequently reiterated the position that the extermination had to be confronted directly by the gentile world, as well as by the Jews. *San Francisco Examiner*, May 17, 1944, Aug. 1, 1944.

8. Ben-Ami, *Years of Wrath, Days of Glory*, p. 293.

9. Ibid.

10. State Department draft message 740.00116 EW 1939/1135.

11. Lerner's speech, Emergency Conference file, Institute of Mediterranean Affairs. *The Answer*, 7/5/43, 8/43.

12. Morgenthau message, Emergency Conference file, Institute of Mediterranean Affairs. Messages of encouragement also came from Mrs. Roosevelt and Wendell Wilkie. *The Answer*, 7/5/43, 8/43; *New York Times*, July 13; 21, 1943; *New York Herald Tribune*, July 26, 1943.

13. Lerner, *PM*, July 22, 1943.

14. Ibid.

15. Max Lerner letter to author, Dec. 22, 1982.

16. Ibid.

17. Eleanor Roosevelt to Lerner, July 23, 1943 ER 1689/100. Eleanor Roosevelt to Bromfield, June 25, 1943 ER 1640/100.

18. Bergson speech, *The Answer* 7/5/43, 8/43; *New York Herald Tribune*, July 26, 1943. Emergency Conference file, Institute of Mediterranean Affairs.

19. Ibid.

20. Wyman, op. cit., pp. 187-188.

21. Ben-Ami, op. cit., p. 295.

22. Ben-Ami letter to author, Feb. 17, 1984.

23. Helen Brown Sherman letter to author, Apr. 28, 1983.

24. Kook – Rapoport interviews, July 1982.

25. Zar, *Rescue and Liberation*, p. 72.

26. Ibid.

27. Ibid.

28. Bauer, *American Jewry and the Holocaust*, p. 194.

29. Urofsky, *A Voice That Spoke for Justice*, p. 335.

30. Silver – Wise fight, ibid.

31. Silver's speech in Hertzberg, *The Zionist Idea*, pp. 597-599. Urofsky, op. cit., p. 339.

32. Goldmann in Minutes of Palestine Committee, American Jewish Conference, Aug. 31 – Sept. 3, 1943, pp. 73-77.

33. Ibid.

34. Wyman, op. cit., pp. 166

35. *New York Times*, Aug. 30, 1943.

36. Rogers, "War Congress," *American Hebrew*, Sept. 17, 1943, 152:20, 45.

37. Rogers felt (then and years later) that the Jewish and Zionist establishment, directly or indirectly, contributed to the Roosevelt administration's dismal record regarding rescue. "By no manner nor means was Roosevelt doing all he could to alleviate the situation. Nor was Churchill. They had what they called their 'higher' priorities and I called 'lower' priorities of activity. They wanted to win the war, period. Roosevelt did what he could, but as a humanitarian, he was nowhere near brilliant... many people just wanted us to sweep our issues under the rug. The established Jews were the supposedly wiser heads, we were the idealists. In retrospect, I think they were foolish, very foolish. I think we could have saved hundreds of thousands of people if there had been more action. But we really should not blame them from hindsight, I suppose. There were tricky decisions to be made."

Rogers thought Bergson was the most persistent character he had ever met, a man who "saw more clearly than any of us the full ramifications of what was going on and what had to be done... I remember telling Peter Bergson, 'Go away, leave me alone; it's too problematical for me,' when he tried to get me involved. He succeeded though, and I am glad he did." – Unpublished interview with Charley Levine, 197.

38. Kook – Rapoport interviews, July 1982. Bergson probably hoped that these encounters would lead to a meeting with FDR.

39. Eleanor Roosevelt Collection, Container 2899, Folder 190 (1943), BA-BE, Hyde Park, p. 8. FDR to Thompson, Aug. 16, 1943.

40. Morgenthau Diary, Container 688, Part L, May 7 – Dec. 9, 1943, p. 35, Hyde Park.

41. Cavendish quoted in Wasserstein, *Britain and the Jews of Europe*, p. 296.

42. Morgenthau Diary, Container 718, Folder 173, p. 222.

43. Wyman, op. cit., p. 191.

44. Long in Friedman, *No Haven for the Oppressed*, p. 167.

45. Kook – Rapoport interviews, Apr. 1983.

46. Threat to Japan cited in *The War Diary of Breckinridge Long*, Fred L. Israel, ed., p. 269, June 5, 1942.

47. Kook – Rapoport interviews, Apr. 1983. Bergson was told that FDR had written "What about this?" in the margin of the cable, but that nothing ever came of it.

48. Bergson to Joint Chiefs, RG218 CCS 385-3 B96936 Sept. 16, 1944.

49. Leaky, RG218 CCS 385-3 B103967 Oct. 4, 1944.

50. First draft reply, RG218 CCS385-3 Sept. 16, 1944 E.B. 2793 B103049.

51. Ibid.

52. Second draft reply, RG 218 CCS 385-3 E.B. 2793 B99906 Sept. 16, 1944.

53. Ibid.

54. Kook – Rapoport interviews, Apr. 1983.

55. Ibid.

56. Bergson letter to Halifax, Oct. 28, 1944, Halifax file, Institute of Mediterranean Affairs.

57. Reitlinger, *The Final Solution*, pp. 446ff.

58. Ibid., p. 130.

59. Borkin, *The Crime and Punishment of I.G. Farben*, pp. 131-133.

5. *The Hoskins Affair*

1. During the war era, there were between five and six million Jews in a population of some 135 million.

2. Isaiah Berlin letter to author, Nov. 2, 1983.

3. *Foreign Relations of the United States* (hereafter abbreviated FRUS), 1943, vol. IV, p. 747ff; and Michael J. Cohen, "American Influence on British Policy in the Middle East During World War Two: First Attempts at Coordinating Allied Policy on Palestine," *Jewish Historical Quarterly*, vol. 67, Sept. 1977.

4. Biographical material on Hoskins obtained by author from FBI files under FOIA. Also, R. Harris Smith, *O.S.S.*, University of California Press, 1972.

5. Berle to Welles, FRUS, 1942, vol. IV, p. 544ff. Information on Hoskins' 1942 duties in FBI file, 77-83159-7, p. 9, May 18, 1960.

6. FRUS, 1942, vol. IV, p. 539.

7. Ibid. The Axis had won Moslem support in Iraq, in Egypt, Palestine and elsewhere in the Arab world, long before the Bergson campaign or increased activities by the establishment Zionists.

8. FRUS, 1942, vol. IV, p. 35.

9. FRUS, 1943, vol. IV, p. 748.

10. Ibid., p. 749.

11. Ibid., pp. 781-782.

12. Ibid., p. 783.

13. Ibid., p. 782.

14. Ibid., p. 784.

15. Ibid.

16. Ibid.; also "Summary of [Hoskins'] Report on the Near East," and cover letter from FDR, July 30, 1943, Rosenman Collection, Hyde Park, Palestine File, Container no. 3.

Under Hoskins' plan, "the Holy Places, including Jerusalem, Jaffa and Bethlehem," were to be an enclave under United Nations control.

17. Ibid.

18. Ibid., p. 785.

19. Berlin letters to author: Nov. 2, 1983; May 7, 1984; Dec. 10, 1984.

20. Public Record Office FO 371/35037 xc/a/049358.

21. Ibid. Berlin's report passed through several hands. Wright, Head of the Chancery, was, in Berlin's view, "a passionate anti-Zionist and pro-Arab. Berlin explains how his reports were tampered with in a book edited by H.G. Nicholas, *Washington Dispatches 1941-1945: Weekly Political Reports from the British Embassy*, Chicago, 1981.

22. Ibid. (frontispiece of report).

23. Ibid.

24. Prof. Monty Penkower letter to author, Dec. 4, 1984, and Penkower's monograph, "The 1943 Joint Anglo-American Statement on Palestine," *Herzl Year Book 8* (1978), pp. 212-241.

25. Peter Grose, *Israel in the Mind of America*, pp. 141-144. Penkower on Hurley, op. cit.

26. Berlin letter to author, Nov. 2, 1983.

27. Ibid.

28. FO 371/35037 xc/a/049358.

29. Ibid.

30. Ibid.

31. Ibid.

32. Ibid.

33. Ibid.

34. Kook – Rapoport interviews, Apr. 1983. Bergson did not remember the exact date of the meeting but believes it took place in early July. Other sources believe the meeting took place in late July, but Bergson says this was not possible, since Wise was the first to inform him about the Hoskins plan. A mid-July letter from General Marshall to Hoskins, inspired by Bergson, and a press release about the same time by Congressman Emanuel Celler attacking the Hoskins proposal appear to confirm Bergson's chronology.

35. FO 371/35037 xc/a/049358. There was an earlier parallel in a British government request to Chaim Weizmann to stop the Jewish Army campaign, and his reply to Lord Halifax that the Bergsonites would not listen to him (Weizmann's *Collected Letters*, 1942 volume). The Zionist establishment nevertheless tried to do the bidding of both the U.S. and British governments in stanching the movement for a Jewish army.

36. Kook – Rapoport interviews, Apr. 1983.

37. Ibid.

38. Ibid.

39. Wise to Weizmann, Weizmann's *Collected Letters*, 1943 volume, p. 64.

40. Kook – Rapoport interviews, op. cit.

41. Ibid.

42. Ibid.

43. I.F. Stone, *The Nation*, Mar. 18, 1944.

44. Marshall's letter in Hoskins File at Institute of Mediterranean Affairs. According to researcher Penkower, there is no copy of Marshall's "reprimand" in the Joint Chiefs papers (Penkower letter to author, Dec. 4, 1984.).

45. FO 371/35037 xc/a/049358.

46. Ibid.

47. Wise biographer Urofsky, in his one-paragraph reference to the affair (in which Hoskins' name is not mentioned), erroneously states that the joint declaration was a British proposal to the State Department. Using Penkower as his source, Urofsky states that Wise did not know about the proposal until July 27, but this date appears to be incorrect, given Wise's July 22 reference in his letter to Weizmann and other contradictory evidence. Urofsky also manages to give all the credit to Wise for forcing the State Department to "back down." See Urofsky, *A Voice That Spoke for Justice*, p. 341.).

48. FO 371/35037 xc/a/049358. Swope, who in 1917 won the first Pulitzer Prize for reporting, was the brother of General Electric tycoon Gerald Swope.

49. Ibid.

50. Frankfurter and Swope approached Stimson's assistant, Robert Patterson, while Morgenthau spoke to Stimson, according to Penkower letter to author, Dec. 4, 1984, and his previously cited monograph.

51. According to Berlin's Aug. 9, 1943, report, Nahum Goldmann also huddled with FDR aides Ben Cohen and David Niles, and other prominent Jews, all of whom viewed the prospect of a joint declaration "with disquiet."

52. Hull to Rosenman, Rosenman Collection, Hyde Park, Palestine File, Container no. 13.

53. FO 371/35037 xc/a/049358.

54. Berlin letter to author, May 24, 1984.

55. Berlin letter to author, May 7, 1984.

56. Researchers up to now have found no documentary evidence of why FDR backed down, but given the President's keen political sense of which way the wind was blowing, it is not implausible to surmise that the "united front" among the Jews made an impression. Over a year after the Hoskins affair, Roosevelt, in private conversations, expressed strong support for a Jewish commonwealth in Palestine.

57. FO 371/35037 xc/a/049358.

58. Kook – Rapoport interviews, Apr. 1983.

59. Kook – Rapoport interview, Aug. 26, 1986. J. Edgar Hoover flip-flopped between terming the Bergsonites "fascists" and "communists."

60. Kook – Rapoport interviews, Apr. 1983.

61. Hoskins' success in scuttling a Palestine scheme by Britain's St. John Philby is worthy of a book in itself. Peter Grose renders a fascinating description of the affair in *Israel in the Mind of America.*

62. Penkower letter to author, Dec. 4, 1984. Penkower also said that Roosevelt and Churchill discussed the aborted joint declaration at the Quebec Conference in mid-August 1943 and decided to hold it "in abeyance." But Churchill biographer Martin Gilbert, in an Aug. 27, 1986, telephone interview with the author, said that the principals at the conference did not discuss the Hoskins proposal.

63. Only Monty Penkower and Michael J. Cohen have written monographs on the affair. In the decades after the affair, no articles appeared in Jewish magazines. Neither Hoskins' name nor his potentially disastrous plan appears in the *Encyclopaedia Judaica.*

64. Berlin letter to author, Sept. 19, 1983.

65. Berlin letter to author, Nov. 2, 1983.

66. Berlin letter to author, May 7, 1984.

67. Israel Goldstein Papers at Zionist Archives, Jerusalem, A364/1951.

---

6. *Jew Against Jew*

1. Kook – Rapoport interviews, July 1982. April 1983; Merlin – Rapoport interview, Sept. 10, 1982; Isaac Zar, *Rescue and Liberation*, p. 62; *New York Herald Tribune*, Oct. 7, 1943. *Time* magazine, Oct. 18, 1943.

2. Eri Jabotinsky to Altman, Palestine Statehood Committee Papers, Oct. 12, 1943, Box 1, Folder 10.

3. Wyman, *The Abandonment of the Jews*, p. 152; Zar, op. cit; *Washington Times Herald*, Oct. 7, 1943.

4. *Washington Times Herald*, op. cit.

5. Kook – Rapoport interviews, op. cit.

6. Ibid.; Public Record Office FO 371/35041.

7. *Time* magazine, Oct. 18, 1943, p. 21; Langer's remarks in Yitshaq Ben-Ami, *Years of Wrath, Days of Glory*, pp. 575-576.

8. Ben-Ami, op. cit.

9. *New York Post*, Oct. 7, 1943; *New York Herald Tribitune*, Oct. 7, 1943; Kook – Rapoport interview, April 1983.

10. *New York Times*, Oct. 12, 1943, Nov. 2, 1943.

11. Berman – Rapoport interview, Feb. 25, 1983.

12. Wyman, op. cit., Appendix B.

13. Helen Brown Sherman letter to author, April 28, 1983; a long list of examples of pressure and harassment is noted in Appendix B of Wyman's book.

14. David E. Pinsky, *Cooperation Among American Jewish Organizations in Their Efforts to Rescue European Jewry During the Holocaust*. Ph. D. dissertation, Yeshiva University, pp. 342, 356.

15. Long quoted in Saul S. Friedman, *No Haven for the Oppressed*, p. 148.

16. Wyman, op. cit., pp. 167-168.

17. Berman – Rapoport interview, op. cit. Rabbi Berman became a Wise disciple in 1917 and was "like a son to him. Wise was far more antagonistic toward Silver than to Bergson, because Silver betrayed him." But Wise definitely "hated the Bergsonite gang."

18. Merlin letter to author, March 22, 1983.

19. *New Palestine*, Jan. 23, 1943.

20. Reinhold Niebuhr, "Jews After the War," *The Nation*, Feb. 21, 1942, p. 214.

21. Pinsky, op. cit., p. 360.

22. Public Record Office FO 371/35041 xc/a/047702, Nov. 15, 1943.

23. Ibid.

24. Ibid.

25. Goldmann's reports on Bergson (those that survived "sanitization," at any rate) in Peter Bergson File Z5/395, Zionist Archives, Jerusalem. Isaiah Berlin would say of Goldmann years later: "Yes, I suspect he did exaggerate – he had a lively imagination, at times very creative. But I have no direct evidence of this: I had no way (and no particular wish) to check his stories. I enjoyed them for what they were." Berlin letter to author, Nov. 2, 1983. In a May 7, 1984, letter to the author, Berlin stated that Goldmann made it clear "that he only told me things which he hoped that I would report to my superiors."

26. Goldmann quoted in Lucy Dawidowicz, "American Jewry and the Holocaust," *New York Times Magazine*, April 18, 1982.

27. Berlin letter to author, Nov. 2, 1983.

28. Merlin letter to author, Mar. 22, 1983.

29. Melvin Urofsky, *A Voice That Spoke for Justice*, pp. 339, 344. What they loved was the power, and the benefits that went along with it. As Wise's aide, Rabbi Morton Berman would recall: "Wise had many peccadillos with women, including a member of my congregation and a journalist I knew – but Goldmann was the one who always had a beautiful girl on his arm at all of these congresses. Wise's wife was much older; his children knew about his affairs and were not concerned by them. Extra-marital affairs are the norm among these leaders." Berman – Rapoport interview, op. cit.

30. Isaiah Berlin, "Zionist Politics in Wartime Washington," Ya'acov Herzog Memorial Lecture, Hebrew University, Jerusalem, October 1972.

31. Berlin letter to author, May 7, 1983: "I am not clear even now how much difference Bergson's agitation actually made – whether, e.g., the petitions signed by Senators, Congressmen and influential persons in fact made a significant difference to the policies of the Roosevelt administration." Sir Isaiah conceded that he may have been wrong in his "acceptance of the official Zionist view of Bergson's activities."

32. Pehle's remark in Laurence Jarvik's documentary film, *Who Shall Live and Who Shall Die?*, 1978.

33. Kook – Rapoport interviews, July 1982.

34. Raul Hilberg, *The Destruction of European Jews*, p. 201ff.

35. Wyman, op. cit., p. 82.

36. Minutes of ZOA Executive Committee, Feb. 20, 1943, Stephen Wise Papers, *B'nai B'rith Messenger*, Apr. 9, 1943.

37. *New York Times*, Feb. 16, 1943, p. 11.

38. Ben-Ami, op. cit., p. 413; Urofsky, op. cit., p. 413; Morgenthau Diary, Container 611, p. 275; Welles to Wagner, Mar. 10, 1943; Robert Wagner Papers, Palestine File; Wise to Holmes, *Personal Letters*, pp. 265-266; Weizmann to Halifax, Feb. 16, 1943, Weizmann Archives, Rehovot. A Jewish Agency representative in Istanbul was informed of the offer by a go-between in early December 1942. Hull to Ankara embassy, Feb. 17, 1943, State Department R/3604; Morgenthau Diary, Container 611, pp. 276-277.

39. Kook – Rapoport interview, July 1982.

40. *New York Times*, Mar. 10, 1943, p. 10; *New York Herald Tribune*, Feb. 22, 1943, p. 16; *Philadelphia Inquirer*, Feb. 23, 1943.

41. Ben-Ami, op. cit., p. 413.

42. Wise, *Challenging Years*, p. 239.

43. Urofsky, op. cit., p. 413.

44. Ibid.

45. Wise, *Personal Letters*, p. 266.

46. *Manchester Guardian*, Feb. 9, 1943.

47. Urofsky, op. cit., p. 413; Friedman, op. cit., p. 150; Wise, *Challenging Years*, pp. 277-278.

48. *Foreign Relations of the U.S.*, 1941, vol. 2, pp. 875-876.

49. Cable of Feb. 26, 1943, Public Record Office FO 371/36676 (W3019/880/48); Eden quoted in Robert Sherwood's *Roosevelt and Hopkins*, p. 717.

50. Friedman, op. cit., p. 150.

51. Wise, *Challenging Years*, pp. 277-278.

52. Peter Grose, *Israel in the Mind of America*, p. 163.

53. Bergson on Wise in Jarvik's film, op. cit.

54. Wyman, op. cit., p. 93.

55. Haskell Lookstein, *American Jewry's Public Response to the Holocaust 1938-44*, Ph. D. dissertation, p. 186.

56. Hoover's report on Bergsonites to Lawrence M. Smith, Dept. of Justice Division of Records: No. 149-178, and F4173.

57. Weizmann to Wise, May 29, 1943. Weizmann Archives, Rehovot.

58. Berman – Rapoport interview, op. cit.

59. Peter Grose noted in his book that Kook was a name in Jewish Palestine [and among Orthodox Jews around the world] "that connotes something like Cabot in New England."

60. Voss letter to author, Apr. 6, 1983.

61. Wise's testimony in *Problems of World War II and Its Aftermath*, Part 2, U.S. House of Representatives historical series, Washington, 1976.

62. Wise to Ickes, Dec. 27, 1943, American Jewish Conference File, Institute of Mediterranean Affairs.

63. Ickes Diary, Jan. 1, 1944, Jan. 2, 1944 and Jan. 22, 1944, Library of Congress. Ickes added in his Jan. 1 entry that Wise in a letter had asked him to withdraw from the "irresponsible" committee which "had not done a thing which may result in the saving of a single Jew." Ickes also got a call from Judge Harry M. Fisher in Chicago, who told him that "the Jews associated with this group were not well regarded by Zionists. The suggestion was made that they were financial adventurers... Yesterday, I had a call from Rabbi Wise to the same effect." Wise was averse to mentioning Bergson by name only in *written* correspondence.

64. Kook – Rapoport interviews, Sept. 1982; Ickes Diary, Jan. 22, 1944. Ickes told Congressman Rogers that he had written to Wise, saying "that I did not consider his criticisms to be valid."

65. Pehle quote in Morgenthau Diary, May 20, 1944, Container 734, p. 5.

66. Robinson's autobiography, *All My Yesterdays*, p. 176.

67. Merlin – Rapoport interviews, Sept. 1982; Kook – Rapoport interview, July 1982, February 1983.

68. Grose, op. cit., p. 176.

69. Rafaeli – Rapoport interview, Feb. 12, 1984.

70. Goldmann File at Institute of Mediterranean Affairs.

71. Jarvik, op. cit.

72. Kook – Rapoport interviews, April 1983.

73. Goldmann File, Institute of Mediterranean Affairs. The Zionists did not press hard for temporary havens. They never publicly denounced the idea.

74. Goldmann to Mead, Peter Bergson File, Zionist Archives, June 28, 1944, Z5/395.

75. Goldmann quoted in State Department Memorandum 867 N. 01/2347.

76. Ibid.

77. G. Reitlinger, *The Final Solution*, p. 454ff.

78. Goldmann's letters in Peter Bergson File, Zionist Archives.

79. Levinthal's 1943 pamphlets: "Pragmatic Realism" and "The Credo of an American Zionist," Zionist Organization of America, Washington.

80. Feuer, "The Birth of the Jewish Lobby," *American Jewish Archives*, Nov. 1976, vol. xxviii. The statement that Eleanor Roosevelt protected him was incorrect. The Zionists played on the phobia of aliens in wartime America by stressing that Bergson was a foreigner who should be deported.

81. Ibid. By implication, Feuer's article may be viewed as an indictment of his superiors who *did* inform on Bergson.

82. Kook – Rapoport interviews, April 1983.

83. Wise to Bloom, Dec. 30, 1943, American Jewish Congress, Wise Papers.

84. Pehle on Wise, Morgenthau Diary, May 24, 1944, Container 735, p. 6.

7. *Bloomsday*

1. Senate Resolution 203, *Congressional Record*, Nov. 9, 1943.

2. Kook – Rapoport interviews, July 1982.

3. *New York Times*, Nov. 10, 1943, p. 19.

4. Ibid., Nov. 2, 1943, pp. 1, 14.

5. Ibid., Nov. 5, 1943, p. 14. *Washington Post*, Nov. 8, 1943, p. 9.

6. David Wyman, *The Abandonment of the Jews*, pp. 155-156. Wyman suggests that Roosevelt "was moving at last to confront the extermination issue. Or perhaps he was maneuvering to cut the ground from under the Rescue Resolution."

7. Long to Rosenman, Rosenman Papers, Refugees File, Oct. 15, 1943, Container 13, Hyde Park. Long said he told Bergson that the committee's ads "made it very difficult for the department, and injured the cause which they professed to have so much at heart." He urged an end to publicity.

8. E. Silver to Sol Bloom, Nov. 25, 1943, Legis. 16432; Union of Orthodox Rabbis to Gillette, Nov. 14, 1943, Vaad HaHatzala Papers, B24.

9. Minutes of Executive Committee, Oct. 31, 1943, American Jewish Historical Society Archives, I-67, B6.

10. The American Jewish Conference press release was issued on Dec. 29, 1943. *New York Times*, Dec. 31, 1943; State Department R/5025.

11. Wyman, op. cit., p. 199.

12. Merlin – Rapoport interviews, Sept. 1982.

13. HIAS and Bloom in Saul Friedman, *No Haven for the Oppressed*, p. 150. Long's State Department colleague George Warren said years later, Bloom and other officials did not speak out for the Jewish refugees because "we were afraid of fifth columnists,

that is, spies." Warren in Laurence Jarvik's film, *Who Shall Live and Who Shall Die?*, 1978.

14. Friedman, op. cit., p. 162.
15. Sol Bloom, *The Autobiography of Sol Bloom*, 1948.
16. Melvin Urofsky, *A Voice That Spoke for justice*, p. 305.
17. *Problems of World War II and Its Aftermath, Part 2*, transcript of testimony before the Committee on Foreign Affairs, U.S. House of Representatives, 1976.
18. Ibid., pp. 62-63.
19. Ibid., p. 65.
20. Ibid., p. 70.
21. Ibid., p. 67.
22. Ibid., p. 86f. Only 6,000 of the 22,000 were Jews.
23. Ibid., p. 87.
24. Ibid., p. 35f., p. 96f. The telegram stated: "The campaign to save the Jewish people of Europe from annihilation is a race against time. Our representatives in England, Palestine, Turkey cable us favorable possibilities for rescue. Considerable funds needed by them for work in those countries. Our tremendous efforts and activities in the United States exhausting available funds..." Under Bloom's questioning, Alfange conceded that the committee's offices abroad were a relatively minor expense compared to the cost of the giant ads in U.S. newspapers and magazines. Bergson himself felt that the hastily-drafted telegram was poorly worded, exaggerating the overseas operation. At this time, for example, the committee had only one full-time representative and one associated representative in Turkey.
25. Ibid., p. 101.
26. Ibid., p. 99.
27. Ibid., pp. 101, 105.
28. Ibid., p. 99.
29. Ibid., p. 100, footnote.
30. Ibid.
31. Ibid., p. 106.
32. G. Reitlinger, *The Final Solution*, p. 408f; *Problems of World War II and Its Aftermath, Part 2*, p. 121.
33. Ibid., pp. 110-111.
34. Ibid.
35. Ibid., p. 111.
36. Ibid., pp. 113, 197.
37. Ibid., p. 113.
38. Ibid., p. 152.

39. The Nov. 1, 1943, Moscow Declaration, signed by FDR, Churchill and Stalin, warned the Germans that the victorious Allies would track down all who participated in massacres and mass executions and try them in the countries where the crimes were committed. Besides mentioning all of the violated countries and their peoples, the Allied leaders included in the list of war crimes the shooting of Polish officers, hostages, and Cretan peasants. The declaration did not mention the extermination of hundreds of thousands of Gypsies, who, like the Jews, had no motherland to call their own. Ibid., Appendix III, p. 368.

40. Ibid., p. 135.

41. Ibid., p. 113.

42. Ibid. "...the Jews of Poland had political status even before the war, before Germany came there," Bergson said. "They had a certain national status. They were a national minority, whose treatment was recognized by the Versailles Treaty. There are no Jews politically in the United States, as there are no Irish, no Germans, no nothing: they are Americans – when we [in America] speak about Jews, Irish, Greeks and Italians, and about Jews, Protestants and Catholics, we are speaking in social terms, not in political terms."

43. Ibid., p. 119.

44. Ibid., p. 120f.

45. Ibid., pp. 123-124.

46. Ibid., p. 124.

47. Ibid., pp. 218-219, 235. Wise also said of himself: "I happen to have been fairly active in Jewish life – I am the rabbi of a free synagogue and the president of the Jewish Institute, the religious president of the American Jewish Congress, and chairman of the Emergency Zionist Council. I know something of Jewish life..."

48. Ibid., p. 220.

49. Ibid., p. 221.

50. Ibid., p. 227.

51. Ibid., pp. 227-228.

52. Ibid., p. 231.

53. Ibid., p. 235.

54. Ibid.

55. Ibid., pp. 235-236.

56. "On the Question of Rescue," *Congress Weekly*, Dec. 10, 1943.

57. *Problems of World War II and Its Aftermath, Part 2*, p. 171. The American Jewish Conference figure was 166,843; HIAS 157,927, and the Yiddish Scientific Institute, 138,000; *New Republic*, Dec. 20, 1943, pp. 867-868; *New York Post*, Dec. 11, Dec. 13, 1943; Celler quoted in Wyman, op. cit., p. 197.

58. *Problems of World War II and Its Aftermath, Part 2*, p. 201.

59. Long to Rosenman, op. cit.

60. *Problems of World War II and Its Aftermath, Part 2*, p. 191.

61. Ibid., p. 196.

62. Ibid.

63. Ibid., pp. 184-185.

64. Ibid., p. 243. Rabbi Herzog, father of future Israeli President Chaim Herzog, was a close friend and colleague of Peter Bergson's father, Rabbi Dov Kook.

65. Ibid.

66. Ibid., Foreword. Bloom could not keep the transcripts of the hearings secret forever. Surviving House committee members gave their permission for publication of the 33-year-old transcripts. The State Department also approved.

67. One of the anti-Long ads appeared in *The Nation*, Dec. 25, 1943.

68. Attack on Bloom in *The Answer*, June 1944.

69. Bloom's autobiography, op. cit.; and Stephen Wise, *Challenging Years: The Autobiography of Stephen Wise*, 1949.

70. Goldstein to Bloom, Nov. 9, 1944, Goldstein Collection, Zionist Archives, Jerusalem: A364/10030. Max Maneschewitz to Goldstein, June 1, 1944. Bloom was honored for his "outstanding public service... which has won wide acclaim from heads of government, statesmen and lovers of liberty and freedom throughout the world."

8. *An Agency of Rescue*

1. American Jewish Conference press release, Dec. 29, 1943; *New York Times*, Dec. 31, 1943; State Department R/5025; David Wyman, *The Abandonment of the Jews*, p. 203.

2. *The Answer*, January 1944.

3. *The War Diary of Breckinridge Long*, Jan. 11, 1944, p. 335-336.

4. *New Palestine*, Jan. 7, 1944; *Congress Weekly*, Jan. 7, 1944; Zvi Ganin, *Truman, American Jewry and Israel*, p. 5.

5. Saul Friedman, *No Haven for the Oppressed*, p. 147.

6. David Pinsky, *Cooperation Among American Jewish Organizations in Their Efforts to Rescue European Jewry During the Holocaust*, pp. 361-362.

7. Ibid., p. 351.

8. Kook – Rapoport interviews, April 1983.

9. Ibid.

10. Haskel Lookstein, *American Jewry's Public Response to the Holocaust, 1938-44*, p. 206.

11. Ibid., p. 294; *The Reconstructionist*, Jan. 21, 1944.

12. *The Answer*, June 15, 1944.

13. Helen Brown Sherman letter to author, Apr. 28, 1983.

14. Public Record Office FO/371/42727, Jan. 5, 1944.

15. Arthur Morse, *Whie Six Million Died*, pp. 70-97; Henry Feingold, *The Politics of Rescue*, pp. 239-244; Morgenthau Diary, Container 694, p. 197; Yitshaq Ben-Ami, *Years of Wrath, Days of Glory*, pp. 573-585. The report said that, "Unless remedial steps of a drastic nature are taken, and taken immediately, I am certain that no effective action will be taken by this Government to prevent the complete extermination of the Jews in German controlled Europe, and that this Government will have to share for all time responsibility for this extermination."

16. Morgenthau Diary, op. cit.

17. Ibid., pp. 197-198.

18. Morse, op. cit., p. 70; Merlin – DuBois interview, Aug. 13, 1981.

19. Kook – Rapoport interviews, April 1983, Sept. 1983.

20. Source unknown.

21. Cox – Bergson meeting, Cox Collection, Hyde Park, Container no. 2.

22. Kook – Rapoport interviews, Sept. 1983.

23. Morgenthau Diary, op. cit., pp. 180-192.

24. *The Nation*, Jan. 15, 1944; *The New Republic*, Jan. 17, 1944.

25. Morgenthau Diary, op. cit.; WRB file, Institute of Mediterranean Affairs.

26. Luxford-Morgenthau, Morgenthau Diary, Container 735, May 24, 1944.

27. Luxford-Morgenthau, Morgenthau Diary, Container 735, May 24, 1944.

28. Morse, op. cit., pp. 363-364; Yehuda Bauer, *American Jewry and the Holocaust*, pp. 444-447.

29. Kook – Rapoport interviews, April 1983, Sept. 1983; Merlin – Rapoport interviews, Sept. 1983.

30. Wyman, op. cit., p. 213ff. Bergson, however, always insisted that the money should come from the President's $50 million emergency fund, and believed that there was no reason to worry about whether or not Congress would agree to pay the bills.

31. Bauer, op. cit., p. 194. According to Wyman's figures in *Abandonment of the Jews*, other contributions to the WRB came from the Orthodox body Vaad HaHatzala ($1 m.), the World Jewish Congress ($300,000), HIAS ($100,000), President's Emergency Funds ($1,150,000), and other government funds ($547,000).

32. *Final Summary Report of the U.S. War Refugee Board*, pp. 8, 9, 12.

33. *The Nation*, Feb. 19, 1944; *The New Republic*, Feb. 21, 1944.

34. *Final Summary Report of the U.S. War Refugee Board*, p. 9.

35. Wyman, op. cit., p. 210.

36. *Final Summary Report of the U.S. War Refugee Board*, p. 11.

37. Ibid., p. 1.

38. Yehuda Bauer, *A History of the Holocaust*, p. 31.

39. Lookstein, op. cit., pp. 298-299.

40. *Christian Science Monitor*, Jan. 24, 1944.

41. Thackery to Bergson, Jan. 25, 1944, WRB File, Institute of Mediterranean Affairs; Isaac Zar, *Rescue and Liberation*, p. 78.

42. Ickes in Zar, ibid.; *Washington Post*, Jan. 25, 1944.

43. Zionist rescue aims: Jewish Labor Committee letter to American Jewish Conference, Jan. 12, 1944, Zionist Archives, Jerusalem, A364/1954; Zionist rescue claims: Ibid., Jan. 23, 1944; also, *American Hebrew*, Feb. 4, 1944, 153:14.4.

44. Morgenthau Diary, March 8, 1944, Container 707, pp. 220-221. Morgenthau and his Treasury aides, armed with the threat of the Rescue Resolution, did "force" FDR to move, but of course Morgenthau would not be so impolitic as to say so publicly, or in a written communication that might reach the hands of a Sol Bloom.

45. Ibid. Nowhere in the vast Morgenthau Diary does one find any suggestion that Roosevelt acted because of pressure from, or "negotiations" with, establishment Jewish organizations.

46. Ibid.

47. Kook – Rapoport interviews, April 1983; Merlin – Rapoport interviews, September 1983; *The Answer*, June 15, 1944.

48. Wyman has produced the most comprehensive picture so far of the WRB's work in *The Abandonment of the Jews*. His approximate 200,000 figure is broken down thus: 15,000 evacuated from Axis territory (as were 20,000 non-Jews), over 10,000 protected within Axis territory by WRB-financed underground activities, 48,000 Jewish survivors in Transnistria and over 120,000 Jews in Hungary saved by WRB diplomatic efforts.

49. Ibid., p. 286.

50. DuBois – Jarvik interview, Oct. 23, 1978, *Who Shall Live and Who Shall Die?* documentary film.

51. Isaiah Berlin, "Zionist Politics in Wartime Washington," Ya'acov Herzog Memorial Lecture, Oct. 1972, Hebrew University, Jerusalem.

52. Morgenthau Diary, May 24, 1944, Container 735, p. 24.

53. Ibid., pp. 12, 26, 31.

54. Ibid.

55. Ibid., p. 77.

56. Ibid., p. 83.

57. Ibid., pp. 35-36, 56.

58. Ben-Ami, op. cit., pp. 326, 329-330, 409; Dept. of Justice letter Aug. 25, 1943, no. 149-718.

59. Bloom to Goldstein, Feb. 12, 1944, Goldstein Collection, Zionist Archives, A364/10030; and Bloom to Goldstein, Sept. 8, 1944, A364/1570. "What is all this talk I hear about you and Mr. Merlin of the Emergency Committee to Save the Jewish

People of Europe?" Bloom wrote in his Feb. 12 letter. "I have been told that Mr. Merlin states that a lot of these erroneous statements that his committee gets come either from you or through you. This surprises me very much."

60. U.S. Government memo, March 24, 1945, No. 100-316012-40-64494.

61. Nahum Goldmann, in his less than honest autobiography, claimed that "Jewish public opinion was roused chiefly at two conferences" that his World Jewish Congress called. There is no historical evidence of this, nor does Goldmann offer any.

62. Tandy to Taub Cohen, Bergson File, Zionist Archives, Z5/395, Aug. 8, 1945. A Sept. 7, 1945, *Washington Post* report quoted a Justice Department source as saying that the State Department had refused to extend Bergson's visitor's visa and that he must leave the U.S. by Nov. 1, 1945. Bergson appealed the decision and won.

63. The four-part series ran in the *Washington Post* Oct. 3-6, 1944.

64. Kook – Rapoport interviews, April 1983. In the wake of the Hoskins affair, Rabbi Wise had asked Meyer to meet with FDR on Palestine, which he did in October 1943. Peter Grose, *Israel in the Mind of America*, p. 145. Given Wise's friendly relations with Meyer and the fact that the rabbi's organizations were the main source of "information" about the Bergsonites, it is not farfetched to surmise that Wise was instrumental in getting Meyer to "expose" the Bergson group.

65. Kook – Rapoport interviews, April 1983.

66. Van Paassen had accepted the argument of the official Zionists that Bergson's Emergency Committee was "a cruel hoax perpetrated on the American public." The one-time disciple of Jabotinsky accused Bergson's organizations of being fronts for the "Fascist" party in Palestine, the Irgun. *Washington Post*, Oct. 3, 1944. After the war, however, Van Paassen would work again with Bergson.

67. *Washington Post*, Oct. 4, 1944.

68. Ibid. According to the transcripts of the hearings on the Rescue Resolution (*Problems of World War II and Its Aftermath, Part 2*, p. 100), Bloom did not use the word "hell" or otherwise "swear."

69. Harper's letter, *Washington Post*, Oct. 6, 1944.

70. Bergson press conference, Oct. 3, 1944, *Washington Post*, letter, *Washington Post*, Oct. 10, 1944; Kook – Rapoport interviews, April 1983.

71. In this implied attack on Wise, Goldman, Muldmann and their colleagues, Bergson said: "We abandoned this system of secret bargaining with this or that government official and we brought the whole problem out into the open... a revolutionary change in behalf of our people."

72. Editorial, *Washington Post*, Oct. 13, 1944.

73. *Washington Post*, Oct. 6, 1944.

74. *Washington Post*, Oct. 13, 1944.

75. Merlin – Rapoport interviews, Sept. 1983.

76. "IB" letter in Bergson File, Zionist Archives Z5/395. (Isaiah Berlin, another "IB," says – in a letter to the author, Sept. 19, 1983 – he had nothing whatsoever to do with the *Washington Post* and never discussed that newspaper with Goldmann.)

77. Goldmann to Meyer, Dec. 1, 1944, Bergson File, Zionist Archives, Z5/395; Jewish Agency to Meyer, ibid., Oct. 12, 1944.

78. *New York Post*, July 11, 1944.

79. Kook – Rapoport interviews, July 1983; "a cheap publicity stunt" in Melvin Urofsky, *A Voice That Spoke for Justice*, p. 337; "moral blackmail" in Lookstein, op. cit., p. 294.

80. *Commentary*, Sept. 1982, p. 12.

81. *The War Diary of Breckinridge Long*, Jan. 24, 1944, p. 336.

---

9. The Survivors and the Hebrew Nation

1. The national/cultural aspect was stressed in the "Hebrew" University. "Hebrew" originally meant Israelite, "one who is from across (the river)." In modern times, the words Jew and Hebrew were often used interchangeably, with Hebrew appearing to have been a more "dignified" term. "Are you of the Hebrew persuasion?" an anti-Semitic hotel clerk asks Mr. Greene in *Gentleman's Agreement* (the book's author, Laura Hobson, was a supporter of the Bergson group). Although the Jews of Palestine were called "Palestinians," there was no particular affection for the term or allegiance to it.

2. Kook – Rapoport interviews, April 1983, Sept. 10, 1986.

3. Merlin – Rapoport interviews, September 1983; Ben-Ami letter to author, Feb. 17, 1984; Rafaeli – Rapoport interview, Nov. 26, 1982.

4. *The Answer*, June 15, 1944; *Washington Post*, May 19, 1944; *New York Post*, May 19, 1944.

5. Bergson believed in democratic principles as embodied by Jabotinsky and Thomas Jefferson, two of his heroes, and was antagonistic to leftist as well as rightist authoritarianism. He would find any comparison to young Trotsky, for instance to be invidious. The revolt of the Jews in Palestine was much closer to the American rebellion against the British than to the Russian Revolution.

6. *The Answer*, op. cit.; Bergson to Hull, June 19, 1944, Hull File, Institute of Mediterranean Affairs.

7. The American League for a Free Palestine was launched on May 24, 1944, in New York. Another related Bergsonite group, the National Jewish Council, was set up in January 1944. Rabbis made up its membership, and it concentrated its efforts on the Yiddish-speaking community.

8. Ben Hecht, *A Child of the Century*, p. 515ff.

9. *Washington Post* editorial, Oct. 13, 1944. Hecht and Rogers in *The Answer*, op. cit. In a comment on Hecht's attacks on Wise, Zionist Judd Teller would write that

however disappointed American Jews may have been in Wise's wartime leadership, they still revered him for a lifetime of service, and "Ben Hecht was hardly fit to sit in judgment on him." (Cited in Melvin Urofsky, *A Voice That Spoke for Justice*, p. 337).

10. Morgenthau Diary, May 24, 1944, Container 735, p. 75.

11. Goldmann, *New York Post*, May 19, 1944; Feuer, United Press dispatch, May 19, 1944; Grossman, *Congress Weekly*, May 26, 1944; Goldstein, *Washington Post*, May 19, 1944.

12. David Pinsky, *Cooperation Among American Jewish Organizations in Their Efforts to Rescue European Jews During the Holocaust*, p. 429.

13. David Wyman, *The Abandonment of the Jews*, p. 234.

14. The Answer, June 15 and Aug. 29, 1944.

15. March 27, 1944, draft for FDR to Teller, under cover of Bohlen to Early, FDR Papers, OF76C.

16. Even after the war, humanists wishing to stress the commonality of peoples also tended to substitute "humanity" or "mankind" for the word "Jews," as in the play based on Anne Frank's diary, in which her mention of Jews was changed to suit the internationalist views of the playwrights. But the victims themselves chose to identify themselves as Jews: Like Anne Frank, the Marxist Jewish Socialist Bund in Poland did not describe themselves as "Marxists" or "human beings" but as "Jews" in their 1942 report detailing the mass gassing. Marie Syrkin, then co-editor of the Labor Zionist organ *Jeiwsh Frontier*, buried the Bund report in the back pages of the magazine's Sept. 1942 issue. (*Commentary*, letter from Irving Howe, p. 5).

17. UNRRA and UNWCC Files, Institute of Mediterranean Affairs. The term "Hebrew" sounds dated and somewhat pedantic today, but in the context of the forties, it was virtually the only appropriate term with which to define the national identity of those Jews in Palestine and Europe who were pressing for political recognition, and the thinking behind the distinction – between Israeli and Jew – remains critically important today.

18. Kook – Rapoport interviews, April 1983.

19. Hecht, op. cit.

20. *New York Post*, July 7, 1944.

21. On Dec. 18, 1944, according to FBI files, attorney Irving D. Lipkowitz of New York wrote on behalf of the Zionists to a justice Ministry official in charge of foreign agents registration. The lawyer said that the HCNL was clearly using its registration as a foreign agent to give itself a status it did not have: "The Committee should be required to file a supplement to its registration statement" that would show it was "self-constituted and self-appointed and has not been authorized by any person or body to act on behalf of... the 'Hebrew nation.'"

22. *The Answer*, June 15, 1944.

23. Charles E. Stein – Rapoport interview, July 18, 1983.

24. Harry Louis Selden letter to author, July 25, 1983.

25. Ibid.

26. Ibid.

27. The quoting of Jefferson was not an affectation. Bergson and Eri Jabotinsky would one day publish translations of Jefferson's work in Israel.

28. *New York Times*, Aug. 5, 7, 9, 1944.

29. Sharon Lowenstein, "A New Deal for Refugees: The Promise and Reality of Oswego," *American Jewish History*, March 1982, p. 328ff.

30. Arthur Hertzberg, *The Zionist Idea*, p. 328. The Lithuanian-born Silver remained throughout his life a Zionist outside Zion.

31. Lowenstein, op. cit., p. 330.

32. Bergson to Viscount Halifax, June 10, 1944, Halifax File, Institute for Mediterranean Affairs.

33. *Summary of the Final Report of the U.S. War Refugee Board*, p. 5. Arthur Morse, *While Six Million Died*, p. 261; Kook – Rapoport interviews, July 1983.

34. Morse, op. cit.

35. *Summary of the Final Report of the U.S. War Refugee Board*, p. 11

36. Wyman, op. cit., p. 256ff.; Lowenstein, op. cit., pp. 327, 329; Gillette resolution, cable to Bergson, Oswego file, Institute of Mediterranean Affairs.

37. FDR to Hun, Aug. 14, 1944, FDR Papers, OF3186.

38. *The Answer*, Aug. 29, 1944; Wyman, op. cit., p. 252. The Zionists did not openly denounce the idea of temporary havens, but neither did they press for it. Wise, for example, commented (Urofsky, op. cit., p. 325) that he had no objection to temporary sanctuary in the Virgin Islands, but that (permanent) settlement in Palestine would be better. The Zionists' attitude was akin to the one they assumed toward the Rescue Resolution.

39. Wyman, op. cit., p. 235ff.; G. Reitlinger, *The Final Solution*, pp. 447-487.

40. Halifax to State Department, June 5, 1944, Weizmann Archives, Rehovot.

41. Wyman, op. cit.

42. Ibid., pp. 251-252.

43. Saul Friedman, *No Haven for the Oppressed*, pp. 221, 293.

44. *The Answer*, Aug. 29, 1944; Wyman, op. cit., pp. 252-253; Kook – Rapoport interview, Sept. 4, 1986.

45. Bergson cable to Churchill, July 9, 1944, Hungary file, Institute of Mediterranean Affairs.

46. *The Answer*, Aug. 15, 1944.

47. Wyman, op. cit., p. 253.

48. Goldman at State, Sept. 13, 1944, Palestine Statehood Committee Papers, 3/67; Wyman, ibid.

49. Eichmann and Nazi ideologue Alfred Rosenberg arranged a reception for the Mufti
    as the Hungarian Jews were being shipped to Auschwitz. At the Eichmann trial,
    documents were submitted showing that the Mufti proposed using Nazi
    extermination methods to rid the entire Middle East of Jews. (Reitlinger, op. cit., p.
    467n.; Quentin Reynolds, *Eichmann: Minister of Death*; and Haifa Documentation
    Center report on the Mufti, July 1974).

50. Dov Joseph's stand cited in Prof. Michael J. Cohen's letter, *Midstream*, March 1982,
    p. 61.

51. Kook – Rapoport interviews, September 1982, April 1983. Eri Jabotinsky's
    assessments on the Danube transit route for refugees differed sharply from
    Hirschmann's. Jabotinsky was indignant that Hirschmann, the WRB's
    representative, refused to recommend the Danube route because it was "too
    dangerous." Jabotinsky believed the Jews in Hungary had at best a 50-50 chance of
    survival and that they were ready to take any risk on the navigability of the Danube.
    Hirschmann was considered by most of the parties concerned, other than the State
    Department and U.S. Ambassador to Turkey Laurence Steinhardt, to be an
    ineffective emissary, a "rather flamboyant figure" whose work was castigated not
    only by Eri Jabotinsky, but also by the Joint Distribution Committee and Jewish
    Agency representatives (Yehuda Bauer, *American Jewry and the Holocaust*, p. 404).
    Hirschmann would eventually write a series of books about how he reputedly saved
    50,000 Jews. Bergson thought he was a weak, vainglorious, ineffective man and
    greatly regretted the Emergency Committee's role in obtaining his appointment.

52. Menachem Begin, *The Revolt*, p. 63; Kook – Rapoport interviews, Sept. 1982.

53. Shoshana Raziel – Rapoport interview, Oct. 28, 1982.

---

10. *A Flag is Born*

1. Bergson to Weizmann, April 2, 1945, Bergson file, Weizmann Archives, Rehovot, and
   HNCL file, Jabotinsky Institute, Tel Aviv. Weizmann at least saved the letter and did
   not try, like Wise, to eliminate all mention of the man in his personal archives.

2. Ibid.

3. Ibid.

4. Ibid.

5. Ibid.

6. The hysteria Bergson referred to in his letter never subsided. According to Jesse Zel
   Lurie, who says he was put in charge of the Haganah's PR after the war, "my chief
   function was to attack Bergson." (Lurie letter to author, Aug. 7, 1986.) Typically, Lurie
   gets his facts all wrong, asserting, for example, that Menachem Begin sent Bergson
   and the other Palestinians to the US. to raise money for the Irgun (Begin was still a
   soldier in the Polish army when Raziel and Jabotinsky sent the core group of
   Palestinians to America). Lurie also maintains, as he did forty years ago, that the
   funds raised by the "Rumanian Jews for Sale" ad were used "to buy office furniture."

He says money was squandered on "costly publicity events. Some, like the Ben Hecht pageant, were successful; others, like bringing 500 rabbis to Washington, were expensive duds."

7. Morgenthau Diary, May 24, 1944, Container 735, pp. 24, 79-80.

8. Kook – Rapoport interviews, April 1983; Walter Laqueur, *A History of Zionism*, pp. 564f.; Isaiah Berlin, "Zionist Politics in Wartime Washington," pp. 24-28.

9. Menachem Begin, *The Revolt*, p. 178.

10. Kook – Rapoport interviews, Sept. 1982, April 1983.

11. Ibid.; Ben-Ami letter to author, Feb. 17, 1984.

12. Yitzhaq Ben-Ami, *Years of Wrath, Days of Glory*, p. 358.

13. Merlin – Rapoport interview, Oct. 12, 1982.

14. Shmuel Katz, *Days of Fire*, p. 72.

15. In a Dec. 15, 1944, memo, Hoover described the Hebrew Committee as a group that "has been the subject of considerable public criticism and has been branded as 'the brazen fraud' of a half dozen adventurists without any standing, credentials or mandate except from the 'pistol-packing Irgun.'" On Feb. 22, 1945, Assistant Attorney General Herbert Wechsler wrote to Hoover recommending a thorough probe of the HCNL in regard to possible violations of the Foreign Agents Registration Act because of the committee's ties to "Revisionist groups in Palestine." Wechsler expressed suspicion that the money was going to the Irgun. (Both letters in FBI file at Institute of Mediterranean Affairs). The term "adventurists," used by Hoover, was a favorite of the Zionists. (*The Record*, American Jewish Conference, Dec. 13, 1946). The frequent Zionist charges of Bergsonite fraud in fund-raising continued not only in America, but also over the Haganah's clandestine Voice of Israel radio (Nov. 13, 1946 broadcast).

16. Kook – Rapoport interviews, Sept. 1982, April, July 1983.

17. *New Palestine*, May 18, 1945.

18. Epstein to Jewish Agency quoted in Zvi Ganin, *Truman, American Jewry and Israel*, p. 4; Elath file, Institute for Mediterranean Affairs.

19. Epstein quoted in Melvin Urofsky, *We Are One*, p. 98. Ben Hecht was pleased by such expressions, proud of his performance in a circus as a teenager.

20. Kook – Rapoport interviews, July 1983; Urofsky, *A Voice That Spoke for Justice*, pp. 348-349.

21. Bergson meeting with Yugoslavian Foreign Minister M. Ivan Subask, June 6, 1945, Hadj Amin al-Husseini file, Institute for Mediterranean Affairs. According to the testimony of Auschwitz survivor M. Ben-Haim of Belgium, the Mufti toured the death camp with Eichmann and a suite of senior Nazi officials in June 1944 (*Jerusalem Post*, July 27, 1961). According to the Nuremberg testimony of Eichmann aide Dieter Wisliceny, the Mufti prevailed upon Himmler to cancel a plan to trade some Jewish children for German nationals under detention in Allied countries. As noted, the Mufti sought the extermination of Middle East Jews (See note 49, Chapter 9).

Although the Mufti was reponsible for the deaths of thousands of Serbs and Croats, after Arab League pressure was applied on Tito, Belgrade quietly dropped its demand that the Mufti be brought to justice. (*The Mufti*, p. 175).

22. *New York Herald Tribune*, Mar. 3, 1945; *The New Republic*, Mar. 12, 1945; Ben-Ami, op. cit., pp. 308-312. A quarter of a century earlier, Eri's father had also been held at the Acre fortress, for organizing Jewish defense units during the 1920 Arab riots. Eri, a mathematician-engineer who had been educated in Russia, England and France, held regular lectures for the other prisoners on topics ranging from "Modern Revolutionary Techniques" to "Recent Currents in Mathematics." Scores of his fellow inmates would escape in May 1947 when the Irgun mounted a celebrated attack on "the Bastille" and freed the Jewish fighters.

23. *Congressional Record*, May 15, 1945; Merlin – Rapoport interviews, Sept. 1983.

24. Peter Grose, *Israel in the Mind of America*, pp. 199-200; Isaac Zar, *Rescue and Liberation*, p. 143; Saul Friedman, *No Haven for the Oppressed*, p. 223.

25. Truman file, Institute for Mediterranean Affairs; Michael J. Cohen, *Palestine and the Great Powers*, p. 58.

26. Cohen, op. cit.; Kook – Rapoport interviews, July 1983.

27. Peter Grose in his otherwise excellent book asserts that Bergson's motive for leaking the news was to make it appear "as though the presidential demarche had resulted from Bergson's own efforts" (op. cit., p. 202), but this surmise, which follows the Zionist line in assessing all of Bergson's motives, is patently unfair – self-aggrandizement was simply never Bergson's primary aim during his long years of activism.

28. Kook – Rapoport interviews, op. cit.; Merlin – Rapoport interviews, op. cit.

29. Kook – Rapoport interviews, op. cit.

30. Bevin to Halifax, Oct. 12, 1945, E7757 FO 371/45381; Bevin and Weizmann in Walter Laqueur, *A History of Zionism*, p. 565.

31. Bevin file, Nov. 15, 1945, Institute for Mediterranean Affairs; *New York Times*, Nov. 13, 1945. But Bevin would go back on his promise to the delegation – no interim reports were issued.

32. *Congressional Record*, Dec. 17, 1945, Dec. 19, 1945; Merlin – Rapoport interviews, op. cit.

33. Gavin, op. cit., pp. 46-47.

34. Kook – Rapoport interviews, Sept. 1982, July 1983.

35. Ibid.

36. Grose, op. cit., p. 226.

37. Kook – Rapoport interviews, op. cit.

38. Ibid.

39. Hecht file, April 27, 1947, Institute for Mediterranean Affairs.

40. Cohen, op. cit., p. 27.

41. Bergson's testimony, Anglo-American Commission file, Institute for Mediterranean Affairs; news agency reports, Reuters, Jan. 16, 1946.

42. Ibid.

43. Ibid.

44. Ibid.

45. Ibid.

46. Ibid. Bergson was never sure whether he was born in 1914 or 1915. He may have been ten, not eleven as stated, when his family left Russia for Palestine.

47. Ibid.

48. Laqueur, op. cit., pp. 570-571; Crum quoted in Zar, op. cit., p. 183.

49. Arthur Koestler, *Promise and Fulfilment*, p. 111; Bergson press conference, May 3, 1946, Anglo-American Commission file, Institute for Mediterranean Affairs; Cohen, op. cit., p. 30. The American Zionists, at the last minute, decided in the interests of Western solidarity not to campaign against the loan.

50. *The Answer*, September 1946.

51. R. Crossman, *Palestine Mission: A Personal Record*, p. ? Bergson in his testimony did not use the term "new" Hebrew nation.

52. Adler letter to author, Feb. 7, 1986.

53. Ben-Ami, op. cit., p. 383ff; *The Answer*, September 1946.

54. Ibid.

55. *The Answer*, September 1946.

56. Leonard Slater, *The Pledge*, p. 96.

57. *New York Herald Tribune*, Dec. 27, 1946. Nov. 13, 1946, broadcast, Haganah file, Institute for Mediterranean Affairs.

58. *New York Times*, Nov. 14, 1946.

59. Agronsky's editorial and letter about its censorship, original document in possession of Harry Louis Selden.

60. Kook – Rapoport interviews, April, July 1983; Merlin – Rapoport interviews, op. cit.

11. To Nationhood

1. *New York Post*, Dec. 27, 1946; *New York Herald Tribune*, Dec. 29, 1946; *Washington Star*, Dec. 29, 1946; Kook – Rapoport interview, Sept. 20, 1986.

2. Ben-Ami, op. cit., p. 435ff; *The Answer*, August 1946; Koestler letter to author, Jan. 3, 1983.

3. Bergson's speech, *The Answer*, Jan. 1947.

4. Kook – Rapoport interviews, April, July 1983; Merlin – Rapoport interviews, op. cit.

5. Mar. 7, 1947, report, Elath file, Institute for Mediterranean Affairs; *The Record*, editorial, Dec. 13, 1946. Labor Zionism was equally dismissive of the Irgun, for many years, and could not really accept the reality when the veterans of that organization took power in Israel in 1977.

6. Kook – Rapoport interviews, April, July 1983.

7. Ibid.

8. Ibid.; Ben-Ami, op. cit., p. 436.

9. Basle resolution, *New York Times*, Dec. 24, 1946.

10. Shertok's report quoted in Ganin, op. cit., p. 123.

11. Merlin – Rapoport interviews, op. cit.; Kook – Rapoport interviews, July 1983; Ben-Ami, op. cit., pp. 390-391, 403-408. The journey of the *Ben Hecht* is described fully in Jacques Mery's 1947 account, with preface by Albert Camus, *Laissez Passer Mon Peuple.*

12. Merlin – Rapoport interviews, op. cit. In the years between 1937 – 1940, the Irgunists and their associates had brought more "illegal" refugees from Europe to Palestine than did the far bigger and richer mainstream Zionists. But after the war, illegal immigration was almost exclusively a project of the labor Zionists, and the Haganah brought about 70,000 people to Palestine between August 1945 and May 1948. (Haganah figures in Yehuda Bauer, *A History of the Holocaust*, p. 344.)

13. Kook – Rapoport interviews, July 1983.

14. Ibid.; Ben-Ami, op. cit., p. 407ff.

15. *New York Herald Tribune*, May 14, 1947; *New York Post*, May 18, 1947; Ben-Ami, op. cit., pp. 414-415.

16. Kook – Rapoport interviews, February 1983.

17. Ben Hecht, *A Child of the Century*, p. 515ff.

18. Ibid.; Ben-Ami, op. cit.; *New York Post*, May 19, 1947. Hecht was profiled in the *Post* a few days after returning from a stay in Hollywood where he wrote "five movie scripts for half a million dollars." Hecht undoubtedly *did* embarrass Bergson on some counts: for example, when he enlisted the support of Jewish gangsters, such as Mickey Cohen, in Hollywood benefits for the Irgun.

19. *New York Herald Tribune*, June 5, June 8, 1947.

20. Ben-Ami, op. cit., pp. 434, 437.

21. The term "bursting forth" – in Hebrew, *peritzat hamedinah* – reflects a popular appreciation of a historical truism: nations are generally born suddenly, violently and without warning. That most histories of the establishment of the State of Israel present a studied, even logical progression of events that, it is claimed, naturally culminated in Israeli independence, leads one to suspect that a true history of Israel – unburdened by political and ideological baggage – has yet to be written.

22. Grose, op. cit., p. 175.

23. Laqueur, op. cit., pp. 483-485.

24. Hebrew Committee statement of Dec. 15, 1947, HNCL file, Jabotinsky Institute, Tel Aviv.

25. Ibid.

26. Ibid.

27. Rafaeli – Rapoport interview, Nov. 26, 1982.

28. Kook – Rapoport interviews, September 1982, July 1983.

29. Ibid.; Ben-Ami, op. cit., p. 506; Koestler, op. cit., p. 248ff.

30. Ben-Ami, op. cit., p. 517.

31. Nakdimon-Rapoport interview, Oct. 26, 1982.

32. Ibid.; Kook – Rapoport interviews, September 1982, July 1983; *Palestine Post*, Aug. 27, 1948.

33. Ben-Ami, who had become an American citizen through his army service, was traumatized by the *Altalena* incident, after which he opted to live in New York. He remained a Begin supporter throughout his life. Rafaeli became a member of the Herut party's Central Committee, and a leading Israeli industrialist.

34. Kook – Rapoport interviews, September 1982, April, July 1983.

35. Ibid.

36. Rafaeli – Rapoport interview, op. cit.

A Political Epilogue

1. "Jewish National Identity Today," *Forum*, Spring 1983.

Afterword: Historical Amnesia and Jewish Coventry

1. Weizmann quoted in Walter Laqueur, *A History of Zionism*, p. 551.

2. Lucy Dawidowicz, "American Jewry and the Holocaust," *New York Times Magazine*, April 18, 1982.

3. Ibid.; *Commentary*, Dawidowicz review of Ben Hecht's *Perfidy*, June 1962.

4. Dawidowicz on the Bergson group, *The American Jewish Year Book*, 1982; Dawidowicz, "Indicting American Jews," *Commentary*, June 1983.

5. Dawidowicz Letter, *Commentary*, September 1983.

6. Dawidowicz, *New York Times Magazine*, op. cit.

7. Dawidowicz, *Jewish Prescence*, p. 278.

8. Dawidowicz, *The Holocaust and the Historians*, p. 1.

9. Bernard Wasserstein, "The Myth of 'Jewish Silence,'" *Midstream*, August/September 1980.

10. David Wyman letter, *New York Times Magazine*, May 2, 1982.

11. Paul O'Dwyer letter, *New York Times Magazine*, May 2, 1982.

12. Charles Liebman letter, *Midstream*, March 1982.

13. Samuel Haber letter, *Midstream*, June 1982.

14. Melvin Urofsky, *A Voice That Spoke for Justice*, p. 317; Marie Syrkin, "What American Jews Did During the Holocaust," *Midstream*, Oct. 1982; Wasserstein, op. cit.

15. Dawidowicz, *New York Times Magazine*, op. cit.

16. *Problems of World War II and Its Aftermath, Part 2*, p. 9ff.

17. Nathan Kaganoff letter to author, Oct. 27, 1983. Given Wise's habit of not directly mentioning the Bergson group in written correspondence, there may not have been all that much to eliminate in the first place.

18. Menachem Begin, *The Revolt*, p. 63; Kook – Rapoport interviews, September 1982.

19. Dawidowicz, *The Holocaust and the Historians*, p. 142.

20. Michael J. Cohen letter, *Midstream*, March 1982. Cohen himself comes out of a Hashomer Hatzair labor Zionist background and shows no prejudice in favor of the "Jabotinsky camp" – which is to say that not all defenders of the Bergson group's historical record are "Revisionists."

21. Ibid.

22. Wasserstein, op. cit.

23. Dawidowicz, *New York Times Magazine*, op. cit.; Yehuda Bauer, *American Jewry and the Holocaust*, p. 458.

24. Isaiah Berlin letter to author, Nov. 2, 1983; Berlin, "Zionist Politics in Wartime Washington," Hebrew University, 1972.

25. Syrkin, "What American Jews Did During the Holocaust," op. cit.

26. Berlin, *Historical Inevitability*, pp. 58-59, 7.

27. Ibid.

28. Michael J. Cohen, op. cit.

29. David Pinsky, *Cooperation Among American Jewish Organizations in Their Efforts to Rescue European Jewry During the Holocaust*, pp. 375, 387.

30. Wise Street, *Jerusalem Post*, July 6, 1962.

SELECTED BIBLIOGRAPHY

Agassi, John: *Between Religion and Nationality*, Tel Aviv, 1984 (Hebrew).

The Answer, 1943-1948, Palestine Statehood Committee papers, Sterling Memorial Library, Yale University.

Barlas, Haim: *Rescue in the Days of the Holocaust*, Tel Aviv, 1975 (Hebrew).

Bauer, Yehuda: *American Jewry and the Holocaust*, Detroit, 1981.

——— *A History of the Holocaust*, New York, 1982.

Begin, Menachem: *The Revolt*, New York, 1951.

Ben-Ami, Yitshaq: *Years of Wrath, Days of Glory*, New York, 1982.

Berlin, Isaiah: "Zionist Politics in Wartime Washington," Ya'acov Herzog Memorial Lecture at Hebrew University, Jerusalem, Oct. 1972.

——— "Historical Inevitability," August Comte Lectures, London, 1954.

Bloom, Sol: *The Autobiography of Sol Bloom*, New York, 1948.

Borkin, Joseph: *The Crime and Punishment of I. G. Farben*, New York, 1978.

Briscoe, Robert: *For the Life of Me*, Boston, 1958.

Cohen, Michael J.: *Palestine: Retreat from the Mandate*, London, 1978.

——— *Palestine and the Great Powers*, Princeton, 1982.

——— "American Influence on British Policy in the Middle East During World War Two: First Attempts at Coordinating Allied Policy on Palestine," *American Jewish Historical Quarterly*, V. 67, September 1977.

Crossman, Richard: *Palestine Mission: A Personal Account*, London, 1946.

Dawidowicz, Lucy: "American Jewry and the Holocaust," *New York Times Magazine*, April 18, 1982.

——— Review of *Perfidy, Commentary*, March 1962.

——— *The Holocaust and the Historians*, Cambridge, Mass., 1981.

—— "Indicting American Jews," *Commentary*, June 1983; and letters, Sept. 1983.

—— "A Century of Jewish History, 1881-1981: The View From America," *American Jewish Year Book 1982*, American Jewish Committee.

Elath (Epstein), Eliahu: *Zionism at the UN*, Philadelphia, 1976.

Feingold, Henry L.: *The Politics of Rescue*, New Brunswick, N.J., 1970.

—— *Zion in America*, New York, 1974.

Feuer, Leon: "The Birth of the Jewish Lobby," *American Jewish Archives*, V. xxxviii, November 1976.

Final Summary Report of the U.S. War Refugee Board, Washington, 1945.

Friedman, Saul S.: *No Haven for the Oppressed*, Detroit, 1972.

Ganin, Zvi: *Truman, American Jewry and Israel*, New York, 1979.

Gilbert, Martin: *Auschwitz and the Allies*, London, 1981.

Goldmann, Nahum: *The Autobiography of Nahum Goldmann*, New York, 1978.

—— *The Jewish Paradox*, New York, 1978.

Grose, Peter: *Israel in the Mind of America*, New York 1983.

Hecht, Ben: *A Child of the Century*, New York, 1954.

Hertzberg, Arthur: *The Zionist Idea*, New York, 1960.

Hilberg, Raul: *The Destruction of European Jews*, Chicago, 1961.

Hirschmann, Ira: *Caution to the Winds*, New York, 1962.

Israel, Fred (editor): *The War Diary of Breckinridge Long*, University of Nebraska, 1966.

Jabotinsky, Vladimir: *The War and the Jew*, Philadelphia, 1942.

Jarvik, Laurence: "Who Shall Live and Who Shall Die," film, 1978.

Katz, Samuel: *Days of Fire*, London, 1968.

Koestler, Arthur: *Promise and Fulfillment*, New York, 1949.

Kurzman, Dan: *Ben-Gurion: Prophet of Fire*, New York, 1983.

Laqueur, Walter: *A History of Zionism*, New York, 1976.

—— *The Terrible Secret*, Boston, 1981.

Levine, Daniel: *David Raziel, the Man and His Times*, Ph. D. dissertation, Yeshiva University, New York, 1969.

Levinthal, Louis: "The Credo of an American Zionist," Zionist Organization of America, Washington, 1943.

Lookstein, Haskel: *American Jewry's Public Response to the Holocaust 1938-1944*, Ph. D. dissesrtation, 1979.

Lowenstein, Sharon: "A New Deal for Refugees: The Promise and Reality of Oswego," *American Jewish History*, March 1982, p. 328ff.

Matzozsky, Eli, "An Episode: Roosevelt and the Mass Killing," *Midstream*, August/September 1980.

Mery, Jacques: *Laisser Passer Mon Peuple*, Paris, 1947.

Morse, Arthur D.: *While Six Million Died*, New York, 1968.

Neumann, Emanuel: *In the Arena: An Autobiograhical Memoir*, New York, 1976.

Nicholas, H.G. (editor): *Washington Dispatches 1941-1945; Weekly Political Reports from the British Embassy*, Chicago, 1981.

Pearlman, Maurice: *Mufti of Jerusalem*, London, 1947.

Peck, Sara E.: "The Campaign for an American Response to the Nazi Holocaust (1943-1945)," *Journal of Contemporary History*, V. 15, 1980.

Penkower, Monty: "In Dramatic Dissent: The Bergson Boys," *American Jewish History*, March 1981.

—— *The Jews Were Expendable: Free World Diplomacy and the Holocaust*, Urbana and Chicago, 1983.

—— "The 1943 Joint Anglo-American Statement on Palestine," *Herzl Yearbook 8*, 1978, pp. 212-241.

Pinsky, David E.: *Cooperation Among American Jewish Organizations in Their Efforts to Rescue European Jewry During the Holocaust*, Ph. D. dissertation, New York University, 1980.

Problems of World War II and Its Aftermath, Part 2, House Committee on International Relations, U.S. Government Printing Office, Washington, 1976.

Schechtman, Joseph B.: *The Vladimir Jabotinsky Story*, 2 vols., New York and London, 1961.

Slater, Leonard: *The Pledge*, New York, 1970.

Syrkin, Marie: "What American Jews Did During the Holocaust," *Midstream*, October 1982.

Urofsky, Melvin: *A Voice That Spoke for Justice: The Life and Times of Stephen S. Wise*, Albany, 1982.

Voss, Carl H.: *Rabbi and Minister: The Friendship of Stephen S. Wise and John Haynes Holmes*, Cleveland, 1964.

—— *Servant of the People*, Selected Letters, Philadelphia, 1969.

Wasserstein, Bernard: *Britain and the Jews of Europe 1939-1945*, New York, 1979.

—— "The Myth of 'Jewish Silence,'" *Midstream*, August/September 1980; letters March 1981, March 1982.

Wise, Stephen S.: *Challenging Years: The Autobiography of Stephen Wise*, New York, 1949.

Wyman, David S.: *The Abandonment of the Jews*, New York, 1984.

—— *Paper Walls: America and the Refugee Crisis 1938-1941*, Amherst, Mass., 1968.

Young-Bruehl, Elisabeth: *Hannah Arendt: For Love of the World*, New Haven, 1982.

Zar, Isaac: *Rescue and Liberation*, New York, 1954.

INDEX